The Unabridged Collected Works

of
Jeanne Guyon

The Unabridged Collected Works

of
Jeanne Guyon

Edited By
Glenn Kahley

Copyright © 2006 by Glenn Kahley

"The Unabridged Collected Works of Jeanne Guyon," edited by Glenn Kahley. All rights reserved under Title 17, U.S. Code, International and Pan-American Copyright Conventions. No part of this work, whether in printed or digital form, may be reproduced or transmitted in any form or by any means, electronic or mechanical, including (but not limited to) photocopying, scanning, recording, live performance or broadcast, or duplication by any information storage or retrieval system without prior written permission from Glenn Kahley.

While every precaution has been taken in the preparation of this book, the publisher assumes no responsibilities for errors of omissions, or for damages resulting from the use of information contained herein.

ISBN: 978-0-9788914-1-1

For my wife Lisa and my daughter Hannah

Table of Contents

Preface	xi
Autobiography	1
Method of Prayer	233
Way to God	279
Spiritual Torrents	299
Poetry	366

PREFACE

About Jeanne Guyon

In the history of the world few persons have attained that high degree of spirituality reached by Madame Guyon. However lofty this may seem, when we admire Madame Guyon (1648-1717), we're in good company, for John Wesley said of her, "How few such instances do we find of exalted love to God, and our neighbor; of genuine humility; of invincible meekness and unbounded resignation." Born in a corrupt age, in a nation marked for its degeneracy; nursed and reared in a church, as decadent as the world in which it was embedded; persecuted at every step of her career; groping as she did in spiritual desolation and ignorance, nevertheless, she arose to the highest pinnacle of pre-eminence in spirituality and Christian devotion. She lived and died in the Catholic Church; yet was tormented and afflicted; was maltreated and abused; and was imprisoned for years by the highest authorities of that church. Her sole crime was that of loving God. The ground of her offense was found in her supreme devotion, and unmeasured attachment to Christ. When they demanded her money and estate, she gladly surrendered them, even to her impoverishment, but it availed nothing. The crime of loving Him in whom her whole being was absorbed, never could be mitigated, or forgiven. She loved only to do good to her fellow-creatures, and to such an extent was she filled with the Holy Ghost, and with the power of God, that she produced wonders in her day, and has not ceased to influence the ages that have followed. Viewed from a human standpoint, it is a sublime spectacle, to see a solitary woman subvert all the maneuverings of kings and courtiers; laugh to scorn all the wicked energy of the papal inquisition, and silence, and confound the pretensions of the most learned individuals. She not only saw more clearly the most sublime truths of our most holy Christianity, but she basked in the clearest and most beautiful sunlight while they groped in darkness. She grasped with ease the deepest and most sublime truths of scripture, while they were lost in the mazes of their own profound ignorance. One distinguished individual was delighted to sit at her feet. At first he heard her with distrust; then with admiration. Finally he opened his heart to the truth, and stretched forth his hand to be led by this saint of God into the Holy of Holies where she dwelt. We allude to the distinguished Archbishop Fenelon, whose sweet spirit and charming writings have been a blessing to every generation following him. There can be no doubt that God caused her to commit her life so minutely to writing. The duty was put upon her by her spiritual director, whom the rules of her church made it obligatory upon her to obey. It was written while she was incarcerated in the cell of a lonely prison. God preserved it from destruction. We have not a shadow of doubt that it is destined to accomplish tenfold more in the future than it has accomplished in the past. Indeed, the Christian world is only beginning to understand and appreciate it, and our hope and prayer is that thousands may, through its instrumentality, be brought into the same intimate communion and fellowship with God, that was so richly enjoyed by Madame Guyon. Let us take a closer look at this intimate communion under the heading mystical Union.

About Mystical Union

There is a mystical union of God and the believer, which is taught in the Scriptures and experienced by the Christian, but which is difficult to describe. Saint Paul declares of the Christians that they are in Christ (Romans 8:1) and again that Christ is in them (Galatians 2:20). What this union meant to Paul he tells us when he says, "Nevertheless I live, yet not I, but Christ lives in me; and the life which I now live in the flesh, I live by faith of the Son of God who loved me and gave Himself for me" (Galatians 2:20). The indwelling of God in the believer must not be understood in the pantheistic sense, as though the person of the believer were absorbed by Christ. On the contrary it is a close personal union in which the believer rests in Christ and draws strength from Him. Nor must the union be understood in such a way as to make man divine. The personality of man is not changed in any way, but it is united in a mystical and indescribable yet real and comforting way with Christ, or with God in Christ, so that Christ lives in him and he in Christ. Even the Reformer Martin Luther writes of this union. He says in his commentary on Galatians, 2:20: "Christ therefore, joined and united unto me and abiding in me, lives this life in me which I now live. Yes, Christ Himself is this life which now I live. Wherefore Christ and I in this behalf are both one. You are so entirely and nearly joined unto Christ that He and you are made as it were one person." Though the mystical union cannot be fully described because it is a mystery, it is nevertheless not to be regarded as a figure of speech, but as a reality. It is not to be understood as denoting merely that harmony has been established between man's will and God's, or that there simply exists a union of God and man in love, such as might exist between two human persons. Nor is it to be understood as denoting merely that the believer receives special and peculiar gifts from the Holy Spirit. It is a real indwelling of God in man.

AUTOBIOGRAPHY
ೲ

PART ONE

Chapter One

There were omissions of importance in the former narration of my life. I willingly comply with your desire, in giving you a more circumstantial relation; though the labor seems rather painful, as I cannot use much study or reflection. My earnest wish is to paint in true colors the goodness of God to me, and the depth of my own ingratitude - but it is impossible, as numberless little circumstances have escaped my memory. You are also unwilling I should give you a minute account of my sins. I shall, however, try to leave out as few faults as possible. I depend on you to destroy it, when your soul has drawn those spiritual advantages which God intended, and for which purpose I am willing to sacrifice all things. I am fully persuaded of His designs toward you, as well for the sanctification of others, as for your own sanctification.

Let me assure you, this is not attained, save through pain, weariness and labor; and it will be reached by a path that will wonderfully disappoint your expectations. Nevertheless, if you are fully convinced that it is on the nothing in man that God establishes his greatest works, - you will be in part guarded against disappointment or surprise. He destroys that he might build; for when He is about to rear His sacred temple in us, He first totally razes that vain and pompous edifice, which human art and power had erected, and from its horrible ruins a new structure is formed, by His power only.

Oh, that you could comprehend the depth of this mystery, and learn the secrets of the conduct of God, revealed to babes, but hid from the wise and great of this world, who think themselves the Lord's counselor's, and capable of investigating His procedures, and suppose they have attained that divine wisdom hidden from the eyes of all who live in self, and are enveloped in their own works. Who by a lively genius and elevated faculties mount up to Heaven, and think to comprehend the height and depth and length and breadth of God.

This divine wisdom is unknown, even to those who pass in the world for persons of extraordinary illumination and knowledge. To whom then is she known, and who can tell us any tidings concerning her? Destruction and death assure us, that they have heard with their ears of her fame and renown. It is, then, in dying to all things, and in being truly lost to them, passing forward into God, and existing only in Him, that we attain to some knowledge of the true wisdom. Oh, how little are her ways known, and her dealings with her most chosen servants. Scarce do we discover anything thereof, but surprised at the dissimilitude betwixt the truth we thus discover and our former ideas of it, we cry out with Saint Paul, "Oh, the depth of the knowledge and wisdom of God! How unsearchable are his judgments, and his ways past finding out." The Lord judges not of things as men do, who call good evil and evil good, and account that as righteousness which is abominable in His sight, and which according to the prophet He regards as filthy rags. He will enter into strict judgment with these self-righteous, and they shall, like the Pharisees, be rather subjects of His wrath, than objects of His love, or inheritors of His rewards. Does not Christ Himself assure us, that "except our righteousness exceed that of the scribes and Pharisees we shall in no case enter into the kingdom of heaven." And which of us even approaches them in righteousness; or, if we live in the practice of virtues, though much inferior to theirs, are we not tenfold more ostentatious? Who is not pleased to behold himself righteous in his own eyes, and in the eyes of others? Who doubts that such righteousness is sufficient to please God? Yet, we see the indignation of our Lord manifested against such. He who was the perfect pattern of tenderness and meekness, such as flowed from the depth of the heart, and not that affected meekness, which under the form of a dove, hides the hawk's heart. He appears severe only to these self-righteous people, and He publicly dishonored them. In what strange colors does He represent them, while He beholds the poor sinner with mercy, compassion and love, and declares that for them only He was come, that it was the sick who needed the physician; and that He came only to save the lost sheep of the house of Israel.

O thou Source of Love! You do indeed seem so jealous of the salvation You have purchased, that You do prefer the sinner to the righteous! The poor sinner beholds himself vile and wretched, is in a manner constrained to detest himself; and finding his state so horrible, casts himself in his desperation into the arms of his Savior, and plunges into the healing fountain, and comes forth "white as wool." Then confounded at the review of his disordered state, and overflowing with love for Him, who having alone the power, had also the compassion to save him -- the excess of his love is proportioned to the enormity of his crimes, and the fullness of his gratitude to the extent of the debt remitted. The self-righteous, relying on the many good works he imagines he has performed, seems to hold salvation in his own hand, and considers Heaven as a just reward of his merits. In the bitterness of his zeal he exclaims against all sinners, and represents the gates of mercy as barred against them, and Heaven as a place to which they have no claim. What need have such self-righteous persons of a Savior? They are already burdened with the load of their own merits. Oh, how long they bear the flattering load, while sinners divested of everything, fly rapidly on the wings of faith and love into their Savior's arms, who freely bestows on them that which he has so freely promised!

How full of self-love are the self-righteous, and how void of the love of God! They esteem and admire themselves in their works of righteousness, which they suppose to be a fountain of happiness. These works are no sooner exposed to the Sun of Righteousness, than they discover all to be so full of impurity and baseness, that it frets them to the heart. Meanwhile the poor sinner, Magdalene, is pardoned because she loves much, and her faith and love are accepted as righteousness. The inspired Paul, who so well understood these great truths and so fully investigated them, assures us that "the faith of Abraham was imputed to him for righteousness." This is truly beautiful for it is certain that all of that holy patriarch's actions were strictly righteous; yet, not seeing them as such, and being devoid of the love of them, and divested of selfishness, his faith was founded on the coming Christ. He hoped in Him even against hope itself, and this was imputed to him for righteousness, (Romans 41:18,22,) a pure, simple and genuine righteousness, wrought by Christ, and not a righteousness wrought by himself, and regarded as of himself.

You may imagine this a digression wide of the subject, but it leads insensibly to it. It shows that God accomplishes His work either in converted sinners, whose past iniquities serve as a counterpoise to their elevation, or in persons whose selfrighteousness He destroys, by totally overthrowing the proud building they had reared on a sandy foundation, instead of the Rock -- Christ.

The establishment of all these ends, which He proposed in coming into the world, is effected by the apparent overthrow of that very structure which in reality He would erect. By means which seem to destroy His Church, He establishes it. How strangely does He found the new dispensation and give it His sanction! The legislator Himself is condemned by the learned and great, as a malefactor, and dies an ignominious death. Oh, that we fully understood how very opposite our selfrighteousness is to the designs of God -- it would be a subject for endless humiliation, and we should have an utter distrust in that which at present constitutes the whole of our dependence.

From a just love of His supreme power, and a righteous jealousy of mankind, who attribute to each other the gifts He Himself bestows upon them, it pleased Him to take one of the most unworthy of the creation, to make known the fact that His graces are the effects of His will, not the fruits of our merits. It is the property of His wisdom to destroy what is proudly built, and to build what is destroyed; to make use of weak things to confound the mighty and to employ in His service such as appear vile and contemptible.

This He does in a manner so astonishing, as to render them the objects of the scorn and contempt of the world. It is not to draw public approbation upon them, that He makes them instrumental in the salvation of others; but to render them the objects of their dislike and the subjects of their insults; as you will see in this life you have enjoined upon me to write.

Chapter Two

I was born on April 18, 1648. My parents, particularly my father, was extremely pious; but to him it was a manner hereditary. Many of his forefathers were saints.

My mother, in the eighth month, was accidentally frightened, which caused an abortion. It is generally imagined that a child born in that month cannot survive. Indeed, I was so excessively ill, immediately after my birth, that all about me despaired of my life, and were apprehensive I should die without baptism. Perceiving some signs of vitality, they ran to acquaint my father, who immediately brought a priest; but on entering the chamber they were told those symptoms which had raised their hopes were only expiring struggles, and all was over.

I had no sooner shown signs of life again, than I again relapsed, and remained so long in an uncertain state, that it was some time before they could find a proper opportunity to baptize me. I continued very unhealthy until I was two and a half years old, when they sent me to the convent of the Ursulines, where I remained a few months.

On my return, my mother neglected to pay due attention to my education. She was not fond of daughters and abandoned me wholly to the care of servants. Indeed, I should have suffered severely from their inattention to me had not an all-watchful Providence been my protector: for through my liveliness, I met with various accidents. I frequently fell into a deep vault that held our firewood; however, I always escaped unhurt.

The Dutchess of Montbason came to the convent of the Benedictines, when I was about four years old. She had a great friendship for my father, and obtained his permission that I should go to the same convent. She took peculiar delight in my sportiveness and certain sweetness in my external deportment. I became her constant companion.

I was guilty of frequent and dangerous irregularities in this house, and committed serious faults. I had good examples before me, and being naturally well inclined, I followed them, when there were none to turn me aside. I loved to hear God spoken of, to be at church, and to be dressed in a religious garb. I was told of terrors of Hell which I imagined was intended to intimidate me as I was exceedingly lively, and full of a little petulant vivacity which they called wit. The succeeding night I dreamed of Hell, and though I was so young, time has never been able to efface the frightful ideas impressed upon my imagination. All appeared horrible darkness, where souls were punished, and my place among them was pointed out. At this I wept bitterly, and cried, "Oh, my God, if You will have mercy upon me, and spare me yet a little longer, I will never more offend You." And You did, O Lord, in mercy hearken unto my cry, and pour upon me strength and courage to serve You, in an uncommon manner for one of my age. I wanted to go privately to confession, but being little, the mistress of the boarders carried me to the priest, and stayed with me while I was heard. She was much astonished when I mentioned that I had suggestions against the faith, and the confessor began to laugh, and inquire what they were. I told him that till then I had doubted there was such a place as Hell, and supposed my mistress had spoken of it merely to make me good, but now my doubts were all removed. After confession my heart glowed with a kind of fervor, and at one time I felt a desire to suffer martyrdom. The good girls of the house, to amuse themselves, and to see how far this growing fervor would carry me, desired me to prepare for martyrdom. I found great fervency and delight in prayer, and was persuaded that this ardor, which was as new as it was pleasing, was a proof of God's love. This inspired me with such courage and resolution, that I earnestly besought them to proceed, that I might thereby enter into His sacred presence. But was there not latent hypocrisy here? Did I not imagine that it was possible they would not kill me, and that I would have the merit of martyrdom without suffering it? Indeed, it appeared there was something of this nature in it. Being placed kneeling on a cloth spread for the purpose, and seeing behind me a large sword lifted up which they had prepared to try how far my ardor would carry me I cried, "Hold! it is not right I should die without first obtaining my father's permission." I was quickly upbraided with having said this that I might escape, and that I was no longer a martyr. I continued long disconsolate, and would receive no comfort; something inwardly reproved me, for not having embraced that opportunity of going to Heaven, when it rested altogether on my own choice.

At my solicitation, and on account of my falling so frequently sick, I was at length taken home. On my return, my mother having a maid in whom she placed confidence, left me again to the care of servants. It is a great fault, of which mothers are guilty, when under pretext of external devotions, or other engagements, they suffer their daughters to be absent from them. I forbear not condemning that unjust partiality with which parents treat some of their children. It is frequently productive of divisions in families, and even the ruin of some. Impartiality, by uniting children's hearts together, lays the foundation of lasting harmony and unanimity.

I would I were able to convince parents, and all who have the care of youth, of the great attention they require, and how dangerous it is to let them be for any length of time from under their eye, or to suffer them to be without some kind of employment. This negligence is the ruin of multitudes of girls.

How greatly it is to be lamented, that mothers who are inclined to piety, should pervert even the means of salvation to their destruction -- commit the greatest irregularities while apparently pursuing that which should produce the most regular and circumspect conduct.

Thus, because they experience certain gains in prayer, they would be all day long at church; meanwhile their children are running to destruction. We glorify God most when we prevent what may offend Him. What must be the nature of that sacrifice which is the occasion of sin! God should be served in His own way. Let the devotion of mothers be regulated so as to prevent their daughters from straying. Treat them as sisters, not as slaves. Appear pleased with their little amusements. The children will delight then in the presence of their mothers, instead of avoiding it. If they find so much happiness with them, they will not dream of seeking it elsewhere. Mothers frequently deny their children any liberties. Like birds constantly confined to a cage, they no sooner find means of escape than off they go, never to return. In order to render them tame and docile when young, they should be permitted sometimes to take wing, but as their flight is weak, and closely watched, it is easy to retake them when they escape. Little flight gives them the habit of naturally returning to their cage which becomes an agreeable confinement. I believe young girls should be treated in a manner something similar to this. Mothers should indulge them in an innocent liberty, but should never lose sight of them.

To guard the tender minds of children from what is wrong, much care should be taken to employ them in agreeable and useful matters. They should not be loaded with food they cannot relish. Milk suited to babies should be administered to them not strong meat which may so disgust them, that when they arrive at an age when it would be proper nourishment, they will not so much as taste it. Every day they should be obliged to read a little in some good book, spend some time in prayer, which must be suited rather to stir the affections, than for meditation. Oh, were this method of education pursued, how speedily would many irregularities cease! These daughters becoming mothers, would educate their children as they themselves had been educated.

Parents should also avoid showing the smallest partiality in the treatment of their children. It begets a secret jealousy and hatred among them, which frequently augments with time, and even continues until death. How often do we see some children the idols of the house, behaving like absolute tyrants, treating their brothers and sisters as so many slaves according to the example of father and mother. And it happens many times, that the favorite proves a scourge to the parents while the poor despised and hated one becomes their consolation and support. My mother was very defective in the education of her children. She suffered me whole days from her presence in company with the servants, whose conversation and example were particularly hurtful to one of my disposition.

My mother's heart seemed wholly centered in my brother. I was scarcely ever favored with the smallest instance of her tenderness or affection. I therefore voluntarily absented myself from her. It is true, my brother was more amiable than I but the excess of her fondness for him, made her blind even to my outward good qualities. It served only to discover my faults, which would have been trifling had proper care been taken of me.

Chapter Three

My father who loved me tenderly and seeing how little my education was attended to sent me to a convent of the Ursulines. I was near seven years old. In this house were two half sisters of mine, the one by my father, the other by my mother. My father placed me under his daughter's care, a person of the great capacity and most exalted piety, excellently qualified for the instruction of youth. This was a singular dispensation of God's providence and love toward me, and proved the first means of my salvation. She loved me tenderly, and her affection made her discover in me many amiable qualities, which the Lord had implanted in me. She endeavored to improve these good qualities, and I believe that had I continued in such careful hands, I should have acquired as many virtuous habits as I afterward contracted evil ones.

This good sister employed her time in instructing me in piety and in such branches of learning as were suitable to my age and capacity. She had good talents and improved them well. She was frequent in prayer and her faith was as great as that of most persons. She denied herself every other pleasure to be with me and to instruct me. Such was her affection for me that it made her find more pleasure with me than anywhere else.

If I made her agreeable answers, though more from chance than from judgment, she thought herself well paid for all her labor. Under her care I soon became mistress of most studies suitable for me. Many grown persons of rank could not have answered the questions.

As my father often sent for me, desiring to see me at home, I found at one time the Queen of England there. I was near eight years of age. My father told the Queen's confessor that if he wanted a little amusement he might entertain himself with me. He tried me with several very difficult questions, to which I returned such pertinent answers that he carried me to the Queen, and said, "Your majesty must have some diversion with this child." She also tried me and was so well pleased with my lively answers, and my manners, that she demanded me of my father with no small importunity. She assured him that she would take particular care of me, designing me for maid of honor to the princess. My father resisted. Doubtless it was God who caused this refusal, and thereby turned off the stroke which might have probably intercepted my salvation. Being so weak, how could I have withstood the temptations and distractions of a court?

I went back to the Ursulines where my good sister continued her affection. But as she was not the mistress of the boarders, and I was obliged sometimes to go along with them, I contracted bad habits. I became addicted to lying, peevishness and indevotion, passing whole days without thinking on God; though He watched continually over me, as the sequel will manifest. I did not remain long under the power of such habits because my sister's care recovered me. I loved much to hear of God, was not weary of church, loved to pray, had tenderness for the poor, and a natural dislike for persons whose doctrine was judged unsound. God has always continued to me this grace, in my greatest infidelities.

There was at the end of the garden connected with this convent, a little chapel dedicated to the child Jesus. To this I betook myself for devotion and, for some time, carrying my breakfast thither every morning, I hid it all behind this image. I was so much a child, that I thought I made a considerable sacrifice in depriving myself of it. Delicate in my choice of food, I wished to mortify myself, but found self-love still too prevalent, to submit to such mortification. When they were cleaning out this chapel, they found behind the image what I had left there and presently guessed that it was I. They had seen me every day going thither. I believe that God, who lets nothing pass without a recompense, soon rewarded me with interest for this little infantine devotion.

I continued some time with my sister, where I retained the love and fear of God. My life was easy; I was educated agreeably with her. I improved much while I had my health, but very often I was sick, and seized with maladies as sudden as they were uncommon. In the evening well; in the morning swelled and full of bluish marks, symptoms of a fever which soon followed. At nine years, I was taken with so violent a hemorrhage that they thought I was going to die. I was rendered exceedingly weak.

A little before this severe attack, my other sister became jealous, wanting to have me in turn. Though she led a good life, yet she had not a talent for the education of children. At first she caressed me, but all her caresses made no impression upon my heart. My other sister did more with a look, than she with either caresses or threatenings. As she saw that I loved her not so well, she changed to rigorous treatment. She would not allow me to speak to my other sister. When she knew I had spoken to her, she had me whipped, or beat me herself. I could no longer hold out against severe usage, and therefore requited with apparent ingratitude all the favors of my paternal sister, going no more to see her. But this did not hinder her from giving me marks of her usual goodness, in the severe malady just mentioned. She kindly construed my ingratitude to be rather owing to my fear of chastisement, than to a bad heart. Indeed, I believe this was the only instance in which fear of chastisement operated so powerfully upon me. From that time I suffered more in occasioning pain to One I loved, than in suffering myself at their hand.

You know, O my Beloved, that it was not the dread of Your chastisements that sunk so deep, either into my understanding or my heart; it was the sorrow for offending You which ever constituted the whole of my distress; which was so great. I imagine if there were neither Heaven nor Hell, I should always have retained the same fear of displeasing You. You know that after my faults, when, in forgiving mercy, You were pleased to visit my soul, Your caresses were a thousand-fold more insupportable than Your rod.

My father being informed of all that passed, took me home again. I was nearly ten years of age. I stayed only a little while at home. A nun of the order of Saint Dominic, of a great family, one of my father's intimate friends, solicited him to place me in her convent. She was the prioress and promised she would take care of me and make me lodge in her room. This lady had conceived a great affection for me. She was so taken up with her community, in its many troublesome events that she was not at liberty to take much care of me. I had the chickenpox, which made me keep to my bed three weeks, in which I had very bad care, though my father and mother thought I was under excellent care. The ladies of the house had such a dread of the smallpox, as they imagined mine to be, that they would not come near me. I passed almost all the time without seeing anybody. A lay-sister who only brought me my allowance of diet at the set hours immediately went off again. I providentially found a Bible and having both a fondness for reading and a happy memory, I spent whole days in reading it from morning to night. I learned entirely the historical part. Yet I was really very unhappy in this house. The other boarders, being large girls, distressed me with grievous persecutions. I was so much neglected, as to food, that I became quite emaciated.

Chapter Four

After about eight months my father took me home. My mother kept me more with her, beginning to have a higher regard for me than before. She still preferred my brother; every one spoke of it. Even when I was sick and there was anything I liked, he demanded it. It was taken from me, and given to him, and he was in perfectly good health. One day he made me mount the top of the coach; then threw me down. By the fall I was very much bruised. At other times he beat me. But whatever he did, however wrong, it was winked at, or the most favorable construction was put upon it. This soured my temper. I had little disposition to do good, saying, "I was never the better for it."

It was not then for You alone, O God, that I did good; since I ceased to do it, when it met not with such a reception from others as I wanted. Had I known how to make a right use of this you're crucifying conduct, I should have made a good progress. Far from turning me out of the way, it would have made me turn more wholly to You.

I looked with jealous eyes on my brother, seeing the difference between him and me. Whatever he did was considered well; but if there were blame, it fell on me. My stepsisters by the mother, gained her goodwill by caressing him and persecuting me. True, I was bad. I relapsed into my former faults of lying and peevishness. With all these faults I was very tender and charitable to the poor. I prayed to God assiduously, loved to hear any one speak of Him and to read good books.

I doubt not that you will be amazed at such a series of inconsistencies; but what succeeds will surprise you yet more, when you see this manner of acting gain ground with my years. As my reason ripened, it was so far from correcting this irrational conduct. Sin grew more powerful in me.

O my God, your grace seemed to be redoubled in proportion to the increase of my ingratitude! It was with me as with a city besieged, You did surround my heart, and I only studied how to defend myself against your attacks. I raised fortifications about the wretched place, adding every day to the number of my iniquities to prevent You taking it. When there was an appearance of Your becoming victorious over this ungrateful heart, I raised a counter-battery, and threw up ramparts to keep off your goodness, and to hinder the course of your grace. None other could have conquered than Yourself.

I cannot bear to hear it said, "We are not free to resist grace." I have had too long and fatal an experience of my liberty. I closed up the avenues of my heart, that I might not so much as hear that secret voice of God, which was calling me to Himself. I have indeed, from tenderest youth, passed through a series of grievances, either by maladies or by persecutions. The girl to whose care my mother left me, in arranging my hair used to beat me, and did not make me turn it except with rage and blows.

Everything seemed to punish me, but this instead of making me turn unto You, O my God, only served to afflict and embitter my mind.

My father knew nothing of all this; his love to me was such that he would not have suffered it. I loved him very much, but at the same time I feared him, so that I told him nothing of it. My mother was often teasing him with complaints of me, to which he made no other reply than, "There are twelve hours in the day; she'll grow wiser." This rigorous proceeding was not the worst for my soul, though it soured my temper, which was otherwise mild and easy. But what caused my greatest hurt was, that I chose to be among those who caressed me, in order to corrupt and spoil me.

My father, seeing I was now grown tall, placed me in Lent among the Ursulines, to receive my first communion at Easter, at which time I was to complete my eleventh year. And here my most dear sister, under whose inspection my father placed me, redoubled her cares, to cause me to make the best preparation possible for this act of devotion. I thought now of giving myself to God in good earnest. I often felt a combat between my good inclinations and my bad habits. I even did some penances. As I was almost always with my sister, and as the boarders in her class, which was the first, were very reasonable and civil, I became such also, while among them. It had been cruel to educate me badly; for my very nature was strongly disposed to goodness. Easily won with mildness, I did with pleasure whatever my good sister desired. At length Easter arrived; I received the communion with much joy and devotion. In this house I staid until Whitsuntide. But as my other sister was mistress of the second class, she demanded that in her week I should be with her in that class. Her manners, so opposite to the other's, made me relax my former piety. I felt no more that new and delightful ardor which had seized my heart at my first communion. Alas, it held but a short time. My faults and failings were soon reiterated and drew me from the care and duties of religion.

As I now grew very tall for my age, and more to my mother's liking than before, she took care to deck and dress me, to make me see company, and to take me abroad. She took an inordinate pride in that beauty with which God had formed me, to bless and praise Him. However it was perverted by me into a source of pride and vanity. Several suitors came to me; but as I was not yet twelve years my father would not listen to any proposals. I loved reading and shut myself up alone every day to read without interruption.

What proved effectual to gain me entirely to God, at least for a time, was that a nephew of my father's passed by our home on a mission to Cochin China. I happened at that time to be taking a walk with my companions, which I seldom did. At my return he was gone. They gave me an account of his sanctity, and the things he had said. I was so touched that I was overcome with sorrow. I cried all the rest of the day and night. Early in the morning I went in great distress to seek my confessor. I said to him, "What, my father, am I the only person in our family to be lost? Alas; help me in my salvation." He was greatly surprised to see me so much afflicted, and comforted me in the best manner he could, not thinking me so bad as I was. In my backslidings I was docile, punctual in obedience, careful to confess often. Since I went to him my life was more regular.

O God of love, how often have You knocked at the door of my heart! How often terrified me with appearances of sudden death! All these only made a transient impression. I presently returned again to my infidelities. This time you did take and quite carried off my heart. Alas, what grief I now sustained for having displeased You! what regrets, what exclamations, what sobbings! Who would have thought, to see me, but that my conversion would have lasted as long as my life? Why did you not, O my God, utterly take this heart to yourself, when I gave it to You so fully. Or, if You did take it then, oh, why did You let it revolt again? You were surely strong enough to hold it, but You would perhaps, in leaving me to myself, display your mercy that the depth of my iniquity might serve as a trophy to your goodness.

I immediately applied myself to every part of my duty. I made a general confession with great compunction of heart. I frankly confessed all that I knew with many tears. I became so changed that I was scarcely known. I would not for ever so much have made the least voluntary slip. They found not any matter for absolution when I confessed. I discovered the very smallest faults and God did me the favor to enable me to conquer myself in many things. There were left only some remains of passion, which gave me some trouble to conquer. But as soon as I had by means thereof, given any displeasure, even to the domestics, I begged their pardon, in order to subdue my wrath and pride; for wrath is the daughter of pride. A person truly humbled permits not anything to put him in a rage. As it is pride which dies the last in the soul, so it is passion which is last destroyed in the outward conduct. A soul thoroughly dead to itself, finds nothing of rage left.

There are persons who, being very much filled with grace and with peace, at their entrance of the resigned path of light and love, think they are come thus far. But they are greatly mistaken, in this view of their state. This they will readily discover, if they are heartily willing to examine two things. First, if their nature is lively, warm and violent, (I speak not of stupid tempers) they will find, from time to time, that they make slips, in which trouble and emotion have some share. Even then they are useful to humble and annihilate them. (But when annihilation is perfected all passion is gone - it is incompatible with this state.) They will find that there often arises in them certain motions of anger, but the sweetness of grace holds them back. They would easily transgress, if in any wise they gave way to these motions. There are persons who think themselves very mild because nothing thwarts them. It is not of such that I am speaking. Mildness which has never been put to the proof, is often only counterfeit. Those persons who, when unmolested, appear to be saints are no sooner exercised by vexing occurrences than there starts up in them a strange number of faults. They had thought them dead which only lay dormant because nothing awakened them.

I followed my religious exercises. I shut myself up all day to read and pray. I gave all I had to the poor taking even linen to their houses. I taught them the catechism and when my parents dined out I made them eat with me and served them with great respect. I read the works of Saint Francis de Sales and the life of Madam de Chantal. There I first learned what mental prayer was, and I besought my confessor to teach me that kind of prayer. As he did not, I used my own endeavors to practice it, though without success, as I then thought, because I could not exercise the imagination, I persuaded myself, that that prayer could not be made without forming to one's self certain ideas and reasoning much. This difficulty gave me no small trouble, for a long time. I was very assiduous and prayed earnestly to God to give me the gift of prayer. All that I saw in the life of M. de Chantal charmed me. I was so much a child, that I thought I ought to do everything I saw in it. All the vows she had made I made also. One day as I was reading that she had put the name of Jesus on her heart, to follow the counsel, "Set me as a seal upon thy heart." For this purpose she had taken a hot iron, whereupon the holy name was engraven. I was very much afflicted that I could not do the same. I decided to write that sacred and adorable name, in large characters, on paper, then with ribbons and a needle I fastened it to my skin in four places. In that position it continued a long time.

After this, I turned all my thoughts to become a nun. Because the love which I had for Saint Francis de Sales did not permit me to think of any other community than the one of which he was the founder, I frequently went to beg the nuns there to receive me into their convent. Often I stole out of my father's house to go and repeatedly solicit my admission there. Though it was what they eagerly desired, even as a temporal advantage, yet they never dared let me enter, as they very much feared my father, to whose fondness for me they were no strangers.

There was at that house a niece of my father's, to whom I am under great obligations. Fortune had not been very favorable to her father. It had reduced her in some measure to depend on mine, to whom she made known my desire. Although he would not for anything in the world have hindered a right vocation, yet he could not hear of my design without shedding tears. As he happened at this time to be abroad, my cousin went to my confessor, to desire him to forbid my going to the visitation. He dared not, however, do it plainly, for fear of drawing on himself the resentment of that community. I still wanted to be a nun, and importuned my mother excessively to take me to that house. She would not do it, for fear of grieving my father, who was absent.

Chapter Five

No sooner was my father returned home, than he became violently ill. My mother was at the same time indisposed in another part of the house. I was all alone with him, ready to render him every kind of service I was capable of, and to give him all the dutiful marks of a most sincere affection. I do not doubt but my assiduity was very agreeable to him. I performed the most menial offices unperceived by him taking the time for it when the servants were not at hand; as well to mortify myself as to pay due honor to what Jesus Christ said, that He came not to be ministered to, but to minister. When father made me read to him, I read with such heartfelt devotion that he was surprised. I remembered the instruction my sister had given me, and the ejaculatory prayers and praises I had learned.

She had taught me to praise You, O my God, in all Your works. All that I saw called upon me to render You homage. If it rained, I wished every drop to be changed into love and praises. My heart was nourished insensibly with Your love; and my spirit was incessantly engrossed with the remembrance of You. I seemed to join and partake in all the good that was done in the world, and could have wished to have the united hearts of all men to love You. This habit rooted itself so strongly in me, that I retained it throughout my greatest wanderings.

My cousin helped not a little, to support me in these good sentiments; I was often with her, and loved her, as she took great care of me, and treated me with much gentleness. Her fortune being equal neither to her birth nor her virtue, she did with charity and affection what her condition obliged her to do. My mother grew jealous, fearing I should love my cousin too well and herself too little. She who had left me in my young years to the care of her maids, and since that to my own, only requiring if I was in the house. Troubling herself no further, now required me always to stay with her, and never suffered me to be with my cousin but with great reluctance. My cousin fell ill. My mother took that occasion to send her home, which was a very severe stroke to my heart, as well as to that grace which began to dawn in me. My mother was a very virtuous woman. She was one of the most charitable women of her age. She not only gave the surplus, but even the necessities of the house. Never were the needy neglected. Never any wretched one came to her without succor. She furnished poor mechanics wherewith to carry on their work, and needy tradesmen wherewith to supply their shops. From her, I think, I inherited my charity and love for the poor. God favored me with the blessing of being her successor in that holy exercise. There was not one in the town, or its environs, who did not praise her for this virtue. She sometimes gave to the last penny in the house, though she had a large family to maintain, and yet she did not fail in her faith.

My mother's only care about me had been all along to have me in the house, which indeed is one material point for a girl. This habit of being so constantly kept within, proved of great service after my marriage. It would have been better had she kept me more in her own apartment, with an agreeable freedom and inquired oftener what part of the house I was in.

After my cousin left me, God granted me the grace to forgive injuries with such readiness, that my confessor was surprised. He knew that some young ladies had, out of envy, traduced me and that I spoke well of them as occasion offered. I was seized with an ague, which lasted four months, in which I suffered much. During that time, I was enabled to suffer with much resignation and patience. In this frame of mind and manner of life I persevered, so long as I continued the practice of mental prayer.

Later we went to pass some days in the country. My father took along with us one of his relations, a very accomplished young gentleman. He had a great desire to marry me; but my father, resolved not to give me to any near kinsman on account of the difficulty obtaining dispensations, put him off, without alleging any false or frivolous reasons for it. As this young gentleman was very devout, and every day said the office of the Virgin, I said it with him. To have time for it, I left off prayer which was to me the first inlet of evils. Yet, I kept up for a long time some share of the spirit of piety; for I went to seek out the little shepherdesses, to instruct them in their religious duties. This spirit gradually decayed, not being nourished by prayer. I became cold toward God. All my old faults revived to which I added an excessive vanity. The love I began to have for myself extinguished what remained in me of the love of God.

I did not wholly leave off mental prayer, without asking my confessor's leave. I told him I thought it better to say the office of the Virgin every day than to practice prayer; I had not time for both. I saw not that this was a stratagem of the enemy to draw me from God, to entangle me in the snares he had laid for me. I had time sufficient for both, as I had no other occupation than what I prescribed to myself. My confessor was easy in the matter. Not being a man of prayer he gave his consent to my great hurt.

Oh, my God, if the value of prayer were but known, the great advantage which accrues to the soul from conversing with You, and what consequence it is of to salvation, everyone would be assiduous in it. It is a stronghold into which the enemy cannot enter. He may attack it, besiege it, make a noise about its walls; but while we are faithful and hold our station, he cannot hurt us. It is alike requisite to dictate to children the necessity of prayer as of their salvation. Alas, unhappily, it is thought sufficient to tell them that there is a Heaven and a Hell; that they must endeavor to avoid the latter and attain the former; yet they are not taught the shortest and easiest way of arriving at it. The only way to Heaven is prayer; a prayer of the heart, which every one is capable of, and not of reasonings which are the fruits of study, or exercise of the imagination, which, in filling the mind with wandering objects, rarely settle it; instead of warming the heart with love to God, they leave it cold and languishing. Let the poor come, let the ignorant and carnal come; let the children without reason or knowledge come, let the dull or hard hearts which can retain nothing come to the practice of prayer and they shall become wise.

O you great, wise and rich, Have you not a heart capable of loving what is proper for you and of hating what is destructive? Love the sovereign good, hate all evil, and you will be truly wise. When you love anyone, is it because you know the reasons of love and its definitions? No, certainly. You love because your heart is formed to love what it finds amiable. Surely you cannot but know that there is nought lovely in the universe but God. Know you not that He has created you, that He has died for you? But if these reasons are not sufficient, which of you has not some necessity, some trouble, or some misfortune? Which of you does not know how to tell his malady, and beg relief? Come, then, to this Fountain of all good, without complaining to weak and impotent creatures, who cannot help you; come to prayer; lay before God your troubles, beg His grace -- and above all, that you may love Him. None can exempt himself from loving; for none can live without a heart, nor the heart without love.

Why should any amuse themselves, in seeking reasons for loving Love itself? Let us love without reasoning about it, and we shall find ourselves filled with love, before the others have learned the reasons which induced to it. Make trial of this love, and you will be wiser in it than the most skillful philosophers. In love, as in everything else, experience instructs better than reasoning. Come then, drink at this fountain of living waters, instead of the broken cisterns of the creature, which far from allaying your thirst, only tend continually to augment it. Did you once drink at this fountain, you would not seek elsewhere for anything to quench your thirst; for while you still continue to draw from this source, you would thirst no longer after the world. But if you quit it, alas, the enemy has the ascendant. He will give you of his poisoned draughts, which may have an apparent sweetness, but will assuredly rob you of life.

I forsook the fountain of living water when I left off prayer. I became as a vineyard exposed to pillage, hedges torn down with liberty to all the passengers to ravage it. I began to seek in the creature what I had found in God. He left me to myself, because I first left him. It was His will by permitting me to sink into the horrible pit, to make me feel the necessity I was in of approaching Him in prayer.

You have said, that You will destroy those adulterous souls who depart from You. Alas, it is their departure alone which causes their destruction, since, in departing from You, O Sun of Righteousness, they enter into the regions of darkness and the coldness of death, from which they would never rise, if You did not revisit them. If You did not by your divine light, illuminate their darkness, and by your enlivening warmth, melt their icy hearts, and restore them to life, they would never rise. I fell then into the greatest of all misfortunes. I wandered yet farther and farther from You, O my God, and you did gradually retire from a heart which had quitted You. Yet such is your goodness, that it seemed as if You had left me with regret; and when this heart was desirous to return again unto You, with what speed did You come to meet it. This proof of Your love and mercy, shall be to me an everlasting testimony of your goodness and of my own ingratitude.

I became still more passionate than I had ever been, as age gave more force to nature. I was frequently guilty of lying. I felt my heart corrupt and vain. The spark of divine grace was almost extinguished in me, and I fell into a state of indifference and indevotion, though I still carefully kept up outside appearances. The habit I had acquired of behaving at church made me appear better than I was. Vanity, which had been excluded to my heart now resumed its seat. I began to pass a great part of my time before a looking glass. I found so much pleasure in viewing myself, that I thought others were in the right who practiced the same. Instead of making use of this exterior, which God had given me, that I might love Him the more, it became to me only the means of a vain complacency. All seemed to me to look beautiful in my person, but I saw not that it covered a polluted soul. This rendered me so inwardly vain, that I doubt whether any ever exceeded me therein. There was an affected modesty in my outward deportment that would have deceived the world.

The high esteem I had for myself made me find faults in everyone else of my own sex. I had no eyes but to see my own good qualities, and to discover the defects of others. I hid my own faults from myself, or if I remarked any, yet to me they appeared little in comparison of others. I excused, and even figured them to myself as perfections. Every idea I had of others and of myself was false. I loved reading to such excess, particularly romances, that I spent whole days and nights at them. Sometimes the day broke while I continued to read, insomuch, that for a length of time I almost lost the habit of sleeping. I was ever eager to get to the end of the book, in hopes of finding something to satisfy a certain craving which I found within me. My thirst for reading was only increased the more I read. Books are strange inventions to destroy youth. If they caused no other hurt than the loss of precious time, is not that too much? I was not restrained, but rather encouraged to read them under this fallacious pretext, that they taught one to speak well.

Meanwhile, through your abundant mercy, O my God, You came to seek me from time to time, You did indeed knock at the door of my heart. I was often penetrated with the most lively sorrow and shed abundance of tears. I was afflicted to find my state so different from what it was when I enjoyed Your sacred presence; but my tears were fruitless and my grief in vain. I could not of myself get out of this wretched state. I wished some hand as charitable as powerful would extricate me; as for myself I had no power. If I had had any friend, who would have examined the cause of this evil, and made me have recourse again to prayer, which was the only means of relief, all would have been well. I was (like the prophet) in a deep abyss of mire, which I could not get out off. I met with reprimands for being in it, but none were kind enough to reach out to free me. And when I tried vain efforts to get out, I only sunk the deeper, and each fruitless attempt only made me see my own impotence, and rendered me more afflicted.

Oh, how much compassion has this sad experience given me for sinners. It has taught me why so few of them emerge from the miserable state into which they have fallen. Such as see it only cry out against their disorders, and frighten them with threats of future punishment! These cries and threats at first make some impression, and they use some weak efforts after liberty, but, after having experienced their insufficiency, they gradually abate in their design, and lose their courage for trying any more. All that man can say to them afterward is but lost labor, though one preach to them incessantly. When any for relief run to confess, the only true remedy for them is prayer; to present themselves before God as criminals, beg strength of Him to rise out of this state. Then would they soon be changed, and brought out of the mire and clay. But the devil has falsely persuaded the doctors and the wise men of the age, that, in order to pray, it is necessary first to be perfectly converted. Hence people are dissuaded from it, and hence there is rarely any conversion that is durable. The devil is outrageous only against prayer, and those that exercise it; because he knows it is the true means of taking his prey from him. He lets us undergo all the austerities we will. He neither persecutes those that enjoy them nor those that practice them. But no sooner does one enter into a spiritual life, a life of prayer, but they must prepare for strange crosses. All manner of persecutions and contempt in this world are reserved for that life.

Miserable as the condition was to which I was reduced by my infidelities, and the little help I had from my confessor, I did not fail to say my vocal prayers every day, to confess pretty often, and to partake of the communion almost every fortnight. Sometimes I went to church to weep, and to pray to the Blessed Virgin to obtain my conversion. I loved to hear anyone speak of God, and would never tire of the conversation. When my father spoke of Him, I was transported with joy; and when he and my mother went on any pilgrimage, and were to set off early in the morning, I either did not go to bed the night before, or hired the girls to awake me early. My father's conversation at such times was always of divine matters, which afforded me the highest delight, and I preferred that subject to any other. I also loved the poor, and was charitable, even while I was so very faulty. How strange may this seem to some, and how hard to reconcile things so very opposite.

Chapter Six

Afterward we came to Paris where my vanity increased. No course was spared to make me appear to advantage. I was forward enough to show myself and expose my pride, in making a parade of this vain beauty. I wanted to be loved of everyone and to love none. Several apparently advantageous offers of marriage were made for me; but God unwilling to have me lost did not permit matters to succeed. My father still found difficulties, which my all-wise Creator raised for my salvation. Had I married any of these persons, I should have been much exposed, and my vanity would have had means to extend itself.

There was one person who had asked for me in marriage for several years. My father, for family reasons, had always refused him. His manners were opposite to my vanity. A fear lest I should leave my country, together with the affluent circumstances of this gentleman, induced my father, in spite of both his own and my mother's reluctance, to promise me to him. This was done without consulting me. They made me sign the marriage articles without letting me know what they were. I was well pleased with the thoughts of marriage, flattering myself with a hope of being thereby set at full liberty, and delivered from the ill-treatment of my mother which I drew upon myself. God ordered it far otherwise. The condition which I found myself in afterward, frustrated my hopes.

Pleasing as marriage was to my thoughts, I was all the time, after my being promised, and even long after my marriage, in extreme confusion, which arose from two causes. First, my natural modesty, which I did not lose. I had much reserve toward men. The other, my vanity. Though the husband provided was a more advantageous match than I merited, yet I did not think him such. The figure which the others made, who had offered to me before, was vastly more engaging. Their rank would have placed me in view. Whatever did not flatter my vanity, was to me insupportable. Yet this very vanity was, I think, of some advantage; it hindered me from falling into such things as cause the ruin of families. I would not do anything which in the eye of the world, might render me culpable. As I was modest at church and had not been used to go abroad without my mother, as the reputation of our house was great, I passed for virtuous.

I did not see my spouse elect (at Paris) till two or three days before our marriage. I caused masses to be said all the time after my being contracted, to know the will of God. I wished to do it in this affair at least.

Oh, my God, how great was your goodness, to bear with me at this time, and to allow me to pray to You with as much boldness, as if I had been one of your friends, I who had rebelled against You as your greatest enemy.

The joy of our nuptials was universal through our village. Amid this general rejoicing, there appeared none sad but myself. I could neither laugh as others did, nor even eat; so much was I depressed. I knew not the cause. It was a foretaste which God gave me of what was to befall me. The remembrance of the desire I had of being a nun, came pouring in. All who came to compliment me, the day after, could not forbear rallying me. I wept bitterly. I answered, "Alas, I had desired so much to be a nun; why then am I now married? By what fatality has such a revolution befallen me? No sooner was I at the house of my new spouse, than I perceived that it would be for me a house of mourning.

I was obliged to change my conduct. Their manner of living was very different from that in my father's house. My mother-inlaw, who had long been a widow, regarded nothing else but economy. At my father's house they lived in a noble manner and great elegance. What my husband and mother-in-law called pride, and I called politeness, was observed there. I was very much surprised at this change, and so much the more, as my vanity wished to increase, rather than to be diminished.

At the time of my marriage I was a little past fifteen years of age. My surprise increased greatly, when I saw I must lose what I had acquired with so much application. At my father's house we were obliged to behave in a genteel way, and to speak with propriety. All that I said was applauded. Here they never hearkened to me, but to contradict and find fault. If I spoke well, they said it was to give them a lesson. If any questions were started at my father's, he encouraged me to speak freely. Here, if I spoke my sentiments, they said it was to enter into a dispute. They put me to silence in an abrupt and shameful manner, and scolded me from morning till night.

I should have some difficulty to give you an account, which cannot be done without wounding charity, if you had not forbidden me to omit any one. I request you not to look at things on the side of the creature, which would make these persons appear worse than they were. My mother-in-law had virtue, my husband had religion, and not any vice. It is requisite to look at everything on the side of God. He permitted these things only for my salvation, and because He would not have me lost. I had beside so much pride, that had I received any other treatment, I should have continued therein, and should not, perhaps, have turned to God as I was induced to do, by the oppression of a multitude of crosses.

My mother-in-law conceived such a desire to oppose me in everything, that, in order to vex me, she made me perform the most humiliating offices. Her disposition was so extraordinary, having never surmounted it in her youth, that she could hardly live with anybody. Saying none than vocal prayers, she did not see this fault; or seeing it, and not drawing from the forces of prayer, she could not get the better of it. It was a pity, for she had both sense and merit. I was made the victim of her humors. All her occupation was to thwart me and she inspired the like sentiments in her son. They would make persons my inferiors take place above me. My mother, who had a high sense of honor, could not endure that. When she heard it from others (for I told her nothing) she chided me thinking I did it because I did not know how to keep my rank and had no spirit. I dared not tell her how it was; but I was almost ready to die with the agonies of grief and continual vexation. What aggravated all was the remembrance of the persons who had proposed for me, the difference of their dispositions and manners, the love they had for me, with their agreeableness and politeness. All this made my burden intolerable. My mother-in-law upbraided me in regard to my family, and spoke to me incessantly to the disadvantage of my father and mother. I never went to see them, but I had some bitter speeches to bear on my return.

My mother complained that I did not come often enough to see her. She said I did not love her, that I was alienated from my family by being too much attached to my husband.

What augmented my crosses was that my mother related to my mother-in-law the pains I had cost her from infancy. They then reproached me, saying, I was a changeling, and an evil spirit. My husband obliged me to stay all day long in my mother-in-law's room, without any liberty of retiring into my own apartment. She spoke disadvantageously of me, to lessen the affection and esteem which some had entertained for me. She galled me with the grossest affronts before the finest company. This did not have the effect she wanted; the more patiently they saw me bear it, the higher esteem they had for me.

She found the secret of extinguishing my vivacity, and rendering me stupid. Some of my former acquaintances hardly knew me. Those who had not seen me before said, "Is this the person famed for such abundance of wit? She can't say two words. She is a fine picture." I was not yet sixteen years old. I was so much intimidated, that I dared not go out without my mother-in-law, and in her presence I could not speak. I knew not what I said; so much fear had I.

To complete my affliction, they presented me with a waitingmaid who was everything with them. She kept me in sight like a governess. For the most part I bore with patience these evils which I had no way to avoid. But sometimes I let some hasty answer escape me, a source of grievous crosses to me. When I went out, the footmen had orders to give an account of everything I did. It was then I began to eat the bread of sorrows, and to mingle tears with my drink. At the table they always did something which covered me with confusion. I could not forbear tears. I had no one to confide in who might share my affliction, and assist me to bear it. When I would impart some hint of it to my mother, I drew upon myself new crosses. I resolved to have no confidant. It was not from any natural cruelty that my husband treated me thus; he loved me passionately, but he was warm and hasty, and my mother-in-law continually irritated him about me.

It was in a condition so deplorable, O my God, that I began to perceive the need I had of Your assistance. For this situation was perilous for me. I met with none but admirers abroad, those that flattered me to my hurt. It were to be feared lest at such a tender age, amid all the strange domestic crosses I had to bear, I might be drawn away. But You, by Your goodness and love, gave it quite another turn. By these redoubled strokes You did draw me to Yourself, and by Your crosses effected what Your caresses could not effect. Nay, You made use of my natural pride, to keep me within the limits of my duty. I knew that a woman of honor ought never to give suspicion to her husband. I was so very circumspect that I often carried it to excess, so far as to refuse my hand to such as in politeness offered me theirs. There happened to me an adventure which, by carrying my prudence too far, might have ruined me, for things were taken contrary to their intent. My husband was sensible both of my innocence and of the falsehood of the insinuations of my mother-in-law.

Such weighty crosses made me return to God. I began to deplore the sins of my youth. Since my marriage I had not committed any voluntarily. Yet I still had some sentiments of vanity remaining, which I did not wish. However, my troubles now counter-balanced them. Moreover, many of them appeared my just dessert according to the little light I then had. I was not illuminated to penetrate the essence of my vanity; I fixed my thoughts only on its appearance. I tried to amend my life by penance, and by a general confession, the most exact that I ever yet had made. I laid aside the reading of romances, for which I lately had such a fondness. Though some time before my marriage that had been dampened by reading the Gospel, I was so much affected therewith, and discovered truth therein, that put me out of patience with all the other books. Novels appeared then to me only full of lies and deceit. I now put away even indifferent books, to have none but such as were profitable. I resumed the practice of prayer, and endeavored to offend God no more. I felt His love gradually recovering the ascendant in my heart, and banishing every other. Yet I had still an intolerable vanity and self-complacency, which has been my most grievous and obstinate sin.

My crosses redoubled. What rendered them more painful was, that my mother-in-law, not content with the bitterest speeches which she uttered against me, both in public and private, would break out in anger about the smallest trifles, and scarcely be pacified for a fortnight. I used a part of my time in bewailing myself when I could be alone; and my grief became every day more bitter. Sometimes I could not contain myself, when the girls, my domestics, who owed me submission, treated me ill. I did what I could to subdue my temper which has cost me not a little.

Such stunning blows so impaired the vivacity of my nature, that I became like a lamb that is shorn. I prayed to our Lord to assist me, and He was my refuge. As my age differed from theirs (for my husband was twenty-two years older than I) I saw well that there was no probability of changing their dispositions, which were fortified with years. I found that whatever I said was offensive, not excepting those things which others would have been pleased with.

One day, weighed down with grief and in despair, about six months after I was married, being alone, I was tempted even to cut out my tongue so I might no longer irritate those who seized every word I uttered with rage and resentment.

But You, O God, did stop me short and showed me my folly. I prayed continually, and wished even to become dumb, so simple and ignorant was I. Though I have had my share of crosses, I never found any so difficult to support as that of perpetual contrariety without relaxation of doing all one can to please, without succeeding, but still offending by the very means designed to oblige. Being kept with such persons, in a most severe confinement, from morning till night, without ever daring to quit them is most difficult. I have found that great crosses overwhelm, and stifle all anger. Such a continual contrariety irritates and stirs up sourness in the heart. It has such strange effect, that it requires the utmost efforts of self-restraint, not to break out into vexation and rage.

My condition in marriage was rather that of a slave than of a free person. I perceived, four months after my marriage, that my husband was gouty. This malady caused many crosses within and without. He had the gout twice the first year, six weeks each time. He was so much plagued with it, that he came no more out of his room, nor out of his bed. He was in bed usually for several months. I carefully attended him although so very young. I did not fail to exert myself to the utmost in the performance of my duty. Alas, all this did not gain me friendship. I had not the consolation to know whether what I did was agreeable. I denied myself all the most innocent diversions to continue with my husband. I did whatever I thought would please him. Sometimes he quietly suffered me, and then I esteemed myself very happy. At other times I seemed insupportable to him. My particular friends said, "I was of a fine age indeed to be a nurse to an invalid, and that it was a shameful thing that I did not set more value on my talents." I answered, "Since I have a husband, I ought to share his painful as well as his pleasing circumstances." Besides this, my mother, instead of pitying me, reprimanded me sharply for my assiduity to my husband.

But, O my God, how different were Your thoughts from theirs, how different that which was without, from what passed within! My husband had that foible, that when anyone said anything to him against me, he flew into a rage at once. It was the conduct of providence over me; for he was a man of reason and loved me much. When I was sick, he was inconsolable. I believe, had it not been for my mother-in-law, and the girl I have spoken of, I should have been very happy with him. Most men have their moods and emotions, and it is the duty of a reasonable woman to bear them peaceably, without irritating them more by cross replies.

These things You have ordered, O my God, in such a manner, by Your goodness, that I have since seen it was necessary, to make me die to my vain and haughty nature. I should not have had power to destroy it myself, if you had not accomplished it by an all-wise economy of your providence. I prayed for patience with great earnestness; nevertheless, some sallies of my natural liveliness escaped me, and vanquished the resolutions I had taken of being silent. This was doubtless permitted, that my self-love might not be nourished by my patience. Even a moment's slip caused me months of humiliation, reproach and sorrow, and proved the occasion of new crosses.

Chapter Seven

During the first year I was still vain. I sometimes lied to excuse myself to my husband and mother-in-law. I stood strangely in awe of them. Sometimes I fell into a temper, their conduct appeared so very unreasonable, and especially their countenancing the most provoking treatment of the girl who served me. As to my mother-in-law, her age and rank rendered her conduct more tolerable.

But You, O my God, opened my eyes to see things in a very different light. I found in You reasons for suffering, which I had never found in the creature. I afterward saw clearly and reflected with joy, that this conduct, as unreasonable as it seemed, and as mortifying as it was, was quite necessary for me. Had I been applauded here as I was at my father's, I should have grown intolerably proud. I had a fault common to most of our sex - I could not hear a beautiful woman praised, without finding fault, to lessen the good which was said of her. This fault continued long, and was the fruit of gross and malignant pride. Extravagantly extolling anyone proceeds from a like source.

Just before the birth of my first child, they were induced to take great care of me. My crosses were somewhat mitigated. Indeed, I was so ill that it was enough to excite the compassion of the most indifferent. They had so great a desire of having children to inherit their fortunes, that they were continually afraid lest I should any way hurt myself. Yet, when the time of my delivery drew near, this care and tenderness of me abated. Once, as my mother-in-law had treated me in a very grating manner, I had the malice to feign a cholic, to give them some alarm; but as I saw this little artifice gave them too much pain, I told them I was better. No creature could be more heavily laden with sickness than I was. Beside continual heavings, I had so strange a distaste, except for some fruit, that I could not bear the sight of food. I had continual swoonings and violent pains. After my delivery I continued weak a long time. There was indeed sufficient to exercise patience, and I was enabled to offer up my sufferings to our Lord. I took a fever, which rendered me so weak, that after several weeks I could scarcely bear to be moved or to have my bed made. When I began to recover, an abscess fell upon my breast, which was forced to be laid open in two places, which gave me great pain. Yet all the maladies seemed to me only a shadow of troubles, in comparison with those I suffered in the family which daily increased. Indeed, life was so wearisome to me, that those maladies which were thought mortal did not frighten me.

The event improved my appearance, and consequently served to increase my vanity. I was glad to call forth expressions of regard. I went to the public promenades (though but seldom) and when in the streets, I pulled off my mask out of vanity. I drew off my gloves to show my hands. Could there be greater folly? After falling into these weaknesses, I used to weep bitterly at home. Yet, when occasion offered, I fell into them again.

My husband lost considerably. This cost me strange crosses, not that I cared for the losses, but I seemed to be the butt of all the ill-humors of the family. With what pleasure did I sacrifice temporal blessings. How often I felt willing to have begged my bread, if God had so ordered it. But my mother-in-law was inconsolable. She bid me pray to God for these things. To me that was wholly impossible.

O my dearest Lord, never could I pray to You about the world, or the things thereof; nor sully my sacred addresses to Your majesty with the dirt of the earth. No; I rather wish to renounce it all, and everything beside whatsoever, for the sake of Your love, and the enjoyment of Your presence in that kingdom which is not of this world. I wholly sacrificed myself to You, even earnestly begging You rather to reduce our family to beggary, than suffer it to offend you.

In my own mind I excused my mother-in-law, saying to myself, "If I had taken the pains to scrape and save, I would not be so indifferent at seeing so much lost. I enjoy what cost me nothing, and reap what I have not sowed." Yet all these thoughts could not make me sensible to our losses. I even formed agreeable ideas of our going to the hospital. No state appeared to me so poor and miserable, which I should not have thought easy, in comparison with the continual domestic persecutions I underwent. My father who loved me tenderly, and whom I honored beyond expression, knew nothing of it. God so permitted it that I should have him also displeased with me for some time. My mother was continually telling him that I was an ungrateful creature, showing no regard for them, but all for my husband's family. Appearances were against me. I did not go to see them as often as I should. They knew not the captivity I was in; what I was obliged to bear in defending them. These complaints of my mother, and a trivial affair that fell out, lessened a little my father's fond regard for me; but it did not last long. My mother-in-law reproached me, saying, "No afflictions befell them till I came into the house. All misfortunes came with me." On the other hand my mother wanted me to exclaim against my husband which I could never submit to do.

We continued to meet with loss after loss, the king retrenching a considerable share of our revenues, besides great sums of money, which we lost by L'Hotel de Ville. I could have no rest or peace, in such great afflictions. I had no mortal to console me, or to advise me. My sister, who had educated me, had departed this life. She died two months before my marriage. I had no other for a confidant.

I declare, that I find much repugnance in saying so many things of my mother-in-law. I have no doubt that my own indiscretion, my caprice, and the occasional sallies of a warm temper, drew many of the crosses upon me. Although I had what the world calls patience, yet I had neither a relish nor love for the cross. Their conduct toward me, which appeared so unreasonable, should not be looked upon with worldly eyes. We should look higher and then we shall see that it was directed by Providence for my eternal advantage.

I now dressed my hair in the most modest manner, never painted, and to subdue the vanity which still had possession of me, I rarely looked in the glass. My reading was confined to books of devotion, such as Thomas à Kempis, and the works of St. Francis de Sales. I read these aloud for the improvement of the servants, while the maid was dressing my hair. I suffered myself to be dressed just as she pleased, which freed me from a great deal of trouble. It took away the occasions wherein my vanity used to be exercised. I knew not how things were; but they always liked me, and thought all well in point of dress. If on some particular days I wanted to appear better, it proved worse. The more indifferent I was about dress the better I appeared. How often have I gone to church, not so much to worship God as to be seen. Other women, jealous of me, affirmed that I painted; they told my confessor, who chided me for it, though I assured him I was innocent. I often spoke in my own praise, and sought to raise myself by depreciating others. Yet these faults gradually deceased; for I was very sorry afterward for having committed them. I often examined myself very strictly, writing down my faults from week to week, and from month to month, to see how much I was improved or reformed. Alas, this labor, though fatiguing, was of but little service, because I trusted in my own efforts. I wished indeed to be reformed, but my good desires were weak and languid.

At one time my husband's absence was so long, and in the meantime my crosses and vexations at home so great, that I determined to go to him. My mother-in-law strongly opposed it. This once my father interfering, and insisting on it, she let me go. On my arrival I found he had almost died. Through vexation and fretting he was very much changed. He could not finish his affairs, having no liberty in attending to them, keeping himself concealed at the Hotel de Longueville, where Madame de Longueville was extremely kind to me. I came publicly, and he was in great fear lest I should make him known. In a rage he bid me return home. Love and my long absence from him surmounting every other reason, he soon relented and suffered me to stay with him. He kept me eight days without letting me stir out of his sight. Fearing the effects of such a close confinement on my constitution, he desired me to go and take a walk in the garden. There I met Madame de Longueville, who testified great joy on seeing me.

I cannot express all the kindness I met with in this house. All the domestics served me with emulation, and applauded me on account of my appearance, and exterior deportment. Yet I was much on my guard against too much attention. I never entered into discourse with any man when alone. I admitted none into my coach, not even my relations, unless my husband were in it. There was not any rule of discretion which I did not duly observe, to avoid giving suspicion to my husband, or subject of calumny to others. Everyone studied there how to contribute to divert or oblige me. Outwardly everything appeared agreeable. Chagrin had so overcome and ruffled my husband that I had continually something to bear. Sometimes he threatened to throw the supper out of the windows. I said, he would then do me an injury, as I had a keen appetite. I made him laugh and I laughed with him. Before that, melancholy prevailed over all my endeavors, and over the love he had for me. God both armed me with patience and gave me the grace to return him no answer. The devil, who attempted to draw me into some offence, was forced to retire in confusion, through the signal assistance of that grace.

I loved my God and was unwilling to displease Him, and I was inwardly grieved on account of that vanity, which still I found myself unable to eradicate. Inward distresses, together with oppressive crosses, which I had daily to encounter, at length threw me into sickness. As I was unwilling to incommode the Hotel de Longueville I had myself moved to another house. The disease proved violent and tedious, insomuch that the physicians despaired of my life. The priest, a pious man, seemed fully satisfied with the state of my mind. He said, "I should die like a saint." But my sins were too present and too painful to my heart to have such presumption. At midnight they administered the sacrament to me as they hourly expected my departure. It was a scene of general distress in the family and among all who knew me. There were none indifferent to my death but myself. I beheld it without fear, and was insensible to its approach. It was far otherwise with my husband. He was inconsolable when he saw there was no hope. I no sooner began to recover, than notwithstanding all his love, his usual fretfulness returned. I recovered almost miraculously and to me this disorder proved a great blessing. Beside a very great patience under violent pains, it served to instruct me much in my view of the emptiness of all worldly things. It detached me from myself and gave me new courage to suffer better than I had done. The love of God gathered strength in my heart, with a desire to please and be faithful to Him in my condition. I reaped several other advantages from it which I need not relate, I had yet six months to drag along with a slow fever. It was thought that it would terminate in death. Your time, O my God, had not yet arrived for taking me to Yourself. Your designs over me were widely different from the expectations of those about me; it being Your determination to make me both the object of Your mercy and the victim of Your justice.

Chapter Eight

After long languishing, at length I regained my former health. About this time my dear mother departed this life in great tranquility of mind. Beside her other good qualities, she had been particularly charitable to the poor. This virtue, so acceptable to God, He was graciously pleased to commence rewarding even in this life. Though she was but twenty-four hours sick, she was made perfectly easy about everything that was near and dear to her in this world.

I now applied myself to my duties, never failing to practice that of prayer twice a day. I watched over myself, to subdue my spirit continually. I went to visit the poor in their houses, assisting them in their distresses. I did (according to my understanding) all the good I knew.

You, O my God, increased both my love and my patience, in proportion to my sufferings. I regretted not the temporal advantages with which my mother distinguished my brother above me. Yet they fell on me about that, as about everything else. I also had for some time a severe ague. I did not indeed serve You yet with that fervor which You did give me soon after. For I would still have been glad to reconcile Your love with the love of myself and of the creature. Unhappily I always found some who loved me, and whom I could not forbear wishing to please. It was not that I loved them, but it was for the love that I bore to myself.

A lady, an exile, came to my father's house. He offered her an apartment which she accepted, and she stayed a long time. She was one of true piety and inward devotion. She had a great esteem for me, because I desired to love God. She remarked that I had the virtues of an active and bustling life; but I had not yet attained the simplicity of prayer which she experienced. Sometimes she dropped a word to me on that subject. As my time had not yet come, I did not understand her. Her example instructed me more than her words. I observed on her countenance something which marked a great enjoyment of the presence of God. By the exertion of studied reflection and thoughts I tried to attain it but to little purpose. I wanted to have, by my own efforts, what I could not acquire except by ceasing from all efforts.

My father's nephew, of whom I have made mention before, was returned from Cochin China, to take over some priests from Europe. I was exceedingly glad to see him, and remembered what good he had done me. The lady mentioned was no less rejoiced than I. They understood each other immediately and conversed in a spiritual language. The virtue of this excellent relation charmed me. I admired his continual prayer without being able to comprehend it. I endeavored to meditate, and to think on God without intermission, to utter prayers and ejaculations. I could not acquire, by all my toil, what God at length gave me Himself, and which is experienced only in simplicity. My cousin did all he could to attach me more strongly to God. He conceived great affection for me. The purity he observed in me from the corruptions of the age, the abhorrence of sin at a time of life when others are beginning to relish the pleasures of it, (I was not yet eighteen), gave him a great tenderness for me. I complained to him of my faults ingenuously. These I saw clearly. He cheered and exhorted me to support myself, and to persevere in my good endeavors. He would fain have introduced me into a more simple manner of prayer, but I was not yet ready for it. I believe his prayers were more effectual than his words.

No sooner was he gone out of my father's house, than you, O Divine Love, manifested your favor. The desire I had to please You, the tears I shed, the manifold pains I underwent, the labors I sustained, and the little fruit I reaped from them, moved You with compassion. This was the state of my soul when Your goodness, surpassing all my vileness and infidelities, and abounding in proportion to my wretchedness, granted me in a moment, what all my own efforts could never procure. Beholding me rowing with laborious toil, the breath of Your divine operations turned in my favor, and carried me full sail over this sea of affliction.

I had often spoken to my confessor about the great anxiety it gave me to find I could not meditate, nor exert my imagination in order to pray. Subjects of prayer which were too extensive were useless to me. Those which were short and pithy suited me better.

At length, God permitted a very religious person, of the order of Saint Francis, to pass by my father's dwelling. He had intended going another way that was shorter, but a secret power changed his design. He saw there was something for him to do, and imagined that God had called him for the conversion of a man of some distinction in that country. His labors there proved fruitless. It was the conquest of my soul which was designed. As soon as he arrived he came to see my father who rejoiced at his coming. At this time I was about to be delivered of my second son, and my father was dangerously ill, expected to die. For some time they concealed his sickness from me. An indiscreet person abruptly told me. Instantly I arose, weak as I was, and went to see him. A dangerous illness came upon me. My father was recovered, but not entirely, enough to give me new marks of his affection. I told him of the strong desire I had to love God, and my great sorrow at not being able to do it fully. He thought he could not give me a more solid indication of his love than in procuring me an acquaintance with this worthy man. He told me what he knew of him, and urged me to go and see him.

At first I made a difficulty of doing it, being intent on observing the rules of the strictest prudence. However, my father's repeated requests had with me the weight of a positive command. I thought I could not do that amiss, which I only did in obedience to him. I took a kinswoman with me. At first he seemed a little confused; for he was reserved toward women. Being newly come out of a five years' solitude, he was surprised that I was the first to address him. He spoke not a word for some time. I knew not to what attribute his silence. I did not hesitate to speak to him, and to tell him a few words, my difficulties about prayer. Presently he replied, "It is, madame, because you seek without what you have within. Accustom yourself to seek God in your heart, and you will there find Him."

Having said these words, he left me. They were to me like the stroke of a dart, which penetrated through my heart. I felt a very deep wound, a wound so delightful that I desired not to be cured. These words brought into my heart what I had been seeking so many years. Rather they discovered to me what was there, and which I had not enjoyed for want of knowing it.

O my Lord, You were in my heart, and demanded only a simple turning of my mind inward, to make me perceive Your presence. Oh, Infinite Goodness! How was I running hither and thither to seek You, my life was a burden to me, although my happiness was within myself. I was poor in riches, and ready to perish with hunger, near a table plentifully spread, and a continual feast. O Beauty, ancient and new; why have I known You so late? Alas, I sought You where You were not, and did not seek You where you were. It was for want of understanding these words of Your Gospel, "The kingdom of God comes not with observation . . . The kingdom of God is within you." This I now experienced. You became my King, and my heart Your kingdom, wherein You did reign supreme, and performed all Your sacred will.

I told this man, that I did not know what he had done to me, that my heart was quite changed, that God was there. He had given me an experience of His presence in my soul; not by thought or any application of mind, but as a thing really possessed after the sweetest manner. I experienced these words in the Canticles (Song of Solomon): "Your name is as precious ointment poured forth; therefore do the virgins love you." I felt in my soul an unction which, as a salutary balsam, healed in a moment all my wounds.

I slept not that whole night, because Your love, O my God, flowed in me like a delicious oil, and burned as a fire which was going to devour all that was left of self. I was suddenly so altered that I was hardly to be known either by myself or others. I found no longer those troublesome faults or reluctances. They disappeared, being consumed like chaff in a great fire.

I now became desirous that the instrument hereof might become my director, preferable to any other. This good father could not readily resolve to charge himself with my conduct although he saw so surprising a change effected by the hand of God. Several reasons induced him to excuse himself. First, my person, then my youth, for I was only nineteen years. Lastly, a promise he had made to God, from a distrust of himself, never to take upon himself the direction of any of our sex, unless God, by some particular providence, should charge him therewith. However, upon my earnest and repeated request to him to become my director, he said he would pray to God and desired that I should do so. As he was at prayer, it was said to him, "Fear not that charge; she is my spouse." When I heard this, it affected me greatly. "What (said I to myself) a frightful monster of iniquity, who has done so much to offend my God, in abusing His favors, and requiting them with ingratitude, now to be declared his spouse!" After this he consented to my request.

Nothing was more easy to me than prayer. Hours passed away like moments, while I could hardly do anything else but pray. The fervency of my love allowed me no intermission. It was a prayer of rejoicing and possessing, devoid of all busy imaginations and forced reflections; it was a prayer of the will, and not of the head. The taste of God was so great, so pure, unblended and uninterrupted, that it drew and absorbed the power of my soul into a profound recollection without act or discourse. I had now no sight but of Jesus Christ alone. All else was excluded, in order to love with the greater extent, without any selfish motives or reasons for loving.

The will, absorbed the two others, the memory and understanding into itself, and concentrated them in love; - not but that they still subsisted, but their operations were in a manner imperceptible and passive. They were no longer stopped or retarded by the multiplicity, but collected and united in one. So the rising of the sun does not extinguish the stars, but overpowers and absorbs them in the luster of his incomparable glory.

Chapter Nine

Such was the prayer that was given me at once, far above ecstasies, transports or visions. All these gifts are less pure, and more subject to illusion or deceits from the enemy.

Visions are in the inferior powers of the soul, and cannot produce true union. The soul must not dwell or rely upon them, or be retarded by them; they are but favors and gifts. The Giver alone must be our object and aim.

It is of such that Paul speaks, "Satan transforms himself into an angel of light," (2Corinthians 11:18); which is generally the case with such as are fond of visions, and lay a stress on them; because they are apt to convey a vanity to the soul, or at least hinder it from humbly attending to God only.

Ecstasies arise from a sensible relish. They may be termed a kind of spiritual sensuality, wherein the soul letting itself go too far, by reason of the sweetness it finds in them, falls imperceptibly into decay. The crafty enemy presents such sort of interior elevations and raptures for baits to entrap the soul, to fill it with vanity and self-love, to fix its esteem and attention on the gifts of God, and to hinder it from following Jesus Christ in the way of renunciation and of death to all things.

And as to distinct interior words, they too are subject to illusion; the enemy can form and counterfeit them. Or if they come from a good angel (for God Himself never speaks thus) we may mistake and misapprehend them. They are spoken in a divine manner, but we construe them in a human and carnal manner.

But the immediate word of God has neither tone nor articulation. It is mute, silent, and unutterable. It is Jesus Christ Himself, the real and essential Word who in the center of the soul that is disposed for receiving Him, never one moment ceases from His living, fruitful, and divine operation.

Oh, your Word made flesh, whose silence is inexpressible eloquence, You can never be misapprehended or mistaken. You become the life of our life, and the soul of our soul. How infinitely is your language elevated above all the utterances of human and finite articulation. Your adorable power, all efficacious in the soul that has received it, communicates itself through them to others. As a divine seed it becomes fruitful to eternal life.

The revelations of things to come are also very dangerous. The Devil can counterfeit them, as he did formerly in the heathen temples, where he uttered oracles. Frequently they raise false ideas, vain hopes, and frivolous expectations. They take up the mind with future events, hinder it from dying to self, and prevent it following Jesus Christ in His poverty, abnegation, and death.

Widely different is the revelation of Jesus Christ, made to the soul when the eternal Word is communicated. (Galatians 1:16) It makes us new creatures, created anew in Him. This revelation is what the Devil cannot counterfeit. From hence proceeds the only safe transport of ecstasy, which is operated by naked faith alone, and dying even to the gifts of God. As long as the soul continues resting in gifts, it does not fully renounce itself. Never passing into God the soul loses the real enjoyment of the Giver, by attachments to the gifts. This is truly an unutterable loss.

Lest I should let my mind go after these gifts, and steal myself from your love, O my God, You were pleased to fix me in a continual adherence to Yourself alone. Souls thus directed get the shortest way. They are to expect great sufferings, especially if they are mighty in faith, in mortification and deadness to all but

God. A pure and disinterested love, and intenseness of mind for the advancement of your interest alone. These are the dispositions You did implant in me, and even a fervent desire of suffering for You. The cross, which I had hitherto borne only with resignation, was become my delight, and the special object of my rejoicing.

Chapter Ten

I wrote an account of my wonderful change, in point of happiness, to that good father who had been made the instrument of it. It filled him both with joy and astonishment. O my God, what penances did the love of suffering induce me to undergo! I was impelled to deprive myself of the most innocent indulgences. All that could gratify my taste was denied and I took everything that could mortify and disgust it. My appetite, which had been extremely delicate, was so far conquered that I could scarcely prefer one thing to another.

I dressed loathsome sores and wounds, and gave remedies to the sick. When I first engaged in this sort of employment, it was with the greatest difficulty I was able to bear it. As soon as my aversion ceased, and I could stand the most offensive things, other channels of employment were opened to me. For I did nothing of myself, but left myself to be wholly governed by my Sovereign.

When that good father asked me how I loved God, I answered, "Far more than the most passionate lover his beloved; and that even this comparison was inadequate, since the love of the creature never can attain to this, either in strength or in depth." This love of God occupied my heart so constantly and so strongly, that I could think of nothing else. Indeed, I judged nothing else worthy of my thoughts.

The good father mentioned was an excellent preacher. He was desired to preach in the parish to which I belonged. When I came, I was so strongly absorbed in God, that I could neither open my eyes, nor hear anything he said.

I found that Your Word, O my God, made its own impression on my heart, and there had its effect, without the mediation of words or any attention to them. And I have found it so ever since, but after a different manner, according to the different degrees and states I have passed through. So deeply was I settled in the inward spirit of prayer, that I could scarce any more pronounce the vocal prayers.

This immersion in God absorbed all things therein. Although I tenderly loved certain saints, as Saint Peter, Saint Paul, Saint Mary Magdalene, Saint Teresa, yet I could not form to myself images of them, nor invoke any of them out of God.

A few weeks after I had received that interior wound of the heart, which had begun my change, the feast of the Blessed Virgin was held, in the convent in which was that good father my director. I went in the morning to get the indulgences and was much surprised when I came there and found that I could not attempt it; though I stayed above five hours in the church. I was penetrated with so lively a dart of pure love, that I could not resolve to abridge by indulgences, the pain due to my sins. "O my Love," I cried, "I am willing to suffer for You. I find no other pleasure but in suffering for You. Indulgences may be good for those who know not the value of sufferings, who choose not that your divine justice should be satisfied; who, having mercenary souls, are not so much afraid of displeasing You, as of the pains annexed to sin." Yet, fearing I might be mistaken, and commit a fault in not getting the indulgences, for I had never heard of anyone being in such a way before, I returned again to try to get them, but in vain. Not knowing what to do, I resigned myself to our Lord. When I returned home, I wrote to the good father that he had made what I had written a part of his sermon, reciting it verbatim as I had written it.

I now quitted all company, bade farewell forever to all plays and diversions, dancing, unprofitable walks and parties of pleasure. For two years I had left off dressing my hair. It became me, and my husband approved it.

My only pleasure now was to steal some moments to be alone with You, O you who are my only Love! All other pleasure was a pain to me. I lost not Your presence, which was given me by a continual infusion, not as I had imagined, by the efforts of the head, or by force of thought in meditating on God, but in the will, where I tasted with unutterable sweetness the enjoyment of the beloved object. In a happy experience I knew that the soul was created to enjoy its God.

The union of the will subjects the soul to God, conforms it to all His pleasure, causes self-will gradually to die. Lastly in drawing with it the other powers, by means of the charity with which it is filled. It causes them gradually to be reunited in the Center, and lost there as to their own nature and operations.

This loss is called the annihilation of the powers. Although in themselves they still subsist, yet they seem annihilated to us, in proportion as charity fills and inflames; it becomes so strong, as by degrees to surmount all the activities of the will of man, subjecting it to that of God. When the soul is docile, and leaves itself to be purified, and emptied of all that which it has of its own, opposite to the will of God, it finds itself by little and little, detached from every emotion of its own, and placed in a holy indifference, wishing nothing but what God does and wills. This never can be effected by the activity of our own will, even though it were employed in continual acts of resignation. These though very virtuous, are so far one's own actions and cause the will to subsist in a multiplicity, in a kind of separate distinction or dissimilitude from God.

When the will of the creature entirely submits to that of the Creator, suffering freely and voluntarily and yielding only a concurrence to the divine will (which is its absolute submission) suffering itself to be totally surmounted and destroyed, by the operations of love; this absorbs the will into self, consummates it in that of God, and purifies it from all narrowness, dissimilitude, and selfishness.

The case is the same with the other two powers. By means of charity, the two other theological virtues, faith and hope, are introduced. Faith so strongly seizes on the understanding, as to make it decline all reasonings, all particular illuminations and illustrations, however sublime. This sufficiently demonstrates how far visions, revelations and ecstasies, differ from this, and hinder the soul from being lost in God. Although by them it appears lost in Him for some transient moments, yet it is not a true loss, since the soul which is entirely lost in God no more finds itself again. Faith then makes the soul lose every distinct light, in order to place it in its own pure light.

The memory, too, finds all its little activities surmounted by degrees, and absorbed in hope. Finally the powers are all concentrated and lost in pure love. It engulfs them into itself by means of their sovereign, the will. The will is the sovereign of the powers and charity is the queen of the virtues, and unites them all in herself.

This reunion thus made, is called the central union or unity. By means of the will and love, all are reunited in the center of the soul in God who is our ultimate end. According to Saint John, "He who dwells in love, dwells in God, for God is love." This union of my will to Yours, O my God, and this ineffable presence was so sweet and powerful, that I was compelled to yield to its delightful power, power which was strict and severe to my minutest faults.

Chapter Eleven

My senses (as I have described) were continually mortified, and under perpetual restraint. To conquer them totally, it is necessary to deny them the smallest relaxation, until the victory is completed. We see those who content themselves practicing great outward austerities, yet by indulging their senses in what is called innocent and necessary, they remain forever unsubdued. Austerities, however severe, will not conquer the senses. To destroy their power, the most effectual means is, in general, to deny them firmly what will please, and to persevere in this, until they are reduced to be without desire or repugnance. If we attempt, during the warfare, to grant them any relaxation, we act like those, who, under pretext of strengthening a man, who was condemned to be starved to death, should give him from time to time a little nourishment. It indeed would prolong his torments, and postpone his death.

It is just the same with the death of the senses, the powers, the understanding, and self-will. If we do not eradicate every remains of self subsisting in these, we support them in a dying life to the end. This state and its termination are clearly set forth by Paul. He speaks of bearing about in the body the dying of the Lord Jesus. (2 Corinthians 4:10) But, lest we should rest here, he fully distinguishes this from the state of being dead and having our life hid with Christ in God. It is only by a total death to self we can be lost in God.

He who is thus dead has no further need of mortification. The very end of mortification is accomplished in him, and all is become new. It is an unhappy error in those good souls, who have arrived at a conquest of the bodily senses, through this unremitted and continual mortification, that they should still continue attached to the exercise of it. They should rather drop their attention thereto, and remain in indifference, accepting with equality the good as the bad, the sweet as the bitter, and bend their whole attention to a labor of greater importance; namely, the mortification of the mind and self-will. They should begin by dropping all the activity of self, which can never be done without the most profound prayer; no more than the death of the senses can be perfected without profound recollection joined to mortification. Indeed, recollection is the chief means whereby we attain to a conquest of the senses. It detaches and separates us from them, and sweetly saps the very cause from whence they derive their influence over us.

The more You did augment my love, and my patience, O my Lord, the less respite had I from the most oppressive crosses; but love rendered them easy to bear.

O you poor souls, who exhaust yourselves with needless vexation, if you would but seek God in your hearts, there would be a speedy end to all your troubles. The increase of crosses would proportionately increase your delight.

Love, at the beginning, athirst for mortification impelled me to seek and invent various kinds. It is surprising, that as soon as the bitterness of any new mode of mortification was exhausted, another kind was pointed to me, and I was inwardly led to pursue it. Divine love so enlightened my heart, and so scrutinized into its secret springs, that the smallest defects became exposed. If I was about to speak, something wrong was instantly pointed to me, and I was compelled to silence. If I kept silence, faults were presently discovered - in every action there was something defective - in my mortifications, my penances, my alms-giving, my retirement, I was faulty. When I walked, I observed there was something wrong; if I spoke any way in my own favor, I saw pride. If I said within myself, alas, I will speak no more, here was self. If I was cheerful and open, I was condemned. Pure love always found matter for reproof in me, and was jealous that nothing should escape unnoticed. It was not that I was particularly attentive over myself, for it was even with constraint that I could look at all at myself. My attention toward God, by an attachment of my will to His, was without intermission. I waited continually upon Him, and He watched incessantly over me, and He so led me by His providence, that I forgot all things. I knew not how to communicate what I felt to anyone. I was so lost to myself, that I could scarcely go about self-examination. When I attempted it all ideas of myself immediately disappeared. I found myself occupied with my one object without distinction of ideas. I was absorbed in peace inexpressible; I saw by the eye of faith that it was God that thus wholly possessed me; but I did not reason at all about it. It must not, however, be supposed that divine love suffered my faults to go unpunished.

O Lord, with what rigor, do You punish the most faithful, the most loving and beloved of Your children. I mean not externally, for this would be inadequate to the smallest fault, in a soul that God is about to purify radically. The punishments it can inflict on itself, are rather gratifications and refreshments than otherwise. Indeed, the manner in which He corrects His chosen, must be felt, or it is impossible to conceive how dreadful it is. In my attempt to explain it, I shall be unintelligible, except to experienced souls. It is an internal burning, a secret fire sent from God to purge away the fault, giving extreme pain, until this purification is complete. It is like a dislocated joint, which is in incessant torment, until the bone is replaced. This pain is so severe, that the soul would do anything to satisfy God for the fault, and would rather be torn in pieces than endure the torment. Sometimes the soul flies to others, and opens her state that she may find consolation. Thereby she frustrates God's designs toward her. It is of the utmost consequence to know what use to make of the distress. The whole of one's spiritual advancement depends on it. We should at these seasons of internal anguish, obscurity and mourning, co-operate with God, endure this consuming torture in its utmost extent (while it continues) without attempting to lessen or increase it. Bear it passively, nor seek to satisfy God by anything we can do of ourselves. To continue passive at such a time is extremely difficult, and requires great firmness and courage. I knew some who never advanced farther in the spiritual process because they grew impatient, and sought means of consolation.

Chapter Twelve

The treatment of my husband and mother-in-law, however rigorous and insulting, I now bore silently. I made no replies and this was not so difficult for me, because the greatness of my interior occupation, and what passed within, rendered me insensible to all the rest. There were times when I was left to myself. Then I could not refrain from tears. I did the lowest offices for them to humble myself. All this did not win their favor. When they were in a rage, although I could not find that I had given them any occasion, yet I did not fail to beg their pardon, even from the girl of whom I have spoken. I had a good deal of pain to surmount myself, as to the last. She became the more insolent for it; reproaching me with things which ought to have made her blush and have covered her with shame. As she saw that I contradicted and resisted her no more in anything, she proceeded to treat me worse. And when I asked her pardon she triumphed, saying, "I knew very well I was in the right." Her arrogance rose to the height that I would not have treated the meanest slave.

One day, as she was dressing me, she pulled me roughly, and spoke to me insolently. I said, "It is not my account that I am willing to answer you, for you give me no pain, but lest you should act thus before persons to whom it would give offence. Moreover, as I am your mistress, God is assuredly offended with you." She left me that moment, and ran like a mad woman to meet my husband telling him she would stay no longer, I treated her so ill, that I hated her for the care she took of him in his continual indispositions, wanting her not to do any service for him. My husband was very hasty, so he took fire at these words. I finished dressing alone. Since she had left me I dared not call another girl; she would not suffer another girl to come near me. I saw my husband coming like a lion, he was never in such a rage as this. I thought he was going to strike me; I awaited the blow with tranquility; he threatened with his uplifted crutch; I thought he was going to knock me down. Holding myself closely united to God, I beheld it without pain. He did not strike me for he had presence of mind enough to see what indignity it would be. In his rage he threw it at me. It fell near me, but it did not touch me. He then discharged himself in language as if I had been a street beggar, or the most infamous of creatures. I kept profound silence, being recollected in the Lord.

The girl in the meantime came in. At the sight of her his rage redoubled. I kept near to God, as a victim disposed to suffer whatever He would permit. My husband ordered me to beg her pardon, which I readily did, and thereby appeased him. I went into my closet, where I no sooner was, than my divine Director impelled me to make this girl a present, to recompense her for the cross which she had caused me. She was a little astonished, but her heart was too hard to be gained.

I often acted thus because she frequently gave me opportunities. She had a singular dexterity in attending the sick. My husband, ailing almost continually, would suffer no other person to administer to him. He had a very great regard for her. She was artful; in his presence she affected an extraordinary respect for me. When he was not present, if I said a word to her, though with the greatest mildness and if she heard him coming, she cried out with all her might that she was unhappy. She acted like one distressed so that, without informing himself of the truth, he was irritated against me, as was also my mother-in-law.

The violence I did to my proud and hasty nature was so great, that I could hold out no longer. I was quite spent with it. It seemed sometimes as if I was inwardly rent, and I have often fallen sick with the struggle. She did not forbear exclaiming against me, even before persons of distinction, who came to see me. If I was silent, she took offence at that yet more, and said that I despised her. She cried me down, and made complaints to everybody. All this redounded to my honor and her own disgrace. My reputation was so well established, on account of my exterior modesty, my devotion, and the great acts of charity which I did, that nothing could shake it.

Sometimes she ran out into the street, crying out against me. At one time she exclaimed, "Am not I very unhappy to have such a mistress?" People gathered about her to know what I had done to her; and not knowing what to say, she answered that I had not spoken to her all the day. They returned, laughing, and said, "She has done you no great harm then."

I am surprised at the blindness of confessors, and at their permitting their penitents to conceal so much of the truth from them. The confessor of this girl made her pass for a saint. This he said in my hearing. I answered nothing; for love would not permit me to speak of my troubles. I should consecrate them all to God by a profound silence.

My husband was out of humor with my devotion. "What," said he, "you love God so much, that you love me no longer." So little did he comprehend that the true conjugal love is that which the Lord Himself forms in the heart that loves Him.

Oh, You who are pure and holy, You did imprint in me from the first such a love of chastity, that there was nothing in the world which I would not have undergone to possess and preserve it.

I endeavored to be agreeable to my husband in anything, and to please him in everything he could require of me. God gave me such a purity of soul at that time, that I had not so much as a bad thought. Sometimes my husband said to me, "One sees plainly that you never lose the presence of God."

The world, seeing I quit it, persecuted and turned me into ridicule. I was its entertainment, and the subject of its fables. It could not bear that a woman, scarce twenty years of age, should thus make war against it, and overcome. My mother-in-law took part with the world, and blamed me for not doing many things that in her heart she would have been highly offended had I done them. I was as one lost, and alone; so little communion had I with the creature, farther than necessity required. I seemed to experience literally those words of Paul, "I live yet, no more I, but Christ lives in me." His operations were so powerful, so sweet, and so secret, all together, that I could not express them. We went into the country on some business. Oh, what unutterable communications did I there experience in retirement!

I was insatiable for prayer. I arose at four o'clock in the morning to pray. I went very far to the church, which was so situated, that the coach could not come to it. There was a steep hill to go down and another to ascend. All that cost me nothing; I had such a longing desire to meet with my God, as my only good, who on His part was graciously forward to give Himself to His poor creature, and for it to do even visible miracles. Such as saw me lead a life so very different from the women of the world said I was a fool. They attributed it to stupidity. Sometimes they said, "What can all this mean? Some people think this lady has parts, but nothing of them appears." If I went into company, often I could not speak; so much was I engaged within, so inward with the Lord, as not to attend to anything else. If any near me spoke, I heard nothing. I generally took one with me, that this might not appear. I took some work, to hide under that appearance the real employ of my heart. When I was alone, the work dropped out of my hand. I wanted to persuade a relation of my husband's to practice prayer. She thought me a fool, for depriving myself of all the amusements of the age. But the Lord opened her eyes, to make her despise them. I could have wished to teach all the world to love God; and thought it depended only on them to feel what I felt. The Lord made use of my thinking to gain many souls to Himself.

The good father I have spoken of, who was the instrument of my conversion, made me acquainted with

Genevieve Granger, prioress of the Benedictines, one of the greatest servants of God of her time. She proved of very great service to me. My confessor, who had told everyone that I was a saint before, when so full of miseries, and so far from the condition to which the Lord in His mercy had now brought me, seeing I placed a confidence in the father of whom I have spoken, and that I steered in a road which was unknown to him, declared openly against me. The monks of his order persecuted me much. They even preached publicly against me, as a person under a delusion.

My husband and mother-in-law, who till now had been indifferent about this confessor, then joined him and ordered me to leave off prayer, and the exercise of piety; that I could not do. There was carried on a conversation within me, very different from that which passed without. I did what I could to hinder it from appearing, but could not. The presence of so great a Master manifested itself, even on my countenance. That pained my husband, he sometimes told me. I did what I could to hinder it from being noticed, but was not able completely to hide it. I was so much inwardly occupied that I knew not what I ate. I made as if I ate some kinds of meat, though I did not take any. This deep inward attention suffered me scarcely to hear or see anything. I still continued to use many severe mortifications and austerities. They did not in the least diminish the freshness of my countenance.

I had often grievous fits of sickness and no consolation in life, except in the practice of prayer, and in seeing Mother Granger. How dear did these cost me, especially the former! Is this esteeming the cross as I ought? - should I not rather say that prayer to me was recompensed with the cross, and the cross with prayer. Inseparable gifts united in my heart and life! When your eternal light arose in my soul, how perfectly it reconciled me and made you the object of my love! From the moment I received You I have never been free from the cross, nor it seems without prayer - though for a long time I thought myself deprived thereof, which exceedingly augmented my afflictions.

My confessor at first exerted his efforts to hinder me from practicing prayer, and from seeing Mother Granger. He violently stirred up my husband and mother-in-law to hinder me from praying. The method they took was to watch me from morning until night. I dared not go out from my mother-in-law's room, or from my husband's bedside. Sometimes I carried my work to the window, under a pretense of seeing better, in order to relieve myself with some moment's repose. They came to watch me very closely, to see if I did not pray instead of working. When my husband and mother-in-law played cards, if I did turn toward the fire, they watched to see if I continued my work or shut my eyes. If they observed I closed them, they would be in a fury against me for several hours. What is most strange, when my husband went out, having some days of health, he would not allow me to pray in his absence. He marked my work, and sometimes, after he was just gone out, returning immediately, if he found me in prayer he would be in a rage. In vain I said, "Surely, sir, what matters it what I do when you are absent, if I be assiduous in attending you when you are present?" That would not satisfy him; he insisted that I should no more pray in his absence than in his presence.

I believe there is hardly a torment equal to that of being ardently drawn to retirement, and not having it in one's power to be retired.

O my God, the war they raised to hinder me from loving You did but augment my love. While they were striving to prevent my addresses to You, you drew me into an inexpressible silence. The more they labored to separate me from You, the more closely did You unite me to Yourself. The flame of Your love was kindled, and kept up by everything that was done to extinguish it.

Often through compliance I played at piquet with my husband. At such times I was even more interiorly attracted than if I had been at church. I was scarce able to contain the fire which burned in my soul, which had all the fervor of what men call love, but nothing of its impetuosity. The more ardent, the more peaceable it was. This fire gained strength from everything that was done to suppress it. And the spirit of prayer was nourished and increased from their contrivances and endeavors to disallow me any time for practicing it. I loved without considering a motive or reason for loving. Nothing passed in my head, but much in the innermost recesses of my soul. I thought not about any recompense, gift, or favor, which He could bestow or I receive. The Well-beloved was Himself the only object which attracted my heart. I could not contemplate His attributes. I knew nothing else, but to love and to suffer. Ignorance more truly learned than any science of the doctors, since it taught me so well Jesus Christ crucified and brought me to be in love with His holy cross. I could then have wished to die, in order to be inseparably united to Him who so powerfully attracted my heart. As all this passed in the will, the imagination and the understanding being absorbed in it, I knew not what to say, having never read or heard of such a state as I experienced. I dreaded delusion and feared that all was not right, for before this I had known nothing of the operations of God in souls. I had only read Saint Francis de Sales, Thomas à Kempis, The Spiritual Combat, and the Holy Scriptures. I was quite a stranger to those spiritual books wherein such states are described.

Then all those amusements and pleasures that are prized and esteemed appeared to me dull and insipid. I wondered how it could be that I had ever enjoyed them. And indeed since that time, I could never find any satisfaction or enjoyment out of God. I have sometimes been unfaithful enough to find it. I was not astonished that martyrs gave their lives for Jesus Christ. I thought them happy, and sighed after their privilege of suffering for Him. I so esteemed the cross that my greatest trouble was the want of suffering as much as my heart thirsted for.

This respect and esteem for the cross continually increased. Afterward I lost the sensible relish and enjoyment, yet the love and esteem no more left me than the cross itself. Indeed, it has ever been my faithful companion, changing and augmenting, in proportion to the changes and dispositions of my inward state. O blessed cross, you have never quitted me, since I surrendered myself to my divine, crucified Master. I still hope that you will never abandon me. So eager was I for the cross, that I endeavored to make myself feel the utmost rigor of every mortification. This only served to awaken my desire for suffering, and to show me that it is God alone that can prepare and send crosses suitable to a soul that thirsts for a following of His sufferings, and a conformity to His death. The more my state of prayer augmented, my desire of suffering grew stronger, as the full weight of heavy crosses from every side came thundering upon me.

The peculiar property of this prayer of the heart is to give a strong faith. Mine was without limits, as was also my resignation to God, and my confidence in Him -- my love of His will, and of the order of His providence over me. I was very timorous before, but now feared nothing. It is in such a case that one feels the efficacy of these words, "My yoke is easy, and my burden is light" (Matthew 11:30).

Chapter Thirteen

I had a secret desire given me from that time to be wholly devoted to the disposal of my God, let that be what it would. I said, "What could You demand of me, that I would not willingly offer You? Oh, spare me not." The cross and humiliations were represented to my mind in the most frightful colors, but this deterred me not. I yielded myself up as willing and indeed our Lord seemed to accept of my sacrifice, for His divine providence furnished me incessantly with occasions and opportunities for putting it to the test.

I had difficulty to say vocal prayers I had been used to repeat. As soon as I opened my lips to pronounce them, the love of God seized me strongly. I was swallowed up in a profound silence and an inexpressible peace. I made fresh attempts but still in vain. I began again and again, but could not go on. I had never before heard of such a state, I knew not what to do. My inability increased because my love to the Lord was growing more strong, more violent and more overpowering. There was made in me, without the sound of words, a continual prayer. It seemed to me to be the prayer of our Lord Jesus Christ Himself; a prayer of the Word, which is made by the Spirit. According to Saint Paul it "asks for us that which is good, perfect, and conformable to the will of God" (Rom. 8:26-27).

My domestic crosses continued. I was prevented from seeing or even writing to Mrs. Granger. My very going to divine service or the sacrament, were a source of woeful offences. The only amusement I had left me, was the visiting and attending the sick poor, and performing the lowest offices for them.

My prayer-time began to be exceedingly distressing. I compelled myself to continue at it, though deprived of all comfort and consolation. When I was not employed therein, I felt an ardent desire and longing for it. I suffered inexpressible anguish in my mind, and endeavored with the severest inflictions of corporeal austerities to mitigate and divert it – but in vain. I found no more that enlivening vigor which had hitherto carried me on with great swiftness. I seemed to myself to be like those young brides, who find a great deal of difficulty to lay aside their self-love, and to follow their husbands to the war. I relapsed into a vain complacency and fondness for myself. My propensity to pride and vanity, which seemed quite dead, while I was so filled with love of God, now showed itself again, and gave me severe exercise. This made me lament the exterior beauty of my person, and pray to God incessantly, that he would remove from me that obstacle, and make me ugly. I could even have wished to be deaf, blind and dumb, that nothing might divert me from my love of God.

I set out on a journey, which we had then to make, and I appeared more than ever like those lamps which emit a glimmering flash, when they are just on the point of extinguishing. Alas, how many snares were laid in my way! I met them at every step. I even committed infidelities through unwatchfulness.

O my Lord, with what rigor did You punish them! A useless glance was checked as a sin. How many tears did those inadvertent faults cost me, through a weak compliance, and even against my will! You know that Your rigor, exercised after my slips, was not the motive of those tears which I shed. With what pleasure would I have suffered the most rigorous severity to have been cured of my infidelity. To what severe chastisement did I not condemn myself! Sometimes You did treat me like a father who pities the child, and caresses it after its involuntary faults.

How often did You make me sensible of Your love toward me, notwithstanding my blemishes! It was the sweetness of this love after my falls which caused my greatest pain; for the more the amiableness of Your love was extended to me, the more inconsolable I was for having departed ever so little from You. When I had let some inadvertence escape me, I found You ready to receive me. I have often cried out, "O my Lord, is it possible you can be so gracious to such an offender, and so indulgent to my faults; so propitious to one who has wandered astray from You, by vain complaisances, and an unworthy fondness for frivolous objects? Yet no sooner do I return, than I find You waiting, with open arms ready to receive me.

O sinner, sinner, have you any reason to complain of God? If there yet remains in thee any justice, confess the truth, and admit that it is owing to yourself if you go wrong; that in departing from Him you disobey His call. When you return, He is ready to receive you; and if you return not, He makes use of the most engaging motives to win you. Yet you turn a deaf ear to His voice; you will not hear Him. You say He speaks not to you, though He calls loudly. It is therefore only because you daily rebel, and art growing daily more and more deaf to the voice.

When I was in Paris, and the clergy saw me so young, they appeared astonished. Those to whom I opened my state told me, that I could never enough thank God for the graces conferred on me; that if I knew them I should be amazed at them; and that if I were not faithful, I should be the most ungrateful of all creatures. Some declared that they never knew any woman whom God held so closely, and in so great a purity of conscience.

I believe what rendered it so was the continual care You have over me, O my God, making me feel Your presence, even as You have promised it to us in Your Gospel, - "if a man love me, my Father will love him, and we will come unto him, and make our abode with him" (John 14:23). The continual experience of Your presence in me was what preserved me. I became deeply assured of what the prophet had said, "Except the Lord keep the city, the watchman wakes but in vain" (Psalm 127:1). You, O my Love, were my faithful keeper, who did defend my heart against all sorts of enemies, preventing the least faults, or correcting them when vivacity had occasioned their being committed. But alas, when You did cease to watch for me, or left me to myself, how weak was I, and how easily did my enemies prevail over me! Let others ascribe their victory to their own fidelity. As for me, I shall never attribute them to anything else than your paternal care. I have too often experienced, to my cost, what I should be without You, to presume in the least on any cares of my own. It is to You, and to You only, that I owe everything, O my Deliverer; and my being indebted to You for it gives me infinite joy.

While in Paris, I relaxed and did many things which I should not. I knew the extreme fondness which some had for me, and suffered them to express it without checking it as I ought. I fell into other faults too, as having my neck a little too bare, though not near so much as others had. I plainly saw I was too remiss; and that was my torment. I sought all about for Him who had secretly inflamed my heart. But alas, hardly anybody knew Him. I cried, "Oh, You best beloved of my soul, had You been near me these disasters had not befallen me." When I say that I spoke thus to Him, it is but to explain myself. In reality, it all passed almost in silence, for I could not speak. My heart had a language which was carried on without the sound of words, understood of Him, as He understands the language of the Word, which speaks incessantly in the innermost recesses of the soul. Oh, sacred language! Experience only gives the comprehension of it! Let not any think it a barren language, and effect of the mere imagination. Far different - it is the silent expression of the Word in the soul. As He never ceases to speak, so He never ceases to operate. If people once came to know the operations of the Lord, in souls wholly resigned to His guiding, it would fill them with reverential admiration and awe.

I saw that the purity of my state was like to be sullied by too great a commerce with the creatures, so I made haste to finish what detained me in Paris, in order to return to the country. "Tis true, O my Lord, I felt that You have given me strength enough to avoid the occasions of evil - but when I had so far yielded as to get into them, I found I could not resist the vain complaisances, and a number of other foibles which they ensnared me into." The pain which I felt after my faults was inexpressible. It was not an anguish that arose from any distinct idea or conception, from any particular motive or affection - but a kind of devouring fire which ceased not, till the fault was consumed and the soul purified. It was a banishment of my soul from the presence of its Beloved. I could have no access to Him, neither could I have any rest out of Him. I knew not what to do. I was like the dove out of the ark, which finding no rest for the soul of her foot, was constrained to return to the ark; but, finding the window shut, could only fly about. In the meantime, through an infidelity which will ever render me culpable, I strove to find some satisfaction without, but could not. This served to convince me of my folly and of the vanity of those pleasures which are called innocent. When I was prevailed on to taste them, I felt a strong repulse which, joined with my remorse for the transgression, changed the diversion into torment. "Oh, my Father," said I, "this is not You; and nothing else, beside You, can give solid pleasure."

One day, as much through unfaithfulness as complaisance, I went to take a walk at some of the public parks, rather from excess of vanity to show myself than to take the pleasure of the place. Oh, my Lord! How did You make me sensible of this fault? But far from punishing me in letting me partake of the amusement, You did it in holding me so close to Yourself, that I could give no attention to anything but my fault and Your displeasure. After this I was invited with some other ladies to an entertainment at Saint Cloud. Through vanity and weak compliance, I yielded and went. The affair was magnificent; they, though wise in the eye of the world, could relish it. I was filled with bitterness. I could eat nothing, I could enjoy nothing. Oh, what tears! For beyond three months my Beloved withdrew His favoring presence, and I could see nothing but an angry God.

I was on this occasion, and in another journey which I took with my husband into Touraine, like those animals destined for slaughter. On certain days people adorn them with greens and flowers, and bring in pomp into the city before they kill them. This weak beauty, on the eve of decline, shone forth with new brightness, in order to become the sooner extinct. I was shortly after afflicted with the smallpox.

One day as I walked to church, followed by a footman I was met by a poor man. I went to give him alms; he thanked me but refused them and then spoke to me in a wonderful manner of God and of divine things. He displayed to me my whole heart, my love to God, my charity, my too great fondness for my beauty and all my faults; he told me it was not enough to avoid Hell, but that the Lord required of me the utmost purity and height of perfection. My heart assented to his reproofs. I heard him with silence and respect, his words penetrated my very soul. When I arrived at the church I fainted away. I have never seen the man since.

Chapter Fourteen

My husband enjoying some intermission of his almost continual ailments, had a mind to go to Orleans, and then into Touraine. In this journey my vanity made its last blaze. I received abundance of visits and applauses. But how clearly did I see the folly of men who are so taken with vain beauty! I disliked the disposition, yet not that which caused it, though I sometimes ardently desired to be delivered from it. The continual combat of nature and grace cost me no small affliction. Nature was pleased with public applause; grace made me dread it. What augmented the temptation was that they esteemed in me virtue, joined with youth and beauty. They did not know that all the virtue is only in God, and His protection, and all the weakness in myself.

I went in search of confessors, to accuse myself of my failing, and to bewail my backslidings. They were utterly insensible of my pain. They esteemed what God condemned. They treated as a virtue what to me appeared detestable in His sight. Far from measuring my faults by His graces, they only considered what I was, in comparison of what I might have been. Hence, instead of blaming me, they only flattered my pride. They justified me in what incurred His rebuke, or only treated as a slight fault what in me was highly displeasing to Him, from whom I had received such signal mercies.

The heinousness of sins is not to be measured singly by their nature, but also by the state of the person who commits them. The least unfaithfulness in a spouse is more injurious to her husband, than far greater ones in his domestics. I told them all the trouble I had been under for not having entirely covered my neck. It was covered much more than was covered by other women of my age. They assured me that I was very modestly dressed. As my husband liked my dress there could be nothing amiss in it. My inward Director taught me quite the contrary. I had not courage enough to follow Him, and to dress myself differently from others, at my age. My vanity furnished me with pretenses seemingly just for following fashions. If pastors knew what hurt they do in humoring female vanity, they would be more severe against it! Had I found but one person honest enough to deal plainly with me, I should not have gone on. But my vanity, siding with the declared opinion of all others, induced me to think them right, and my own scruples mere fancy.

We met with accidents in this journey, sufficient to have terrified anyone. Though corrupt nature prevailed so far as I have just mentioned, yet my resignation to God was so strong, that I passed fearless, even where there was apparently no possibility of escape. At one time we got into a narrow pass, and did not perceive, until we were too far advanced to draw back, that the road was undermined by the river Loire, which ran beneath, and the banks had fallen in; so that in some places the footmen were obliged to support one side of the carriage. All those around me were terrified to the highest degree, yet God kept me perfectly tranquil. I secretly rejoiced at the prospect of losing my life by a singular stroke of His providence.

On my return, I went to see Mrs. Granger, to whom I related how it had been with me while abroad. She strengthened and encouraged me to pursue my first design. She advised me to cover my neck, which I have done ever since notwithstanding the singularity of it.

The Lord, who had so long deferred the chastisement merited by such a series of infidelities, now began to punish me for the abuse of his grace. Sometimes I wished to retire to a convent, and thought it lawful. I found wherein I was weak, and that my faults were always of the same nature. I wished to hide myself in some cave, or to be confined in a dreary prison, rather than enjoy a liberty by which I suffered so much. Divine love gently drew me inward, and vanity dragged me outward. My heart was rent asunder by the contest, as I neither gave myself wholly up to the one nor the other.

I besought my God to deprive me of power to displease Him, and cried, "Are you not strong enough wholly to eradicate this unjust duplicity out of my heart?" For my vanity broke forth when occasions offered; yet I quickly returned to God. He, instead of repulsing or upbraiding me, often received me with open arms, and gave me fresh testimonials of His love. They filled me with the most painful reflections on my offense. Though this wretched vanity was still so prevalent, yet my love to God was such, that after my wanderings, I would rather have chosen His rod than His caresses. His interests were more dear to me than my own, and I wished He would have done Himself justice upon me. My heart was full of grief and of love. I was stung to the quick for offending Him, who showered His grace so profusely upon me. That those who know not God should offend Him by sin is not to be wondered at, but that a heart which loved Him more than itself and so fully experienced His love, should be seduced by propensities which it detests, is a cruel martyrdom.

When I felt most strongly Your presence, and Your love, O Lord, said I, how wonderfully You bestow Your favors on such a wretched creature, who requites You only with ingratitude. For if anyone reads this life with attention, he will see on God's part, nothing but goodness, mercy, and love; on my part, nothing but weakness, sin and infidelity. I have nothing to glory in but my infirmities and my unworthiness, since, in that everlasting marriage-union you have made with me, I brought with me nothing but weakness, sin and misery. How I rejoice to owe all to You, and that You favor my heart with a sight of the treasures and boundless riches of Your grace and love! You have dealt by me, as if a magnificent king should marry a poor slave, forget her slavery, give her all the ornaments which may render her pleasing in his eyes, and freely pardon her all the faults and ill qualities which her ignorance and bad education had given her. This You have made my case. My poverty is become my riches, and in the extremity of my weakness I have found my strength. Oh, if any knew, with what confusion the indulgent favors of God cover the soul after its faults! Such a soul would wish with all its power to satisfy the divine justice. I made verses and little songs to bewail myself. I exercised austerities, but they did not satisfy my heart. They were like those drops of water which only serve to make the fire hotter. When I take a view of God, and myself, I am obliged to cry out, "Oh, admirable conduct of Love toward an ungrateful wretch! Oh, horrible ingratitude toward such unparalleled goodness." A great part of my life is only a mixture of such things as might be enough to sink me to the grave between grief and love.

Chapter Fifteen

On my arrival at home I found my husband taken with the gout, and his other complaints. My little daughter ill, and like to die of the smallpox; my eldest son, too, took it; and it was of so malignant a type, that it rendered him as disfigured, as before he was beautiful. As soon as I perceived the smallpox was in the house, I had no doubt but I should take it. Mrs. Granger advised me to leave if I could. My father offered to take me home, with my second son, whom I tenderly loved. My mother-in-law would not suffer it. She persuaded my husband it was useless, and sent for a physician, who seconded her in it, saying, "I should as readily take it at a distance as here, if I were disposed to take it." I may say, she proved at that time a second Jephtha, and that she sacrificed us both, though innocently. Had she known what followed, I doubt not but she would have acted otherwise. All the town stirred in this affair. Everyone begged her to send me out of the house, and cried out that it was cruel to expose me thus. They set upon me, too, imagining I was unwilling to go. I had not told that she was so averse to it. I had at that time no other disposition than to sacrifice myself to divine Providence. Though I might have removed, notwithstanding my mother-in-law's resistance, yet I would not without her consent; because it looked to me as if her resistance was an order of Heaven.

I continued in this spirit of sacrifice to God, waiting from moment to moment in an entire resignation, for whatever He should be pleased to ordain. I cannot express what nature suffered. I was like one who sees both certain death and an easy remedy, without being able to avoid the former, or try the latter. I had no less apprehension for my younger son than for myself. My mother-in-law so excessively doted on the eldest, that the rest of us were indifferent to her. Yet I am assured, if she had known the younger would have died of the smallpox, she would not have acted as she did. God makes use of creatures, and their natural inclinations to accomplish His designs. When I see in the creatures a conduct which appears unreasonable and mortifying, I mount higher, and look upon them as instruments both of the mercy and justice of God. His justice is full of mercy.

I told my husband that my stomach was sick, and that I was taking the smallpox. He said it was only imagination. I let Mrs. Granger know the situation I was in. As she had a tender heart, she was affected by the treatment I met with, and encouraged me to offer myself up to the Lord. At length, nature finding there was no resource, consented to the sacrifice which my spirit had already made. The disorder gained ground apace. I was seized with a great shivering, and pain both in my head and stomach. They would not yet believe that I was sick. In a few hours it went so far, that they thought my life in danger. I was also taken with an inflammation on my lungs, and the remedies for the one disorder were contrary to the other. My mother-in-law's favorite physician was not in town, nor the resident surgeon. Another surgeon said that I must be bled; but my mother-in-law would not suffer it at that time. I was on the point of death for the want of proper assistance. My husband, not being able to see me, left me entirely to his mother. She would not allow any physician but her own to prescribe for me, and yet did not send for him, though he was within a day's journey. In this extremity I opened not my mouth. I looked for life or death from the hand of God, without testifying the least uneasiness. The peace I enjoyed within, on account of that perfect resignation, in which God kept me by His grace, was so great, that it made me forget myself, in the midst of oppressive disorders.

The Lord's protection was indeed wonderful. How oft have I been reduced to extremity, yet He never failed to succor, when things appeared most desperate. It pleased Him so to order it, that the skillful surgeon, who had attended me before, passing by our house, inquired after me. They told him I was extremely ill. He alighted immediately, and came in to see me. Never was a man more surprised, when he saw the condition I was in. The smallpox, which could not come out, had fallen on my nose with such force, that it was quite black. He thought there had been gangrene and that it was going to fall off. My eyes were like two coals; but I was not alarmed. At that time I could have made a sacrifice of all things, and was pleased that God should avenge Himself on that face, which had betrayed me into so many infidelities. He also was so affrighted that he went into my mother-in-law's room and told her, that it was most shameful to let me die in that manner, for want of bleeding. She still opposed it violently so that in short she told him flatly that she would not suffer it, until the physician returned. He flew into such a rage at seeing me thus left without sending for the physician that he reproved my mother-in-law in the severest manner. But it was all in vain. He came up again presently and said, "If you choose, I will bleed you, and save your life." I held out my arm to him; and though it was extremely swelled, he bled me in an instant. My mother-in-law was in a violent passion. The smallpox came out immediately. He ordered that they should have me bled again in the evening, but she would not suffer it. Fear of displeasing my mother-in-law, and a total resignation of myself into the hands of God, I did not retain him.

I am more particular to show how advantageous it is to resign one's self to God without reserve. Though in appearance He leaves us for a time to prove and exercise our faith, yet He never fails us, when our need of Him is the more pressing. One may say with the Scripture, "It is God who brings down to the gates of death, and raises up again." The blackness and swelling of my nose went away and I believe, had they continued to bleed me, I had been pretty easy. For want of that I grew worse again.

The malady fell into my eyes, and inflamed them with such severe pain, that I thought I should lose them both.

I had violent pains for three weeks during which time I got little sleep. I could not shut my eyes, they were so full of the smallpox, nor open them by reason of the pain. My throat, palate, and gums were likewise so filled with the pock, that I could not swallow broth, or take nourishment without suffering extremely. My whole body looked leprous. All that saw me said that they had never seen such a shocking spectacle. But as to my soul, it was kept in a contentment not to be expressed. The hopes of its liberty, by the loss of that beauty, which had so frequently brought me under bondage, rendered me so satisfied, and so united to God, that I would not have changed my condition for that of the most happy prince in the world.

Everyone thought I would be inconsolable. Several expressed their sympathy in my sad condition, as they judged it. I lay still in the secret fruition of a joy unspeakable, in this total deprivation of what had been a snare to my pride, and to the passions of men. I praised God in profound silence. None ever heard any complaints from me, either of my pains or the loss I sustained. The only thing that I said was, that I rejoiced at, and was exceedingly thankful for the interior liberty I gained thereby; and they construed this as a great crime. My confessor, who had been dissatisfied with me before, came to see me. He asked me if I was not sorry for having the smallpox; and he now taxed me with pride for my answer.

My youngest little boy took the distemper the same day with myself, and died for want of care. This blow indeed struck me to the heart, but yet, drawing strength from my weakness, I offered him up, and said to God as Job did, "You gave him to me, and you take him from me; blessed be your holy name." The spirit of sacrifice possessed me so strongly, that, though I loved this child tenderly, I never shed a tear at hearing of his death. The day he was buried, the doctor sent to tell me he had not placed a tombstone upon his grave, because my little girl could not survive him two days. My eldest son was not yet out of danger, so that I saw myself stripped of all my children at once, my husband indisposed, and myself extremely so. The Lord did not take my little girl then. He prolonged her life some years.

At last my mother-in-law's physician arrived, at a time wherein he could be of but little service to me. When he saw the strange inflammation in my eyes, he bled me several times; but it was too late. And those bleedings which would have been so proper at first, did nothing but weaken me now. They could not even bleed me in the condition I was in but with the greatest difficulty. My arms were so swelled that the surgeon was obliged to push in the lance to a great depth. Moreover, the bleeding being out of season had liked to have caused my death. This, I confess, would have been very agreeable to me. I looked upon death as the greatest blessing for me. Yet I saw well I had nothing to hope in that side; and that, instead of meeting with so desirable an event, I must prepare myself to support the trials of life.

After my eldest son was better, he got up and came into my room. I was surprised at the extraordinary change I saw in him. His face, lately so fair and beautiful, was become like a coarse spot of earth, all full of furrows. That gave me the curiosity to view myself. I felt shocked, for I saw that God had ordered the sacrifice in all its reality.

Some things fell out by the contrariety of my mother-in-law that caused me severe crosses. They put the finishing stroke to my son's face. However, my heart was firm in God, and strengthened itself by the number and greatness of my sufferings. I was as a victim incessantly offered upon the altar, to Him who first sacrificed Himself for love. "What shall I render to the Lord, for all his benefits toward me? I will take the cup of salvation, and call upon the name of the Lord." These words, I can truly say, O my God, have been the delight of my heart, and have had their effect on me, through my whole life; for I have been continually heaped with your blessings and your cross. My principal attraction, besides that of suffering for You, has been to yield myself up without resistance, interiorly and exteriorly, to all Your divine disposals. These gifts which I was favored with from the beginning, have continued and increased until now. You have guided my continual crosses, and led me through paths impenetrable to all but you.

They sent me pomatums to recover my complexion and to fill up the hollows of the smallpox. I had seen wonderful effects from it upon others, and therefore at first had a mind to try them. But, jealous of God's work, I would not suffer it. There was a voice in my heart which said, "If I would have had you fair, I would have left you as you were." I was therefore obliged to lay aside every remedy, and to go into the air, which made the pitting worse; to expose myself in the street when the redness of the smallpox was at the worst, in order to make my humiliation triumph, where I had exalted my pride.

My husband kept to his bed almost all that time, and made good use of his indisposition. Only as he now lost that, which before gave him so much pleasure in viewing me, he grew much more susceptible to impressions which any gave him against me. In consequence of this, the persons who spoke to him to my disadvantage, finding themselves now better hearkened to, spoke more boldly and more frequently. There was only You, O my God, who changed not for me. You did redouble my interior graces, in proportion as You did augment my exterior crosses.

Chapter Sixteen

My maid became every day more haughty. Seeing that her scoldings and outcries did not now torment me, she thought, if she could hinder me from going to the communion, she would give me the greatest of all vexations.

She was not mistaken, O divine Spouse of pure souls, since the only satisfaction of my life was to receive and to honor You. I gave everything, of the finest I had, to furnish the churches with ornaments, and contributed to the utmost extent of my abilities to make them have silver plates and chalices.

"Oh, my Love," I cried, "let me be your victim! Spare nothing to annihilate me." I felt an inexpressible longing to be more reduced, and to become, as it were, nothing.

This girl then knew my affection for the holy sacrament, where, when I could have liberty for it, I passed several hours on my knees. She took it in her head to watch me daily. When she discovered me going, she ran to tell my mother-in-law and my husband. They needed no more to chagrin them. Their invectives lasted the whole day. If a word escaped me in my own justification, it was enough to make them say that I was guilty of sacrilege, and to raise an outcry against all devotion. If I made them no answer at all, they still heightened their indignation, and said the most grating things they could devise. If I fell sick, which often happened, they took occasion to come to quarrel with me at my bed, saying, my communion and prayers were what made me sick. They spoke as if there had been nothing else could make me ill, but my devotion to You, O my Beloved!

She told me one day that she was going to write to my director to get him to stop me from going to the communion. When I made no answer, she cried out as loud as she could, that I treated her ill and despised her. When I went to prayers, (though I had taken care to arrange everything about the house) she ran to tell my husband that I was going and had left nothing in order. When I returned home his rage fell on me in all its violence. They would hear none of my reasons, but said, "they were all a pack of lies." My mother-in-law persuaded my husband that I let everything go to wreck. If she did not take the care of things he would be ruined. He believed it, and I bore all with patience, endeavoring, as well as I could, to do my duty. What gave most trouble was the not knowing what course to take; for when I ordered anything without her, she complained that I showed her no respect, that I did things of my own head and that they were done always the worse for it. Then she would order them contrary. If I consulted her to know what, or how she would have anything to be done, she said that I compelled her to have the care and trouble of everything.

I had scarcely any rest but what I found in the love of Your will, O my God, and submission to Your orders, however rigorous they might be. They incessantly watched my words and actions, to find occasion against me. They chided me all the day long, continually repeating, and harping over and over the same things, even before the servants. How often have I made my meals on my tears, which were interpreted as the most criminal in the world! They said, I would be damned; as if the tears would open Hell for me, which surely they were more likely to extinguish. If I recited anything I had heard, they would render me accountable for the truth of it. If I kept silence, they taxed me with contempt and perverseness; if I knew anything without telling it, that was a crime; if I told it, then they said I had forged it. Sometimes they tormented me for several days successively, without giving me any relaxation. The girls said, "I ought to feign sickness, to get a little rest." I made no reply. The love of God so closely possessed me, that it would not allow me to seek relief by a single word, or even by a look. Sometimes I said in myself, "Oh, that I had but any one who could take notice of me, or to whom I might unburden myself, - what a relief it would be to me!" But it was not granted me.

Yet, if I happened to be for some days freed from the exterior cross, it was a most sensible distress to me, and indeed a punishment more difficult to bear than the severest trials. I then comprehended what Saint Teresa says, "Let me suffer or die." For this absence of the cross was so grievous to me, that I languished with desire for its return. But no sooner was this earnest longing granted, and the blessed cross returned again, than strange as it may seem, it appeared so weighty and burdensome, as to be almost insupportable.

Though I loved my father extremely, and he loved me tenderly, yet I never spoke to him of my sufferings. One of my relations, who loved me very much, perceived the little moderation they used toward me. They spoke very roughly to me before him. He was highly displeased, and told my father of it, adding, that I would pass for a fool. Soon after I went to see my father, who, contrary to his custom, sharply reprimanded me, "for suffering them to treat me in such a manner, without saying anything in my own defense." I answered, "If they knew what my husband said to me, that was confusion enough for me, without my bringing any more of it on myself by replies; that if they did not notice it, I ought not to cause it to be observed, nor expose my husband's weakness; that remaining silent stopped all disputes, whereas I might cause them to be continued and increased by my replies." My father answered that I did well, and that I should continue to act as God should inspire me. And after that, he never spoke to me of it any more.

They were ever talking to me against my father, against my relations, and all such as I esteemed most. I felt this more keenly than all they could say against myself. I could not forbear defending them, and therein I did wrong; as whatever I said served only to provoke them. If any complained of my father or relations, they were always in the right. If any, whom they had disliked before, spoke against them, they were presently approved of. If any showed friendship to me, such were not welcome. A relation whom I greatly loved for her piety, coming to see me, they openly bid her be gone. They treated her in such a manner as obliged her to go, which gave me no small uneasiness. When any person of distinction came, they would speak against me; even to those who knew me not, which surprised them. But when they saw me they pitied me.

It mattered not what they said against me, love would not allow me to justify myself. I spoke not to my husband of what either my mother-in-law or the girl did to me, except the first year, when I was not sufficiently touched with the power of God to suffer. My mother-in-law and my husband often quarreled. Then I was in favor, and to me they made their mutual complaints. I never told the one what the other had said. And though it might have been of service to me, humanly speaking, to take advantage of such opportunities, I never made use of them to complain of either. Nay, on the contrary, I did not rest till I had reconciled them. I spoke many obliging things of the one to the other, which made them friends again. I knew by frequent experience that I should pay dear for their reunion. Scarcely were they reconciled when they joined together against me.

I was so deeply engaged within, as often to forget things without, yet not anything which was of consequence. My husband was hasty, and inattention frequently irritated him. I walked into the garden, without observing anything. When my husband, who could not go thither, asked me about it, I knew not what to say, at which he was angry. I went thither on purpose to notice everything, in order to tell him and yet when there did not think of looking. I went ten times one day, to see and bring him an account and yet forgot it. But when I did remember to look, I was much pleased. Yet it happened I was then asked nothing about them.

All my crosses to me would have seemed little, if I might have had liberty to pray, and to be alone, to indulge the interior attraction which I felt. But I was obliged to continue in their presence, with such a subjection as is scarcely conceivable. My husband looked at his watch, if at any time I had liberty allowed me for prayer, to see if I stayed more than half an hour. If I exceeded, he grew very uneasy. Sometimes I said, "Grant me one hour to divert and employ myself as I have a mind." Though he would have granted it to me for other diversions, yet for prayer he would not. I confess that inexperience caused me much trouble. I have often thereby given occasion for what they made me suffer. For ought I not to have looked on my captivity as an effect of the will of my God, to content myself and to make it my only desire and prayer? But I often fell back again into the anxiety of wishing to get time for prayer, which was not agreeable to my husband. Those faults were more frequent in the beginning. Afterward I prayed to God in His own retreat, in the temple of my heart, and I went out no more.

Chapter Seventeen

We went into the country where I committed many faults. I thought I might do it then because my husband diverted himself with building. If I stayed from him he was dissatisfied. That sometimes happened as he was continually talking with the workmen. I set myself in a corner, and there had my work with me, but could scarcely do anything by reason of the force of the attraction which made the work fall out of my hands. I passed whole hours this way, without being able either to open my eyes or know what passed; but I had nothing to wish for, nor yet to be afraid of. Everywhere I found my proper center, because everywhere I found God.

My heart could then desire nothing but what it had. This disposition extinguished all its desires; and I sometimes said to myself, "What do you want? What do you fear?" I was surprised to find upon trial that I had nothing to fear. Every place I was in was my proper place. As I had generally no time allowed me for prayer but with difficulty, and would not be suffered to rise till seven o'clock, I stole up at four, and kneeling in my bed, I wished not to offend my husband and strove to be punctual and assiduous in everything. But this soon affected my health and injured my eyes, which were still weak. It was but eight months since I had the smallpox. This loss of rest brought a heavy trial upon me. Even my sleeping hours were much broken, by the fear of not waking in time. I insensibly dropped asleep at my prayers. In the half hour that I got after dinner, though I felt quite wakeful, the drowsiness overpowered me. I endeavored to remedy this by the severest bodily inflictions, but in vain.

As we had not yet built the chapel, and were far from any church, I could not go to prayers or sacrament without the permission of my husband. He was very reluctant to permit me, except on Sundays and holidays. I could not go out in the coach, so that I was obliged to make use of some stratagems, and to get service performed very early in the morning, to which, feeble as I was, I made an effort to creep on foot. It was a quarter of a league distant. Really God wrought wonders for me. Generally, in the mornings when I went to prayers, my husband did not awake until after I was returned. Often, as I was going out, the weather was so cloudy, that the girl I took with me told me that I could not go; or if I did, I should be soaked with the rain. I answered her with my usual confidence, "God will assist us." I generally reached the chapel without being wet. While there the rain fell excessively. When I returned it ceased. When I got home it began again with fresh violence. During several years that I have acted this way, I have never been deceived in my confidence. When I was in town, and could find nobody, I was surprised that there came to me priests to ask me if I was willing to receive the communion, and that if I was they would give it to me. I had no mind to refuse the opportunity which You yourself offered me; for I had no doubt of its being You who inspired them to propose it. Before I had contrived to get divine service at the chapel I have mentioned, I have often suddenly awoke with a strong impulse to go to prayers. My maid would say, "But, madam, you are going to tire yourself in vain. There will be no service." For that chapel was not yet regularly served. I went full of faith and at my arrival have found them just ready to begin. If I could particularly enumerate the remarkable providences which were hereupon given in my favor there would be enough to fill whole volumes.

When I wanted to hear from, or write to Mother Granger, I often felt a strong propensity to go to the door, there to find a messenger with a letter from her. This is only a small instance of these kind of continual providences. She was the only person I could be free to open my heart to, when I could get to see her, which was with the greatest difficulty. It was through providential assistance; because prohibited by my confessor and husband. I placed an extreme confidence in Mother Granger. I concealed nothing from her either of sins or pains. I did not now practice any austerities but those she was willing to allow me. My interior dispositions I was scarcely able to tell because I knew not how to explain myself, being very ignorant of those matters, having never read or heard of them.

One day when they thought I was going to see my father, I ran off to Mother Granger. It was discovered, and cost me crosses. Their rage against me was so excessive, that it would seem incredible. Even my writing to her was extremely difficult. I had the utmost abhorrence of a lie, so I forbade the footman to tell any. When they were met they were asked whither they were going, and if they had any letters. My mother-in-law set herself in a little passage, through which those who went out must necessarily pass. She asked them whither they were going and what they carried. Sometimes going on foot to the Benedictines, I caused shoes to be carried, that they might not perceive by the dirty ones that I had been far. I dared not go alone; those who attended me had orders to tell of every place I went. If they were discovered to fail, they were either corrected or discharged.

My husband and mother-in-law were always inveighing against that good woman, though in reality they esteemed her. I sometimes made my own complaint and she replied, "How should you content them, when I have been doing all in my power for twenty years to satisfy them without success?" For as my mother-in-law had two daughters under her care, she was always finding something to say against everything she did in regard to them.

But the most sensible cross to me now was the revolting of my own son against me. They inspired him with so great a contempt for me, that I could not bear to see him without extreme affliction. When I was in my room with some of my friends, they sent him to listen to what we said. As he saw this pleased them, he invented a hundred things to tell them. If I caught him in a lie, as I frequently did, he would upbraid me, saying, "My grandmother says you have been a greater liar than I." I answered, "Therefore I know the deformity of that vice, and how hard a thing it is to get the better of it; and for this reason, I would not have you suffer the like." He spoke to me things very offensive. Because he saw the awe I stood in of his grandmother and his father, if in their absence I found fault with him for anything, he insultingly upbraided me. He said that now I wanted to be set up over him because they were not there. All this they approved of. One day he went to see my father and rashly began talking against me to him, as he was used to doing to his grandmother. But there it did not meet with the same recompense. It affected my father to tears. Father came to our house to desire he might be corrected for it. They promised it should be done, and yet they never did it. I was grievously afraid of the consequences of so bad an education. I told Mother Granger of it, who said that since I could not remedy it, I must suffer and leave everything to God. This child would be my cross.

Another great cross was the difficulty I had in attending my husband. I knew he was displeased when I was not with him; yet when I was with him, he never expressed any pleasure. On the contrary, he only rejected with scorn whatever office I performed. He was so difficult with me about everything, that I sometimes trembled when I approached him. I could do nothing to his liking; and when I did not attend him he was angry. He had taken such a dislike to soups, that he could not bear the sight of them. Those that offered them had a rough reception. Neither his mother nor any of the domestics would carry them to him. There was none but I who did not refuse that office. I brought them and let his anger pass; then I tried in some agreeable manner to prevail on him to take them. I said to him, "I had rather be reprimanded several times a day, than let you suffer by not bringing you what is proper." Sometimes he took; at other times he pushed them back.

When he was in a good humor and I was carrying something agreeable to him, then my mother-in-law would snatch it out of my hands. She would carry it herself. As he thought I was not so careful and studious to please him he would fly in a rage against me and express great thankfulness to his mother. I used all my skill and endeavors to gain my mother-in-law's favor by my presents, my services; but could not succeed.

"How bitter and grievous, O my God, would such a life be were it not for You! You have sweetened and reconciled it to me." I had a few short intervals from this severe and mortifying life. These served only to make the reverses more keen and bitter.

Chapter Eighteen

About eight or nine months after my recovery from the smallpox, Father LaCombe, passing by our house, brought me a letter from Father de la Motte, recommending him to my esteem, and expressing the highest friendship for him. I hesitated because I was very loath to make new acquaintances. The fear of offending my brother prevailed. After a short conversation we both desired a farther opportunity. I thought that he either loved God, or was disposed to love Him, and I wished everybody to love Him. God had already made use of me for the conversion of three of his order. The strong desire he had of seeing me again induced him to come to our country house about half a league from the town. A little incident which happened opened a way for me to speak to him. As he was in discourse with my husband, who relished his company, he was taken ill and retired into the garden. My husband bade me go and see what was the matter. He told me he had noticed in my countenance a deep inwardness and presence of God, which had given him a strong desire of seeing me again. God then assisted me to open to him the interior path of the soul, and conveyed so much grace to him through this poor channel that he went away changed into quite another man. I preserved an esteem for him; for it appeared to me that he would be devoted to God; but little did I then foresee, that I should ever be led to the place where he was to reside.

My disposition at this time was a continual prayer, without knowing it to be such. The presence of God was so plentifully given that it seemed to be more in me than my very self. The sensibility thereof was so powerful, so penetrating, it seemed to me irresistible. Love took from me all liberty of my own. At other times I was so dry, I felt nothing but the pain of absence, which was the keener to me, as the divine presence had before been so sensible. In these alternatives I forgot all my troubles and pains. It appeared to me as if I had never experienced any. In its absence, it seemed as if it would never return again. I still thought it was through some fault of mine it was withdrawn, and that rendered me inconsolable. Had I known it had been a state through which it was necessary to pass, I should not have been troubled. My strong love to the will of God would have rendered everything easy to me. The property of this prayer was to give a great love to the order of God, with so sublime and perfect a reliance on Him, as to fear nothing, whether danger, thunders, spirits, or death. It gives a great abstraction from one's self, our own interests and reputation, with an utter disregard to everything of the kind -- all being swallowed up in the esteem of the will of God.

At home, I was accused of everything that was ill done, spoiled or broken. At first I told the truth, and said it was not I. They persisted, and accused me of lying. I then made no reply. Besides, they told all their tales to such as came to the house. But when I was afterward alone with the same persons, I never undeceived them. I often heard such things said of me, before my friends, as were enough to make them entertain a bad opinion. My heart kept its habitation in the tacit consciousness of my own innocence, not concerning myself whether they thought well or ill of me; excluding all the world, all opinions or censures, out of my view, I minded nothing else but the friendship of God.

If through infidelity I happened at any time to justify myself, I always failed, and drew upon myself new crosses, both within and without. But notwithstanding all this, I was so enamored with it, that the greatest cross of all would have been to be without any. When the cross was taken from me for any short space, it seemed to me that it was because of the bad use I made of it; that my unfaithfulness deprived me of so great an advantage. I never knew its value better than its loss.

I cried punish me any way, but take not the cross from me. This amiable cross returned to me with so much the more weight, as my desire was more vehement. I could not reconcile two things, they appeared to me so very opposite. 1) To desire the cross with so much ardor. 2) To support it with so much difficulty and pain.

God knows well, in the admirable economy he observes, how to render the crosses more weighty, conformable to the ability of the creature to bear them. Hereby my soul began to be more resigned, to comprehend that the state of absence, and of wanting what I longed for, was in its turn more profitable than that of always abounding. This latter nourished self-love. If God did not act thus, the soul would never die to itself. That principle of self-love is so crafty and dangerous, that it cleaves to everything.

What gave me most uneasiness, in this time of darkness and crucifixion, both within and without was an inconceivable readiness to be quick and hasty. When any answer a little too lively escaped me, (which served not a little to humble me,) they said "I was fallen into a mortal sin." A conduct no less rigorous than this was quite necessary for me. I was so proud, passionate, and of a humor naturally thwarting, wanting always to carry matters my own way, thinking my own reasons better than those of others. Have you, O my God, spared the strokes of your hammer, I should never have been formed to Your will, to be an instrument for Your use; for I was ridiculously vain. Applause rendered me intolerable. I praised my friends to excess, and blamed others without reason. But, the more criminal I have been, the more I am indebted to You, and the less of any good can I attribute to myself. How blind are men who attribute to others the holiness that God gives them! I believe, my God, that you have had children, who under your grace, owed much to their own fidelity. As for me, I owe all to You; I glory to confess it; I cannot acknowledge it too much.

In acts of charity I was very assiduous. So great was my tenderness for the poor, that I wished to have supplied all their wants. I could not see their necessity without reproaching myself for the plenty I enjoyed. I deprived myself of all I could to help them. The very best at my table was distributed. There were few of the poor where I lived, who did not partake of my liberality. It seemed as if You had made me your only almoner there, for being refused by others, they came to me. I cried, "it is Your substance; I am only the steward. I ought to distribute it according to Your will." I found means to relieve them without letting myself be known, because I had one who dispensed my alms privately. When there were families who were ashamed to take it in this way, I sent it to them as if I owed them a debt. I clothed such as were naked, and caused young girls to be taught how to earn their livelihood, especially those who were handsome; to the end that being employed, and having whereon to live, they might not be under a temptation to throw themselves away. God made use of me to reclaim several from their disorderly lives. I went to visit the sick, to comfort them, to make their beds. I made ointments, dressed their wounds, buried their dead. I privately furnished tradesmen and mechanics wherewith to keep up their shops. My heart was much opened toward my fellow creatures in distress. Few indeed could carry charity much farther than our Lord enabled me to do, according to my state, both while married and since.

To purify me the more from the mixture I might make of His gifts with my own self-love, He gave me interior probations, which were very heavy. I began to experience an insupportable weight, in that very piety which had formerly been so easy and delightful to me; not that I did not love it extremely, but I found myself defective in that noble practice of it. The more I loved it, the more I labored to acquire what I saw failed in. But, alas, I seemed continually to be overcome by that which was the contrary to it. My heart, indeed, was detached from all sensual pleasures. For these several years past, it has seemed to me that my mind is so detached and absent from the body, that I do things as if I did them not. If I eat, or refresh myself, it is done with such an absence, or separation, as I wonder at, with an entire mortification of the keenness of sensation in all the natural functions.

Chapter Nineteen

To resume my history, the smallpox had so much hurt one of my eyes, that it was feared I would lose it. The gland at the corner of my eye was injured. An imposthume arose from time to time between the nose and the eye, which gave me great pain till it was lanced. It swelled all my head to that degree that I could not bear even a pillow. The least noise was agony to me, though sometimes they made a great commotion in my chamber. Yet this was a precious time to me, for two reasons. First, because I was left in bed alone, where I had a sweet retreat without interruption; the other, because it answered the desire I had for suffering, - which desire was so great, that all the austerities of the body would have been but as a drop of water to quench so great a fire. Indeed the severities and rigors which I then exercised were extreme, but they did not appease this appetite for the cross. It is You alone, O Crucified Savior, who can make the cross truly effectual for the death of self. Let others bless themselves in their ease or gaiety, grandeur or pleasures, poor temporary heavens; for me, my desires were all turned another way, even to the silent path of suffering for Christ, and to be united to Him, through the mortification of all that was of nature in me, that my senses, appetites and will, being dead to these, might wholly live in Him.

I obtained leave to go to Paris for the cure of my eye; and yet it was much more through the desire I had to see Monsieur Bertot, a man of profound experience, whom Mother Granger had lately assigned to me for my director. I went to take leave of my father, who embraced me with peculiar tenderness, little thinking then that it would be our last adieu.

Paris was a place now no longer to be dreaded as in times past. The throngs only served to draw me into a deep recollection, and the noise of the streets augmented my inward prayer. I saw Monsieur Bertot, who did not prove of that service to me, which he would have been if I had then the power to explain myself. Though I wished earnestly to hide nothing from him, yet God held me so closely to Him, that I could scarcely tell anything at all. As soon as I spoke to him, everything vanished from my mind, so that I could remember nothing but some few faults. As I saw him very seldom, and nothing stayed in my recollection, and as I read of nothing any way resembling my case, I knew not how to explain myself. Besides, I desired to make nothing known, but the evil which was in me. Therefore Monsieur Bertot knew me not, even till his death. This was of great utility to me, by taking away every support, and making me truly die to myself.

I went to pass the ten days, from the Ascension to Whitsuntide, at an abbey four leagues from Paris, the abbess of which had a particular friendship for me. Here my union with God seemed to be deeper and more continued, becoming always simple, at the same time more close and intimate.

One day I awoke suddenly at four o'clock in the morning, with a strong impression on my mind that my father was dead. At the same time my soul was in a very great contentment, yet my love for him affected it with sorrow, and my body with weakness. Under the strokes and daily troubles which befell me, my will was so subservient to Yours, O my God, that it appeared absolutely united to it. There seemed, indeed, to be no will left in me but Yours only. My own disappeared, and no desires, tendencies or inclinations were left, but to the one sole object of whatever was most pleasing to You, be it what it would. If I had a will, it was in union with yours, as two well tuned lutes in concert. That which is not touched renders the same sound as that which is touched; it is but one and the same sound, one pure harmony. It is this union of the will which establishes in perfect peace. Yet, though my own will was lost I have found since, in the strange states I have been obliged to pass through, how much it had yet to cost me to have it totally lost. How many souls are there which think their own wills quite lost, while they are yet very far from it! They would find they still subsist, if they met with severe trials. Who is there who does not wish something for himself, either of interest, wealth, honor, pleasure, conveniences and liberty. He who thinks his mind loose from all these objects, because he possesses them, would soon perceive his attachment to them, were he stripped of those he possessed. If there are found in a whole age three persons so dead to everything, as to be utterly resigned to providence without any exception, they may well pass for prodigies of grace.

In the afternoon as I was with the abbess, I told her I had strong presentiments of my father's death. Indeed I could hardly speak, I was so affected within. Presently one came to tell her that she was wanted in the parlor. It was a messenger come in haste, with an account from my husband that my father was ill. And as I afterward found, he suffered only twelve hours. He was therefore by this time dead. The abbess returning, said, "Here is a letter from your husband, who writes that your father is taken violently ill." I said to her, "He is dead, I cannot have a doubt about it."

I sent away to Paris immediately, to hire a coach, to go the sooner; mine waited for me at the midway. I went off at nine o'clock at night. They said I "was going to destroy myself." I had no acquaintance with me as I had sent away my maid to Paris, to put everything in order there. Being in a religious house, I had no mind to keep a footman with me. The abbess told me, that "since I thought my father was dead, it would be rashness in me to expose myself, and run the risk of my life in that manner. Coaches could hardly pass the way I was going, it being no beaten road." I answered, "It was my indispensable duty to go to assist my father, and that I ought not, on a bare apprehension, to exempt myself from it." I then went alone, abandoned to Providence, with people unknown. My weakness was so great, that I could hardly keep my seat in the coach. I was often forced to alight, on account of dangerous places in the road.

In this way I was obliged, about midnight, to cross a forest, notorious for murders and robberies. The most intrepid dreaded it; but my resignation left me scarce any room to think at all about it. What fears and uneasiness does a resigned soul spare itself! All alone I arrived within five leagues of my own habitation, where I found my confessor who had opposed me, with one of my relations, waiting for me. The sweet consolation I had enjoyed, when alone, was now interrupted. My confessor, ignorant of my state, restrained me entirely. My grief was of such a nature that I could not shed a tear. And I was ashamed to hear a thing which I knew but too well, without giving any exterior mark of grief. The inward and profound peace I enjoyed dawned on my countenance. The state I was in did not permit me to speak, or to do such things as are usually expected from persons of piety. I could do nothing but love and be silent.

I found on my arrival at home, that my father was already buried because of the excessive heat. It was ten o'clock at night. All wore the habit of mourning. I had traveled thirty leagues in a day and a night. As I was very weak, not having taken any nourishment, I was instantly put to bed.

About two o'clock in the morning my husband got up, and having gone out of my chamber, he returned presently, crying out with all his might, "My daughter is dead!" She was my only daughter, as dearly beloved as truly lovely. She had so many graces both of body and mind conferred on her, that one must have been insensible not to have loved her. She had an extraordinary share of love to God. Often was she found in corners at prayer. As soon as she perceived me at prayer, she came and joined. If she discovered that I had been without her, she would weep bitterly and cry, "Ah, mamma, you pray but I don't." When we were alone and she saw my eyes closed she would whisper, "Are you asleep?" Then she would cry out, "Ah no, you are praying to our dear Jesus." Dropping on her knees before me she would begin to pray too. She was several times whipped by her grandmother, because she said, she would never have any other husband but our Lord. She could never make her say otherwise. She was innocent and modest as a little angel; very dutiful and endearing, and withal very beautiful. Her father doted on her, to me she was very dear, much more for the qualities of her mind than those of her beautiful person. I looked upon her as my only consolation on earth. She had as much affection for me, as her brother had aversion and contempt. She died of an unseasonable bleeding. But what shall I say? She died by the hands of Him who was pleased, for wise reasons of His own, to strip me of all.

There now remained to me only the son of my sorrow. He fell ill to the point of death, but was restored at the prayer of Mother Granger who was now my only consolation after God. I no more wept for my child than for my father. I could only say, "You, O Lord, gave her to me; it pleases You to take her back again, for she was Yours." As for my father, his virtue was so generally known, that I must rather be silent, than enter upon the subject. His reliance on God, his faith and patience were wonderful. Both died in July, 1672. Henceforth crosses were not spared me, and though I had abundance of them hitherto, yet they were only the shadows of those which I have been since obliged to pass through. In this spiritual marriage I claimed for my dowry only crosses, scourges, persecutions, ignominies, lowliness, and nothingness of self, which in God's great goodness, and for wise ends, as I have seen, has been pleased to grant and confer upon me.

One day, being in great distress on account of the redoubling of outward and inward crosses, I went into my closet to give vent to my grief. M. Bertot was brought into my mind, with this wish, "Oh, that he was sensible of what I suffer!" Though he wrote but very seldom, and with great difficulty, yet he wrote me a letter dated the same day about the cross. It was the finest and most consolatory he ever wrote me on that subject. Sometimes my spirit was so oppressed with continual crosses, which scarcely gave me any relaxation, that when alone my eyes turned every way, to see if they could find anything to give relief. A word, a sigh, a trifle, or to know that anyone took part in my grief, would have been some comfort. That was not granted me, not even to look toward Heaven, or to make any complaint. Love held me then so closely, that it would have this miserable nature to perish, without giving it any support or nourishment.

Oh, my dearest Lord! You yet gave my soul a victorious support, which made it triumph over all the weaknesses of nature, and seized Your knife to sacrifice it without sparing. And yet this nature so perverse, and full of artifices to save its life, at last took the course of nourishing itself on its own despair, on its fidelity under such heavy and continual oppression. It sought to conceal the value it attributed thereto. But your eyes were too penetrating not to detect the subtlety. Wherefore, you, O my Shepherd, changed Your conduct toward it. You sometimes comforted it with your crook and Your staff; that is to say, by Your conduct as loving as crucifying; but it was only to reduce it to the last extremity, as I shall show hereafter.

Chapter Twenty

A lady of rank whom I sometimes visited, took a particular liking to me, because (as she was pleased to say) my person and manners were agreeable. She said that she observed in me something extraordinary and uncommon. I believe it was the inward attraction of my soul that appeared on my very countenance. One day a gentleman of fashion said to my husband's aunt, "I saw the lady your niece; and it is very evident that she lives in the presence of God." I was surprised at this, as I little thought such a one as he could know what it was to have God thus present. This lady of rank began to be touched with the sense of God. Wanting once to take me to the play, I refused to go; (I never went to plays) making use of the pretext of my husband's continual indispositions. She pressed me exceedingly, and said, "I should not be prevented by his sickness from taking some amusement and I was not of an age to be confined with the sick like a nurse." I told her my reasons. She then perceived that it was more from a principle of piety, than the indispositions of my husband. Insisting to know my sentiment of plays, I told her, I entirely disapproved of them, and especially for a Christian woman. And as she was far more advanced in years than I was, what I then said made such an impression on her mind, she never went again.

Once with her and another lady, who was fond of talking and who had read "the fathers," they spoke much of God. This lady spoke learnedly of Him. I said scarcely anything, being inwardly drawn to silence, and troubled at this conversation about God. My acquaintance came next day to see me. The Lord had so touched her heart, she could hold out no longer. I attributed this to something the other lady had said, but she said to me, "Your silence had something in it which penetrated to the bottom of my soul. I could not relish what the other said." We spoke to one another with open hearts.

It was then that God left indelible impressions of His grace on her soul, and she continued so athirst for Him, that she could scarcely endure to converse on any other subject. That she might become wholly His, He deprived her of a most affectionate husband. He visited her with such severe crosses, and at the same time poured His grace so abundantly into her heart, that He soon became the sole master thereof. After the death of her husband, and the loss of most of her fortune, she went to reside four leagues from our house, on a small estate, which was left. She obtained my husband's consent to my going to spend a week with her, to console her. God gave her by my means all she wanted. She had a great share of understanding, but was surprised at my expressing things to her so far above my natural capacity. I should have been surprised at it myself. It was God who gave me the gift for her sake, diffusing a flood of grace into her soul, without regarding the unworthiness of the channel of which He was pleased to make use. Since that time her soul has been the temple of the Holy Ghost, and our hearts have been indissolubly united.

My husband and I took a little journey together, in which both my resignation and humility were exercised, yet without difficulty or constraint, so powerful was the influence of divine grace. We had all liked to have perished in a river. The rest of the company in desperate fright threw themselves out of the coach, which sunk in the moving sand. I continued so much inwardly occupied, that I did not once think of the danger. God delivered me from it without my thought of avoiding it. I was quite content to be drowned, had He permitted it. It may be said, "I was rash." I believe I was so; yet I rather chose to perish, trusting in God, than make my escape in a dependence on myself. What say I? We do not perish, but for want of trusting Him. My pleasure is to be indebted to Him for everything. This renders me content in my miseries, which I would rather endure all my life long, in a state of resignation to Him, than put an end to them, in a dependence on myself. However, I would not advise others to act thus, unless they were in the same disposition which I was in.

As my husband's maladies daily increased, he resolved to go to Saint Reine. He appeared very desirous of having none but me with him, and told me one day, "If they never spoke to me against you, I should be more easy, and you more happy." In this journey I committed many faults of self-love and selfseeking. I was become like a poor traveler that had lost his way in the night and could find no way, path, or track. My husband, in his return from Saint Reine, passed by Saint Edm. Having now no children but my firstborn son, who was often at the gates of death, he wished exceedingly for heirs, and prayed for them earnestly. God granted his desire, and gave me a second son. As I was several weeks without any one daring to speak to me, on account of my great weakness, it was a time of retreat and of silence. I tried to indemnify myself for the loss of time I had sustained in the others, to pray to You, O my God, and to continue alone with You. I may say that God took a new possession of me, and left me not. It was a time of continual joy without interruption. As I had experienced many inward difficulties and weaknesses it was a new life. It seemed as if I was already in the fruition of beatitude. How dear did this happy time cost me, since it was only a preparative to a total privation of comfort for several years, without any support, or hope of return! It began with the death of Mrs. Granger, who had been my only consolation under God. Before my return from Saint Reine I heard she was dead.

When I received this news, I confess it was the most afflicting stroke I had ever felt. I thought that had I been with her at her death I might have spoken to her and received her last instructions. God has so ordered it that I was deprived of her assistance in almost all my losses, in order to render the strokes more painful. Some months indeed before her death, it was shown to me, that though I could not see her but with difficulty, and suffering for it, yet she was still some support to me. The Lord let me know that it would be profitable for me to be deprived of her. But at the time she died I did not think so. It was in that trying season when my paths were all blocked up, she was taken from me. She who might have guided me in my lonesome and difficult road, bounded as it were with precipices, and entangled with briars and thorns.

Adorable conduct of my God! There must be no guide for the person whom You are leading into the regions of darkness and death, no conductor for the man whom you are determined to destroy, (that is, to cause to die totally to himself). After having saved me with much mercy, after having led me by the hand in rugged paths, it seems You were bent on my destruction. May it not be said that You do not save but to destroy, nor go to seek the lost sheep, but to cause it to be yet more lost; that You are pleased in building what is demolished, and in demolishing what is built. You would overturn the temple built by human endeavors, with so much care and industry, in order as it were miraculously to erect a divine structure, a house not built with hands, eternal in the Heavens. Secrets of the incomprehensible wisdom of God, unknown to any besides Himself! Man, sprung up only of a few days, wants to penetrate, and to set bounds to it. Who is it that has known the mind of the Lord, or who has been His counselor? Is it a wisdom only to be known through death to everything, and through the entire loss of all self?

My brother now openly showed his hatred for me. He married at Orleans and my husband had the complaisance to go to his marriage. He was in a poor state of health, the roads bad, and so covered over with snow, that we had like to have been overturned twelve or fifteen times. Yet far from appearing obliged by his politeness, my brother quarreled with him more than ever, and without reason. I was the butt of both their resentments. While I was at Orleans, meeting with one whom at that time I thought highly of, I was too forward and free in speaking to him of spiritual things, thinking I was doing well, but had a remorse for it afterwards. How often we mistake nature for grace! One must be dead to self, when such forwardness comes from God only.

My brother treated me with the utmost contempt. Yet, my mind was so fully drawn inward, that although we had much more danger on the road than when going, I had no thought about myself, but all about my husband. Seeing the coach overturning, I said, "Fear not, it is on my side that it falls; it will not hurt you." I believe, had all perished, I should not have been moved. My peace was so profound that nothing could shake it. If these times continued, we should be too strong. They now began to come but seldom and were followed with long and wearisome privations. Since that time my brother has changed for the better, and has turned on the side of God, but he has never turned to me. It has been by particular permission of God, and the conduct of His providence over my soul, that has caused him and other religious persons, who have persecuted me, to think they were rendering glory to God, and doing acts of justice therein. Indeed, it is just that all creatures should be treacherous to me, and declare against me, who have too many times been treacherous to God, and sided with His enemy.

After this there was a very perplexing affair. To me it caused great crosses, and seemed designed for nothing else. A certain person conceived so much malice against my husband, that he was determined to ruin him if possible. He found no other way to attempt it, but by entering into a private engagement with my brother. He obtained a power to demand, in the name of the king's brother, two hundred thousand livres, which he pretended that my brother and I owed him. My brother signed the processes, upon an assurance given him that he should not pay anything. I think his youth engaged him in what he did not understand. This affair so chagrined my husband, that I have reason to believe it shortened his days. He was so angry with me (although I was innocent), that he could not speak to me except in a fury. He would give me no light into the affair, and I did not know in what it consisted. In the height of his rage, he said he would not meddle with it, but give me my portion, and let me live as I could. On the other side, my brother would not move in it, nor suffer anything to be done. The day of the trial, after prayer, I felt myself strongly pressed to go to the judges. I was wonderfully assisted even so as to discover and unravel all the turns and artifices of this affair, without knowing how I could have been able to do it. The first judge was so surprised to see the affair so different from what he had thought it before, that he himself exhorted me to go to the other judges, and especially to the intendant, who was just then going to court. He was quite misinformed about the matter. God enabled me to manifest the truth in so clear a light, and gave such power to my words, that the intendant thanked me for having so seasonably come to undeceive, and set him right. Had I not done this, he assured me the cause had been lost. As they saw the falsehood of every point, they would have condemned the plaintiff to pay the costs, if he had not been so great a prince, who lent his name to the scheme. To save the honor of the prince they ordered us to pay him fifty crowns. Hereby the two hundred thousand livres were reduced to only one hundred and fifty. My husband was exceedingly pleased at what I had done. My brother appeared as outrageous against me, as if I had caused him some great loss. Thus moderately and at once ended an affair, which had at first appeared so very weighty and alarming.

Chapter Twenty-one

About this time I fell into a state of total privation which lasted nearly seven years. I seemed to myself cast down like Nebuchadnezzar, to live among beasts; a deplorable state, yet of the greatest advantage to me, by the use which divine wisdom made of it. This state of emptiness, darkness, and impotency, went far beyond any trials I had ever yet met. I have since experienced, that the prayer of the heart when it appears most dry and barren, nevertheless is not ineffectual nor offered in vain. God gives what is best for us, though not what we most relish or wish for. Were people but convinced of this truth, they would be far from complaining all their lives. By causing us death He would procure us life; for all our happiness, spiritual, temporal and eternal, consists in resigning ourselves to God, leaving it to Him to do in us and with us as He pleases, and with so much the more submission; as things please us less. By this pure dependence on His Spirit, everything is given us admirably. Our very weaknesses, in His hand, prove a source of humiliation. If the soul were faithful to leave itself in the hand of God, sustaining all His operations whether gratifying or mortifying, suffering itself to be conducted, from moment to moment, by His hand, and annihilated by the strokes of His Providence, without complaining, or desiring anything but what it has; it would soon arrive at the experience of the eternal truth, though it might not at once know the ways and methods by which God conducted it there.

People want to direct God instead of resigning themselves to be directed by Him. They want to show Him a way, instead of passively following that wherein He leads them. Hence many souls, called to enjoy God Himself, and not barely His gifts, spend all their lives in running after little consolations, and feeding on them - resting there only, making all their happiness to consist therein.

If my chains and my imprisonment in any way afflict you, I pray that they may serve to engage you to seek nothing but God for Himself alone, and never to desire to possess Him but by the death of your whole selves, never to seek to be something in the ways of the Spirit, but choose to enter into the most profound nothingness.

I had an internal strife, which continually racked me – two powers which appeared equally strong seemed equally to struggle for the mastery within me. On the one hand, a desire of pleasing You, O my God, a fear of offending, and a continual tendency of all my powers to You - on the other side, the view of all my inward corruptions, the depravity of my heart, and the continual stirring and rising of self. What torrents of tears, what desolations have these cost me? "Is it possible," I cried, "that I have received so many graces and favors from God only to lose them; - that I have loved Him with so much ardor, but to be eternally deprived of Him; that His benefits have only produced ingratitude; His fidelity been repaid with infidelity; that my heart has been emptied of all creatures, and created objects, and filled with His blessed presence and love, in order now to be wholly void of divine power, and only filled with wanderings and created objects!"

I could now no longer pray as formerly. Heaven seemed shut to me, and I thought justly. I could get no consolation or make any complaint; nor had I any creature on earth to apply to. I found myself banished from all beings without finding a support of refuge in anything. I could no more practice any virtue with facility. "Alas!" said I, "is it possible that this heart, formerly all on fire, should now become like ice!" I often thought all creatures combined against me. Laden with a weight of past sins, and a multitude of new ones, I could not think God would ever pardon me, but looked on myself as a victim designed for Hell. I would have been glad to do penances, to make use of prayers, pilgrimages, and vows. But still, whatever I tried for a remedy seemed only to increase the malady. I may say that tears were my drink, and sorrow my food. I felt in myself such a pain as I never could bring any to comprehend, but such as have experienced it. I had within myself an executioner who tortured me without respite. Even when I went to church, I was not easy there. To sermons I could give no attention; they were now of no service or refreshment to me. I scarcely conceived or understood anything in them, or about them.

Chapter Twenty-two

As my husband drew near his end, his distempers had no intermission. No sooner was he recovered from one when he fell into another. He bore great pains with much patience offering them to God and making a good use of them. Yet his anger toward me increased, because reports and stories of me were multiplied to him, and those about him did nothing but vex him. He was the more susceptible of such impressions, as his pains gave him a stronger bent to vexation. At this time, the maid, who used to torment me sometimes took pity on me. She came to see me as soon as I was gone into my closet, and said, "Come to my master that your mother-in-law may not speak any more to him against you." I pretended to be ignorant of it all but he could not conceal his displeasure, nor even suffer me near him. My mother-in-law at the same time kept no bounds. All that came to the house were witnesses of the continual scoldings, which I was forced to bear, and which I bore with much patience, notwithstanding my being in the condition I have mentioned.

My husband having, sometime before his death, finished the building of the chapel in the country, where we spent a part of the summer, I had the convenience of hearing prayers every day, and of the communion. Not daring to do it openly every day, the priest privately admitted me to the communion. They solemnized the dedication of this little chapel. I felt myself all on a sudden inwardly seized, which continued more than five hours, all the time of the ceremony, when our Lord made a new consecration of me to Himself. I then seemed to myself a temple consecrated to Him, both for time and for eternity. I said within myself, (speaking both of the one and the other) "May this temple never be profaned; may the praises of God be sung therein forever!" It seemed to me at that time as if my prayer was granted. But soon all this was taken from me, and not so much as any remembrance left to console me.

When I was at this country house, which was only a little place of retreat before the chapel was built, I retired for prayer to woods and caverns. How many times, here, has God preserved me from dangerous and venomous beasts! Sometimes, unawares, I kneeled upon serpents, which were there in great plenty; they fled away without doing me any harm. Once I happened to be alone in a little wood wherein was a mad bull; but he betook himself to flight. If I could recount all the providences of God in my favor, it would appear wonderful. They were indeed so frequent and continual, that I could not but be astonished at them. God everlastingly gives to such as have nothing to repay Him. If there appears in the creature any fidelity or patience, it is He alone who gives it. If He ceases for an instant to support, if He seems to leave me to myself, I cease to be strong, and find myself weaker than any other creature. If my miseries show what I am, His favors show what He is, and the extreme necessity I am under of ever depending on Him.

After twelve years and four months of marriage, crosses as great as possible, except poverty which I never knew, though I had much desired it, God drew me out of that state to give me still stronger crosses of such a nature as I had never met with before. For if you give attention, sir, to the life which you have ordered me to write, you will remark that my crosses have been increasing till the present time, one removed to give place to another to succeed it, still heavier than the former. Amid the troubles imposed upon me, when they said, I "was in a mortal sin," I had nobody in the world to speak to. I could have wished to have had somebody for a witness of my conduct; but I had none. I had no support, no confessor, no director, no friend, no counselor. I had lost all. And after God had taken from me one after another, He withdrew also Himself. I remained without any creature; and to complete my distress, I seemed to be left without God, who alone could support me in such a deeply distressing state.

My husband's illness grew every day more obstinate. He apprehended the approach of death, and even wished for it, so oppressive was languishing life. To his other ills was great dislike to every sort of nourishment; he did not take anything necessary to sustain life. I alone had the courage to get him to take what little he did. The doctor advised him to go to the country. There for a few days at first he seemed to be better, when he was suddenly taken with a complication of diseases. His patience increased his pain. I saw plainly he could not live long. It was a great trouble to me, that my mother-in-law kept me from him as much as she could. She infused into his mind such a displeasure against me, that I was afraid lest he should die in it. I took a little interval of time when she happened not to be with him, and drawing near his bed, I kneeled down and said to him, "That if I had ever done any thing that displeased him I begged his pardon, assuring him it had not been voluntary." He appeared very much affected. As he had just come out of a sound sleep, he said to me, "It is I who beg your pardon, I did not deserve you." After that time he was not only pleased to see me, but gave me advice what I should do after his death; not to depend on the people on whom now I depended. He was for eight days very resigned and patient. I sent to Paris for the most skillful surgeon; but when he arrived my husband was dead.

No mortal could die in a more Christian disposition, or with more courage than he did, after having received the sacrament in a manner truly edifying. I was not present when he expired, for out of tenderness he made me retire. He was above twenty hours unconscious and in the agonies of his death. It was in the morning of July 21, 1676, that he died. Next day I entered into my closet, in which was the image of my divine spouse, the Lord Jesus Christ. I renewed my marriage-contract, and added thereto a vow of chastity, with a promise to make it perpetual, if M. Bertot my director, would permit me. After that I was filled with great joy, which was new to me, as for a long time past I had been plunged in the deepest bitterness.

As soon as I heard that my husband had expired, "Oh, my God," I cried, "you have broken my bonds, and I will offer you a sacrifice of praise." After that I remained in a deep silence, both exterior and interior, quite dry and without any support. I could neither weep nor speak. My mother-in-law said very fine things, and was very much commended for it by everyone. They were offended at my silence, which they attributed to want of resignation. A friar told me, that everyone admired the fine acts which my mother-in-law did; but as for me, they heard me say nothing; that I must sacrifice my loss to God. But I could not say one single word, let me strive as I would. I was indeed very much exhausted. Although I was but recently delivered of my daughter, yet I attended and sat up with my husband four and twenty nights before his death. I was more than a year after in recovering from fatigue, joined to my great weakness and pain both of body and of mind. The great depression, or dryness and stupidity which I was in, was such that I could not say a word about God. It bore me down in such a manner that I could hardly speak. However, I entered for some moments into the admiration of your goodness, O my God. I saw well that my crosses would not fail, since my mother-in-law had survived my husband. Also I was still tied, in having two children given me in so short a time before my husband's death, which evidently appeared the effect of divine wisdom; for had I only my eldest son, I would have put him in a college; and have gone myself into the convent of the Benedictines, and so frustrated all the designs of God upon me.

I was willing to show the esteem I had for my husband, in causing the most magnificent funeral to be made for him at my own expense. I paid off the legacies he had left. My mother-in-law violently opposed everything I could do for securing my own interests. I had nobody to apply to for advice or help; for my brother would not give me the least assistance. I was ignorant of business affairs; but God, independent of my natural understandings, always made me fit for everything that pleased Him, and supplied me with such a perfect intelligence that I succeeded. I omitted not the least minutia, and was surprised that in these matters I should know without ever having learned. I digested all my papers, and regulated all my affairs, without assistance from any one. My husband had abundance of writings deposited in his hands. I took an exact inventory of them, and sent them severally to their owners, which, without divine assistance, would have been very difficult for me; because, my husband having been a long time sick, everything was in the greatest confusion. This gained me the reputation of being a skillful woman.

There was one matter of great importance. A number of persons, who had been contending at law for several years, applied to my husband to settle their affairs. Though it was not properly the business of a gentleman, yet they applied to him, because he had both understanding and prudence; and as he had a love for several of them, he consented. There were twenty actions one upon another, and in all twenty-two persons concerned, who could not get any end put to their differences, by reason of new incidents continually falling out. My husband charged himself with getting lawyers to examine their papers, but died before he could make any procedure therein. After his death I sent for them to give them their papers; but they would not receive them, begging of me that I would accommodate them, and prevent their ruin. It appeared to me as ridiculous, as impossible, to undertake an affair of so great consequence, and which would require so long a discussion. Nevertheless, relying on the strength and wisdom of God, I consented. I shut myself up about thirty days for all these affairs, without ever going out, but to mass and to my meals. The arbitration being at length prepared, they all signed it without seeing it. They were all so well satisfied therewith, that they could not forbear publishing it everywhere. It was God alone who did those things; for after they were settled I knew nothing about them; and if I now hear any talk of such things, to me it sounds like Arabic.

Chapter Twenty-three

Being now a widow, my crosses, which one would have thought should have abated, only increased. That turbulent domestic I have often mentioned, instead of growing milder, now that she depended on me became more furious than ever. In our house she had amassed a good fortune, and I settled on her, besides, an annuity for the remainder of her life, for the services she had done my husband. She swelled with vanity and haughtiness. Having been used to sit up so much with an invalid, she had taken to drink wine, to keep up her spirits. This had now passed into a habit. As she grew aged and weak, a very little of it affected her. I tried to hide this fault, but it grew so that it could not be concealed. I spoke of it to her confessor, in order that he might try, softly and artfully to reclaim her from it; but instead of profiting by her director's advice, she was outrageous against me. My mother-in-law, who could hardly bear the fault of intemperance, and had often spoken to me about it, now joined in reproaching me and vindicating her. This strange creature, when any company came, would cry out with all her might, that I had dishonored her, thrown her into despair, and would be the cause of her damnation, as I was taking the ready course to my own. Yet God gave me an unbounded patience. I answered only with mildness and charity all her passionate invectives, giving her besides every possible mark of my affection. If any other maid came to wait on me, she would drive her back in a rage, crying out, that I hated her on account of the affection with which she had served my husband. When she had not a mind to come, I was obliged to serve myself; and when she did come, it was to chide me and make a noise. When I was very unwell, as was often the case, this girl would appear to be in despair. From hence I thought it was from You, O Lord, that all this came upon me. Without your permission, she was scarcely capable of such unaccountable conduct. She seemed not sensible of any faults, but always to think herself in the right. All those whom You have made use of to cause me to suffer, thought they were rendering service to You in so doing.

Before my husband's death, I went to Paris on purpose to see Monsieur Bertot, who had been of very little service to me as a director. Not knowing my state, and I being incapable of telling him of it, he grew weary of the charge. At length he gave it up, and wrote to me to take another director. I made no doubt but God had revealed to him my wicked state; and this desertion of me seemed a most certain mark of my reprobation. This was during the life of my husband. But now my renewed solicitations, and his sympathy with me on my husband's death, prevailed on him to resume my direction, which to me still proved of very little service. I went again to Paris to see him. While there, I visited him twelve or fifteen times, without being able to tell him anything of my condition. I told him, indeed, that I wanted some ecclesiastic to educate my son, to rid him of his bad habits, and of the wrong impressions he had conceived against me. He found one for me, of whom he had received very good recommendations.

I went to make a retreat with M. Bertot and Madame de C. All that time he spoke to me not a quarter of an hour at most. As he saw that I said nothing to him, for indeed I knew not what to say, as I had not spoken to him of the favors which God had conferred on me (not from a desire to conceal them, but because the Lord did not permit me to do it, as He had over me only the designs of death) he therefore spoke to such as he looked upon to be more advanced in grace. He let me alone as one for whom there was nothing to be done. So well did God hide from him the situation of my soul, in order to make me suffer, that he wanted to refer me, thinking that I had not the spirit of prayer, and that Mrs. Granger was mistaken when she told him I had. I did what I could to obey him, but it was entirely impossible. On this account I was displeased with myself, because I believed M. Bertot rather than my experience. Through this whole retreat my inclination, which I discerned only by my resistance to it, was to rest in silence and nakedness of thought. In the settling of my mind therein I feared I was disobeying the orders of my director. This made me think that I had fallen from grace. I kept myself in a state of nothingness, content with my poor low degree of prayer, without envying the higher degree of others, of which I judged myself unworthy. I would have, however, desired much to do the will of God, and to please Him, but despaired altogether of ever attaining that desirable end.

There was in the place where I lived, and had been for some years, one whose doctrine was suspected. He possessed a dignity in the church, which always obliged me to have a deference for him. As he understood how averse I was to all who were suspected of unsoundness in the faith, and knowing that I had some credit in the place, he used his utmost efforts to engage me in his sentiments. I answered him with so much clearness and energy, that he had not a word to reply. This increased his desire to win me in order to do it, to contract a friendship for me. He continued to importune me for two years and a half. As he was very polite, and of an obliging temper, and had a good share of learning, I did not mistrust him. I even conceived a hope of his conversion, in which I found myself mistaken. I then ceased going near him. He came to inquire why he could see me no more. At that time he was so agreeable to my sick husband, in his assiduities about him, that I could not avoid him though I thought the shortest and best way for me would be break off all acquaintance with him, which I did after the death of my husband. M. Bertot would not permit me to do it before. When he now saw that he could not renew it, he and his party raised up strong persecutions against me.

These gentlemen had at that time a method among them, by which they soon knew who were of their party, and who were opposite. They sent to one another circular letters, by means of which, in a very little time, they cried me down on every side, after a very strange manner. Yet this gave me little trouble. I was glad of my new liberty, intending never again to enter into an intimacy with anyone, which would give me so much difficulty to break.

This inability I was now in, of doing those exterior acts of charity I had done before, served this person with a pretext to publish that it was owing to him I had formerly done them. Willing to ascribe to himself the merit of what God alone, by His grace, had made me do, he went so far as to preach against me publicly, as one who had been a bright pattern to the town, but was now become a scandal to it. Several times he preached very offensive things. Though I was present at those sermons, and they were enough to weigh me down with confusion, for they offended all that heard them, I could not be troubled. I carried in myself my own condemnation beyond utterance. I thought I merited abundantly worse than all he could say of me, and that, if all men knew me, they would trample me under their feet. My reputation then was blasted by the industry of this ecclesiastic. He caused all such as passed for persons of piety to declare against me. I thought he and they were in the right and therefore quietly bore it all. Confused like a criminal that dares not lift up his eyes, I looked upon the virtue of others with respect. I saw no fault in others and no virtue in myself. When any happened to praise me, it was like a heavy blow struck at me, and I said in myself, "They little know my miseries, and from what state I have fallen." When any blamed me, I agreed to it, as right and just. Nature wanted sometimes to get out of such an abject condition, but could not find any way. If I tried to make an outward appearance of righteousness, by the practice of some good thing, my heart in secret rebuked me as guilty of hypocrisy, in wanting to appear what I was not; and God did not permit that to succeed. Oh, how excellent are the crosses of Providence! All other crosses are of no value.

I was often very ill and in danger of death, and knew not how to prepare myself for it. Several persons of piety, who had been acquainted with me, wrote to me about those things which the gentleman spread about me. I did not offer to justify myself, although I knew myself innocent of the things whereof they accused me. One day being in the greatest desolation and distress, I opened the New Testament on these words, "My grace is sufficient for you, for my strength is made perfect in weakness." That for a little time gave me some relief.

Chapter Twenty-four

The Lord took from me all the sensibility which I had for the creatures, or things created, even in an instant, as one takes off a robe. After that time I had none for any whatsoever. Though He had done me that favor, for which I can never be sufficiently grateful, I was, however, neither more contented nor less confused by it. My God seemed to be so estranged and displeased with me, that there remained nothing but the grief of having lost His blessed presence through my fault. The loss of my reputation every day increasing, became sensible to my heart, though I was not allowed to justify or bewail myself.

As I became always more impotent for every kind of exterior works, as I could not go to see the poor, nor stay at church, nor practice prayer; as I became colder toward God, in proportion as I was more sensible of my wrong steps, all this destroyed me the more both in my own eyes and in those of others. There were some very considerable gentlemen who made proposals for me, and even such persons as according to the rules of fashion ought not to think of me. They presented themselves during the very depth of my outward and inward desolation. At first it appeared to me a means of drawing me out of the distress I was in. But it seemed to me then notwithstanding my pains of body and mind, that if a king had presented himself to me, I would have refused him with pleasure, to show you, O my God, that with all my miseries I was resolved to be yours alone.

If You would not accept of me, I should at least have the consolation of having been faithful to You to the utmost of my power. For as to my inward state, I never mentioned it to anybody. I never spoke thereof, nor of the suitors, though my mother-in-law would say that if I did not marry, it was because none would have me. It was sufficient for me that You, O my God, knew that I sacrificed them to You, (without saying a word to anybody) especially one whose high birth and amiable exterior qualities might have tempted both my vanity and inclination. Oh, could I but have hoped, to become agreeable to You, such a hope would have been like a change from Hell to Heaven. So far was I from presuming to hope for it, that I feared this sea of affliction might also be followed by everlasting misery, in the loss of You. I dared not even desire to enjoy You - I only desired not to offend You.

I was for five or six weeks at the last extremity. I could not take any nourishment. A spoonful of broth made me faint. My voice was so gone, that when they put their ears close to my mouth, they could scarcely distinguish my words. I could not see any hope of salvation, yet was not unwilling to die. I bore a strong impression that the longer I lived the more I would sin. Of the two, I thought I would rather choose Hell than sin. All the good, which God made me do, now seemed to me evil or full of faults. All my prayers, penances, alms and charities, seemed to rise up against me, and heighten my condemnation. I thought there appeared on the side of God, on my own, and from all creatures, one general condemnation, my conscience was a witness against me, which I could not appease. What may appear strange, the sins of my youth did not then give me any pain at all. They did not rise up in judgment against me, but there appeared one universal testimony against all the good I had done, and all the sentiments of evil I had entertained. If I went to confessors, I could tell them nothing of my condition. If I could have told them, they would have not understood me. They would have regarded as eminent virtues, what, O my God, your eyes all pure and chaste rejected as infidelity. It was then that I felt the truth of what You have said, that You judge our righteousness. Oh, how pure you are! Who can comprehend it? It was then that I turned my eyes on every side, to see what way succor might come to me; but my succor could come no way but from Him who made Heaven and earth. As I saw there was no safety for me, or spiritual health in myself, I entered into a secret complacency in seeing no good in myself whereon to rest, or presume for salvation. The nearer my destruction appeared, the more I found in God Himself, wherewith to augment my trust and confidence, notwithstanding He seemed so justly irritated against me. It seemed to me that I had in Jesus Christ all that was wanting in myself. Oh, you stout and righteous men! Observe as much as you please of excellence in what you have done to the glory of God. As for me, I only glory in my infirmities, since they have merited for me such a Savior!

All my troubles, joined to the loss of my reputation, which yet was not so great as I apprehended, (it being only among a party) rendered me so unable to eat, that it seemed wonderful how I lived. In four days I did not eat as much as would make one very moderate repast. I was obliged to keep my bed through mere weakness, my body being no longer able to support the burden laid upon it. If I had thought, known, or heard tell, that there had ever been such a state as mine, it would have exceedingly relieved me. My very pain appeared to me to be sin. Spiritual books, when I tried to read them, all contributed only to augment it. I saw in myself none of those states which they set down. I did not so much as comprehend them. And when they treated the pains of certain states, I was very far from attributing any of them to myself. I said to myself, "These persons feel the pains of divine operations; but as to me, I sin, and feel nothing but my own wicked state." I could have wished to separate the sin from the confusion of sin, and provided I had not offended God, all would have been easy to me.

A slight sketch of my last miseries, which I am glad to let you know, because in their beginning I omitted many infidelities, having had too much of an earnest attachment, vain complaisance, unprofitable and tedious conversations, though self-love and nature made a sort of necessity for them; but toward the latter part I could not have borne a speech too human, nor the least thing of the kind.

Chapter Twenty-five

The first religious person that God made use of to draw me to Himself, to whom (according to his desire) I had written from time to time, wrote to me in the depth of my distress, desiring me to write to him no more, signifying his disapprobation of what came from me, and that I displeased God greatly. A father, a Jesuit, who had esteemed me much, wrote to me in like manner. No doubt, it was by Your permission, they thus contributed to complete my desolation. I thanked them for their charity, and commended myself to their prayers. It was then so indifferent to me to be decried of everybody, even of the greatest saints, that it added but little to my pain. The pain of displeasing God, and the strong propensity I felt in myself to all sorts of faults, caused me most lively and sensible pain.

I had been accustomed from the beginning to dryness and privation. I even preferred it to the state of abounding, because I knew that I must seek God above all. I had even at the first beginnings, an instinct of my inmost soul to pass over every manner of thing whatsoever, and to leave the gifts to run after the Giver. But at this time my spirit and senses were in such a manner struck, by Your permission, O my Lord, who was pleased to destroy me without mercy, that the farther I went, the more everything appeared to me a sin; even crosses appeared to me no more crosses but real faults. I thought I drew them all on myself by my imprudent words and actions. I was like those, who, looking through a colored glass, behold everything of the same color with which it is stained. Had I been able to perform any exterior acts as formerly, or penances for my evil, it would have relieved me. I was forbidden to do the latter, besides I grew so timorous, and felt in myself such a weakness, as made it appear impossible for me to do them. I looked on them with horror, I found myself now so weak and incapable of anything of the kind.

I omit many things, both of providences of the Lord in my favor, and of rugged paths through which I was obliged to pass. But as I have only one general view, I leave them in the knowledge of the Lord only. Afterward, being forsaken of my director, the coldness toward me which I remarked in the persons conducted by him, gave me no more trouble, nor indeed the estrangement of all the creatures, on account of my inward humiliation. My brother also joined with those who exclaimed against me, even though he had never seen them before. I believe it was the Lord who conducted things in this way, for my brother has worth, and undoubtedly thought he did well in acting thus.

I was obliged to go about some business to a town where some near relations of my mother-in-law lived. How did I find things changed there! When I was there before, they entertained me in a most elegant and obliging manner, regaling me from house to house with emulation. Now they treated me with the utmost contempt, saying, they did it to revenge what I made their relation suffer. As I saw the thing went so far, and that notwithstanding all my care and endeavors to please her, I had not been able to succeed, I resolved to come to an explanation with her. I told her that there was a current report that I treated her ill, though I made it my study to give her every mark of my esteem. If the report were true, I desired her to allow me to remove from her; for that I would not choose to stay to give her pain, but only with a quite contrary view. She answered very coldly, "I might do what I would; for she had not spoken about it, but was resolved to live apart from me." This was fairly giving me my discharge, and I thought of taking my measures privately to retire. As I had not, since my widowhood, made any visits but such as were of pure necessity, or charity, there were found too many discontented spirits, who made a party with her against me. The Lord required of me an inviolable secrecy of all my pains, both exterior and interior. There is nothing which makes nature die so much, as to find neither support nor consolation. In short I saw myself obliged to go out, in the middle of winter, with my children and my daughters' nurse. At that time there was no house empty in the town, so the Benedictines offered me an apartment in theirs.

I was now in a great strait; on one side fearing lest I was shunning the cross, on the other side thinking it unreasonable to impose my stay on one to whom it was only painful. Besides what I have related of her behavior, which still continued, when I went into the country to take a little repose she complained that I left her alone. If I desired her to come thither she would not. If I said, "I dare not ask her to come, for fear of incommoding her by changing her bed," She replied, "It was only an excuse, because I would not have her go; and that I only went to be away from her." When I heard that she was displeased at my being in the country, I returned to the town. Then she could not bear to speak to me, or to see me. I accosted her without appearing to notice how she received it. Instead of making me any answer, she turned her head another way. I often sent her my coach, desiring her to come and spend a day in the country. She sent it back empty, without any answer. If I passed some days there without sending it, she complained aloud. In short, all I did to please her soured her, God so permitting it. She had in the main a good heart, but was troubled with an uneasy temper: And I do not fail to think myself under much obligation to her.

Being with her on Christmas day, I said to her with much affection: "My mother, on this day was the King of peace born, to bring it to us; I beg peace of you in His name." I think that touched her, though she would not let it appear. The ecclesiastic, whom I had met with at home, far from strengthening and comforting me, did nothing but weaken and afflict me, telling me that I ought not to suffer certain things. I had not credit enough to discharge any domestic, however defective or culpable. As soon as any of them were warned to go away, she sided with them, and all her friends interfered. As I was ready to go off, one of my mother-in-law's friends, a man of worth, who had always an esteem for me, without daring to show it, having heard it, was much afraid lest I should leave the town; for the removal of my alms, he thought, would be a loss to the country. He resolved to speak to my mother-in-law in the softest manner he could for he knew her. After he had spoken to her, she said, that she would not put me away, but if I went, she would not hinder me. After this he came to see me, and desired me to go and make an excuse to her, in order to content her. I told him, I should be willing to make a hundred, although "I did not know about what; that I did it continually about everything, which made her uneasy. But that was not now the matter, for I make no complaint of her, but thought it not proper for me to continue with her, to give her pain; that it was but just that I should contribute to her ease." However, he went with me into her room. Then I told her, that I begged her pardon, if ever I had displeased her in anything, that it had never been my intention to do it; that I desired her, before this gentleman, who was her friend, to tell me wherein I had given her any offense. Here God permitted; she made a declaration of the truth in his presence. She said, "She was not a person to suffer herself to be offended; that she had no other complaint against me but that I did not love her, and that I wished her dead." I answered her that these thoughts were far from my heart, so far from it, that I should be glad, by my best care and attendance on her, to prolong her days; that my affection was real, but that she never would be persuaded to believe it, whatever testimonies I could give, so long as she hearkened to people who spoke to her against me; that she had with her a maid, who, far from showing me any respect, treated me ill, so far as to push me when she wanted to pass by. She had done it at church, making me give way to her with as much violence as contempt, several times, also, in my room grating me with her words: that I had never complained of it, because such a temper might one day give her trouble." She took the girl's part. Nevertheless we embraced and it was left so. Soon after, when I was in the country, this maid, having me no more to vent her chagrins on behaved in such a manner to my mother-in-law that she could not bear it. She immediately put her out of doors. I must say here on my mother-in-law's behalf, that she had both sense and virtue, and except certain faults, which persons who do not practice prayer are liable to, she had good qualities. Perhaps I caused crosses to her without intending it, and she to me without knowing it. I hope what I write will not be seen by any who may be offended with it, or who may not be in a condition to see these matters in God.

That gentleman who had used me so ill, for breaking off my acquaintance with him, among his penitents had one who, for affairs which befell her husband, was obliged to quit the country. He himself was accused of the same things which he had so liberally and unjustly accused me, and even things much worse, and with more noise and outcry. Though I well knew all this, God granted me the favor never to make his downfall the subject of my discourse. On the contrary, when any spoke to me of it, I pitied him, and said what I could in mitigation of his case. And God governed my heart so well, that it never offered to go into any vain joy at seeing him overtaken, and oppressed, with those kind of evils which he had been so assiduous in endeavoring to bring upon me. Though I knew that my mother-in-law was informed of it all, I never spoke to her about it, or about the sad confusions he had caused in a certain family.

Chapter Twenty-six

One day during my husband's lifetime, laden with sorrow, not knowing what to do, I wished to speak to a person of distinction, and merit, who came often into the country. I wrote to request an opportunity with him, for that I wanted his instruction and advice. But soon after I felt remorse for it; this voice spoke in my heart, "What, - do you seek for ease, and to shake off my yoke?" Hereupon I instantly sent a note again to desire him to excuse me, adding that what I had written was only from self-love, not necessity; that as he knew what it was to be faithful to God, I hoped he would not disapprove my acting with this Christian simplicity. Yet he resented it, which surprised me much, as I had conceived a high idea of his virtue. Virtues he had, but such as are full of the life and activities of nature, and unacquainted with the paths of mortification and death.

You, O my God, have been my conductor even in these paths, as with admiration I have discovered since they are past. Blessed be Your name forever. I am obliged to bear this testimony to Your goodness.

Before I continue my narration, I must add one remark, which the Lord gave me to make upon the way by which He, in His goodness, was pleased to conduct me; which is, that this obscure path is the surest to mortify the soul, as it leaves it not any prop to lean upon for support. Though it has no application to any particular state of Jesus Christ; yet, at its coming out, it finds itself clothed with all His dispositions. The impure and selfish soul, is hereby purified, as gold in the furnace. Full of its own judgment and its own will before, but now obeys like a child and finds no other will in itself. Before, it would have contested for a trifle; now it yields at once, not with reluctance and pain by way of practicing virtue, but as it were naturally. Its own vices are vanished. This creature so vain before now loves nothing but poverty, littleness and humiliation. Before, it preferred itself above everybody; now everybody above itself, having a boundless charity for its neighbor, to bear with his faults and weaknesses, in order to win him by love, which before it could not do but with very great constraint. The rage of the wolf is changed to the meekness of the lamb.

During all the time of my experiencing my miseries and my deep trials, I went after no fine sights or recreations. I wanted to see and know nothing but Jesus Christ. My closet was my only diversion. Even when the queen was near me, whom I had never seen, and whom I had desire enough to see; I had only to open my eyes, and look out to see her; yet did not do it. I had been fond of hearing others sing; yet I was once four days with one who passed for the finest voice in the world, without ever desiring her to sing; which surprised her, because she was not ignorant that, knowing her name, I must know the charming excellence of her voice. However, I committed some infidelities, in inquiring what others said of me by way of blame. I met with one who told me everything. Though I showed nothing of it, it served only to mortify me. I saw I was yet too much alive to self.

I shall never be able to express the number of my miseries. They are so vastly surmounted by the favors of God, and so swallowed up in these that I can see them no more. One of the things which gave me most pain in the seven years I have spoken of, especially the last five, was so strange a folly of my imagination that it gave me no rest. My senses bore it company. I could no more shut my eyes at church. Thus having all the gates and avenues open, I was like a vineyard exposed, because the hedges which the father of the family had planted were torn away. I saw every one that came and went, and everything that passed in the church. For the same force, which had drawn me inward to recollection, seemed to push me outward to dissipation.

Laden with miseries, weighed down with oppressions, and crushed under continual crosses, I thought of nothing but ending my days thus. There remained in me not the least hope of ever emerging. Notwithstanding, I thought I had lost grace forever, and the salvation which it merits for us, I longed at least to do what I could for God, though I feared I should never love Him. Seeing the happy state from whence I had fallen, I wished in gratitude to serve Him, though I looked on myself as a victim doomed to destruction. Sometimes the view of that happy period caused secret desires to spring up in my heart, of recovering it again. I was instantly rejected and thrown back into the depth of the abyss; I judged myself to be in a state which was due to unfaithful souls. I seemed, my God, as if I was forever cast off from Your regard, and from that of all creatures. By degrees my state ceased to be painful. I became even insensible to it, and my insensibility seemed like the final hardening of my reprobation. My coldness appeared to me a mortal coldness. It was truly so, O my God, since I thus died to self, in order to live wholly in You, and in your precious love.

To resume my history, a servant of mine wanted to become a Barnabite. I wrote about it to Father de la Mothe. He answered me, that I must address Father La Combe, who was then the superior of the Barnabites of Tonon. That obliged me to write to him. I had always preserved secret respect and esteem for him, as one under grace. I was glad of this opportunity of recommending myself to his prayers. I wrote to him about my fall from the grace of God, that I had requited His favors with the blackest ingratitude; that I was miserable, and a subject worthy of compassion; and far from having advanced toward God, I was become entirely alienated from Him. He answered in such a manner, as if he had known, by a supernatural light, the frightful description I had given of myself.

In the midst of my miseries, Geneva came into my mind, a singular manner, which caused me many fears. "What," said I, "to complete my reprobation, shall I go to such an excess of impiety, as to quit the faith through apostasy? (The inhabitants of Geneva being generally Protestant Calvinists.) Am I then about quitting that church, for which I would give a thousand lives? Or, shall I ever depart from that faith which I would even wish to seal with my blood?" I had such a distrust of myself, that I dared hope for nothing, but had a thousand reasons for fear. Nevertheless the letter which I had received from Father La Combe, in which he wrote me an account of his present disposition, somewhat similar to mine, had such an effect, as to restore peace and calmness to my mind. I felt myself inwardly united to him, as to a person of great fidelity to the grace of God. Afterward a woman appeared to me in a dream to be come down from Heaven, to tell me that God demanded me at Geneva.

About eight or ten days before Magdalene's day, 1680, it came into my mind to write to Father La Combe, and to request him, if he received my letter before that day, to pray particularly for me. It was so ordered, contrary even to my expectations, that he received my letter on St. Magdalene's eve, and when praying for me the next day, it was said to him, thrice over, with much power, "You shall both dwell in one and the same place." He was very much surprised, as he never had received interior words before. I believe, O my God, that that has been much more verified, both in our inward sense and experience, and in the same crucifying events which have befallen us, pretty much alike; and in Yourself, who are our dwelling, than in any temporal abode.

Chapter Twenty-seven

On that happy Magdalene's day my soul was perfectly delivered from all its pains. It had already begun since the receipt of the first letter from Father La Combe, to recover a new life. It was then only like that of a dead person raised, though not yet unbound from grave clothes. On this day I was, as it were, in perfect life, and set wholly at liberty. I found myself as much raised above nature, as before I had been depressed under its burden. I was inexpressibly overjoyed to find Him, whom I thought I had lost forever, returned to me again with unspeakable magnificence and purity. It was then, O God, that I found again in You with new advantages, in an ineffable manner, all I had been deprived of; the peace I now possessed was all holy, heavenly and inexpressible. All I had enjoyed before was only a peace, a gift of God, but now I received and possessed the God of peace. Yet the remembrance of my past miseries still brought a fear upon me, lest nature should find means to take to itself any part therein. As soon as it wanted to see or taste anything, the Spirit ever watchful crossed and repelled it. I was far from elevating myself, or attributing to myself anything of this new state. My experience made me sensible of what I was.

I hoped I should enjoy this happy state for some time, but little did I think my happiness so great and immutable as it was. If one may judge of a good by the trouble which precedes it, I leave mine to be judged of by the sorrows I had undergone before my attaining it. The apostle Paul tells us, that "the sufferings of this life are not to be compared with the glory that is prepared for us." How true is that of this life! One day of this happiness was worth more than years of suffering. It was indeed, at that time well worth all I had undergone, though it was then only dawning. An alacrity for doing good was restored to me, greater than ever. It seemed to me all quite free and natural to me. At the beginning, this liberty was less extensive; but as I advanced it grew greater. I had occasion to see Mon. Bertot for a few moments, and told him, I thought my state much changed. He, seemingly attentive to something else, answered, "No." I believed him; because grace taught me to prefer the judgment of others, and rather believe them than my own opinions or experience. This did not give me any kind of trouble. Every state seemed equally indifferent if I only had the favor of God. I felt a kind of beatitude every day increasing in me. I did all sorts of good, without selfishness or premeditation. Whenever a self-reflective thought was presented to my mind, it was instantly rejected, and as it were a curtain in the soul drawn before it. My imagination was kept so fixed, that I had now very little trouble on that. I wondered at the clearness of my mind and the purity of my whole heart.

I received a letter from Father La Combe, wherein he wrote that God had discovered to him that he had great designs in regard to me. "Let them be," then said I to myself, "either of justice or mercy, all is equal to me." I still had Geneva deeply at heart; but said nothing of it to anybody, waiting for God to make known to me His all powerful will and fearing lest any stratagem of the Devil should be concealed therein, that might tend to draw me out of my proper place, or steal me out of my condition. The more I saw my own misery, incapacity and nothingness, the plainer it appeared that they rendered me fitter for the designs of God, whatever they might be. "Oh, my Lord," said I, "take the weak and the wretched to do your works, that You may have all the glory and that man may attribute nothing of them to himself. If You should take a person of eminence and great talents, one might attribute to him something; but if You take me, it will be manifest that you alone are the Author of whatever good shall be done." I continued quiet in my spirit, leaving the whole affair to God, being satisfied, if He should require anything of me, that He would furnish me with the means of performing it. I held myself in readiness with a full resolution to execute His orders, whenever he should make them known, though it were to the laying down of my life. I was released from all crosses. I resumed my care of the sick, and dressing of wounds, and God gave me to cure the most desperate. When surgeons could do no more, it was then that God made me cure them.

Oh, the joy that accompanied me everywhere, finding still Him who had united me to Himself, in His own immensity and boundless vastitude! Oh, how truly did I experience what He said in the Gospel, by the four evangelists, and by one of them twice over, "Whosoever will lose his life for my sake shall find it; and whosoever will save his life shall lose it."

When I had lost all created supports, and even divine ones, I then found myself happily compelled to fall into the pure divine, and to fall into it through all those very things which seemed to remove me further from it. In losing all the gifts, with all their supports, I found the Giver. In losing the sense and perception of You in myself - I found You, O my God, to lose You no more in Yourself, in Your own immutability. Oh, poor creatures, who pass all your time in feeding upon the gifts of God, and think therein to be the most favored and happy. How I pity you if you stop here, short of the true rest, and cease to go forward to God Himself, through the loss of those cherished gifts which you now delight in! How many pass all their lives in this way, and think highly of themselves! There are others who, being called of God to die to themselves, yet pass all their time in a dying life, in inward agonies, without ever entering into God through death and a total loss of self, because they are always willing to retain something under plausible pretexts, and so never lose themselves to the whole extent of the designs of God. They never enjoy God in all His fullness; which is a loss that cannot be perfectly known in this life.

Oh, my Lord, what happiness did I not largely taste in my solitude, and with my little family, where nothing interrupted my tranquility! As I was in the country, the slender age of my children did not require my application too much, they being in good hands, I retired a great part of the day into a wood. I passed as many days of happiness as I had had months of sorrow. You, O my God, dealt by me as by your servant Job, rendering me double for all you had taken, and delivering me from all my crosses. You gave me a marvelous facility to satisfy everyone. What was surprising now was that my mother-in-law, who had ever been complaining of me, without my doing anything more than usual to please her, declared that none could be better satisfied with me than she was. Such as before had cried me down the most, now testified their sorrow for it and became full of my praises. My reputation was established with much more advantage, in proportion as it had appeared to be lost. I remained in an entire peace, as well without as within. It seemed to me that my soul was become like New Jerusalem, spoken of in the Apocalypse, prepared as a bride for her husband and where there is no more sorrow, or sighing. I had a perfect indifference to everything that is here, a union so great with the will of God, that my own will seemed entirely lost. My soul could not incline itself on one side or the other, since another will had taken the place of its own, but only nourished itself with the daily providences of God. It now found a will all divine, yet was so natural and easy that it found itself infinitely more free than ever it had been in its own.

These dispositions have still subsisted, and still grown stronger, and more perfect even to this hour. I could neither desire one thing nor another, but was content with whatever fell. If any in the house asked me, "Will you have this, or that?" then I was surprised to find that there was nothing left in me which could desire or choose. I was as if everything, of smaller matters, quite disappeared, a higher power having taken up and filled all their place. I even perceived no more that soul which He had formerly conducted by His crook and His staff, because now He alone appeared to me, my soul having given up its place to Him. It seemed to me, as if it was wholly and altogether passed into its God, to make but one and the same thing with Him; even as a little drop of water, cast into the sea, receives the qualities of the sea. Oh, union of unity, demanded of God by Jesus Christ for men and merited by him! How strong is this in a soul that is become lost in its God! After the consummation of this divine unity, the soul remains hid with Christ in God. This happy loss is not like those transient ones which ecstasy operates, which are rather an absorption than union because the soul afterwards finds itself again with all its own dispositions. Here she feels that prayer fulfilled - John 17:21: "That they all may be one as you Father are in me, and I in you; that they also may be one in us."

Chapter Twenty-eight

I was obliged to go to Paris about some business. Having entered into a church, that was very dark, I went up to the first confessor I found, whom I did not know, nor have ever seen since. I made a simple and short confession; but to the confessor himself I said not a word. He surprised me saying, "I know not who you are whether maid, wife or widow; but I feel a strong inward motion to exhort you to do what the Lord has made known to you, that he requires of you. I have nothing else to say." I answered him, "Father, I am a widow who have little children. What else could God require of me, but to take due care of them in their education?" He replied, "I know nothing about this. You know if God manifests to you that He requires something of you; there is nothing in the world which ought to hinder you from doing His will. One may have to leave one's children to do that." This surprised me much. However, I told him nothing of what I felt about Geneva. I disposed myself submissively to quit everything, if the Lord required it of me. I did not look upon it as a good I aspired to, or a virtue I hoped to acquire, or as anything extraordinary, or as an act that would merit some return on God's part; but only gave myself up to be led in the way of my duty, whatever it might be, feeling no distinction between my own will and the will of God in me.

In this disposition, I lived with my family in the greatest tranquility, until one of my friends had a great desire to go on a mission to Siam. He lived twenty leagues from my house. As he was ready to make a vow to this purpose, he found himself stopped, with an impulse to come and speak to me. He came immediately, and as he had some reluctance to declare his mind to me, he went to read prayers in my chapel, hoping God would be satisfied with his making the vow. As he was performing divine service in my hearing, he was stopped again. He left the chapel to come and speak to me. He then told me his intention.

Though I had no thought of saying anything positive to him, I felt an impression in my soul to relate to him my case, and the idea I had for a long time past for Geneva. I told him a dream I had, which appeared to me supernatural. When I had done, I felt a strong impulse to say to him, "You must go to Siam; and you must also serve me in this affair. It is for that end God has sent you hither; I desire you to give me your advice." After three days, having considered the matter, and consulted the Lord in it, he told me that he believed I was to go thither; but to be the better assured of it, it would be needful to see the Bishop of Geneva. If he approved of my design, it would be a sign that it was from the Lord; if not, I must drop it. I agreed with his sentiment. He then offered to go to Annecy, to speak to the Bishop, and to bring me a faithful account. As he was advanced in years, we were deliberating in what way he could take so long a journey, when there came two travelers, who told us the Bishop was at Paris. This I looked on as an extraordinary providence. He advised me to write to Father La Combe, and recommend the affair to his prayers, as he was in that country. He then spoke to the Bishop at Paris. I, having occasion to go thither, spoke to him also.

I told him, that "my design was to go into the country, to employ there my substance, to erect an establishment for all such as should be willing truly to serve God, and to give themselves unto him without reserve; and that many of the servants of the Lord had encouraged me thereto." The bishop approved of the design. He said, "there were New Catholics going to establish themselves at Gex, near Geneva, and that it was providential thing. I answered him, "that I had no vocation for Gex, but for Geneva." He said, "I might go from hence to that city."

I thought this was a way which divine Providence had opened, for my taking this journey with the less difficulty. As I yet knew nothing positive of what the Lord would acquire at my hand, I was not willing to oppose anything. "Who knows," said I, "but the will of the Lord is only that I should contribute to this establishment?"

I went to see the prioress of the New Catholics at Paris. She seemed much rejoiced, and assured me she would gladly join me. As she is a great servant of God, this confirmed me. When I could reflect a little, which was but seldom, I thought God would make choice of her for her virtue, and me for my worldly substance. When I inadvertently looked at myself, I could not think God would make use of me; but when I saw the things in God, then I perceived that the more I was nothing, the fitter I was for His designs. As I saw nothing in myself extraordinary, and looked on myself as being in the lowest stage of perfection, and imagined that an extraordinary degree of inspiration was necessary for extraordinary designs, this made me hesitate, and fear deception. It was not that I was in fear of anything, as to my perfection and salvation which I had referred to God; but I was afraid of not doing His will by being too ardent and hasty in doing it. I went to consult Father Claude Martin. At that time he gave me no decisive answer, demanding time to pray about it; saying he would write to me what should appear to him to be the will of God concerning me.

I found it hard to get to speak to M. Bertot, both on account of his being difficult of access, and of my knowing how he condemned things extraordinary, or out of the common road. Being my director, I submitted, against my own views or judgment, to what he said, laying down all my own experiences when duty required me to believe and obey. I thought, however, than in an affair of this importance, I ought to address myself to him, and prefer his sense of the matter to that of every one beside. Persuaded, he would infallibly tell me the will of God. I went to him then, and he told me that my design was of God, and that he had had a sense given him of God for some time past, that he required something of me. I therefore returned home to set everything in order. I loved my children much, having great satisfaction in being with them, but resigned all to God to follow His will.

On my return from Paris, I left myself in the hands of God, resolved not to take any step, either to make the thing succeed or to hinder it, either to advance or retard it, but singly to move as He should be pleased to direct me. I had mysterious dreams, which portended nothing but crosses, persecutions and afflictions. My heart submitted to whatever it should please God to ordain. I had one which was very significant.

Being employed in some necessary work, I saw near me a little animal which appeared to be dead. This animal I took to be the envy of some persons, which seemed to have been dead for some time. I took it up, and as I saw it strove hard to bite me, and that it magnified to the eye, I cast it away. I found thereupon that it filled my fingers with sharp-pointed prickles like needles. I came to one of my acquaintance to get him to take them out; but he pushed them deeper in, and left me so, till a charitable priest of great merit, (whose countenance is still present with me, though I have not yet seen him, but believe I shall before I die) took this animal up with a pair of pincers. As soon as he held it fast, those sharp prickles fell off, of themselves. I found that I easily entered into a place, which before had seemed inaccessible. And although the mire was up to my girdle, in my way to a deserted church, I went over it without getting any dirt. It will be easy to see in the sequel what this signified.

Doubtless you will wonder that I, who makes so little account of things extraordinary, relate dreams. I do it for two reasons; first out of fidelity, having promised to omit nothing of what should come to my mind; secondly, because it is the method God makes use of to communicate Himself to faithful souls, to give them foretokens of things to come, which concern them. Thus mysterious dreams are found in many places of the holy Scriptures. They have singular properties, as – 1. To leave a certainty that they are mysterious, and will have their effect in their season. 2. To be hardly ever effaced out of the memory, though one forgets all others. 3. To redouble the certainty of their truth every time one thinks of them. 4. They generally leave a certain unction, a divine sense or savor at one's waking.

I received letters from sundry religious persons, some of whom lived far from me, and from one another, relating to my going forth in the service of God, and some of them to Geneva in particular, in such a manner as surprised me. One of them intimated that I must there bear the cross and be persecuted; and another of them that I should be eyes to the blind, feet to the lame, and arms to the maimed.

The ecclesiastic, or chaplain, of our house was much afraid lest I was under a delusion. What at that time greatly confirmed me was Father Claude Martin, whom I mentioned above, wrote to me that, after many prayers, the Lord had given him to know that He required me at Geneva, and to make a free sacrifice of everything to Him. I answered him, "that perhaps the Lord required of me nothing more than a sum of money to assist in founding an institution which was going to be established there." He replied, that the Lord had made him know that He wanted not my worldly substance but myself. At the very same time with this letter I received one from Father La Combe, who wrote to me that the Lord had given him a certainty, as he had done to several of his good and faithful servants and handmaids, that he wanted me at Geneva. The writers of these two letters lived above a hundred and fifty leagues from each other; yet both wrote the same thing. I could not but be somewhat surprised to receive at the same time two letters exactly alike, from two persons living so far distant from each other.

As soon as I became fully convinced of its being the will of the Lord, and saw nothing on earth capable of detaining me, my senses had some pain about leaving my children. And upon reflecting thereon a doubt seized my mind. O my Lord! Had I rested on myself, or on the creatures, I would have revolted; "leaned on a broken reed, which would have pierced my hand." But relying on You alone, what needed I to fear? I resolved then to go, regardless of the censures of such as understand not what it is to be a servant of the Lord, and to receive and obey His orders. I firmly believed that He, by His Providence, would furnish the means necessary for the education of my children. I put everything by degrees in order, the Lord alone being my guide.

Chapter Twenty-nine

While providence on the one hand, appointed my forsaking all things, it seemed on the other to make my chains the stronger, and my separation the more blamable. None could receive stronger marks of affection from one's own mother than those which I received at this time from my mother-in-law. Even the least sickness which befell me made her very uneasy. She said, "she had veneration for my virtue." I believe what contributed not a little to this change was, that she had heard that three persons had offered suit to me, and that I had refused them, although their fortune and quality were quite superior to mine. She remembered how she had upbraided me on this head, and I answered her not a word, whereby she might understand that it depended on myself to marry to advantage. She began to fear lest such rigorous treatment, as hers had been toward me, might excite me to deliver myself by such means, with honor, from her tyranny, and was sensible what damage that might be to my children. So she was now very tender to me on every occasion.

I fell extremely ill. I thought that God had accepted of my willingness to sacrifice all to him, and required that of my life. During this illness, my mother-in-law went not from my bedside; her many tears proved the sincerity of her affection. I was very much affected at it, and thought I loved her as my true mother. How, then, should I leave her now, being so far advanced in age? The maid, who till then had been my plague, took an inconceivable friendship for me. She praised me everywhere, extolling my virtue to the highest and served me with extraordinary respect. She begged pardon for all that she had made me suffer, and died of grief after my departure.

There was a priest of merit, a spiritual man, who had fallen in with temptation of taking upon him employment which I was sensible God did not call him to do. Fearing it might be a snare to him, I advised him against it. He promised me he would not do it, and yet accepted it. He then avoided me, joined in calumniating me, gradually fell away from grace, and died soon after.

There was a nun in a monastery I often went to, who was entered into a state of purification, which everyone in the house looked on as distraction. They locked her up and all who went to see her called it frenzy or melancholy. I knew her to be devout I requested to see her. As soon as I approached, I felt an impression that she sought purity. I desired of the Superior that she should not be locked up, nor should people be admitted to see her, but that she would confide her to my care. I hoped things would change. I discovered that her greatest pain was at being counted a fool. I advised her to bear the state of foolishness, since Jesus Christ had been willing to bear it before Herod. This sacrifice gave her a calmness at once. But as God was willing to purify her soul, He separated her from all those things for which she had before the greatest attachment. At last, after she had patiently undergone her sufferings, her Superior wrote to me that "I was in the right, and that she had now come out of that state of dejection, in greater purity than ever." The Lord gave to me alone at that time to know her state. This was the commencement of the gift of discerning spirits, which I afterward received more fully.

The winter before I left home was one of the longest and hardest that had been for several years (1680). It was followed with extreme scarcity, which proved to me an occasion of exercising charity. My mother-in-law joined me heartily and appeared to me so much changed. I could not but be both surprised and overjoyed at it. We distributed at the house ninety-six dozen loaves of bread every week, but private charities to the bashful poor were much greater. I kept poor boys and girls employed. The Lord gave such blessings to my alms, that I did not find that my family lost anything by it. Before the death of my husband, my mother-in-law told him that I would ruin him with my charities, though he himself was so charitable, that in a very dear year, while he was young, he distributed a considerable sum. She repeated this to him so often, that he commanded me to set down in writing all the money I laid out, both what I gave for the expense of the house, and all that I caused to be bought, that he might better judge of what I gave to the poor. This new obligation, which I was brought under, appeared to me so much the harder, as for above eleven years we had been married I never before had this required of me. What troubled me most was the fear of having nothing to give to such as wanted. However, I submitted to it, without retrenching any part of my charities. I did not indeed set down any of my alms, and yet my account of expenses was found to answer exactly. I was much surprised and astonished, and esteemed it one of the wonders of Providence. I saw plainly it was simply given out of Your treasury, O my Lord, that made me more liberal of what I thought was the Lord's, and not mine. Oh, if we but knew how far charity, instead of wasting or lessening the substance of the donor, blessed, increased and multiplied it profusely. How much is there in the world of useless dissipation, which, if properly applied, might amply serve for the subsistence of the poor, and would abundantly be restored, and amply rewarded to the families of those who gave it.

In the time of my greatest trials, some years after my husband's death (for they began three years before my widowhood, and lasted four years after) my footman came one day to tell me, (I was then in the country) that there was in the road a poor soldier dying. I had him brought in, and ordering a separate place to be made ready for him, I kept above a fortnight. His malady was a flux, which he had taken in the army. It was so nauseous, that though the domestics were charitably inclined, nobody could bear to come near him. I went myself to take away his vessels. But I never did anything of the kind which was so hard. I frequently made efforts for a full quarter of an hour at a time. It seemed as if my very heart was going to come up; yet I never desisted. I sometimes kept the poor people at my house to dress their putrid sores; but never met with anything so terrible as this. The poor man, after I had made him receive the sacrament, died.

What gave me now no small concern was the tenderness I had for my children, especially my younger son, whom I had strong reasons for loving. I saw him inclined to be good; everything seemed to favor the hopes I had conceived of him. I thought it running a great risk to leave him to another's education. My daughter I designed to take with me, though she was at this time ill of a very tedious fever. Providence was pleased, however, so to order it that she speedily recovered. The ties, with which the Lord held me closely united to Himself, were infinitely stronger than those of flesh and blood. The laws of my sacred marriage obliged me to give up all, to follow my spouse whithersoever it was His pleasure to call me after Him. Though I often hesitated, and doubted much before I went, I never doubted after my going of its being His will; and though men, who judge of things only according to the success they seem to have, have taken occasion from my disgraces and sufferings, to judge of my calling, and to run it down as error, illusion and imagination; it is that very persecution, and a multitude of strange crosses it has drawn upon me, (of which this imprisonment I now suffer is one,) which have confirmed me in the certainty of its truth and validity. I am more than ever convinced that the resignation which I have made of everything is in pure obedience to the divine will.

The gospel effectually in this point shows itself to be true, which has promised to those that shall leave all for the love of the Lord, "an hundred fold in this life, and persecutions also." And have not I infinitely more than an hundred fold, in so entire a possession as my Lord has taken of me; in that unshaken firmness which is given me in my sufferings, in a perfect tranquility in the midst of a furious tempest, which assaults me on every side; in an unspeakable joy, enlargedness and liberty which I enjoy in a most straight and rigorous captivity. I have no desire that my imprisonment should end before the right time. I love my chains. Everything is equal to me, as I have no will of my own, but purely the love and will of Him who possesses me. My senses indeed have not any relish for such things, but my heart is separated from them. My perseverance is not of myself, but of Him who is my life; so that I can say with the apostle, "It is no more I that live, but Jesus Christ that lives in me." It is He in whom I live, move, and have my being.

To return to the subject, I say that I was not so reluctant to go with the New Catholics, as I was to engage with them, not finding a sufficient attraction, though I sought for it. I longed indeed to contribute to the conversion of wandering souls, and God made use of me to convert several families before my departure, one of which was composed of eleven or twelve persons. Besides, Father La Combe had written to me, to make use of this opportunity for setting off, but did not tell me whether I ought to engage with them or not. Thus it was the Providence of my God alone, which ordered everything, to which I was resigned without any reserve; and that hindered me from engaging with them.

One day reflecting humanly on this undertaking of mine, I found my faith staggering, weakened with a fear lest I were under a mistake, which slavish fear was increased by an ecclesiastic at our house, who told me it was a rash and ill-advised design. Being a little discouraged, I opened the Bible, and met with this passage in Isaiah, "Fear not you worm Jacob, and you men of Israel. I will help you says the Lord, and your Redeemer, the holy one of Israel." And near it, "Fear not; for I have redeemed you, I have called you by your name; you are mine. When you pass through the waters, I will be with you."

I had a very great courage given me for going, but could not persuade myself that it would be best to settle with the New Catholics. It was, however, necessary to see Sister Garnier, their superior at Paris, in order to take our measures together. But I could not go to Paris, because that journey would have hindered me from taking another, which I had to take. She then, though much indisposed, resolved to come and see me. In what a wonderful manner, O my God, did You conduct things by Your Providence, to make everything come to the point of Your will! Every day I saw new miracles, which both amazed and still more confirmed me; for with a paternal goodness You took care of even the smallest things. As she intended setting off, she fell sick. And You permitted it to fall out so, to give room thereby for a person, who would have discovered everything, in the meantime to take a journey to see me. As this person had given me notice of the day she intended to set off, seeing that day was excessively hot, and so sultry that I imagined that being taken so much tender care of as she was at home, they would not suffer her to begin her journey, (which really proved to be the case, as she afterward told me,) I prayed to the Lord to be pleased to grant a wind to rise, to moderate the violent heat. Scarce had I prayed, but there arose suddenly so refreshing a wind, that I was surprised and the wind did not cease during her whole journey.

I went to meet her, and brought her to my country house, in such a way that she was not seen or known of anybody. What embarrassed me a little was, that two of my domestics knew her. But as I was then endeavoring the conversion of a lady, they thought that it was on this account I had sent for her, and that it was necessary to keep it secret, that the other lady might not be discouraged from coming. Though I knew nothing of controversial points, yet God so furnished me that I did not fail to answer all her objections, and resolve all her doubts, to such a degree, that she could not but give herself up entirely to God. Though Sister Garnier had a good share of both of grace and natural understanding, yet her words had not such an effect on this soul as those with which God furnished me, as she assured me herself. She even could not forbear speaking of it. I felt a movement to beg her of God, as a testimony of His holy will concerning me. But He was pleased not to grant it then, being willing that I should go off alone without any other assurance than His divine Providence was conducting all things. Sister Garnier did not declare her thoughts to me for four days. Then she told me she would not go with me. At this I was the more surprised, as I had persuaded myself that God would grant to her virtue what He might refuse to my demerits. Besides, the reason she gave appeared to me to be merely human, and void of supernatural grace. That made me hesitate a little; then, taking new courage, through the resignation of my whole self, I said, "As I go not thither for your sake, I will not fail to go even without you." This surprised her, as she acknowledged to me; for she thought that, on her refusal, I would decline my purpose of going.

I regulated everything, wrote down the contract of association with them as I thought proper. No sooner had I done it, but I felt great perturbation and trouble of mind. I told her my pain, and that I had no doubt but the Lord demanded me at Geneva, yet did not let me see that He would have me to be of their congregation. She desired to have some time till after prayers and communion, and that then she would tell me what she thought the Lord required of me. Accordingly. He directed her contrary both to her interests and inclination. She then told me that I ought not to connect myself with her, that it was not the Lord's design; that I only ought to go with her sister's, and that when I should be there, Father La Combe, (whose letter she had seen) would signify to me the divine will. I entered at once into these sentiments, and my soul then regained the sweets of inward peace.

My first thought had been (before I heard of the New Catholics going to Gex) to go directly to Geneva. At this time there were Catholics there in service, and otherwise; to take some little room without any noise, and without declaring myself at first; and as I knew how to make up all sorts of ointments to heal wounds and especially the king's evil, of which there is abundance in that place, and for which I had a most certain cure. I hoped easily to insinuate myself by this way and with the charities which I should have done to have won over many of the people. I have no doubt but, if I had followed this impulse, things would have succeeded better. But I thought I ought to follow the sentiments of the Bishop rather than my own. What am I saying? Has not Your eternal Word, O my Lord, had its effect and accomplishment in me? Man speaks as man; but when we behold things in the Lord, we see them in another light. Yes, my Lord, Your design was to give Geneva not to my cares, words or works, but to my sufferings; for the more I see things appear hopeless, the more do I hope for the conversion of that city by a way known to You only.

Father La Combe has told me since, that he had a strong impulse to write to me, not to engage with the New Catholics. He believed it not to be the will of the Lord concerning me; but he omitted doing it. As to my director, M. Bertot, he died four months before my departure. I had some intimations of his death, and it seemed as if he bequeathed me a portion of his spirit to help his children.

I was seized with a fear, that the check I had felt, at giving so largely in favor of the New Catholics, what I had designed for Geneva, was a stratagem of nature, which does not love to be stripped. I wrote to Sister Garnier to get a contract drawn up according to my first memorial. God permitted me to commit this fault, to make me the more sensible of His protection over me.

Part Two

Chapter One

I went off in a strange renunciation, and in great simplicity, scarcely able to render the reason why I should in such a manner quit my family, which I most tenderly love, being without any positive assurance, yet hoping even against hope itself. I went to the New Catholics at Paris, where Providence wrought wonders to conceal me. They sent for the notary, who had drawn up the contract of engagement. When he read it to me, I felt such a repugnance to it, that I could not bear to hear it to the end, much less sign it. The notary wondered and much more so when Sister Garnier came in, and told him, that they needed no contract of engagement. I was enabled through divine assistance, to put my affairs in very good order, and to write sundry letters by the inspiration of the Spirit of God, and not by my own. This was what I had never experienced before. It was given me at that time only as a beginning, and has since been granted me much more perfectly.

I had two domestics, whom it was very difficult for me to discharge, as I did not think to take them with me. If I had left them, they would have told of my departure; and I should have been sent after. I was when it became known. But God so ordered it that they were willing to follow me. They were of no use to me, and soon after turned into France. I took with me only my daughter, and two maids to serve us both. We set off in a boat upon the river, though I had taken places in the stagecoach, in order that, if they searched for me in the coach, they might not find me. I went to Melun to wait for it there.

It was surprising that in this boat the child could not forbear making crosses, employing a person to cut rushes for her to use for that purpose. She then put around, and all over me, above three hundred of them. I let her do it, and inwardly apprehended that it was not without its meaning. I felt an interior certainty that I was going to meet with crosses in abundance and that this child was sowing the cross for me to reap it. Sister Garnier, who saw that they could not restrain her from covering me with crosses, said to me, "What that child does appears to be significant." Turning to the little girl, she said, "Give me some crosses, too, my pretty pet." "No," she replied, "they are all for my dear mother." Soon she gave her one to stop her importunity, then continued putting more on me; after which she desired some river-flowers, which floated on the water, to be given her. Braiding a garland she put it on my head, and said to me, "After the cross you shall be crowned." I admired all this in silence, and offered myself up to the pure love of God, as a victim, free and willing to be sacrificed to Him.

Some time before my departure, a particular friend, a true servant of God, related to me a vision she had respecting me. "She saw my heart surrounded with thorns; that our Lord appeared in it well pleased; that, though the thorns seemed likely to tear it, yet, instead of doing that, they only rendered it fairer, and our Lord's approbation the stronger.

At Corbeil, (a little town on the river Seine, sixteen miles south of Paris,) I met with the priest whom God had first made use of so powerfully to draw me to His love. He approved of my design to leave all for the Lord; but he thought I should not be well suited with the New Catholics. He told me some things about them, to show that our leadings were incompatible. He cautioned me not to let them know that I walked in the inward path. If I did, I must expect nothing but persecution from them. But it is in vain to contrive to hide, when God sees it best for us to suffer, and when our wills are utterly resigned to Him, and totally passed into His.

While at Paris I gave the New Catholics all the money I had. I reserved not to myself a single penny, rejoicing to be poor after the example of Jesus Christ. I brought from home nine thousand livres. As by my donation I had reserved nothing to myself and by a contract lent them six thousand; this six thousand has returned to my children but none of it to me. That gives me no trouble; poverty, thus procured, constitutes my riches. The rest I gave entirely to the sisters that were with us, as well to supply their traveling expenses, for the purchase of furniture. I did not reserve so much as my linen for my own use, putting it in the common fund. I had neither a locked coffer, nor purse. I had brought but little linen for fear of mistrust. In wanting to carry off clothes I should have been discovered. My persecutors did not fail to report that I had brought great sums from home, which I had imprudently expended, and given to the friends of Father La Combe. False as I had not a penny. On my arrival at Annecy a poor man was asking alms. I, having nothing else, gave him the buttons from my sleeves. At another time I gave a poor man a little plain ring, in the name of Jesus Christ. I had worn it as a token of marriage with Him.

We joined the flying stage at Melun where I left Sister Garnier. I went on with the other sisters with whom I had no acquaintance. The carriages were very fatiguing; I got no sleep through so long a journey. My daughter, a very tender child, only five years of age, got scarcely any. We bore great fatigue without falling sick by the way. My child had not an hour's uneasiness, although she was only three hours in bed every night. At another time half this fatigue, or even the want of rest, would have thrown me into a fit of sickness. God only knows both the sacrifices which He induced me to make, and the joy of my heart in offering up everything to Him. Had I kingdoms and empires, I think I would yield them up with still more joy, to give Him the higher marks of my love. As soon as we arrived at the inn, I went to church and stayed there till dinner time. In the coach, my divine Lord communed with me, and in me, in a manner which the others could not comprehend, indeed not perceive. The cheerfulness I showed in the greatest dangers encouraged them. I even sang hymns of joy at finding myself disengaged from the riches, honors and entanglements of the world. God in such a manner protected us. He seemed to be to us "a pillar of fire by night, and a pillar of a cloud by day." We passed over a very dangerous spot between Lyons and Chamberry. Our carriage broke as we were coming out of it. Had it happened a little sooner, we would have perished.

We arrived at Annecy on Magdalene's eve, 1681. On Magdalene's day the Bishop of Geneva performed divine service for us, at the tomb of St. Francis de Sales. There I renewed my spiritual marriage with my Redeemer, as I did every year on this day. There also I felt a sweet remembrance of that saint, with whom our Lord gives me a singular union. I say union, for it appears to me that the soul in God is united with saints, the more so in proportion as they are conformable to Him. It is a union which it pleases God sometimes to revive after death, and awaken in the soul for His own glory. At such times departed saints are rendered more intimately present to that soul in God; and this revival is as it were an holy intercourse of friend with friend, in Him who unites them all in one immortal tie.

That day we left Annecy, and on the next went to prayers at Geneva. I had much joy at the communion. It seemed to me as if God more powerfully united me to Himself. There I prayed to Him for the conversion of that great people. That evening we arrived late at Gex, where we found only bare walls. The Bishop of Geneva had assured me that the house was furnished; undoubtedly he believed it to be. We lodged at the house of the sisters of charity, who were so kind as to give us their beds.

I was in great pain of mind for my daughter, who visibly lost weight. I had a strong desire to place her with the Ursulines at Tonon. My heart was so affected on her behalf, that I could not forbear weeping in secret for her. Next day I said, "I would take my daughter to Tonon, and leave her there, till I should see how we might be accommodated." They opposed it strongly, after a manner which seemed very hard-hearted as well as ungrateful, seeing she was a skeleton. I looked upon the child as a victim whom I had imprudently sacrificed. I wrote to Father La Combe, entreating him to come and see me, to consult together about it. I thought I could not in conscience keep her in this place any longer. Several days passed without my having any answer. In the meantime I became resigned to the will of God, whether to have succor or not.

Chapter Two

Our Lord took pity on the lamentable condition of my daughter, and so ordered it, that the Bishop of Geneva wrote to Father La Combe, to come as speedily as possible to see us, and to console us. As soon as I saw that father, I was surprised to feel an interior grace, which I may call communication; such as I had never had before with any person. It seemed to me that an influence of grace came from him to me, through the innermost of the soul; returned from me to him, in such a way that he felt the same effect. Like a tide of grace it caused a flux and reflux, flowing on into the divine and invisible ocean. This is a pure and holy union, which God alone operates, and which has still subsisted, and even increased. It is a union exempt from all weakness, and from all self-interest. It causes those who are blessed with it to rejoice in beholding themselves, as well as those beloved, laden with crosses and afflictions - a union which has no need of the presence of the body. At certain times absence makes not more absent, nor presence more present; a union unknown to men, but such as are come to experience it. It can never be experienced but between such souls as are united to God. As I never before felt a union of this sort with any one, it then appeared to me quite new. I had no doubt of its being from God; so far from turning the mind from Him, it tended to draw it more deeply into Him. It dissipated all my pains, and established me in the most profound peace.

God gave him at first much openness of mind toward me. He related to me the mercies God had shown him, and several extraordinary things, which gave me at first some fear. I suspected some illusion, especially in such things as flatter in regard to the future; little imagining that God would make use of me to draw him from this state and bring him into that naked faith. But the grace, which flowed from Him into my soul, recovered me from that fear. I saw that it was joined with extraordinary humility. Far from being elevated with the gifts which God had liberally conferred upon him, or with his own profound learning, no person could have a lower opinion of himself than he had. He told me as to my daughter, it would be best for me to take her to Tonon, where he thought she would be very well situated. As to myself, after I had mentioned to him my dislike to the manner of life of the New Catholics, he told me, that he did not think it would be my proper place to be long with them. It would be best for me to stay there, free from all engagements, till God, by the guidance of His Providence, should make known to me how he would dispose of me, and draw my mind to the place whither he would have me remove. I had already begun to awake regularly at midnight, in order to pray. I awoke with these words suddenly put in my mind, "It is written of me, I will do your will, O my God." This was accompanied with the most pure, penetrating, and powerful communication of grace that I had ever experienced. Though the state of my soul was already permanent in newness of life; yet this new life was not in that immutability in which it has been since. It was a beginning life and a rising day, which goes on increasing unto the full meridian; a day never followed by night; a life which fears death no more, not even in death itself; because he who has suffered the first death, shall no more be hurt of the second. From midnight I continued on my knees till four o'clock in the morning, in prayer, in a sweet intercourse with God, and did the same also the night following.

The next day, after prayers, Father La Combe told me, that he had a very great certainty, that I was a stone which God designed for the foundation of some great building. What that building was he knew no more than I. After whatever manner then it is to be, whether His divine Majesty will make use of me in this life, for some design known to himself only, or will make me one of the stones of the new and heavenly Jerusalem, it seems to me that such stone cannot be polished, but by the strokes of the hammer. Our Lord has given to this soul of mine the qualities of the stone, firmness, resignation, insensibility, and power to endure hardness under the operations of His hand.

I carried my little daughter to the Ursulines at Tonon. That child took a great fondness for Father La Combe, saying, "He is a good father, one from God." Here I found a hermit, whom they called Anselm. He was a person of the most extraordinary sanctity that had appeared for some time. He was from Geneva; God had miraculously drawn him from thence, at twelve years of age. He had at nineteen years of age taken the habit of hermit of St. Augustine. He and another lived alone in a little hermitage, where they saw nobody but such as came to visit their chapel. He had lived twelve years in this hut, never eating anything but pulse with salt, and sometimes oil. Three times a week he lived on bread and water. He never drank wine, and generally took but one meal in twenty-four hours. He wore for a shirt a coarse hair cloth, and lodged on the bare ground. He lived in a continual state of prayer, and in the greatest humility. God had done by him many signal miracles.

This good hermit had a great sense of the designs of God on Father La Combe and me. But God showed him at the same time that strange crosses were preparing for us both; that we were both destined for the aid of souls. I did not find, as I expected, any suitable place for my daughter at Tonon. I thought myself like Abraham, when going to sacrifice his son. Father La Combe said, "Welcome, daughter of Abraham!" I found little encouragement to leave her and could not keep her with myself, because we had no room. The little girls, whom they took to make Catholics, were all mixed and had contracted habits as were pernicious. To leave her there I thought not right. The language of the country, where scarce anyone understood French, and the food, which she could not take, being far different from ours, were great hardships. All my tenderness for her was awakened, and I looked on myself as her destroyer. I experienced what Hagar suffered when she put away her son Ishmael in the desert that she might not be forced to see him perish. I thought that even if I had ventured to expose myself, I ought at least to have spared my daughter. The loss of her education, even of her life, appeared to me inevitable. Everything looked dark in regard to her.

With her natural disposition and fine qualities, she might have attracted admiration, if educated in France, and been likely to have such offers of marriage, as she could never hope to meet with in this poor country; in which, if she should recover, she would never be likely to be fit for anything. Here she could eat nothing of what was offered her. All her subsistence was a little unpleasant and disagreeable broth, which I forced her to take against her will. I seemed like a second Abraham, holding the knife over her to destroy her. Our Lord would have me make a sacrifice to Him, without any consolation, and plunged in sorrow, night was the time in which I gave vent to it. He made me see, on one side the grief of her grandmother, if she should hear of her death, which she would impute to my taking the child away from her; the great reproach, it would be accounted among all the family. The gifts of nature she was endowed with were now like pointed darts which pierced me. I believe that God so ordered it to purify me from too human an attachment still in me. After I returned from the Ursulines at Tonon, they changed her manner of diet, and gave her what was suitable; in a short time she recovered.

Chapter Three

As soon as it was known in France that I was gone there was a general outcry. Father de la Mothe wrote to me, that all persons of learning and of piety united in censuring me. To alarm me still more, he informed me that my mother-in-law, with whom I had entrusted my younger son and my children's substance, was fallen into a state of childhood. This, however, was false.

I answered all these fearful letters as the Spirit dictated. My answers were thought very just, and those violent exclamations were soon changed into applauses. Father La Mothe appeared to change his censures into esteem; but it did not last. Self interest threw him back again; being disappointed in his hopes of a pension, which he expected I would have settled on him. Sister Garnier, whatever was her reason, changed and declared against me.

I both ate and slept little. The food which was given us was putrid and full of worms, by reason of the great heat of the weather, also being kept too long. What I should have formerly beheld with the greatest abhorrence, now became my only nourishment. Yet everything was rendered easy to me. In God I found, without increase, everything which I had lost for Him. That spirit, which I once thought I had lost in a strange stupidity, was restored to me with inconceivable advantages. I was astonished at myself. I found there was nothing which I was not fit for or in which I did not succeed. Those who observed said that I had a prodigious capacity. I well knew that I had but meager capabilities, but that in God my spirit had received a quality which it had never had before. I thought I experienced something of the state which the apostles were in, after they had received the Holy Ghost. I knew, I comprehended, I understood, I was enabled to do everything necessary. I had every sort of good thing and no want of anything. When Jesus Christ, the eternal wisdom, is formed in the soul, after the death of the first Adam, it finds in Him all good things communicated to it. Sometime after my arrival at Gex, the Bishop of Geneva came to see us. He was so clearly convinced, and so much affected, that he could not forbear expressing it. He opened his heart to me on what God had required of him. He confessed to me his own deviations and infidelities. Every time when I spoke to him he entered into what I said, and acknowledged it to be the truth. Indeed it was the Spirit of truth which inspired me to speak to him, without which I should be only a mere simpleton. Yet as soon as those persons spoke to him, who sought for preeminence, and who could not suffer any good but what came from themselves, he was so weak as to be imposed on with impressions against the truth. This weakness has hindered him from doing all the good which otherwise he might have done.

After I had spoken to him, he said that he had it in his mind to give me Father La Combe for director; he was a man illuminated of God, who well understood the inward path, and had a singular gift of pacifying souls. Greatly was I rejoiced when the Bishop appointed him, seeing thereby his authority united with the grace which already seemed to have given him to me, by a union and effusion of supernatural life and love. The fatigues I had, and watchings with my daughter, threw me into a violent sickness attended with exquisite pain. The physicians judged me in danger, yet the sisters of the house quite neglected me; especially the stewardess. She was so penurious, that she did not give me what was necessary to sustain life. I had not a penny to help myself with, as I had reserved nothing to myself. Besides, they received all the money which was remitted to me from France, which was very considerable. I practiced poverty and was in necessity even among those to whom I had given all. They wrote to Father La Combe, desiring him to come to me, as I was so extremely ill. Hearing of my condition he was so touched with compassion as to walk on foot all night. He traveled not otherwise, endeavoring in that, as in everything else, to imitate our Lord Jesus Christ.

As soon as he entered the house my pains abated; when he had prayed and blessed me, laying his hand on my head, I was perfectly cured, to the great astonishment of my physicians; who were not willing to acknowledge the miracle.

These sisters advised me to return to my daughter. Father La Combe returned with me. A violent storm arose on the Lake, which made me very sick, and seemed likely to upset the boat. But the hand of Providence remarkably appeared in our favor; so much so, that it was taken notice of by the mariners and passengers. They looked upon Father La Combe as a saint. We arrived at Tonon, where I found myself so perfectly recovered, that, instead of making and using the remedies I had proposed, I went into a retreat, and stayed twelve days. Here I made vows of perpetual chastity, poverty and obedience, covenanting to obey whatever I should believe to be the will of God also to obey the church, and to honor Jesus Christ in such a manner as He pleased.

At this time I found that I had the perfect chastity of love to the Lord, it being without any reserve, division, or view of interest. Perfect poverty, by the total privation of everything that was mine, both inwardly and outwardly. Perfect obedience to the will of the Lord, submission to the church, and honor to Jesus Christ in loving Himself only; the effect of which soon appeared. When by the loss of ourselves we are passed into the Lord, our will is made one and the same with that of the Lord, according to the prayer of Christ, "As you Father are in me, and I in you, grant that they also may be one of us." John 17:21. Oh, but it is then that the will is rendered marvelous, both because it is made the will of the Lord, which is the greatest of miracles; also because it works wonders in Him. For as it is the Lord who wills in the soul, that will has its effect. Scarcely has it willed but the thing is done.

But some may say, Why then so many oppressions endured? Why do not these souls, if they have such a power, set themselves free from them? We answer that if they had any will to do anything of that sort against divine providence, that would be the will of flesh, or the will of man, and not the will of God, John 1:13.

I rose generally at midnight, waking at the proper time; but if I wound up my alarm-watch, then I used not to awake in time. I saw that the Lord had the care of a father and a spouse over me. When I had any indisposition, and my body wanted rest, He did not awake me; but at such times I felt even in my sleep a singular possession of Him. Some years have passed wherein I have had only a kind of half-sleep; but my soul waked the more for the Lord, as sleep seemed to steal from it every other attention. The Lord made it known also to many persons, that He designed me for a mother of great people, but a people simple and childlike. They took these intelligences in a literal sense and thought it related to some institution or congregation. But it appeared to me that the persons whom it would please the Lord that I should win over to Him, and to whom I should be as a mother, through His goodness, should have the same union of affection for me as children have for a parent, but a union much deeper and stronger; giving me all that was necessary for them, to bring them to walk in the way by which He would lead them, as I shall show.

Chapter Four

I would willingly suppress what I am now about to write if anything of it were my own, also on account of the difficulty of expressing myself as because few souls are capable of understanding divine leadings which are so little known, and so little comprehended. I have myself never read of anything like it. I shall say something of the interior dispositions I was then in, and I shall think my time well employed, if it serves you who are willing to be of the number of my children; it serves such as are already my children, to induce them to let God glorify Himself in them after His manner, and not after their own. If there be anything which they do not comprehend, let them die to themselves. They will find it much easier to learn by experience than from anything I could say; expression never equals experience.

After I had come out of the trying condition I have spoken of I found it had purified my soul, instead of blackening it as I had feared. I possessed God after a manner so pure, and so immense, as nothing else could equal. In regard to thoughts or desires, all was so clean, so naked, so lost in the divinity, that the soul had no selfish movement, however plausible or delicate; both the powers of the mind and the very senses being wonderfully purified. Sometimes I was surprised to find that there appeared not one selfish thought. The imagination, formerly so restless, now no more troubled me. I had no more perplexity or uneasy reflections. The will, being perfectly dead to all its own appetites, was become void of every human inclination, both natural and spiritual, and only inclined to whatever God pleased, and to whatever manner He pleased. This vastness or enlargedness, which is not bounded by anything, however plain or simple it may be, increases every day. My soul in partaking of the qualities of her Spouse seems also to partake of His immensity. My prayer was in an openness and singleness inconceivable. I was, as it were, borne up on high, out of myself. I believe God was pleased to bless me with this experience. At the beginning of the new life, He made me comprehend, for the good of other souls, the simplicity and desirableness of this passage of the soul into God.

When I went to confess, I felt such an immersion of the soul into Him, that I could scarcely speak. This ascension of the spirit, wherein God draws the soul so powerfully, not into its own inmost recess, but into Himself, is not operated till after the death of self. The soul actually comes out of itself to pass into its divine object. I call it death, that is to say, a passage from one thing to another. It is truly a happy Passover for the soul, and its passage into the promised land. The spirit which is created to be united to its divine Origin, has so powerful a tendency to Him, that if it were not stopped by a continual miracle, its moving quality would cause the body to be drawn after it by reason of its impetuosity and noble ascent. But God has given it a terrestrial body to serve for a counterpoise. This spirit then, created to be united to its Origin, without any medium or interstice, feeling itself drawn by its divine object, tends to it with an extreme violence; in such sort that God, suspending for sometime the power which the body has to hold back the spirit, it follows with ardency. When it is not sufficiently purified to pass into God, it gradually returns to itself; as the body resumes its own quality, it turns to the earth. The saints who have been the most perfect have advanced to that degree, as to have nothing of all this. Some have lost it toward the end of their lives, becoming single and pure as the others, because they then had in reality and permanence what they had at first only as transient fruitions, in the time of the prevalence or dominion of the body. It is certain then that the soul, by death to itself, passes into its divine Object. This is what I then experienced. I found, the farther I went, the more my spirit was lost in its Sovereign, who attracted it more and more to Himself. He was pleased at first that I should know this for the sake of others and not for myself. Indeed He drew my soul more and more into Himself, till it lost itself entirely out of sight, and could perceive itself no more. It seemed at first to pass into Him. As one sees a river pass into the ocean, lose itself in it, its water for a time distinguished from that of the sea, till it gradually becomes transformed into the same sea, and possesses all its qualities; so was my soul lost in God, who communicated to it His qualities, having drawn it out of all that it had of its own. Its life is an inconceivable innocence, not known or comprehended of those who are still shut up in themselves or only live for themselves.

The joy which such a soul possesses in its God is so great, that it experiences the truth of those words of the royal prophet, "All they who are in you, O Lord, are like persons ravished with joy." To such a soul the words of our Lord seem to be addressed, "Your joy no man shall take from you." John 16:22. It is as it were plunged in a river of peace. Its prayer is continual. Nothing can hinder it from praying to God, or from loving Him. It amply verifies these words in the Canticles, "I sleep but my heart wakes;" for it finds that even sleep itself does not hinder it from praying. Oh, unutterable happiness! Who could ever have thought that a soul, which seemed to be in the utmost misery, should ever find a happiness equal to this? Oh, happy poverty, happy loss, happy nothingness, which gives no less than God

Himself in His own immensity, no more circumscribed to the limited manner of the creature, but always drawing it out of that, to plunge it wholly into His own divine essence.

Then the soul knows that all the states of self-pleasing visions, openings, ecstasies and raptures, are rather obstacles; that they do not serve this state which is far above them; because the state which has supports, has pain to lose them; yet cannot arrive at this without such loss. In this are verified the words of an experienced saint; "When I would," says he, "possess nothing through self-love, everything was given me without going after it." Oh, happy dying of the grain of wheat, which makes it produce a hundredfold! The soul is then so passive, so equally disposed to receive from the hand of God either good or evil, as is astonishing. It receives both the one and the other without any selfish emotions, letting them flow and be lost as they come. They pass away as if they did not touch.

After I finished my retreat with the Ursulines at Tonon, I returned through Geneva and, having found no other means of conveyance, the French resident lent me a horse. As I knew not how to ride I made some difficulty of doing it; but as he assured me that it was a very quiet horse, I ventured to mount. There was a sort of a smith, who looking at me with a wild haggard look, struck the horse a blow on the back, just as I had got upon him, which made him give a leap. He threw me on the ground with such force that they thought I was killed. I fell on my temple. My cheekbone and two of my teeth were broken. I was supported by an invisible hand and in a little time I mounted as well as I could on another horse and had a man by my side to keep me up.

My relations left me in peace at Gex. They had heard at Paris of my miraculous cure; it made a great noise there. Many persons in reputation for sanctity then wrote to me. I received letters from Mademoiselle De Lamoignon, and another young lady, who was so moved with my answer, that she sent me a hundred pistoles for our house, and let me know besides that, when we wanted money, I had only to write to her; and that she would send me all I could desire. They talked in Paris of printing an account of the sacrifice I had made, and inserting in it the miracle of my sudden recovery. I don't know what prevented it;

but such is the inconstancy of the creature, that this journey, which drew upon me at that time so much applause, has served for a pretext for the strange condemnation which has since passed upon me.

Chapter Five

My near relations did not signify any eager desire for my return. The first thing they proposed to me, a month after my arrival at Gex, was not only to give up my guardianship, but to make over all my estate to my children and to reserve an annuity to myself. This proposition, coming from people who regarded nothing but their own interest, to some might have appeared very unpleasing; but it was in no wise so to me. I had not any friend to advise with. I knew not anyone whom I could consult about the manner of executing the thing, as I was quite free and willing to do it. It appeared to me that I had now the means of accomplishing the extreme desire I had of being conformable to Jesus Christ, poor, naked, and stripped of all. They sent me an article to execute, which had been drawn under their inspection, and I innocently signed it, not perceiving some clauses which were inserted therein. It expressed that, when my children should die, I should inherit nothing of my own estate, but that it should revolve to my kindred. There were many other things, which appeared to be equally to my disadvantage. Though what I had reserved to myself was sufficient to support me in this place; yet it was scarcely enough to do so in some other places. I then gave up my estate with more joy, for being thereby conformed to Jesus Christ, than they could have who asked it from me. It is what I have never repented of, nor had any uneasiness about. What pleasure to lose all for the Lord! The love of poverty, thus contracted, is the kingdom of tranquility.

I forgot to mention that toward the end of my miserable state of privation, when just ready to enter into newness of life, our Lord illuminated me so clearly to see that the exterior crosses came from Him, that I could not harbor any resentment against the persons who procured me them. On the contrary, I felt the tenderness of compassion for them, and had more pain for those afflictions which I innocently caused to them, than for any which they had heaped upon me. I saw that these persons feared the Lord too much to oppress me as they did, had they known it. I saw His hand in it, and I felt the pain which they suffered, through the contrariety of their humors. It is hard to conceive the tenderness which the Lord gave me for them, and the desire which I have had, with the utmost sincerity, to procure them every sort of advantage.

After the accident which befell me (fall from the horse) from which I soon wonderfully recovered, the Devil began to declare himself more openly mine enemy, to break loose and become outrageous. One night, when I least thought of it, something very monstrous and frightful presented itself. It seemed a kind face, which was seen by a glimmering bluish light. I don't know whether the flame itself composed that horrible face or appearance; for it was so mixed and passed by so rapidly, that I could not discern it. My soul rested in its calm situation and assurance, and it appeared no more after that manner. As I arose at midnight to pray, I heard frightful noises in my chamber and after I had lain down they were still worse. My bed often shook for a quarter of an hour at a time, and the sashes were all burst. Every morning while this continued, they were found shattered and torn, yet I felt no fear. I arose and lighted my wax candle at a lamp which I kept in my room, because I had taken the office of sacristan and the care of waking the sisters at the hour they were to rise, without having once failed in it for my indispositions, ever being the first in all the observances. I made use of my little light to look all over the room and at the sashes, at the very time the noise was strongest. As he saw that I was afraid of nothing, he left off all on a sudden, and attacked me no more in person. But he stirred up men against me, and that succeeded far better with him; for he found them disposed to do what he prompted them to, zealously, inasmuch as they counted it a good thing to do me the worst of injuries.

One of the sisters whom I had brought with me, a very beautiful girl, contracted an intimacy with an ecclesiastic, who had authority in this place. At first he inspired her with an aversion for me, being well assured that if she placed confidence in me, I should advise her not to suffer his visits so frequently. She was undertaking a religious retreat. That ecclesiastic was desirous to induce her to make it, in order to gain her entire confidence, which would have served as a cloak to his frequent visits. The Bishop of Geneva had given Father La Combe for director to our house. As he was going to cause retreats to be made, I desired her to wait for him. As I had gained some share in her esteem, she submitted even against her inclination, which was to have made it under this ecclesiastic. I began to talk to her on the subject of inward prayer, and drew her into the practice of this duty. Our Lord gave such a blessing thereto, that this girl gave herself to God in right earnest, and with her whole heart and the retreat completely won her over. She then became more reserved, and on her guard, toward this ecclesiastic, which exceedingly vexed him. It enraged him both against Father La Combe and me. This proved the source of the persecutions which afterward befell me. The noise in my chamber, which may have been traced to him, ended as these commenced.

This ecclesiastic began to talk privately of me with much contempt. I knew it, but took no notice. There came a certain friar to see him, who mortally hated Father La Combe, on account of his regularity. These combined together to force me to quit the house, that they might become masters of it. All the means they could devise they used for that purpose.

My manner of life was such, that in the house I did not meddle in affairs at all, leaving the sisters to dispose of the temporalities as they pleased. Soon after my entrance into it I received eighteen hundred livres, which a lady, a friend of mine, lent me to complete our furniture, which I had repaid her at my late giving up of my estate. This sum they received, as well as what I had before given them. I sometimes spoke a little to those who retired thither to become Catholics. Our Lord favored with so much benediction what I said to them, that some, whom they knew not before what to make of, became sensible, solid women, and exemplary in piety.

I saw crosses in abundance likely to fall to my lot. At the same time these words came, "Who for the joy that was set before him endured the cross." Heb. 12:2. I prostrated myself for a long time with my face on the ground, earnestly desiring to receive all your strokes. Oh, You who spared not your own son! You could find none but Him worthy of You, and you still find in Him hearts proper for you.

A few days after my arrival at Gex, I saw in a sacred and mysterious dream (for as such I very well distinguished it) Father La Combe fastened up to an enormous cross, stripped in like manner as they paint our Savior. I saw around it a frightful crowd, which covered me with confusion, and threw back on me the ignominy of his punishment. He seemed to have most pain, but I more reproaches than he. I have since beheld this fully accomplished.

The ecclesiastic won over to his party one of our sisters, who was the house-steward and soon after the prioress. I was very delicate, the good inclination which I had did not give strength to my body. I had two maids to serve me; yet, as the community had need of one of them for their cook, and the other to attend the door and other occasions, I gave them up, not thinking but they would allow them to serve me sometimes. Besides this, I let them still receive all my income, they having had my first half of this year's annuity. Yet they would not permit either of my maid-servants, to do anything for me. By my office of sacristan I was obliged to sweep the church, which was large, and they would not let anyone help me. I have several times fainted over the broom and have been forced to rest in corners. This obliged me to beg them, that they would suffer it sometimes to be swept by some of the strong country girls, New Catholics, to which at last they had the charity to consent. What most embarrassed me was that I never had washed. I was now obliged to wash all the vestry linen. I took one of my maids to help me, because in attempting it I had done up the linen most awkwardly. These sisters pulled her by the arms out of my chamber, telling her she should do her own work. I let it quietly pass, without making any objection. The other good sister, the girl I just mentioned, grew more and more fervent. By the practice of prayer in her dedication of herself to the Lord she became more and more tender in her sympathy with me. It irritated this ecclesiastic. After all his impotent attempts here, he went off to

Annecy, in order to sow discord, and to effect more mischief to Father La Combe.

Chapter Six

He went directly to the Bishop of Geneva, who till then had manifested much esteem and kindness for me. He persuaded him, that it would be proper to secure me to that house, to oblige me to give up to it the annual income I had reserved to myself; to engage me thereto, by making me prioress. He had gained such an ascendancy over the Bishop, that the people in the country called him the Little Bishop. He drew him to enter heartily and with zeal into this proposition, and to resolve to bring it about whatever it should cost.

The ecclesiastic, having so far carried his point, and being swelled with his success, no longer kept any measures in regard to me. He began with causing all the letters which I sent, and those which were directed to me, to be stopped. That was in order to have it in his power to make what impressions he pleased on the minds of others, and that I should neither be able to know it, nor to defend myself, nor to give or send to my friends any account of the manner in which I was treated. One of the maids I had brought wanted to return. She could have no rest in this place, the other that remained was infirm, too much taken up by others to help me in anything. As Father La Combe was soon to come, I thought he would soften the violent spirit of this man, and that he would give me proper advice.

In the meantime they proposed to me the engagement, and the post of prioress. I answered, that as to the engagement it was impossible for me, since my vocation was elsewhere. And I could not regularly be the prioress, till after passing through the novitiate, in which they had all served two years before their being engaged. When I should have done as much, I should see how God would inspire me. The prioress replied quite tartly, that if I would ever leave them it were best for me to do it immediately. Yet I did not offer to retire, but continued still to act as usual. I saw the sky gradually thickening and storms gathering on every side. The prioress then affected a milder air.

She assured me, that she had a desire, as well as I, to go to Geneva; that I should not engage, but only promise her to take her with me, if I went thither. She pretended to place a great confidence in me, and professed a high esteem for me. As I am very free, and have nothing but uprightness, I let her know that I had no attraction for the manner of life of the New Catholics, by reason of the intrigues from without. Several things did not please me, because I wanted them to be upright in everything. She signified that she did not consent to such things, but because that ecclesiastic told her they were necessary to give the house a credit in distant parts and to draw charities from Paris. I answered that if we walked uprightly God would never fail us. He would sooner do miracles for us. I remarked to her that when, instead of sincerity, they had recourse to artifice, charity grew cold, and kept herself shut up. It is God alone who inspires charity; how, then, is it to be drawn by disguises?

Soon after, Father La Combe came about the retreats. This was the third and last time that he came to Gex. The prioress, after she had been tampering a good deal with me, having written him a long letter before his coming, and received his answer, which she showed me, now went to ask him whether she would one day be united to me at Geneva. He answered with his usual uprightness, "Our Lord has made it known to me that you shall never be established at Geneva." Soon after she died. When he had uttered this declaration, she appeared enraged against both him and me. She went directly to that ecclesiastic, who was in a room with the house-steward; and they took their measures together, to oblige me either to engage or retire. They thought that I would sooner engage than retire, and they watched my letters.

With a design to lay snares for him, he requested Father La Combe to preach. He did on this text, "The King's daughter is beautiful within." That ecclesiastic, who was present with his confidant, said that it was preached against him, and was full of errors. He drew up eight propositions, and inserted in them what the other had not preached, adjusting them as maliciously as ever he could, then sent them to one of his friends in Rome, to get them examined by the Sacred Congregation, and by the

Inquisition. Though he had very illy digested them, at Rome they were pronounced good. That greatly disappointed and vexed him. After having been treated in this manner, and opprobriously reviled by him in the most offensive terms, the Father, with much mildness and humility, told him that he was going to Annecy about some affairs of the convent. If he had anything to write to the Bishop of Geneva, he would take care of his letter. He then desired him to wait awhile, as he was going to write. The good Father had the patience to wait above three hours, without hearing from him; though he had treated him exceedingly ill, so far as to snatch out of his hands a letter I had given him for that worthy hermit I have mentioned. Hearing he was not gone, but was still in the church, I went to him, and begged him to send to see if the other's packet was ready. The day was so far gone that he would be obliged to lodge by the way. When the messenger arrived, he found a servant of the ecclesiastic on horseback, ordered to go at full speed, to be at Annecy before the Father. He then returned an answer, that he had no letters to send by him. This was so contrived, that he might gain time to prepossess the Bishop for his purposes. Father La Combe then set off for Annecy, and on his arrival found the Bishop prepossessed, and in an ill humor. This was the substance of the discourse

  BISHOP - You must absolutely engage this lady to give what she has to the house at Gex, and make her the prioress of it.

  F. LA COMBE - My lord, you know what she has told you herself of her vocation, both at Paris and in this country. I therefore do not believe that she will engage; nor is there any likelihood that, after quitting her all, in the hope of entering Geneva, she should engage elsewhere, and thereby put it out of her power to accomplish the designs of God in regard to her. She has offered to stay with those sisters as a boarder. If they are willing to keep her as such, she will remain with them; if not, she is resolved to retire into some convent, till God shall dispose of her otherwise.

  BISHOP - I know all that; but I likewise know that she is so very obedient, that, if you order her, she will assuredly do it.

F. LA COMBE - It is for that reason, my lord, that one ought to be very cautious in the commands which they lay on her. Can I induce a foreign lady, who, for all her subsistence, has nothing but a small pittance she has reserved to herself, to give that up in favor of a house which is not yet established, and perhaps never will be? If the house should happen to fail, or be no longer of use, what shall that lady live on? Shall she go to the hospital? And indeed this house will not long be of any use, since there are no Protestants in any part of France near it.

BISHOP - These reasons are good for nothing. If you do not make her do what I have said, I will degrade and suspend you.

This manner of speaking somewhat surprised the Father. He well enough understands the rules of suspension, which is not executed on such things. He replied: "My lord, I am ready, not only to suffer the suspension, but even death, rather than do anything against my conscience." Having said that, he retired.

He directly sent me this account by an express, to the end that I might take proper measures. I had no other course to take but to retire into a convent. I received a letter informing me that the nun to whom I had entrusted my daughter had fallen sick, and desiring me to go to her for some time. I showed this letter to the sisters of our house, telling them that I had a mind to go; but if they ceased to persecute me, and would leave Father La Combe in peace, I would return as soon as the mistress of my daughter should be recovered. Instead of this, they persecuted me more violently, wrote to Paris against me, stopped all my letters, and sent libels against me around the country.

The day after my arrival at Tonon, Father La Combe set off for the valley of Aoust, to preach there in Lent. He had come to take leave of me, and told me that he should go from thence to Rome, and perhaps not return, as his superiors might detain him there; that he was sorry to leave me in a strange country, without succor, and persecuted of everyone. I replied, "My father, that gives me no pain; I use the creatures for God, and by His order. Through His mercy, I do very well without them, when He withdraws them. I am very well contented never to see you, and to abide under persecution, if such be His will." He said he would go well satisfied to see me in such a disposition, and then departed.

As soon as I got to the Ursulines, a very aged and pious priest, who for twenty years past had not come out of his solitude, came to find me. He told me that he had a vision relative to me; that he had seen a woman in a boat on the lake; and that the Bishop of Geneva, with some of his priests, exerted all their efforts to sink the boat she was in, and to drown her; that he continued in this vision above two hours, with pain of mind; that it seemed sometimes as if this woman were quite drowned, as for some time she quite disappeared; but afterward she appeared again, and ready to escape the danger, while the Bishop never ceased to pursue her. This woman was always equally calm; but he never saw her entirely free from him. From whence I conclude, added he, that the Bishop will persecute you without intermission.

I had an intimate friend, wife of that governor of whom I have made some mention. As she saw I had quitted everything for God, she had a warm desire to follow me. With diligence did she dispose of all her effects and settle her affairs in order to come to me; but when she heard of the persecution, she was discouraged from coming to a place, from whence she thought I should be obliged to retire. Soon after she died.

Chapter Seven

After Father La Combe was gone the persecution raised against me became more violent. But the Bishop of Geneva still showed me some civilities, as well to try whether he could prevail on me to do what he desired, as to sound out how matters passed in France, and to prejudice the minds of the people there against me, preventing me from receiving the letters sent me. The ecclesiastic and his family had twenty two intercepted letters, opened, on their table. There was one wherein was sent me a power of attorney to sign, of immediate consequence. They were obliged to put it under another cover, and send it to me. The bishop wrote to Father La Mothe, and had no difficulty to draw him into his party. He was displeased with me on two accounts. First, that I had not settled on him a pension, as he expected, and as he told me very roughly several times. Second, I did not take his advice in everything. He at once declared against me. The bishop made him his confidant. It was he who uttered and spread abroad the news about me. They imagined, as was supposed, that I would annul the donation I had made, if I returned; that, having the support of friends in France, I would find the means of breaking it; but in that they were much mistaken. I had no thought of loving anything but the poverty of Jesus Christ. For some time yet, the Father acted with caution toward me. He wrote me some letters, which he addressed to the Bishop of Geneva, and they agreed so together, that he was the only person from whom I received any letters, to which I returned very moving answers. He, instead of being touched with them, became only more irritated against me.

The bishop continued to treat me with a show of respect; yet at the same time he wrote to many persons in Paris, as did also the sisters of the house, to all those persons of piety who had written letters to me, to bias them as much as possible against me. To avoid the blame which ought naturally to fall upon them for having so unworthily treated a person who have given up everything to devote herself to the service of that diocese. After I had done this, and was not in a condition to return to France, they treated me extremely ill in every respect. There was scarcely any kind of false or fabulous story, likely to gain any credit, which they did not invent to cry me down. Beside my having no way to make the truth known in France, our Lord inspired me with a willingness to suffer everything, without justifying myself; so that in my case nothing was heard but condemnation, without any vindication.

I was in this convent, and had seen Father La Combe no further than I have mentioned; yet they did not cease to publish, both of him and me, the most scandalous stories; as utterly false as anything could be, for he was then a hundred and fifty leagues from me.

For some time I was ignorant of this. As I knew that all my letters were kept from me, I ceased to wonder at receiving none. I lived in this house with my little daughter in a sweet repose, which was a very great favor of Providence. My daughter had forgotten her French, and among the little girls from the mountains had contracted a wild look and disagreeable manners. Her will, sense and judgment, were indeed surprising, and her disposition exceedingly good. There were only some little fits of peevishness, which they had caused to arise in her, through certain contrarieties out of season, caresses ill applied, and for want of knowing the proper manner of education. But the Lord provided in regard to her. During this time my mind was preserved calm and resigned to God. Afterward that good sister almost continually interrupted me; I answered everything she desired of me, both out of condescension, and from a principle which I had to obey like a child.

When I was in my apartment, without any other director than our Lord by His Spirit, as soon as one of my little children came to knock at my door, he required me to admit the interruption. He showed me that it is not the actions in themselves which please Him, but the constant ready obedience to every discovery of His will, even in the minutest things, with such a suppleness, as not to stick to anything, but still to turn with Him at every call. My soul was then, I thought, like a leaf, or a feather, which the wind moves what way soever it pleases and the Lord never suffers a soul so dependent upon, and dedicated to Him, to be deceived.

Most men appear to me very unjust, when they readily resign themselves to another man, and look upon that as prudence. They confide in men who are nothing, and boldly say, "Such a person cannot be deceived." But if one speaks of a soul wholly resigned to God, which follows him faithfully, they cry aloud, "That person is deceived with his resignation." Oh, divine Love! Do you want either strength, fidelity, love, or wisdom, to conduct those who trust in you and who are your dearest children? I have seen men bold enough to say, "Follow me, and you shall not be misled." How sadly are those men misled themselves by their presumption! How much sooner should I go to him who would be afraid of misleading me; who trusting neither to his learning nor experience, would rely upon God only!

Our Lord showed me, in a dream, two ways by which souls steer their course, under the figure of two drops of water. The one appeared to me of an unparalleled beauty, brightness and purity; the other to have also a brightness, yet full of little streaks; both good to quench thirst; the former altogether pleasant, but the latter not so perfectly agreeable. By the former is represented the way of pure and naked faith, which pleases the Spouse much, it is so pure, so clear from all self-love. The way of emotions or gifts is not so; yet it is that in which many enlightened souls walk, and into which they had drawn Father La Combe. But God showed me, that He had given him to me, to draw him into one more pure and perfect. I spoke before the sisters, he being present, of the way of faith, how much more glorious it was to God, and advantageous for the soul, than all those gifts, emotions and assurances, which ever cause us to live to self. This discouraged them at first and him also. I saw they were pained, as they have confessed to me since. I said no more of it at that time. But, as he is a person of great humility, he bid me unfold what I had wanted to say to him. I told him a part of my dream of the two drops of water; yet, he did not then enter into what I said, the time for it being not yet come. When he came to Gex, it was to make the retreats. I told him the circumstances of a certain time past; he recollected that it was the time of so extraordinary a touch with which the Lord favored him, that he was quite overwhelmed with contrition. This gave him such an interior renovation, that, having retired to pray, in a very ardent frame of mind, he was filled with joy, and seized with a powerful emotion, which made him enter into what I had told him of the way of faith. I give these things, as they happen to come to my remembrance, without carrying them on in order.

After Easter, in 1682, the bishop came to Tonon. I had occasion to speak to him, which when I had done, our Lord so pointed my words that he appeared thoroughly convinced. But the persons who had influenced him before returned. He then pressed me very much to return to Gex and to take the place of Prioress. I gave him the reasons against it. I then appealed to him, as a bishop, desiring him to take care to regard nothing but God in what he should say to me. He was struck into a kind of confusion; and then said to me, "Since you speak to me in such a manner, I cannot advise you to it. It is not for us to go contrary to our vocations; but do good, I pray you, to this house." I promised him to do it. Having received my pension, I sent them a hundred pistoles, with a design of doing the same as long as I should be in the diocese. The bishop said to me, "I love Father La Combe. He is a true servant of God and he has told me many things to which I was forced to assent for I felt them in myself. But," added he, "when I say so, they tell me I am mistaken, and that before the end of six months he will run mad." He told me, "he approved of the nuns, which had been under the care and instruction of Father La Combe, finding them to come up fully to what he had heard of them." From thence I took occasion to tell him "that in everything he ought to refer himself to his own breast, or to the instructions there immediately received, and not to others." He agreed to what I said, and acknowledged it to be right; yet no sooner was he returned, than, so great was his weakness that he re-entered into his former dispositions. He sent the same ecclesiastic to tell me that I must engage myself at Gex; that it was his sentiment. I answered, that I was determined to follow the counsel he had given me, when he had spoken to me as from God, since now they made him speak only as man.

Chapter Eight

My soul was in a state of entire resignation and very great content, in the midst of such violent tempests. Those persons came to tell me a hundred extravagant stories against Father La Combe. The more they said to me to his disadvantage, the more esteem I felt for him. I answered them, "Perhaps I may never see him again, but I shall ever be glad to do him justice. It is not he who hinders me from engaging at Gex. It is only because I know it to be none of my vocation." They asked me, "Who could know that better than the bishop?" They further told me, "I was under a deception, and my state was good for nothing." This gave me no uneasiness, having referred to God the care of requiring, and of exacting what He requires, and in whatever manner He demands it.

A soul in this state seeks nothing for itself, but all for God. Some may say, "What, then, does this soul?" It leaves itself to be conducted by God's providences and creatures. Outwardly, its life seems quite common; inwardly, it is wholly resigned to the divine will. The more everything appears adverse, and even desperate, the more calm it is, in spite of the annoyance and pain of the senses and of the creatures, which, for some time after the new life, raise some clouds and obstructions, as I have already signified. But when the soul is entirely passed into its original Being, all these things no more cause any separation or partition. It finds no more of that impurity which came from self-seeking, from a human manner of acting, from an unguarded word, from any warm emotion or eagerness, which caused such a mist, as it then could neither prevent nor remedy, having so often experienced its own efforts, to be useless, and even hurtful, as they did nothing else but still more and more defile it. There is in such case no other way or means of remedy, but in waiting till the Sun of Righteousness dissipate those fogs. The whole work of purification comes from God only. Afterward this conduct becomes natural; then the soul can say with the royal prophet, "Though a host should encamp against me, my heart shall not fear. Though war should rise up against me, in him will I confide." For then, though assaulted on every side, it continues fixed as a rock. Having no will but for what God sees meet to order, be it what it may, high or low, great or small, sweet or bitter, honor, wealth, life, or any other object, what can shake its peace? It is true, our nature is so crafty that it worms itself through everything; a selfish sight is like the basilisk's, it destroys.

Trials are suited to the state of the soul, whether conducted by lights, gifts, or ecstasies, or by the entire destruction of self in the way of naked faith. Both these states are found in the apostle Paul. He tells us, "And lest I should be exalted above measure, through the abundance of revelations, there was given to me a thorn in the flesh, the messenger of Satan to buffet me." He prayed thrice, and it was said to him, "My grace is sufficient for you; for my strength is made perfect in weakness." He proved also another state when he thus expressed himself, "Oh, wretched man that I am! Who shall deliver me from the body of this death?" To which he replies, "I thank God, it is done through Jesus Christ our Lord." It is He who conquers death in us through His own life. Then there is no longer a sting in death, or thorn in the flesh, capable of paining or hurting any more.

At first indeed, and for a pretty long time after, the soul sees that nature wants to take some part with it in its trials; then its fidelity consists in withholding it, without allowing it the least indulgence, till it leaves everything to go on with God in purity as it comes from Him. Till the soul be in this state, it always sullies, by its own mixture, the operation of God; like those rivulets which contract the corruption of the places they pass through, but, flowing in a pure place, they then remain in the purity of their source. Unless God through experience, makes known His guidance to the soul, it can never comprehend it.

Oh, if souls had courage enough to resign themselves to the work of purification, without having any weak and foolish pity on themselves, what a noble, rapid and happy progress would they make! But few are willing to lose the earth. If they advance some steps, as soon as the sea is ruffled they are dejected; they cast anchor, and often desist from the prosecution of the voyage. Such disorders doth selfish interest and self-love occasion. It is of consequence not to look too much at one's own state, not to lose courage, not to afford any nourishment to self-love, which is so deep-rooted, that its empire is not easily demolished. Often the idea which a man falsely conceives of the greatness of his advancement in divine experience, makes him want to be seen and known of men, and to wish to see the very same perfection in others. He conceives too low ideas of others, and too high of his own state. Then it becomes a pain to him to converse with people too human; whereas, a soul truly mortified and resigned would rather converse with the worst, by the order of Providence, than with the best, of its own choice; wanting only to see or to speak to any as Providence directs, knowing well that all beside, far from helping, only hurt it, or at least prove very unfruitful to it.

What, then, renders this soul so perfectly content? It neither knows, nor wants to know, anything but what God calls it to. Herein it enjoys divine content, after a manner vast, immense, and independent of exterior events; more satisfied in its humiliation, and in the opposition of all creatures, by the order of Providence, than on the throne of its own choice.

It is here that the apostolic life begins. But do all reach that state? Very few, indeed, as far as I can comprehend. There is a way of lights, gifts and graces, a holy life in which the creature appears all admirable. As this life is more apparent, so it is more esteemed of such, at least, as have not the purest light. The souls which walk in the other path are often very little known, for a length of time, as it was with Jesus Christ Himself, till the last years of His life. Oh, if I could express what I conceive of this state! But I can only stammer about it.

Chapter Nine

Being as I have said with the Ursulines at Tonon, after having spoken to the Bishop of Geneva, and seeing how he changed, just as others turned him, I wrote to him and to Father La Mothe but all my efforts were useless. The more I endeavored to accommodate matters, the more the ecclesiastic tried to confound them, hence I ceased to meddle.

One day I was told that the ecclesiastic had won over the good girl whom I dearly loved. So strong a desire I had for her perfection that it had cost me much. I should not have felt the death of a child so much as her loss; at the same time I was told how to hinder it, but that human way of acting was repugnant to my inward sense; these words arose in my heart, "Except the Lord build the house."

And indeed He provided herein Himself, hindering her from yielding to this deceitful man, after a manner to be admired, and very thwarting to the designs of him and his associates. As long as I was with her she still seemed wavering and fearful; but oh, the infinite goodness of God, to preserve without our aid what without His we should inevitably lose! I was no sooner separated from her, but she became immovable.

As for me, there scarcely passed a day but they treated me with new insults; their assaults came on me at unawares. The New Catholics, by the instigation of the Bishop of Geneva, the ecclesiastic, and the sisters at Gex, stirred up all the persons of piety against me. I had but little uneasiness on my own account. If I could have had it at all, it would have been on account of Father La Combe, whom they vilely aspersed, though he was absent. They even made use of his absence, to overset all the good he had done in the country, by his missions and pious labors, which were inconceivably great. At first I was too ready to vindicate him, thinking it justice to do it. I did not do it at all for myself; and our Lord showed me that I must cease doing it for him, in order to leave him to be more thoroughly annihilated; because from thence he would draw a greater glory, than ever he had done from his own reputation.

Every day they invented some new slander. No kind of stratagem, or malicious device in their power, did they omit. They came to surprise and ensnare me in my words; but God guarded me so well, that therein they only discovered their own malevolence. I had no consolation from the creatures. She who had the care of my daughter behaved roughly to me. Such are the persons who regulate themselves only by their gifts and emotions. When they do not see things succeed, and as they regard them only by their success, and are not willing to have the affront of their pretensions being thought uncertain, and liable to mistake, they seek without for supports. As for me who pretended to nothing, I thought all succeeded well, inasmuch as all tended to self-annihilation. On another side, the maid I had brought, and who stayed with me, grew tired out. Wanting to go back again, she stunned me with her complaints, thwarting and chiding me from morning till night, upbraiding me with what I had left, and coming to a place where I was good for nothing. I was obliged to bear all her ill-humor and the clamor of her tongue.

My own brother, Father La Mothe, wrote to me that I was rebel to my bishop, staying in his diocese only to give him pain. Indeed, I saw there was nothing for me to do here, so long as the bishop should be against me. I did what I could to gain his goodwill, but this was impossible on any other terms than the engagement he demanded, and that I knew to be my duty not to do. This, joined to the poor education of my daughter, affected my heart. When any glimmering of hope appeared, it soon vanished; and I gained strength from a sort of despair.

During this time Father La Combe was at Rome, where he was received with so much honor, and his doctrine was so highly esteemed, that the Sacred Congregation was pleased to take his sentiments on some points of doctrine, which were found to be so just, and so clear, that it followed them. Meanwhile the sister would take no care of my daughter; when I took care of her she was displeased. I was not able, by any means, to prevail on her to promise me that she would try to prevent her contracting bad habits. However, I hoped that Father La Combe, at his return, would bring everything into order, and renew my consolation. Yet I left it all to God.

About July, 1682, my sister, who was an Ursuline, got permission to come. She brought a maid with her, which was very seasonable. My sister assisted in the education of my daughter, but she had frequent jarring with her tutoress -- I labored but in vain for peace. By some instances which I met with in this place, I saw clearly that it is not great gifts which sanctify, unless they be accompanied with a profound humility; that death to everything is infinitely more beneficial; for there was one who thought herself at the summit of perfection, but has discovered since, by the trials which have befallen her, that she was yet very far from it. O, my God, how true it is that we may have of Your gifts, and yet be very imperfect, and full of ourselves!

How very straight is the gate which leads to a life in God! How little one must be to pass through it, it being nothing else but death to self! But when we have passed through it, what enlargement do we find! David said, (Psalm 18:19) "He brought me forth into a large place." And it was through humiliation and abasement that he was brought thither.

Father La Combe, on his arrival, came to see me: The first thing he said was about his own weakness, and that I must return. He added, "that all seemed dark, and there was no likelihood that God would make use of me in this country." The Bishop of Geneva wrote to Father La Mothe to get me to return; he wrote to me accordingly to do it. The first Lent which I passed with the Ursulines, I had a very great pain in my eyes; for that same imposthume which I formerly had between the eye and the nose, returned upon me three times. The bad air, and the noisome room which I was in, contributed hereto. My head was frightfully swelled, but great was my inward joy. It was strange to see so many good creatures, who did not know me, love and pity me; all the rest enraged against me, and most of them on reports entirely false, neither knowing me, nor why they so hated me. To swell the stream of affliction yet more, my daughter fell sick and was likely to die; there was but little hope of her recovery, when her mistress also fell ill. My soul, leaving all to God, continued to rest in a quiet and peaceable habitation. Oh, Principal and sole object of my love! Were there never any other reward of what little services we do, or of the marks of homage we render You, than this fixed state above the vicissitudes in the world, is it not enough? The senses indeed are sometimes ready to start aside, and to run off like truants; but every trouble flies before the soul which is entirely subjected to God. By speaking of a fixed state, I do not mean one which can never decline or fall, that being only in Heaven. I call it fixed and permanent, compared with the states which have preceded it, which were full of vicissitudes and variations. I do not exclude a state of suffering in the senses, or arising from superficial impurity, which remains to be done away, and which one may compare to refined but tarnished gold. It has no more need to be purified in the fire, having undergone that operation; but needs only to be burnished. So it seemed to be with me at that time.

Chapter Ten

My daughter had the smallpox. They sent for a physician from Geneva, who gave her over. Father La Combe then came in to visit, and pray with her. He gave her his blessing; soon after she wonderfully recovered. The persecution of the New Catholics against me continued and increased; yet, for all that, I did not fail to do them all the good in my power. My daughter's mistress came often to converse with me, but much imperfection appeared in her discourses, though they were on religious subjects. Father La Combe regulated many things in regard to my daughter, which vexed her mistress so much, that her former friendship was turned into coldness. She had grace, but suffered nature too frequently to prevail. I told her my thought on her faults, as I was inwardly directed to do; but though, at that time, God enlightened her to see the truth of what I said, and she has been more enlightened since, yet the return of her coldness toward me ensued upon it. The debates between her and my sister grew more tart and violent. My daughter, who was only six years and a half old, by her little dexterities found a way to please them both, choosing to do her exercises twice over, first with the one, then with the other, which continued not long; for as her mistress generally neglected her, doing things at one time, and leaving them at another, she was reduced to learn only what my sister and I taught her. Indeed the changeableness of my sister was so excessive, that, without great grace, it was hard to suit one's self to it; yet she appeared to me to surmount herself in many things. Formerly, I could scarce bear her manners; but I have since loved everything in God, who has given me a very great facility to bear the faults of my neighbor, with a readiness to please and oblige everyone and such a compassion for their calamities or distresses as I never had before.

I have no difficulty to use condescension with imperfect persons; I should be secretly smitten if I failed therein; but with souls of grace I cannot bear this human manner of acting, nor suffer long and frequent conversations. It is a thing of which few are capable. Some religious persons say that these conversations are of great service. I believe it may be true for some, but not for all; for there is a period wherein it hurts, especially when it is of our own choice; the human inclination corrupting everything. The same things which would be profitable, when God, by His Spirit, draws to them, become quite otherwise, when we of ourselves enter into them. This appears to me so clear, that I prefer being a whole day with the worst of persons, in obedience to God, before being one hour with the best, only from my own choice and inclination.

The order of divine providence makes the whole rule and conduct of a soul entirely devoted to God. While it faithfully gives itself up thereto, it will do all things right and well, and will have everything it wants, without its own care; because God in whom it confides, makes it every moment do what He requires, and furnishes the occasions proper for it. God loves what is of His own order, and of His own will, not according to the idea of the merely rational or even enlightened man; for He hides these persons from the eyes of others, in order to preserve them in that hidden purity for Himself.

But how comes it that such souls commit any faults; because they are not faithful, in giving themselves up to the present moment. Often too eagerly bent on something, or wanting to be over-faithful, they slide into many faults, which they can neither foresee nor avoid. Does God then leave souls which confide in Him? Surely not. Sooner would He work a miracle to hinder them from falling, if they were resigned enough to Him. They may be resigned as to the general will, and yet fail as to the present moment. Being out of the order of God, they fall. They renew such falls as long as they continue out of that divine order. When they return into it, all goes right and well.

Most assuredly if such souls were faithful enough, not to let any of the moments of the order of God slip over, they would not thus fall. This appears to me as clear as the day. As a dislocated bone out of the place in which the economy of divine wisdom had fixed it, gives continual pain till restored to its proper order, so the many troubles in life come from the soul not abiding in its place, and not being content with the order of God, and what is afforded therein from moment to moment. If men rightly knew this secret, they would all be fully content and satisfied. But alas! instead of being content with what they have, they are ever wishing for what they have not; while the soul, which enters into divine light begins to be in paradise. What is it that makes paradise? It is the order of God, which renders all the saints infinitely content, though very unequal in glory! From whence comes it that so many poor indigent persons are so contented, and that princes and potentates, who abound to profusion, are so wretched and unhappy? It is because the man who is not content with what he has, will never be without craving desires; and he who is the prey of an unsatisfied desire, can never be content.

All souls have more or less of strong and ardent desires, except those whose will is lost in the will of God. Some have good desires, so as to suffer martyrdom for God; others thirst for the salvation of their neighbor, and some pant to see God in glory. All this is excellent. But he who rests in the divine will, although he may be exempt from all these desires, is infinitely more content, and glorifies God more. It is written concerning Jesus Christ, when he drove out of the temple those who profaned it. "The zeal of your house has eaten me up." John 2:17. It was in that moment of the order of God, that these words had their effect. How many times had Jesus Christ been in the temple without such a conduct? Does not He occasionally say of himself, His hour was not yet come?

Chapter Eleven

After Father La Combe returned from Rome, well approved, and furnished with testimonials of life and doctrine, he performed his functions of preaching and confessing as usual. I gave him an account of what I had done and suffered in his absence, and what care God had taken of all my concerns. I saw his providence incessantly extended to the very smallest things. After having been several months without any news of my papers, when some pressed me to write, and blamed my neglect, an invisible hand held me back; my peace and confidence were great. I received a letter from the ecclesiastic at home, which informed me that he had orders to come and see me, and bring my papers. I had sent to Paris for a pretty considerable bundle of things for my daughter. I heard they were lost on the lake, and could learn no further tidings about them.

I gave myself no trouble; I always thought they would be found. The man who had taken charge of them made a search after them a whole month, in all the environs, without hearing any news. At the end of three months they were brought to me, having been found in the house of a poor man, who had not opened them, nor knew who brought them there. Once I had sent for all the money which was to serve me a whole year; the person who had been to receive cash for the bill of exchange, having put that money in two bags on horseback, forgot that it was there, and gave the horse to a little boy to lead. The money fell from the horse in the middle of the market at Geneva. That instant I arrived, coming on the other side, and having alighted from my litter, the first thing I found was my money. What was surprising, a great throng was in this place and not one had perceived it. Many such things have attended me. These accounts may suffice to show the continual protection of God.

The Bishop of Geneva continued to persecute me. When he wrote, it was with politeness and thanks for my charities at Gex; while at the same time he said to others that I "gave nothing to that house." He wrote against me to the Ursulines with whom I lived, charging them to hinder me from having any conferences with Father La Combe. The superior of the house, a man of merit, and the prioress, as well as the community, were so irritated at this, that they could not forbear testifying it to him. He then excused himself with a pretended respect, saying, he did not mean it that way. They wrote to him that "I did not see the Father but at the confessional, and not in conference; that they were so much edified by me, as to think themselves happy in having me, and to esteem it a greater favor from God." What they said out of pure charity was not pleasing to the Bishop, who, seeing they loved me in this house, said, that I won over everybody to myself and that he wished I were out of the diocese. Though I knew all this, and these good sisters were troubled at it, I could have no trouble by reason of the calm establishment which I was in. The will of God rendering everything equal to me. The creatures, however unreasonable or passionate they appear, not being regarded in themselves but in God; a habitual faith causes everything to be seen in God without distinction. Thus, when I see poor souls so ruffled for discourses in the air, so uneasy for explanations, I pity them. They have reasons, I know, which self-love causes to appear very just.

To relieve myself a little from the fatigue of continual conversation, I desired Father La Combe to allow me a retreat. It was then that I let myself be consumed by love all the day long. Also I perceived the quality of a spiritual mother; for the Lord gave me what I cannot express for the perfection of souls. This I could not hide from Father La Combe. It seemed to me as if I entered into the inmost recesses of his heart. Our Lord showed me he was His servant, chosen among a thousand, singularly to honor Him; but that He would lead him through total death, and the entire destruction of the old man. He would have me contribute thereto and be instrumental to cause him to walk in the way in which He had led me first; in order that I might be in a condition to direct others, to tell them the way through which I have passed. The Lord would have us to be conformed, and to become both one in Him; though my soul was more advanced now, yet he should one day pass beyond it, with a bold and rapid flight. God knows with what joy I would see my spiritual children surpass their mother.

In this retreat I felt a strong propensity to write, but resisted it till I fell sick. I had nothing to write about, not one idea to begin with. It was a divine impulse, with such a fullness of grace as was hard to contain. I opened this disposition of mine to Father La Combe. He answered that he had a strong impulse to command me to write, but had not dared to do it yet, on account of my weakness. I told him, that "weakness was the effect of my resistance," and I believed it would, through my writing, go off again. He asked, "But what is it you will write?" I replied, "I know nothing of it, nor desire to know, leaving it entirely to God to direct me."

He ordered me to do so. At my taking the pen I knew not the first word I should write; when I began, suitable matter flowed copiously, nay, impetuously. As I was writing I was relieved and grew better. I wrote an entire treatise on the interior path of faith, under the comparison of torrents, or of streams and rivers.

As the way, wherein God now conducted Father La Combe, was very different from that in which he had formerly walked (all light, knowledge, ardor, assurance, sentiment) now the poor, low, despised path of faith, and of nakedness; he found it very hard to submit thereto. Who could express what it has cost my heart before he was formed according to the will of God?

Meanwhile, the possession which the Lord had of my soul became every day stronger, insomuch that I passed whole days without being able to pronounce one word. The Lord was pleased to make me pass wholly into Him by an entire internal transformation. He became more and more the absolute master of my heart, to such a degree as not to leave me a movement of my own. This state did not hinder me from condescending to my sister, and the others in the house. Nevertheless, the useless things with which they were taken up could not interest me. That was what induced me to ask leave to make a retreat, to let myself be possessed of Him who holds me so closely to Himself after an ineffable manner.

Chapter Twelve

I had at that time so ardent a desire for the perfection of Father La Combe, and to see him thoroughly die to himself, that I could have wished him all the crosses and afflictions imaginable, that might conduce to this great and blessed end. Whenever he was unfaithful, or looked at things in any other light than the true one - to tend to this death of self - I felt myself on the rack, which, as I had till then been so indifferent, very much surprised me. To the Lord I made my complaint; He graciously encouraged me, both on this subject and on that entire dependence on Himself which He gave me, which was such that I was like a new born infant.

My sister had brought me a maid, whom God was willing to give me to fashion according to His will, not without some crucifixion to myself. I believe it never is to fall out, that our Lord will give me any persons without giving them wherewith to make me suffer, whether it be for the purpose of drawing them into a spiritual life, or never to leave me without the cross. She was one on whom the Lord had conferred very singular graces. She was in high reputation in the country, where she passed for a saint. Our Lord brought her to me, to let her see the difference between the sanctity conceived and comprised in those gifts, with which she was endowed, and that which is obtained by our entire destruction, even by the loss of those very gifts, and of all that raised us in the esteem of men. Our Lord had given her the same dependence on me, as I had in regard to Father La Combe.

This girl fell grievously sick. I was willing to give her all the assistance in my power, but I found I had nothing to do but to command her bodily sickness, or the disposition of her mind; all that I said was done. It was then that I learned what it was to command by the Word, and to obey by the Word. It was Jesus Christ in me equally commanding and obeying.

She, however, continued sick for sometime. One day, after dinner, I was moved to say to her, "Rise and be no longer sick." She arose and was cured. The nuns were very much astonished. They knew nothing of what had passed, but saw her walking, who in the morning had appeared to be in the last extremity. They attributed her disorder to a vivid imagination.

I have at sundry times experienced, and felt in myself, how much God respects the freedom of man, even demands his free concurrence; for when I said, "Be healed," or, "Be free from your troubles," if such persons acquiesced, the Word was efficacious, and they were healed. If they doubted, or resisted, though under fair pretexts, saying, "I shall be healed when it pleases God, I will not be healed till He wills it;" or, in the way of despair, "I cannot be healed; I will not quit my condition," then the Word had no effect. I felt in myself that the divine virtue retired in me. I experienced what our Lord said, when the woman afflicted with the issue of blood touched him. He instantly asked, "Who touched me?" The apostles said, "Master, the multitude throng you, and press you; and you say, Who touched me?" He replied, "It is because virtue has gone out of me" (Luke 8:45,46). Jesus Christ had caused that healing virtue to flow, through me, by means of His Word. When that virtue met not with a correspondence in the subject, I felt it suspended in its source. That gave me some pain. I should be, as it were, displeased with those persons; but when there was no resistance, but a full acquiescence, this divine virtue had its full effect. Healing virtue has so much power over things inanimate, yet the least thing in man either restrains it, or stops it entirely.

There was a good nun much afflicted and under a violent temptation. She went to declare her case to a sister whom she thought very spiritual, and in a condition capable of assisting her. But far from finding succor, she was very much discouraged and cast down. The other despised and repulsed her, and treating her with contempt and rigor, she said, "Don't come near me, since you are that way." This poor girl, in a frightful distress, came to me thinking herself undone on account of what the sister had said to her. I consoled her and our Lord relieved her immediately. But I could not forbear telling her that assuredly the other would be punished, and would fall into a state worse than hers. The sister who had used her in such a manner came also to me, highly pleased with herself in what she had done, saying, she abhorred such tempted creatures. As for herself, she was proof against such sorts of temptations, and that she never had a bad thought." I said to her, "My sister, from the friendship I have for you I wish you the pain of her who spoke to you, and even one still more violent." She answered haughtily, "If you were to ask it from God for me, and I ask of Him the contrary, I believe I shall be heard at least as soon as you."

I answered with great firmness, "If it be only my own interests which I ask, I shall not be heard; but if it be those of God only, and yours too, I shall be heard sooner than you are aware." That very night she fell into so violent a temptation that one equal to it has seldom been known. It was then she had ample occasion to acknowledge her own weakness, and what she would be without grace. She conceived at first a violent hatred for me, saying that I was the cause of her pain. But it served her, as the clay did to enlighten him who had been born blind. She soon saw very well what had brought on her so terrible a state.

I fell sick even to extremity. This sickness proved a means to cover the great mysteries which it pleased God to operate in me. Scarce ever was a disorder more extraordinary, or of longer continuance in its excess. Several times I saw in dreams Father La Mothe raising persecutions against me. Our Lord let me know that this would be and that Father La Combe would forsake me in the time of persecution. I wrote to him, and it disquieted him greatly. He thought his heart was united to the will of God and too desirous of serving me, to admit such desertion; yet it has since been found quite true. He was now to preach during Lent, and was so much followed, that people came five leagues, to pass several days for the benefit of his ministry. I heard he was so sick that he was thought to die. I prayed to the Lord to restore his health, and enable him to preach to the people, who were longing to hear him. My prayer was heard, and he soon recovered, and resumed his pious labors.

During this extraordinary sickness, which continued more than six months, the Lord gradually taught me that there was another manner of conversing among souls wholly His, than by speech. You made me conceive, O divine Word, that as You are ever speaking and operating in a soul, though therein you appear in profound silence; so there was also a way of communication in your creatures, in an ineffable silence. I heard then a language which before had been unknown to me. I gradually perceived, when Father La Combe entered, that I could speak no more. There was formed in my soul the same kind of silence toward him, as was formed in it in regard to God. I comprehended that God was willing to show me that men might in this life learn the language of angels. I was gradually reduced to speak to him only in silence. It was then that we understood each other in God, after a manner unutterable and divine. Our hearts spoke to each other, communicating a grace which no words can express. It was like a new country, both for him and for me; but so divine, that I cannot describe it. At first this was done in a manner so perceptible, that is to say, God penetrated us with Himself in a manner so pure and so sweet, that we passed hours in this profound silence, always communicative, without being able to utter one word. It was in this that we learned, by our own experience, the operations of the heavenly Word to reduce souls into unity with itself, and what purity one may arrive at in this life. It was given me to communicate this way to other good souls, but with this difference: I did nothing but communicate to them the grace with which they were filled, while near me, in this sacred silence, which infused into them an extraordinary strength and grace; but I received nothing from them; whereas with Father La Combe there was a flow and return of communication of grace, which he received from me, and I from him, in the greatest purity.

In this long malady the love of God, and of Him alone, made up my whole occupation, I seemed so entirely lost to Him, as to have no sight of myself at all. It seemed as if my heart never came out of that divine ocean, having been drawn into it through deep humiliations. Oh, happy loss, which is the consummation of bliss, though operated through crosses and through deaths!

Jesus was then living in me and I lived no more. These words were imprinted in me, as a real state into which I must enter, (Matt. 8:20) "The foxes have holes, and the birds of the air have nests, but the Son of man hath not where to lay his head." This I have since experienced in all its extent, having no sure abode, no refuge among friends, who were ashamed of me, and openly renounced me, when universally decried; nor among my relations, most of whom declared themselves my adversaries, and were my greatest persecutors; while others looked on me with contempt and indignation. I might as David say, "For your sake I have borne reproach; shame has covered my face; I am become a stranger to my brethren, and an alien unto my mother's children; a reproach to men, and despised of the people."

He showed me all the world in a rage against me, without anyone daring to appear for me and assured me in the ineffable silence of His eternal Word, that He would give me vast numbers of children, which I should bring forth by the cross. I left it to Him to do with me whatever He pleased, esteeming my whole and sole interest to be placed entirely in His divine will. He gave me to see how the Devil was going to stir up an outrageous persecution against prayer, yet it should prove the source of the same prayer, or rather the means which God would make use of to establish it. He gave me to see farther how He would guide me into the wilderness, where He would cause me to be nourished for a time. The wings, which were to bear me thither, were the resignation of my whole self to His holy will. I think I am at present in that wilderness, separated from the whole world in my imprisonment. I see already accomplished in part what was then shown me. Can I ever express the mercies which my God has bestowed on me? No; they must ever remain in Himself, being of a nature not to be described, by reason of their purity and immensity.

I was often to all appearance at the point of death. I fell into convulsions from violent pains which lasted a long time with violence. Father La Combe administered the sacrament to me, the Prioress of the Ursulines having desired him to do it. I was well satisfied to die, as was he also in the expectation of my departure. For, being united in God after a manner so pure, and so spiritual, death could not separate us. On the contrary it would have more closely united us. Father La Combe, who was on his knees at my bedside, remarking the change of my countenance, and how my eyes faded, seemed ready to give me up, when God inspired him to lift up his hands, and with a strong voice, which was heard by all who were in my room, at that time almost full, to command death to relinquish its hold. Instantly it seemed to be stopped. Thus God was pleased wonderfully to raise me up again; yet for a long time I continued extremely weak, during all of which our Lord gave me new testimonies of His love. How many times was He pleased to make use of His servant to restore me to life, when I was almost on the very point of expiring! As they saw that my sickness and pain did not entirely end, they judged that the air of the lake on which the convent was situated, was very prejudicial to my constitution. They concluded that it would be necessary for me to remove.

During my indisposition, our Lord put it into the heart of Father La Combe to establish a hospital in this place for the poor people seized with maladies, to institute also a committee or congregation of ladies to furnish such as could not leave their families to go to the hospital with the means of subsistence during their illness, after the manner of France, there having been yet no institution of this kind in that country. Willingly did I enter into it; and without any other fund than Providence and some useless rooms which a gentleman of the town gave us, we began it. We dedicated it to the holy Child Jesus, and He was pleased to give the first beds to it from my pension. He gave such a blessing that several other persons joined us in this charity. In a short time there were nearly twelve beds in it and three persons of great piety gave themselves to this hospital to serve it, who, without any salary, consecrated themselves to the service of the poor patients. I supplied them with ointments and medicines, which were freely given to such of the poor people of the town as had need of them. These good ladies were so hearty in the cause, that, through their charity, and the care of the young women, this hospital was very well maintained and served. These ladies joined together also in providing for the sick who could not go to the hospital. I gave them some little regulations such as I had observed when in France, which they continued to keep up with tenderness and love.

All these little things, which cost but little, and which owed all their success to the blessing which God gave them, drew upon us new persecutions. The Bishop of Geneva was offended with me more than ever, especially in seeing that these small matters rendered me beloved. He said that I won over everybody. He openly declared, "he could not bear me in his diocese," though I had done nothing but good, or rather God by me. He extended the persecution to those good religious women who had been my assistants. The prioress in particular had her own share to bear, though it did not last long. As I was obliged, on account of the air, to remove, after having been there about two years and a half, they were then more in peace and quietness. On another side, my sister was very weary of this house; and as the season for the waters approached, they took occasion from thence to send her away with the maid which I brought with me, who had molested me exceedingly in my late illness. I only kept her whom Providence had sent me by means of my sister. I have ever thought that God had ordered my sister's journey only to bring her to me, as one chosen of Him and proper for the state which it was His pleasure to cause me to bear.

While I was yet indisposed, the Ursulines, with the Bishop of Verceil, earnestly requested the Father-general of the Barnabites, to seek among the religious, a man of merit, piety and learning, in whom he might place confidence, and who might serve him for a prebend and a counselor. At first he cast his eyes on Father La Combe; yet before he absolutely engaged him with the said bishop, he wrote to him, to know whether he had any objection thereto. Father La Combe replied that he had no other will but that of obeying him, and that he might command him herein as he should think best in the case. He gave me an account of this, and that we were going to be entirely separated. I was glad to find that our Lord would employ him, under a bishop who knew him, and would be likely to do him justice. Yet it was some time before he went, matters not being all arranged.

Chapter Thirteen

I then went off from the Ursulines and they sought for a house for me at a distance from the lake. There was but one to be found empty which had the look of the greatest poverty. It had no chimney but in the kitchen, through which one was obliged to pass. I took my daughter with me and gave up the largest room for her and the maid who was to take care of her. I was lodged in a little hole on straw, to which I went up by ladder. As we had no other furniture but our beds, quite plain and homely, I brought some straw chairs and some Dutch earthen and wooden ware. Never did I enjoy a greater content than in this little hole, which appeared so very conformable to the state of Jesus Christ. I fancied everything better on wood than on plate. I laid in all my provisions, hoping to stay there a long time; but the Devil did not leave me long in such sweet peace. It would be difficult for me to tell the persecutions which were stirred up against me. They threw stones in at my windows which fell at my feet. I had put my little garden in order. They came in the night, tore it all up, broke down the arbor, and overturned everything in it, as if it had been ravaged by soldiers. They came to abuse me at the door all night long, making such a racket as if they were going to break it open. These persons have since told who the person was that put them on such work.

Though from time to time I continued my charities at Gex, I was not the less persecuted for it. They offered one person a warrant to compel Father La Combe to stay at Tonon, thinking he would otherwise be a support to me in the persecution, but we prevented it. I knew not then the designs of God, and that He would soon draw me from that poor solitary place, in which I enjoyed a sweet and solid satisfaction, notwithstanding the abuse.

I thought myself happier here than any sovereign on earth. It was for me like a nest and a place of repose and Christ was willing that I should be like Him. The Devil, as I have said, irritated my persecutors. They sent to desire me to go out of the diocese. All the good which the Lord had caused me to do in it was condemned, more than the greatest crimes. Crimes they tolerated, but me they could not endure. All this while I never had any uneasiness or repentance for my having left all; not that I was assured of having done the will of God therein. Such an assurance would have been too much for me. But I could neither see nor regard anything, receiving everything alike from the hand of God, who directed and disposed of these crosses for me either in justice or in mercy.

The Marchioness of Prunai, sister of the chief Secretary of State to his Royal Highness (the Duke of Savoy) and his prime minister, had sent an express from Turin, in the time of my illness, to invite me to come to reside with her; and to let me know that, "being so persecuted as I was in this diocese, I should find an asylum with her; that during that time things might grow better; that when they should be well disposed she would return with me and join me with a friend of mine from Paris, who was willing also to come to labor there, according to the will of God," I was not at that time in a condition to execute what she desired and expected to continue with the Ursulines till things should change. She then wrote to me about it no more. This lady is one of extraordinary piety, who had quitted the splendor and noise of the Court, for the more silent satisfaction of a retired life, and to give herself up to God. With an eminent share of natural advantages, she has continued a widow twenty-two years; has refused every offer of marriage to consecrate herself to our Lord entirely and without any reserve. When she knew that I had been obliged to leave the Ursulines, yet without knowing anything of the manner in which I had been treated, she procured a letter to oblige Father La Combe to go to pass some weeks at Turin, for her own benefit, and to bring me with him thither, where I should find a refuge. All this she did unknown to us. As she has told us since, a superior force moved her to do it, without knowing the cause. If she had deliberately reflected on it, being such a prudent lady, she probably would not have done it; because the persecutions, which the Bishop of Geneva procured us in that place, cost her more than a little of humiliations. Our Lord permitted him to pursue me, after a surprising manner, into all the places I have been in, without giving me any relaxation. I never did him any harm, but on the contrary, would have laid down my life for the good of his diocese.

As this fell out without any design on our part, we, without hesitation, believed it was the will of God; and thought it might be the means of His appointment to draw us out of the reproach and persecution we labored under, seeing myself chased on the one side, desired on the other. It was concluded that Father La Combe should conduct me to Turin, and that he should go from thence to Verceil.

Beside him, I took with me a religious man of merit, who had taught theology for fourteen years past, to take away from our enemies all cause for slander. I also took with me a boy whom I had brought out of France. They took horses, and I hired a carriage for my daughter, my chambermaid and myself. But all precautions are useless, when it pleases God to permit them to be frustrated. Our adversaries immediately wrote to Paris. A hundred ridiculous stories were circulated about this journey; comedies were acted on it, things invented at pleasure, and as false as anything in the world could be. It was my brother, Father de la Mothe, who was so active in uttering all this stuff. Had he believed it to be true, he ought out of charity to have concealed it; much more, being so very false. They said that I was gone all alone with Father La Combe, strolling about the country, from province to province, with many such fables, as weak and wicked as they were incoherent and badly put together. We suffered all with patience, without vindicating ourselves, or making any complaint.

Scarcely were we arrived at Turin, but the Bishop of Geneva wrote against us. As he could pursue us no other way, he did it by letters. Father La Combe repaired to Verceil, and I staid at Turin, with the Marchioness of Prunai. But what crosses was I assaulted with in my own family, from the Bishop of Geneva, from the Barnabites, and from a vast number of persons besides!

My eldest son came to find me on the death of my mother-in-law, which was an augmentation of my troubles. After we had heard all his accounts of things and how they had made sales of all the moveables, chosen guardians, and settled every article, without consulting me. I seemed to be there entirely useless. It was judged not proper for me to return, considering the rigor of the season.

The Marchioness of Prunai, who had been so warmly desirous of my company, seeing my great crosses and reproaches, looked coldly upon me. My childlike simplicity, which was the state wherein God at that time kept me, passed with her for stupidity. For when the question was to help anyone, or about anything which God required of me, He gave me, with the weakness of a child, the evident tokens of divine strength. Her heart was quite shut up to me all the time I was there. Our Lord, however, made me foretell events which should happen, which since that time have actually been fulfilled, as well to herself as to her daughter, and to the virtuous ecclesiastic who lived at her house. She did not fail, at last, to conceive more friendship for me, seeing then that Christ was in me. It was the force of self-love, and fear of reproach, which had closed up her heart. Moreover, she thought her state more advanced than in reality it was, by reason of her being without tests; but she soon saw by experience that I had told her the truth. She was obliged for family reasons to leave Turin, and go to live on her own estate. She solicited me to go with her, but the education of my daughter did not permit. To stay at Turin without her seemed improper, because, having lived very retired in this place, I made no acquaintance in it. I knew not which way to turn. The Bishop of Verceil, where Father La Combe was, most obligingly wrote to me, earnestly entreating me to come, promising me his protection, and assuring me of his esteem, adding, "that he should look upon me as his own sister; that he wished extremely to have me there." It was his own sister, one of my particular friends, who had written to him about me, as had also a French gentleman, an acquaintance of his. But a point of honor kept me from it. I would not have it said that I had gone after Father La Combe, and that I had come to Turin only for the purpose of going to Verceil. He had also his reputation to preserve, which was the cause that he could not agree to my going thither, however importunate the Bishop was for it. Had we believed it to be the will of God, we would both of us have passed over these considerations. God kept us both in so great a dependence on His orders, that He did not let us foreknow them; but the divine moment of His providence determined everything. This proved of very great service to Father La Combe, who had long walked in assurances, to die to them and to Himself. God by an effect of His goodness, that he might thus die without any reserve, took them all from him.

During the whole time of my residence at Turin, our Lord conferred on me very great favors. I found myself every day more transformed into Him, and had continually more knowledge of the state of souls, without ever being mistaken or deceived therein, though some were willing to persuade me to think the contrary. I had used my utmost endeavors to give myself other thoughts, which has caused me not a little pain. When I told, or wrote to Father La Combe about the state of some souls, which appeared to him more perfect and advanced than the knowledge given to me of them, he attributed it to pride. He was angry with me, and prejudiced against my state. I had no uneasiness on account of his esteeming me the less, for I was not in a condition to reflect whether he esteemed me or not. He could not reconcile my willing obedience in most things, with so extraordinary a firmness, which in certain cases he looked upon as criminal. He admitted a distrust of my grace; he was not yet sufficiently confirmed in his way, nor did he duly comprehend, that it did not in any wise depend on me to be one way or another. If I had any such power I should have suited myself to what he said, to spare myself the crosses which my firmness caused me. Or, at least, I would have artfully dissembled my real sentiments. I could do neither. Were all to perish by it, I was in such a manner constrained, that I could not forbear telling him the things, just as our Lord directed me to tell them to him. In this he had given me an inviolable fidelity to the very last. No crosses or pains have ever made me fail a moment therein. These things then, which appeared to him to be the strong prejudice of a conceited opinion, set him at variance against me. Though he did not openly show it, on the contrary tried to conceal it from me; yet how far distant soever he were from me, I could not be ignorant of it. Why spirit felt it, and that more or less, as the opposition was stronger or weaker; as soon as it abated or ended, my pain, occasioned thereby, ceased. He also, on his side, experienced the same. He has told me and written to me many times over, "When I stand well with God, I find I am well with you. When I am otherwise with Him, I then find myself to be so with you also." Thus he saw clearly that when God received him, it was always in uniting him to me, as if He would accept of nothing from him but in this union.

While he was at Turin, a widow who was a good servant of God, all in the brightness of sensibility, came to him to confess. She uttered wonderful things of her state. I was then at the other side of the confessional. He told me, "He had met with a soul given up to God; that it was she who was present; that he was very much edified by her; that he was far from finding the like in me; that I operated nothing but death upon his soul." At first I rejoiced at his having met with such a holy soul. It ever gives me the highest joy to see my God glorified. As I was returning, the Lord showed me clearly the state of that soul, as only a beginning of devotion mixed with affection and a little silence, filled with a new sensation. This and more, as it was set before me, I was obliged to write to him. On his first reading of my letter he discovered the stamp of truth in it; but soon after, letting in again his old reflections, he viewed all I wrote in the light of pride. He still had in his mind the ordinary rules of humility conceived and comprised after our manner. As to me, I let myself be led as a child, who says and does, without distinction, whatever it is made to say and do. I left myself to be led where soever my heavenly Father pleased, high or low; all was alike good to me.

He wrote to me, that, at his first reading of my letter there appeared in it something of truth; but that on reading it over again, he found it to be full of pride, and of preference of my own discernments to that of others. Some time after he was more enlightened in regard to the state I was in. He then said, "continue to believe as you have done; I encourage and exhort you to do it." Some time after he sufficiently discovered, by that person's manner of acting, that she was very far from what he had thought. I give this as only one instance. I might give many others, but this may suffice.

Chapter Fourteen

One night in a dream our Lord showed me, that He would also purify the maid whom He had given me, make her truly enter into death to herself. I freely resolved to suffer for her, as I did for Father La Combe. As she resisted God much more than he, and was much more under the power of self-love, she had more to be purified from. What I could not tolerate in her was her regard for herself. I saw clearly that the devil cannot hurt us only so far as we retain some fondness for this corrupt self. This sight was from God. He gave me the discerning of spirits, which would ever accept what was from Him, or reject what was not; that not from any common methods of judging, not from any outward information, but by an inward principle which is His gift alone.

It is needful to mention here that souls which are yet in themselves, whatever degree of light and ardor they have attained, are unqualified for it. They often think they have this discernment, when it is nothing else but sympathy or antipathy of nature. Our Lord destroyed in me every sort of natural antipathy. The soul must be very pure, and depending on God alone, that all these things may be experienced in Him. In proportion as this maid became inwardly purified, my pain abated, till the Lord let me know her state was going to be changed, which soon happily ensued. In comparison of inward pain for souls, outward persecutions, though ever so violent, scarce gave me any.

The Bishop of Geneva wrote to different persons. He wrote in my favor to such as he thought would show me his letters, and quite the contrary in the letters which he thought I would never see. It was so ordered that these persons, having showed each other their letters received from him, were struck with indignation to see in him so shameful a duplicity. They sent me those letters that I might take proper precautions. I kept them two years, and then burned them, not to hurt the prelate. The strongest battery he raised against me was what he did with the Secretary of State, who held that post in conjunction with the Marchioness of Prunai's brother. He used all imaginable endeavors to render me odious. He employed certain abbots for that purpose, insomuch that, though I appeared very little abroad, I was well known by the description this bishop had given of me. This did not make so much impression as it would have done, if he had appeared in a better light at Court. Some letters of his, which her royal highness found after the prince's death, written to him against her, had effect on the princess, that, instead of taking any notice of what he now wrote against me, she showed me great respect. She sent her request to me to come to see her. Accordingly I waited on her. She assured me of her protection, and that she was glad of my being in her dominions.

It pleased God here to make use of me to the conversion of two or three ecclesiastics. But I had much to suffer from their repugnancies and many infidelities - one of whom had vilified me greatly - and even after his conversion turned aside into his old ways. God at length graciously restored him.

As I was undetermined whether I should place my daughter at the Visitation of Turin, or take some other course; I was exceedingly surprised, at a time I least expected it, to see Father La Combe arrive from Verceil. He told me that I must return to Paris without any delay. It was in the evening, and he said, "set off the next morning." I confess this sudden news startled me. It was for me a double sacrifice to return to a place where they had cried me down so much; also toward a family which held me in contempt, and who had represented my journey, caused by pure necessity, as a voluntary course, pursued through human attachments. Behold me then disposed to go off, without offering a single word in reply, with my daughter and my maid, without anybody to guide and attend us. Father La Combe was resolved not to accompany me, not so much as passing the mountains. The Bishop of Geneva had written on all sides that I was gone to Turin to run after him. But the Father Provincial, who was a man of quality, and well acquainted with the virtue of

Father La Combe, told him, that it was improper and unsafe to venture on these mountains, without some person of acquaintance; the more as I had my little daughter with me. He therefore ordered him to accompany me. Father La Combe confessed to me that he had some reluctance to do it, and only obedience, and the danger to which I should have been exposed, made him surmount it. He was only to accompany me to Grenoble, and from thence to return to Turin. I went off then, designing for Paris, there to suffer whatever crosses and trials it should please God to inflict.

What made me go by Grenoble was the desire I had to spend two or three days with a lady, an eminent servant of God, and one of my friends. When I was there Father La Combe and that lady spoke to me not to go any farther. God would glorify Himself in me and by me in that place. He returned to Verceil, and I left myself to be conducted as a child by Providence. This lady took me to the house of a good widow, there not being accommodations at the inn. As I was ordered to stop at Grenoble, at her house I resided. I placed my daughter in a convent, and resolved to employ all this time in resigning myself to be possessed in solitude by Him who is the absolute Sovereign of my soul. I made not any visit in this place; no more had I in any of the others where I had sojourned. I was greatly surprised when, a few days after my arrival, there came to see me several persons who made profession of a singular devotion to God. I perceived immediately a gift which He had given me, of administering to each that which suited their states. I felt myself invested, all of a sudden, with the apostolic state. I discerned the conditions of the souls of such persons as spoke to me, and that with so much facility, that they were surprised at it, and said one to another, that I gave every one of them "the very thing they had stood in need of." It was you, O my God, who did all these things; some of them sent others to me. It came to such excess, that, generally from six in the morning till eight in the evening, I was taken up in speaking of the Lord. People flocked on all sides, far and near, friars, priests, men of the world, maids, wives, widows, all came one after another. The Lord supplied me with what was pertinent and satisfactory to them all, after a wonderful manner, without any share of my study or meditation therein. Nothing was hid from me of their interior state, and of what passed within them. Here, O my God, You made an infinite number of conquests known to Yourself only. They were instantly furnished with a wonderful facility of prayer. God conferred on them His grace plentifully, and wrought marvelous changes in them. The most advanced of these souls found, when with me, in silence, a grace communicated to them which they could neither comprehend, nor cease to admire. The others found an unction in my words, and that they operated in them what I said. Friars of different orders, and priests of merit, came to see me, to whom our Lord granted very great favors, as indeed He did to all, without exception, who came in sincerity.

One thing was surprising; I had not a syllable to say to such as came only to watch my words, and to criticize them. Even when I thought to try to speak to them, I felt that I could not, and that God would not have me do it. Some of them in return said, "The people are fools to go to see that lady. She cannot speak." Others of them treated me as if I were only a stupid simpleton. After they left me there came one and said, "I could not get hither soon enough to apprize you not to speak to those persons; they come from such and such, to try what they can catch from you to your disadvantage." I answered them, "Our Lord has prevented your charity; for I was not able to say one word to them."

I felt that what I spoke flowed from the fountain and that I was only the instrument of Him who made me speak. Amid this general applause, our Lord made me comprehend what the apostolic state was, with which He had honored me, that to give one's self up to the help of souls, in the purity of His Spirit, was to expose one's self to the most cruel persecutions. These very words were imprinted on my heart: "To resign ourselves to serve our neighbor is to sacrifice ourselves to a gibbet. Such as now proclaim, 'Blessed is he who comes in the name of the Lord,' will soon cry out, 'Away with him, crucify him.'" When one of my friends speaking of the general esteem the people had for me, I said to her, "Observe what I now tell you, that you will hear curses out of the same mouths which at present pronounce blessings." Our Lord made me comprehend that I must be conformable to Him in all His states; and that, if He had continued in a private life with His parents, He never had been crucified; that, when He would resign any of His servants to crucifixion, He employed such in the ministry and service of their neighbors. It is certain that all the souls employed herein by apostolic destination from God, and who are truly in the apostolic state, are to suffer extremely. I speak not of those who put themselves into it, who, not being called of God in a singular manner, and having nothing of the grace of the apostleship, have none of its crosses; but of those only who surrender themselves to God without any reserve, and who are willing with their whole hearts to be exposed, for His sake, to sufferings without any mitigation.

Chapter Fifteen

Among so great a number of good souls, on whom our Lord wrought much by me, some were given me only as plants to cultivate. I knew their state, but had not that near connection with, or authority over them, which I had over others. It was then that I comprehended the true maternity beyond what I had done before; for those of the latter kind were given me as children, of whom some were faithful. I knew they would be so; they were closely united to me in pure charity. Others were unfaithful; I knew that of these some would never return from their infidelity, and they were taken from me. Some, after slipping aside, were recovered. Both of them cost me much distress and inward pain, when, for want of courage to die to themselves, they gave up the point; and revolted from the good beginning they had been favored with.

Our Lord, among such multitudes as followed Him on earth, had few true children. Wherefore He said to His Father, "Those that you gave me I have kept, and none of them is lost but the son of perdition," showing that He lost not any beside of His apostles, or disciples, though they sometimes made false steps.

Among the friars who came to see me, there was one Order which discovered the good effects of grace more than any other. Some of that very order had before this, in a little town where Father La Combe was in the exercise of his mission, been actuated with a false zeal, and violent in persecuting all the good souls which had sincerely dedicated themselves to God, plaguing them after such a manner as can scarce be conceived. They burned all their books which treated of silence and inward prayer, refusing absolution to such as were in the practice of it, driving into consternation, and almost into despair, such as had formerly led wicked lives, but were now reformed, and preserved in grace by means of prayer, becoming spotless and blameless in their conduct. These friars had proceeded to such an excess of wild zeal as to raise a sedition in that town, in which a father of the oratory, a person of distinction and merit, received strokes with a stick in the open street, because he prayed extempore in the evenings, and on Sundays made a short fervent prayer, which insensibly habituated these good souls to the use and practice of the like.

I never had so much consolation as to see in this little town so many pious souls who with a heavenly emulation gave up their whole hearts to God. There were girls of twelve or thirteen years of age, who industriously followed their work almost all the day long, in silence, and in their employments enjoyed a communion with God, having acquired a fixed habit. As these girls were poor, they placed themselves two and two together, and such as could do it read to the others who could not. One saw there the innocence of the primitive Christians revived. There was in that town a poor laundress who had five children, and a husband paralytic, lame in the right arm, and yet worse distempered in mind than in body. He had little strength left for anything else than to beat her. This poor woman bore it with all the meekness and patience of an angel, while she by her labor supported him and his five children. She had a wonderful gift of prayer, and amid her great suffering and extreme poverty, preserved the presence of God, and tranquility of mind. There was also a shopkeeper, and one who made locks, very much affected with God. These were close friends. Sometimes the one and sometimes the other read to this laundress; and they were surprised to find that she was instructed by the Lord Himself in all they read to her, and spoke divinely of it.

Those friars sent for this woman, and threatened her much if she did not leave off prayer, telling her it was only for churchmen to pray, and that she was very bold to practice it. She replied, that "Christ had commanded all to pray," that He had said, "What I say unto you I say unto all" (Mark 13:33, 37), without specifying either priests or friars; that without prayer she could not support her crosses and poverty; that formerly she had lived without it, and then was very wicked; that since she had been in the exercise of it, she had loved God with all her soul; so that to leave off prayer was to renounce her salvation, which she could not do. She added that they might take twenty persons who had never practiced prayer, and twenty of those who were in the practice of it. Then, said she, "Inform yourselves of the lives of both sorts, and you will see if you have any reason to cry out against prayer." Such words as these, from such a woman, one would think might have fully convinced them; but instead of that, it only irritated them the more. They assured her that she should have no absolution till she promised them to desist from prayer. She said that depended not on her, and that Christ is master of what He communicates to His creatures, and of doing with it what He pleases. They refused her absolution; and after railing at a good tailor, who served God with his whole heart, they ordered all the books without exception, which treated on prayer to be brought to them. They burned them with their own hands in the public square. They were very much elated with their performance; but all the town presently arose in an uproar. The principal men went to the Bishop of Geneva, and complained to him of the scandals of these new missionaries, so different from the others. Speaking of Father La Combe, who had been there before them on his mission, they said that these seemed as if they were sent to destroy all the good he had done. The bishop was forced to come himself to that town, and there to mount the pulpit, protesting that he had no share in it, and that these fathers had pushed their zeal too far. The friars, on the other side declared, they had done all they did, pursuant to the orders given them.

There were also at Tonon young women who had retired together, being poor villagers, the better to earn their livelihood and to serve God. One of them read from time to time, while the others were at work, and not one went out without asking leave of the eldest. They wove ribbons, or spun, the strong supporting the weak. They separated these poor girls, and others beside them, in several villages, and drove them out of the church.

It was the friars of the very order whom our Lord made use of to establish prayer in (I know not how) many places. Into the places where they went, they carried a hundred times more books of prayer than those which their brethren had burned. The hand of God appeared to me wonderfully in these things.

One day when I was sick, a brother who had skill in curing diseases, came for a charitable collection, but hearing I was ill, came in to see me, and gave me medicines proper for my disorder. We entered into a conversation which revived in him the love he had for God, which he acknowledged had been too much stifled by his occupations. I made him comprehend that there was no employment which should hinder him from loving God, and from being occupied within himself. He readily believed me, as he already had a good share of piety, and of an interior disposition. Our Lord conferred on him many favors, and gave him to be one of my true children.

I saw at this time, or rather experienced the ground on which God rejects sinners from His bosom. All the cause of God's rejection is in the will of the sinner. If that will submits, how horrible soever he be, God purifies him in his love, and receives him into his grace; but while that will rebels, the rejection continues. For want of ability seconding his inclination, he should not commit the sin he is inclined to, yet he never can be admitted into grace till the cause ceases, which is this wrong will, rebellious to the divine law. If that once submits, God then totally removes the effects of sin, which stain the soul, by washing away the defilements which he has contracted. If that sinner dies in the time that his will is rebellious and turned toward sin, as death fixes forever the disposition of the soul, and the cause of its impurity is ever subsisting, such soul can never be received into God. Its rejection must be eternal, as there is such an absolute opposition between essential purity and essential impurity. And as this soul, from its own nature necessarily tends to its own center, it is continually rejected of the Lord, by reason of its impurity, subsisting not only in the effects, but in their cause. It is the same way in this life. This cause, so long as it subsists, absolutely hinders the grace of God from operating in the soul. But if the sinner comes to die truly penitent, then the cause, which is the wrong will, being taken away, there remains only the effect or impurity caused by it. He is then in a condition to be purified. God of his infinite mercy has provided a laver of love and of justice, a painful laver indeed, to purify this soul. And as the defilement is greater or less, so is the pain; but when the cause is utterly taken away, the pain entirely ceases. Souls, are received into grace, as soon as the cause of sin ceases; but they do not pass into the Lord Himself, till all its effects are washed away. If they have not courage to let Him, in His own way and will, thoroughly cleanse and purify them, they never enter into the pure divinity in this life.

The Lord incessantly solicits this will to cease to be rebellious, and spares nothing on His side for this good end. The will is free, yet grace follows it still. As soon as the will ceases to rebel, it finds grace at the door, ready to introduce its unspeakable benefits. O, the goodness of the Lord and baseness of the sinner, each of them amazing when clearly seen!

Before I arrived at Grenoble, the lady, my friend, saw in a dream that our Lord gave me an infinite number of children all uniformly clad, bearing on their habits the marks of candor and innocence. She thought I was coming to take care of the children of the hospital. But as soon as she told me, I discerned that it was not that which the dream meant; but that our Lord would give me, by a spiritual fruitfulness, a great number of children; that they would not be my true children, but in simplicity, candor and innocence. So great an aversion I have to artifice and disguise.

Chapter Sixteen

The physician of whom I have spoken, was disposed to lay open his heart to me. Our Lord gave him through me all that was necessary for him; for though disposed to the spiritual life, yet for want of courage and fidelity he had not duly advanced in it.

He had occasion to bring to me some of his companions who were friars; and the Lord took hold of them all. It was at the very same time, that the others of the same order were making all the ravages I have mentioned, and opposing with all their might the Holy Spirit of the Lord. I could not but admire to see how the Lord was pleased to make amends for former damages, pouring out His Spirit in abundance on these men, while the others were laboring vehemently against it, doing all they could to destroy its dominion and efficacy in their fellow mortals. But those good souls instead of being staggered by persecutions, grew the stronger by it. The Superior, and the master of the novices of the house in which this doctor was, declared against me, without knowing me. They were grievously chagrined that a woman, as they said, should be so much flocked to, and so much sought after. Looking at things as they were in themselves, and not as they were in the Lord, who does whatever pleases Him, they had contempt for the gift which was lodged in so mean an instrument, instead of esteeming the Lord and His grace. Yet this good brother at length got the superior to come to see me, and thank me for the good which he said I had done. Our Lord so ordered, that he found something in my conversation which reached and took hold of him. At length he was completely brought over. He it was, who some time after, being visitor, dispersed such a number of those books, bought at their own charge, which the others had tried utterly to destroy. Oh, how wonderful you are, my God! In all Your ways how wise, in all Your conduct how full of love! How well You can frustrate all the false wisdom of men, and triumph over their vain pretensions!

There were in this novitiate many novices. The eldest of them grew so very uneasy under his vocation, that he knew not what to do. So great was his trouble that he could neither read, study, pray, nor do scarcely any of his duties. His companion brought him to me. We spoke awhile together, and the Lord discovered to me both the cause of his disorder and its remedy. I told it to him; and he began to practice prayer, even that of the heart. He was on a sudden wonderfully changed, and the Lord highly favored him. As I spoke to him grace wrought in his heart, and his soul drank it in, as the parched ground does the gentle rain. He felt himself relieved of his pain before he left the room. He then readily, joyfully, and perfectly performed all his exercises, which before were done with reluctance and disgust. He now both studied and prayed easily, and discharged all his duties, in such a manner, that he was scarce known to himself or to others. What astonished him most was a remarkable gift of prayer. He saw that there was readily given him what he could never have before, whatever pains he took for it. This enlivening gift was the principle which made him act, gave him grace for his employments, and an inward fruition of the grace of God, which brought all good with it. He gradually brought me all the novices, all of whom partook of the effects of grace, though differently, according to their different temperaments. Never was there a more flourishing novitiate.

The master and superior could not forbear admiring so great a change in their novices, though they did not know the cause of it. One day, as they were speaking of it to the collector, for they esteemed him highly on account of his virtue, he said, "My fathers, if you will permit me, I will tell you the reason of it. It is the lady against whom you have exclaimed so much without knowing her, whom God has made use of for all of this." They were very surprised; and both the master, though advanced in age, and his superior then submitted humbly to practice prayer, after the manner taught by a little book, which the Lord inspired me to write, and of which I shall say more hereafter. They reaped such benefit from it, that the superior said to me, "I am become quite a new man. I could not practice prayer before, because my reasoning faculty was grown dull and exhausted; but now I do it as often as I will, with ease, with much fruit, and a quite different sensation of the presence of God." And the master said, "I have been a friar these forty years, and can truly say that I never knew how to pray; nor have I ever known or tasted of God, as I have done since I read that little book."

Many others were gained to God, whom I looked on to be my children. He gave me three famous friars, of an order by which I have been, and still am, very much persecuted. He made me also of service to a great number of nuns, of virtuous young women, and even men of the world; among the rest a young man of quality, who had quitted the order of the knights of Malta, to take that of the priesthood. He was the relation of a bishop near him, who had other designs of preferment for him. He has been much favored of the Lord, and is constant in prayer. I could not describe the great number of souls which were then given me, as well maids, as wives, priests and friars. But there were three curates, one canon, and one grand-vicar, who were more particularly given me. There was one priest for whom I suffered much, through his not being willing to die to himself, and loving himself too much. With a sad regret I saw him decaying, falling away. As for the others there are some of them who have continued steadfast and immovable, and some whom the tempest has shaken a little, but not torn away. Though these start aside, yet they still return. But those who are snatched quite away return no more.

There was one true daughter given me, whom our Lord made use of to gain many others to Him. She was in a strange state of death when I first saw her, and by me He gave her life and peace. She afterward, fell extremely ill. The doctors said she would die; but I had an assurance of the contrary, and that God would make use of her to gain souls, as he has done. There was in a monastery a young woman confined in a state of distraction. I saw her, knew her case, and that it was not what they thought it was. As soon as I had spoken to her she recovered. But the prioress did not like that I should tell her my thoughts of it, because the person who had brought her thither was her friend. They plagued her more than before, and threw her back again into her distraction.

A sister of another monastery had been for eight years in a deep melancholy, unrelieved by anyone. Her director increased it, by practicing remedies contrary to her disorder. I had never been in that monastery; for I did not go into such places, unless I was sent for, as I did not think it right to intrude, but left myself to be conducted of Providence. I was very much surprised that at eight o'clock at night one came for me from the prioress. It was in the long days of summer, and being near, I went. I met with a sister who told me her case. She had gone to such excess, that seeing no remedy for it, she had taken a knife to kill herself. The knife fell out of her hand and a person coming to see her had advised her to speak to me. Our Lord made me know at first what the matter was; and that He required her to resign herself to Him, instead of resisting Him as they had made her do for eight years. I was instrumental to draw her into such a resignation, that she entered at once into a peace of paradise; all her pains and troubles were instantly banished; and never returned again. She has the greatest capacity of any in the house. She was presently so changed as to be the admiration of the whole community. Our Lord gave her a very great gift of prayer and His continual presence, with a faculty and readiness for everything. A domestic also, who had troubled her for twenty-two years past, was delivered from her troubles. That produced a close tie of friendship between the prioress and me, as the wonderful change and the peace of this sister surprised her, she having so often seen her in her terrible sorrow. I also contracted other such ties in this monastery, where there are souls under the Lord's special regard, whom He drew to Himself by the means He had been pleased to make choice.

I was specially moved to read the Holy Scriptures. When I began I was impelled to write the passage, and instantly its explication was given me, which I also wrote, going on with inconceivable expedition, light being poured in upon me in such a manner, that I found I had in myself latent treasures of wisdom and knowledge which I had not yet known of. Before I wrote I knew not what I was going to write. And after I had written, I remembered nothing of what I had penned; nor could I make use of any part of it for the help of souls. The Lord gave me, at the time I spoke to them (without any study or reflection of mine) all that was necessary for them. Thus the Lord made me go on with an explanation of the holy internal sense of the Scriptures. I had no other book but the Bible, nor ever made use of any but that, and without even seeking for any. When, in writing on the Old Testament, I made use of passages of the New, to support what I had said, it was without seeking them, they were given me along with the explication; and in writing on the New Testament, therein making use of passages of the Old, they were given me in like manner without my seeking anything. I had scarce any time for writing but in the night, allowing only one or two hours to sleep. The Lord made me write with so much purity, that I was obliged to leave off or begin again, as He was pleased to order. When I wrote by day, often suddenly interrupted, I left the word unfinished, and He afterward gave me what He pleased. If I gave way to reflection I was punished for it, and could not proceed. Yet sometimes I was not duly attentive to the divine Spirit, thinking I did well to continue when I had time, even without feeling His immediate impulse or enlightening influence, from whence it is easy to see some places clear and consistent, and others which have neither taste nor unction; such is the difference of the Spirit of God from the human and natural spirit. Although they are left just as I wrote them, yet I am ready, if ordered, to adjust them according to my present light.

Did you not, O my God, turn me a hundred ways, to prove whether I was without any reserve, through every kind of trial, or whether I had not yet some little interest for myself? My soul became hereby readily too pliable to every discovery of the divine will, and whatever kind of humiliations attended me to counterbalance my Lord's favors, till everything, high or low, was rendered alike to me.

Methinks the Lord acts with His dearest friends as the sea with its waves. Sometimes it pushes them against the rocks where they break in pieces, sometimes it rolls them on the sand, or dashes them on the mire, then instantly it retakes them into the depths of its own bosom, where they are absorbed with the same rapidity that they were first ejected. Even among the good the far greater part are souls only of mercy; surely that is well; but to appertain to divine justice, oh, how rare and yet how great! Mercy is all distributive in favor of the creature, but justice destroys everything of the creature, without sparing anything.

The lady, who was my particular friend, began to conceive some jealousy on the applause given me, God so permitting if for the farther purification of her soul, through this weakness, and the pain it caused her. Also some confessors began to be uneasy, saying that "it was none of my business to invade their province, and to meddle in the helps of souls; that there were some of the penitents which had a great affection for me." It was easy for me to observe the difference between those confessors who, in their conducting of souls, seek nothing but God, and those who seek themselves therein. The first came to see me, and rejoiced greatly at the grace of God bestowed on their penitents, without fixing their attention on the instrument. The others, on the contrary, tried underhand to stir up the town against me. I saw that they would be in the right to oppose me, if I had intruded of myself; but I could do nothing but what the Lord made me do. At times there came some to dispute and oppose me. Two friars came, one of them a man of profound learning and a great preacher. They came separately, after having studied a number of difficult things to propose to me. Though they were matters far out of my reach, the Lord made me answer as justly as if I had studied them all my life; after which I spoke to them as He inspired me. They went away not only convinced and satisfied, but affected with the love of God.

I still continued writing with a prodigious swiftness; for the hand could scarcely follow fast enough the Spirit which dictated. Through the whole progress of so long a work I never altered my manner nor made use of any other book than the Bible itself. The transcriber, whatever diligence he used, could not copy in five days what I wrote in one night. Whatever is good in it comes from God only. Whatever is otherwise from myself; I mean from the mixture which I have made, without duly attending to it, of my own impurity with his pure and chaste doctrine. In the day I had scarcely time to eat, by reason of the vast numbers of people which came thronging to me. I wrote the canticles in a day and a half, and received several visits besides.

Here I may add to what I have said about my writings, that a considerable part of the book of Judges happened by some means to be lost. Being desired to render that book complete, I wrote again the places lost. Afterward when the people were about leaving the house, they were found. My former and latter explications, on comparison, were found to be perfectly conformable to each other, which greatly surprised persons of knowledge and merit, who attested the truth of it.

There came to see me a counselor of the parliament, a servant of God, who finding on my table a tract on prayer, which I had written long before, desired me to lend it. Having read it and liked it much, he lent it to some friends, to whom he thought it might be of service. Everyone wanted copies of it. He resolved therefore to have it printed. The impression was begun, and proper approbations given to it. They requested me to write a preface, which I did, and thus was that little book printed. This counselor was one of my intimate friends, and a pattern of piety. The book has already passed through five or six editions; and our Lord has given a very great benediction to it. Those good friars took fifteen hundred of them. The devil became so enraged against me on account of the conquest which God made by me, that I was assured he was going to stir up against me a violent persecution. All that gave me no trouble. Let him stir up against me ever so strange persecutions. I know they will all serve to the glory of my God.

Chapter Seventeen

A poor girl of very great simplicity, who earned her livelihood by her labor, and was inwardly favored of the Lord, came all sorrowful to me, and said, "Oh my mother, what strange things have I seen!" I asked what they were, "Alas" said she, "I have seen you like a lamb in the midst of a vast troop of furious wolves. I have seen a frightful multitude of people of all ranks and robes, of all ages, sexes and conditions, priests, friars, married men, maids and wives, with pikes, halberts and drawn swords, all eager for your instant destruction. You let them alone without stirring, or being surprised and without offering any way to defend yourself. I looked on all sides to see whether anyone would come to assist and defend you; but I saw not one."

Some days after, those, who through envy were raising private batteries against me, broke forth. Libels began to spread. Envious people wrote against me, without knowing me. They said that I was a sorceress, that it was by a magic power I attracted souls, that everything in me was diabolical; that if I did charities, it was because I coined, and put off false money, with many other gross accusations, equally false, groundless and absurd.

As the tempest increased every day, some of my friends advised me to withdraw, but before I mention my leaving Grenoble, I must say something farther of my state while here. It seemed to me that all our Lord made me do for souls, would be in union with Jesus Christ. In this divine union my words, had wonderful effect, even the formation of Jesus Christ in the souls of others. I was in no wise able of myself to say the things I said. He who conducted me made me say what he pleased, and as long as He pleased. To some I was not permitted to speak a word; and to others there flowed forth as it were a deluge of grace, and yet this pure love admitted not of any superfluity, or a means of empty amusement. When questions were asked, to which an answer were useless, it was not given me. It was the same in regard to such as our Lord was pleased to conduct through death to themselves, and who came to seek for human consolation. I had nothing for them but what was purely necessary, and could proceed no farther. I could at least only speak of indifferent things, in such liberty as God allows, in order to suit everyone, and not to be unsociable or disagreeable to any; but for His own word, He Himself is the dispenser of it. Oh, if preachers were duly careful to speak only in that spirit what fruits would they bring forth in the lives of the hearers! With my true children I could communicate best in silence, in the spiritual language of the divine Word. I had the consolation some time before to hear one read in Saint Augustine a conversation he had with his mother. He complains of the necessity of returning from that heavenly language to words. I sometimes said, "Oh, my Love, give me hearts large enough to receive and contain the fullness bestowed on me."

After this manner, when the Holy Virgin approached Elizabeth, a wonderful commerce was maintained between Jesus Christ and Saint John the Baptist, who after this manifested no eagerness to come to see Christ, but was drawn to retire into the desert, to receive the like communications with the greatest plenitude. When he came forth to preach repentance, he said, not that he was the Word, but only a Voice which was sent to make way, or open a passage into the hearts of the people for Christ the Word. He baptized only with water, for that was his function; for, as the water in running off leaves nothing, so does the Voice when it is past. But the Word baptized with the Holy Ghost, because He imprinted Himself on souls, and communicated with them by that Holy Spirit. It is not observed that Jesus Christ said anything during the whole obscure part of His life, though it is true that not any of His words shall be lost. Oh Love, if all you have said and operated in silence were to be written, I think the whole world could not contain the books that should be written. John 21:25.

All that I experienced was shown me in the Holy Scripture. I saw with admiration that there passed nothing within my soul which was not in Jesus Christ and in the Holy Scriptures. I must pass over very many things in silence, because they cannot be expressed. If they were expressed they could not be understood or comprehended.

I often felt much for Father La Combe, who was not yet fixed in his state of interior death, but often rose and fell into alternatives. I was made sensible that Father La Combe was a vessel of election, whom God had chosen to carry His name among the Gentiles, and that He would show him how much he must suffer for that name. A carnal world judges carnally of them, and imputes to human attachment what is from the purest grace. If this union by any deviation be broken, the more pure and perfect it is, the more painfully will it be felt; the separation of the soul from God by sin being worse than that from the body of death. For myself I may say I had a continual dependence on God, in every state; my soul was ever willing to obey every motion of His Spirit. I thought there could not be anything in the world which He could require from me, to which I would not give myself up readily and with pleasure. I had no interest at all for myself. When God requires anything from this wretched nothing, I find no resistance left in me to do His will, how rigorous soever it may appear. If there is a heart in the world of which You are the sole and absolute master, mine seems to be one of that sort. Your will, however rigorous, is its life and its pleasure.

To resume the thread of my story, the Bishop of Grenoble's Almoner persuaded me to go for some time to Marseilles, to let the storm pass over. He told me that I would be well received there, it being his native soil, and that many people of merit were there. I wrote to Father La Combe for his consent. He readily gave it. I might have gone to Verceil; for the Bishop of Verceil had written me very obliging letters, earnestly pressing me to come. But a human respect, and fear of affording a handle to my enemies, gave me an extreme aversion thereto.

Beside the above, the Marchioness of Prunai, who, since my departure from her, had been more enlightened by her own experience, having met with a part of the things which I thought would befall her, had conceived for me a very strong friendship and intimate union of spirit, in such a manner that no two sisters could be more united than we. She was extremely desirous that I would return to her, as I had formerly promised her. But I could not resolve upon this, lest it should be thought that I was gone after Father La Combe. There had been no room given to anybody to accuse me of any indirect attachment to him; for when it depended on myself not to continue with him, I did not do it. The Bishop of Geneva had not failed to write against me to Grenoble, as he had done to other places. His nephew had gone from house to house to cry me down. All this was indifferent to me; and I did not cease to do to his diocese all the good in my power. I even wrote to him in a respectful manner; but his heart was too much closed to yield to anything.

Before I left Grenoble, that good girl I have spoken of came to me weeping, and told me that I was going, and that I hid it from her, because I would have nobody know it; but that the Devil would be before me in all the places I should go to; that I was going to a town, where I would scarce be arrived, before he would stir up the whole town against me, and would do me all the harm he possibly could. What had obliged me to conceal my departure, was my fear of being loaded with visits, and testimonies of friendship from a number of good persons, who had a very great affection for me.

I embarked then upon the Rhone, with my maid and a young woman of Grenoble, whom the Lord has highly favored through my means. The Bishop of Grenoble's Almoner also accompanied me, with another very worthy ecclesiastic. We met with many alarming accidents and wonderful preservations; but those instant dangers, which affrighted others, far from alarming me, augmented my peace. The Bishop of Grenoble's Almoner was much astonished. He was in a desperate fright, when the boat struck against a rock, and opened at the stroke. In his emotion looking attentively at me, he observed that I did not change my countenance, or move my eyebrows, retaining all my tranquility. I did not so much as feel the first emotions of surprise, which are natural to everybody on those occasions, as they depend not on ourselves. What caused my peace in such dangers as terrify others, was my resignation to God, and because death is much more agreeable to me than life, if such were His will, to which I desire to be ever patiently submissive.

A man of quality, a servant of God, and one of my intimate friends had given me a letter for a knight of Malta, who was very devout, and whom I have esteemed since I have known him, as a man whom our Lord designed to serve the order of Malta greatly, and to be its ornament and support by his holy life. I had told him that I thought he should go thither, and that God would assuredly make use of him to diffuse a spirit of piety into many of the knights. He has actually gone to Malta, where the first places were soon given him. This man of quality sent him my little book of prayer and printed at Grenoble. He had a chaplain very averse to the spiritual path. He took this book, and condemning it at once, went to stir up a part of the town, and among the rest a set of men who called themselves the seventy-two disciples of Saint Cyran. I arrived at Marseilles at ten o'clock in the morning, and that very afternoon all was in a noise against me. Some went to speak to the bishop, telling him that, on account of that book, it was necessary to banish me from the city. They gave him the book which he examined with one of his prebends. He liked it well. He sent for Monsieur Malaval and a father Recollect, who he knew had come to see me a little after my arrival, to inquire of them from whence that great tumult had its rise, which indeed had no other effect on me than to make me smile, seeing so soon accomplished what that young woman had foretold me. Monsieur Malaval and that good father told the bishop what they thought of me; after which he testified much uneasiness at the insult given me. I was obliged to go to see him. He received me with extraordinary respect, and begged my excuse for what had happened; desired me to stay at Marseilles, and assured me that he would protect me. He even asked where I lodged, that he might come to see me.

Next day the Bishop of Grenoble's Almoner went to see him, with that other priest who had come with us. The Bishop of Marseilles again testified to them his sorrow for the insults given me without any cause; and told them, that it was usual with those persons to insult all such as were not of their cabal, that they had even insulted himself. They were not content with that. They wrote to me the most offensive letters possible, though at the same time they did not know me. I apprehended that our Lord was beginning in earnest to take from me every place of abode; and those words were renewed in my mind, "The foxes have holes, and the birds of the air have nests, but the Son of man has not where to lay his head."

In the short time of my stay at Marseilles, I was instrumental in supporting some good souls, and among others an ecclesiastic, who till then was unacquainted with me. After having finished his thanksgiving in the church, seeing me go out, he followed me into the house in which I lodged. Then he told me that the Lord had inspired him to address me, and to open his inward state to me. He did it with as much simplicity as humility, and the Lord gave him through me all that was necessary for him, from whence he was filled with joy, and thankful acknowledgments to God. Although there were many spiritual persons there, and even of his intimate friends, he never had been moved to open his mind to any of them. He was a servant of

God, and favored by Him with a singular gift of prayer. During the eight days I was at Marseilles, I saw many good souls there. Through all my persecutions, our Lord always struck some good stroke of His own right hand, and that good ecclesiastic was delivered from an anxiety of mind, which had much afflicted him for some years.

After I had left Grenoble, those who hated me, without knowing me, spread libels against me. A woman for whom I had great love, and whom I had even extricated from an engagement which she had continued in for several years, and contributed to her discarding the person to whom she had been attached, suffered her mind to resume its fondness for that pernicious engagement. She became violently enraged against me for having broken it off. Although I had freely been at some expense to procure her freedom, still she went to the Bishop of Grenoble, to tell him that I had counseled her to do an act of injustice. She then went from confessor to confessor, repeating the same story, to animate them against me. As they were too susceptible of the prejudices infused, the fire was soon kindled in all quarters. There were none but those who knew me, and who loved God, that took my part. They became more closely united to me in sympathy through my persecution. It would have been very easy for me to destroy the calumny, as well with the Bishop of Grenoble. I needed only to tell who the person was, and show the fruits of her disorder. I could not declare the guilty person, without making known at the same time the other who had been her accomplice, who now, being touched of God, was very penitent, I thought it best for me to suffer and be silent. There was a very pious man who knew all her history, from the beginning to the end of it, who wrote to her, that if she did not retract her lies, he would publish the account of her wicked life, to make known both her gross iniquity and my innocence. She continued some time in her malice, writing that I was a sorceress, with many other falsehoods. Some time after she had such a cruel remorse of conscience on this account, that she wrote both to the bishop and others to retract what she had said. She induced one to write to me, to inform me that she was in despair for what she had done; that God had punished her. After these recantations the outcry abated, the bishop disabused, and since that time he has testified a great regard for me. This creature had, among other things, said that I caused myself to be worshipped; also other unparalleled follies.

  From Marseilles I knew not how or whither I should turn next. I saw no likelihood either of staying or of returning to Grenoble, where I had left my daughter in a convent. Father La Combe had written to me that he did not think I ought to go to Paris. I even felt a strong repugnance to the idea of going, which made me think it was not yet the time for it. One morning I felt myself inwardly pressed to go somewhere. I took a conveyance to go to see the Marchioness of Prunai, which was, I thought, the most honorable refuge for me in my present condition. I thought I might pass through Nice on my way to her habitation, as some had assured me I might. But when I arrived at Nice, I was greatly surprised to learn that the conveyance could not pass the mountain. I knew not what to do, nor which way to turn, alone, forsaken of everybody, and not knowing what God required of me. My confusion and crosses seemed to increase. I saw myself, without refuge or retreat, wandering as a vagabond. All the tradesmen, whom I saw in their shops, appeared to me happy, in having a dwelling of their own in which to retire. Nothing in the world seemed harder than this wandering life to me, who naturally loved propriety and decorum. As I was in this uncertainty, not knowing what course to take, one came to tell me that next day a sloop would set off, which used to go in one day to Genoa; and that if I chose it, they would land me at Savona, from whence I might get myself carried to the Marchioness of Prunai's house. To that I consented, as I could not be supplied with any other way.

  I had some joy at embarking on the sea. I said in myself, "If I am the dregs of the earth, the scorn and off scouring of nature, I am now going to embark on the element which above all others is the most treacherous; if it be the Lord's pleasure to plunge me in the waves, it shall be mine to perish in them." There came a tempest in a place dangerous for a small boat; and the mariners were some of the wickedest. The irritation of the waves gave a satisfaction to my mind. I pleased myself in thinking that those mutinous billows might probably supply me with a grave. Perhaps I carried the point too far in the pleasure I took, at seeing myself beaten and bandied by the waters. Those who were with me, took notice of my intrepidity, but knew not the cause of it. I asked some little hole of a rock to be placed in, there to live separate from all creatures. I figured to myself, that some uninhabited island would have terminated all my disgraces, and put me in a condition of infallibly doing Your will. You designed me a prison far different from that of the rock, and quite another banishment than that of the uninhabited island. You reserve me to be battered by billows more irritated than those of the sea. Calumnies proved to be the unrelenting waves, to which I was to be exposed, in order to be lashed and tossed by them without mercy. By the tempest we were kept back, and instead of a short day's passage to Genoa, we were eleven days making it. How peaceable was my heart in so violent an agitation! We could not land at Savona. We were obliged to go on to Genoa. We arrived there in the beginning of the week before Easter.

While I was there I was obliged to bear the insults of the inhabitants, caused by the resentment they had against the French because of the havoc of a late bombardment. The Doge was newly gone out of the city, and had carried off with him all the coaches. I could not get one, and was obliged to stay several days at excessive expenses. The people there demanded of us exorbitant sums, and as much for every single person as they would have asked for a company at the best eating place in Paris. I had little money left, but my store in Providence could not be exhausted. I begged with the greatest earnestness for a carriage at any price, to pass the feast of Easter at the Marchioness of Prunai's house. It was then within three days of Easter. I could scarce any way get myself to be understood. By the force of entreaty, they brought me at length a sorry coach with lame mules, and told me that they would take me readily to Verceil, which was only two days journey, but demanded an enormous sum. They would not engage to take me to the Marchioness of Prunai's house, as they knew not where her estate lay. This was to me a strong mortification; for I was very willing to go to Verceil; nevertheless the proximity of Easter; and want of money, in a country where they used every kind of extortion and tyranny, left me no choice. I was under an absolute necessity of submitting to be thus conveyed to Verceil.

Thus Providence led me whither I would not. Our muleteer was one of the most brutal men; and for an increase of my affliction, I had sent away to Verceil the ecclesiastic who accompanied us, to prevent their surprise at seeing me there, after I had protested against going. That ecclesiastic was very coarsely treated on the road, through the hatred they bore to the French. They made him go part of the way on foot, so that, though he set off the day before me, he arrived there only a few hours sooner than I did. As for the fellow who conducted us, seeing he had only women under his care, he treated us in the most insolent and boorish manner.

We passed through a wood infested with robbers. The muleteer was afraid, and told us, that, if we met any of them on the road, we should be murdered. They spared nobody. Scarcely had he uttered these words, when there appeared four men well armed. They immediately stopped us! The man was exceedingly frightened. I made a light bow of my head, with a smile, for I had no fear, and was so entirely resigned to Providence, that it was all one to die this way or any other; in the sea, or by the hands of robbers. When the dangers were most manifest, then was my faith the strongest, as well as my intrepidity, being unable to wish for anything else than what should fall out, whether to be dashed against the rocks, drowned, or killed in any other way; everything in the will of God being equal to me. The people who used to convey or attend me said that they had never seen a courage like mine; for the most alarming dangers, and the time when death appeared the most certain, were those which seemed to please me the most. Was it not your pleasure, O my God, which guarded me in every imminent danger, and held me back from rolling down the precipice, on the instant of sliding over its dizzy brow? The more easy I was about life, which I bore only because You were pleased to bear it, the more care You took to preserve it. There seemed a mutual emulation between us, on my part to resign it, and on yours to maintain it. The robbers then advanced to the coach; but I had no sooner saluted them, than God made them change their design. Having pushed off one another, as it were, to hinder each of them from doing any harm; they respectfully saluted me, and, with an air of compassion, unusual to such sorts of persons, retired. I was immediately struck to the heart with a full and clear conviction that it was a stroke of Your right hand, who had other designs over me than to suffer me to die by the hand of robbers. It is Your sovereign power which takes away their all from Your devoted lovers; and destroys their lives with all that is of self without pity or sparing anything.

The muleteer, seeing me attended only with two young women, thought he might treat me as he would, perhaps expecting to draw money from me. Instead of taking me to the inn, he brought me to a mill, in which there was a woman. There was but one single room with several beds in it, in which the millers and muleteers lay together. In that chamber they forced me to stay. I told the muleteer I was not a person to lie in such a place and wanted to oblige him to take me to the inn. Nothing of it would he do. I was constrained to go out on foot, at ten o'clock at night, carrying a part of my clothes, and to go a good way more than a quarter of a league in the dark, in a strange place, not knowing the way, crossing one end of the wood infested with robbers, to endeavor to get to the inn. That fellow, seeing us go off from the place, where he had wanted to make me lodge, hooted after us in a very abusive manner. I bore my humiliation cheerfully, but not without feeling it. But the will of God and my resignation to it rendered everything easy to me. We were well received at the inn; and the good people there did the best in their power for our recovery from the fatigue we had undergone. They assured us the place we had left was very dangerous. Next morning we were obliged to return on foot to the carriage for that man would not bring it to us. On the contrary, he gave us a shower of fresh insults. To consummate his base behavior, he sold me to the post, whereby I was forced to go the rest of the way in a post chaise instead of a carriage.

In this equipage I arrived at Alexandria, a frontier town, subject to Spain, on the side of the Milanese. Our driver took us, according to their custom, to the post house. I was exceedingly astonished when I saw the landlady coming out not to receive him, but to oppose his entrance. She had heard there were women in the chaise, and taking us for a different sort of women from what we were, she protested against our coming in. On the other hand, the driver was determined to force his entrance in spite of her. Their dispute rose to such a height, that a great number of the officers of the garrison, with a mob, gathered at the noise, who were surprised at the odd humor of the woman in refusing to lodge us. With earnestness I entreated the post to take us to some other house, but he would not; so obstinately was he bent on carrying his point. He assured the landlady we were persons of honor and piety too; the marks whereof he had seen. At last, by force of pressing entreaties, he obliged her to come to see us. As soon as she had looked at us, she acted as the robbers had done; she relented at once and admitted us. No sooner had I alighted from the chaise, than she said, "Go shut yourselves up in that chamber hard by, and do not stir, that my son may not know you are here; as soon as he knows it he will kill you." She said it with so much force, as did also the servant maid, that, if death had not so many charms for me, I should have been ready to die with fear. The two poor girls with me were under frightful apprehensions. When any stirred, or came to open the door, they thought they were coming to kill them. In short they continued in a dreadful suspense, between life and death, till next day, when we learned that the young man had sworn to kill any woman who lodged at the house. A few days before, an event had fallen out, which had like to have ruined him; a woman of a bad life having there privately murdered a man in some esteem, that had cost the house a heavy fine; and he was afraid of any more such persons coming, not without reason.

Chapter Eighteen

After these adventures and others which it would be tedious to recite, I arrived at Verceil. I went to the inn, where I was badly received. I sent for Father La Combe, who I thought had been already apprised of my coming, by the ecclesiastic whom I had sent before, and who would be of so much service to me. This ecclesiastic was only a little while arrived. How much better on the road should I have fared, if I had him with me! For in that country they look upon ladies, accompanied with ecclesiastics, with veneration, as persons of honor and piety. Father La Combe came in a strange fret at my arrival, God so permitting it. He said that every one would think I was come after him, and that would injure his reputation, which in that country was very high. I had no less pain to go. It was necessity only which had obliged me to submit to such a disagreeable task. The father received me with coolness, and in such a manner as let me sufficiently see his sentiments, and indeed redoubled my pain. I asked him if he required me to return, adding, if he did, "I would go off that moment however oppressed and spent, both with fatigues and fastings." He said that he did not know how the Bishop of Verceil would take my arrival, after he had given over all his expectations of it, and after I had so long, and so obstinately, refused the obliging offers he had made me; since which he no longer expressed any desire to see me.

It seemed to me then as if I were rejected from the face of the earth, without being able to find any refuge, and as if all creatures were combined to crush me. I passed that night without sleep, not knowing what course I should be obliged to take, being persecuted by my enemies, and a subject of disgrace to my friends.

When it was known at the inn, that I was one of Father La Combe's acquaintance, they treated me with greatest respect and kindness. They esteemed him as a saint. The father knew not how to tell the bishop of my arrival, and I felt his pain more than my own. As soon as that Prelate knew that I was arrived, he sent his niece, who took me in her coach, and carried me to her house. These things were only done out of ceremony; and the bishop, not having seen me yet, knew not what to think of a journey so very unexpected, after I had thrice refused, though he sent expresses on purpose to bring me to him. He was out of humor with me. Nevertheless, as he was informed that my design was not to stay at Verceil, but to go to the Marchioness of Prunai's house, he gave orders for me to be well treated. He could not see me till Easter Sunday was over. He officiated all the eve and all that day. After it was over, he came in a chaise to his niece's house to see me. Though he understood French hardly any better than I did Italian, he was very well satisfied with the conversation he had with me. He appeared to have as much favor for me as he had of indifference before.

He conceived as strong a friendship for me as if I had been his sister; and his only pleasure, amid his continual occupations, was to come and pass half an hour with me in speaking of God. He wrote to the Bishop of Marseilles to thank him for having protected me in the persecutions there. He wrote to the Bishop of Grenoble; and he omitted nothing to manifest his regard for me. He now seemed to think alone of finding out means to detain me in his diocese. He would not hear of my going to see the Marchioness of Prunai. On the contrary, he wrote to her to come and settle with me in his diocese. He sent Father La Combe to her, on purpose to exhort her to come; assuring her that he would unite us all to make a congregation. The Marchioness entered into it readily, and so did her daughter. They would have come with Father La Combe, but the Marchioness was sick. The bishop was active and earnest in collecting and establishing a society of us, and found several pious persons and some very devout young ladies, who were all ready to come to join us. But it was not the will of God to fix me thus, but to crucify me yet more.

The fatigue of traveling made me sick. The girl also whom I brought from Grenoble fell sick. Her relations, who were covetous took it in their heads that, if she should die in my service, I would get her to make a will in my favor. They were much mistaken. Far from desiring the property of others, I had given up my own. Her brother, full of this apprehension, came with all speed; the first thing he spoke to her about, although he found her recovered, was to make a will. That made a great noise in Verceil. He wanted her to return with him, but she refused. I advised her to do what her brother desired. He contracted a friendship with some of the officers of the garrison, to whom he told ridiculous stories, as that I wanted to use his sister badly. He pretended she was a person of quality. They gave out what I was still afraid of, that I was come after Father La Combe. They even persecuted him on my account. The bishop was much troubled, but could not remedy it. The friendship he had for me increased every day; because, as he loved God, so he did all those whom he thought desired to love God. As he saw me so much indisposed, he came to see me with assiduity and charity, when at leisure from his occupations. He made me little presents of fruits and other things. His relations were jealous. They said that I was come to ruin him, and to carry off his money into France, which was farthest from my thoughts. The bishop patiently bore these affronts, hoping still to keep me in his diocese, when I should be recovered.

Father La Combe was the bishop's prebend and his confessor. He esteemed him highly. God made use of him to convert several of the officers and soldiers, who, from being men of scandalous lives, became patterns of piety. In that place everything was mixed with crosses, but souls were gained to God. There were some of his friars, who, after his example, were advancing toward perfection. Though I neither understood their language nor they mine, the Lord made us understand each other in what concerned His service. The Rector of the Jesuits took his time, when Father La Combe was gone out of town, to prove me, as he said. He had studied theological matters, which I did not understand. He propounded several questions. The Lord inspired me to answer him in such a manner, that he went away both surprised and satisfied. He could not forbear speaking of it.

The Barnabites of Paris, or rather Father de la Mothe took it in head to try to draw Father La Combe to go and preach at Paris. He wrote to the Father-general about it, because they had no one at Paris to support their house, that their church was deserted; that it was a pity to leave such a man as Father La Combe in a place where he only corrupted his language. It was necessary to make his fine talents appear at Paris, where he himself could not bear the burden of the house, if they did not give him an assistant of such qualifications and experience. Who would not have thought all this to be sincere? The Bishop of Verceil, who was very much a friend of Father-general, having advice thereof, opposed it, and answered that it would be doing him the greatest injury to take from him a man who was so exceedingly useful to him, and at a time when he had the greatest need of him.

The Father-general of the Barnabites would not agree to the request of Father de la Mothe, for fear of offending the Bishop of Verceil. As to me, my indisposition increased. The air, which is there extremely bad, caused me a continual cough, with frequent returns of fever. I grew so much worse that it was thought I could not get over it. The Bishop was afflicted to see it, but, having consulted the physicians, they assured him that the air of the place was mortal to me, whereupon he said to me, "I had rather have you live, though distant from me, than see you die here." He gave up his design of establishing his congregation, for my friend would not settle there without me. The Genoese lady could not easily leave her own city, where she was respected. The Genoese besought her to set up there what the Bishop of Verceil had wanted her to set up. It was a congregation almost like that of Madame de Miramion. When the Bishop had first proposed this, however agreeable it appeared, I had a presentiment that it would not succeed, and that it was not what our Lord required of me, though I submissively yielded to the good proposal, were it only to acknowledge the many special favors of this prelate. I was assured that the Lord would know well how to prevent what He should now require of me. As this good prelate saw he must resign himself to let me go, he said to me, "You were willing to be in the diocese of Geneva, and there they persecuted and rejected you; I, who would gladly have you, cannot keep you." He wrote to Father La Mothe that I should go in the spring, as soon as the weather would permit. He was sorry to be obliged to let me go. Yet he still hoped to have kept Father La Combe, which probably might have been, had not the death of the Father-general given it another turn.

Here it was that I wrote upon the Apocalypse, and that there was given me a greater certainty of all the persecutions of the most faithful servants of God. Here also I was strongly moved to write to Madame De Ch------. I did it with great simplicity; and what I wrote was like the first foundation of what the Lord required of her, having been pleased to make use of me to help to bring her into His ways, being one to whom I am much united, and by her to others.

The Bishop of Verceil's friend, the Father-general of the Barnabites, departed this life. As soon as he was dead, Father La Mothe wrote to the Vicar general who now held his place till another should be elected renewing his request to have Father La Combe as an assistant. The father, hearing that I was obliged on account of my indisposition to return into France, sent an order to Father La Combe to return to Paris, and to accompany me in my journey, as his doing that would exempt their house at Paris, already poor, from the expenses of so long a journey. Father La Combe, who did not penetrate the poison under this fair outside, consented thereto; knowing it was my custom to have some ecclesiastic with me in traveling. Father La Combe went off twelve days before me, in order to transact some business, and to wait for me at the passage over the mountains, as the place where I had most need of an escort. I set off in Lent, the weather then being fine. It was a sorrowful parting to the Bishop. I pitied him; he was so much affected at losing both Father La Combe and me. He caused me to be attended, at his own expense, as far as Turin, giving me a gentleman and one of his ecclesiastics to accompany me.

As soon as the resolution was taken that Father La Combe should accompany me, Father La Mothe reported everywhere "that he had been obliged to do it, to make him return into France." He expatiated on the attachment I had for Father La Combe, pretending to pity me. Upon this everyone said that I ought to put myself under the direction of Father La Mothe. In the meantime he deceitfully palliated the malignity of his heart, writing letters full of esteem to Father La Combe, and some to me of tenderness, "desiring him to bring his dear sister, and to serve her in her infirmities, and in the hardships of so long a journey; that he should be sensibly obliged to him for his care;" with many other things of the like nature.

I could not resolve to depart without going to see my good friend, the Marchioness of Prunai, notwithstanding the difficulty of the roads. I caused myself to be carried, it being scarcely possible to go otherwise on account of the mountains. She was extremely joyful at seeing me arrive. Nothing could be more cordial than what passed between us. It was then that she acknowledged that all I had told her had come to pass. A good ecclesiastic, who lives with her, told me the same. We made ointments and plasters together, and I gave her the secret of my remedies, I encouraged her, and so did Father La Combe, to establish a hospital in that place; which was done while we were there. I contributed my mite to it which has ever been blest to all the hospitals, which have ever been established in reliance on Providence.

I believe I had forgotten to tell, that the Lord had made use of me to establish one near Grenoble, which subsists without any other fund than the supplies of Providence. My enemies made use of that afterward to slander me, saying that I had wasted my children's substance in establishing hospitals, though, far from spending any of their substance, I had even given them my own. All those hospitals have been established only on the fund of divine Providence, which is inexhaustible. But so it has been ordered for my good, that all our Lord has made me to do His glory has ever been turned into crosses for me.

As soon as it was determined that I should come into France, the Lord made known to me, that it was to have greater crosses than I ever had. Father La Combe had the like sense. He encouraged me to resign myself to the divine will, and to become a victim offered freely to new sacrifices. He also wrote to me, "Will it not be a thing very glorious to God, if He should make us serve in that great city, for a spectacle to angels and to men?" I set off then with a spirit of sacrifice, to offer myself up to new kinds of punishments, if pleasing to my dear Lord. All along the road something within me repeated the very words of Saint Paul, "I go bound in the Spirit unto Jerusalem, not knowing the things should befall me there, save that the Holy Ghost witnessed, saying, that bonds and afflictions abide me. But none of these things move me; neither count I my life dear unto myself, so that I might finish my course with joy." (Acts 20: 22,23,24.) I could not forbear to testify it to my most intimate friends, who tried hard to prevail on me to stop, and not to proceed. They were all willing to contribute a share of what they had, for my settlement there, and to prevent my coming to Paris. But I found it my duty to hold on my way, and to sacrifice myself for Him who first sacrificed Himself for me.

At Chamberry we saw Father La Mothe, who was going to the election of a Father-general. Though he affected an appearance of friendship, it was not difficult to discover that his thoughts were different from his words, and that he had conceived dark designs against us. I speak not of his intentions, but to obey the command given me to omit nothing. I shall necessarily be obliged often to speak of him. I could wish with all my heart it were in my power to suppress what I have to say of him. If what he has done respected only myself, I would willingly bury all; but I think I owe it to truth, and to the innocence of Father La Combe, so cruelly oppressed, and grievously crushed so long, by wicked calumnies, by an imprisonment of several years, which in all probability will last as long as life. Though Father La Mothe may appear heavily charged in what I say of him, I protest solemnly, and in the presence of God, that I pass over in silence many of his bad actions.

Chapter Nineteen

Scarcely had I arrived at Paris when I readily discovered the black designs entertained against both Father La Combe and me. Father La Mothe who conducted the whole tragedy, artfully dissembled, according to his custom; flattering me to my face, while he was aiming the keenest wounds behind my back. He and his confederates wanted, for their own interest, to persuade me to go to Montargis (my native place), hoping, thereby, to get the guardianship of my children, and to dispose of both my person and effects. All the persecutions from Father La Mothe and my family have been attended on their part with views of interest; those against Father La Combe have sprung from rage and revenge, because he, as my director, did not oblige me to do what they wanted; as well as out of jealousy. I might enter into a long detail on this, sufficient to convince all the world; but I suppress, to avoid prolixity. I shall only say, that they threatened to deprive me of what little I had reserved to myself. To this I only replied that I would not go to law, that if they were resolved to take from me little I had left (little indeed in comparison of what I had given up) I would surrender it entirely to them; being quite free and willing not only to be poor, but to be even in the very extremity of want in imitation of our Lord Jesus Christ.

I arrived at Paris on Magdalene's eve, 1686, exactly five years after my departure from that city. After Father La Combe arrived, he was soon followed and much applauded. I perceived some jealously in Father La Mothe hereupon, but did not think that matters would be carried so far as they have been. The greater part of the Barnabites of Paris, and its neighborhood, joined against Father La Combe, induced from several causes that particularly related to their order. But all their calumnies and evil attempts were overthrown by the unaffected piety he manifested, and the good which multitudes reaped from his labors.

I had deposited a little sum of money in his hands (with the consent of his superior) to serve for the entrance of a nun. I thought myself obliged in conscience to do it. She had, through my means, quitted the New Catholics. It was that young woman whom I mentioned before, whom the priest of Gex wanted to win over. As she is beautiful, though very prudent, there always continues a cause for fear, when such a one is exposed in the world. La Mothe wanted to have that money, and signified to La Combe that, if he did not make me give it to him for a wall, which he had to rebuild in his convent, he would make him suffer for it. But the latter, who is always upright, answered that he could not in conscience advise me to do anything else, but what I had already resolved, in favor of that young woman. Hence he and the provincial ardently longed to satisfy their desire of revenge. They employed all their thoughts on the means of effecting it.

A very wicked man who was employed for that purpose, wrote defamatory libels, declaring that the propositions of Molinos, which had been current for two year past in France, were the sentiments of Father La Combe. These libels were spread about in the community. Father La Mothe and the provincial, acting as persons well affected to the church, carried them to the official, or judge of the ecclesiastical court, who joined in the dark design. They showed them to the Archbishop, saying, "It was out of their zeal, and that they were exceedingly sorry that one of their fraternity was a heretic, and as such execrable. They also brought me in, but more moderately, saying Father La Combe was almost always at my house, which was false. I could scarcely see him at all except at the confessional, and then for a very short time. Several other things equally false they liberally gave out concerning both of us. They bethought themselves of one thing further likely to favor their scheme. They knew I had been at Marseilles, and thought they had a good foundation for a fresh calumny. They counterfeited a letter from a person at Marseilles (I heard it was from the Bishop) addressed to the Archbishop of Paris, or to his official, in which they wrote the most abominable scandal. Father La Mothe came to try to draw me into his snare, and to make me say, in the presence of the people whom he had brought, that I had been at Marseilles with Father La Combe. "There are," said he, "shocking accounts against you, sent by the Bishop of Marseilles. You have there fallen into great scandal with Father La Combe. There are good witnesses of it." I replied with a smile, "The calumny is well devised; but it would have been proper to know first whether Father La Combe had been at Marseilles, for I do not believe he was ever there in his life. While I was there, Father La Combe was laboring at Verceil." He was confounded and went off, saying, "There are witnesses of its being true." He went immediately to ask Father La Combe if he had not been at Marseilles. He assured him he never had been there. They were struck with disappointment. They then gave out that it was not Marseilles but Seisel. Now this Seisel is a place I have never been at, and there is no bishop there.

Every imaginable device was used to terrify me by threats, forged letters, and by memorials drawn up against me, accusing me of teaching erroneous doctrines, and of living a bad life and urging me to flee the country to escape the consequences of exposure. Failing in all these, at length La Mothe took off the mask, and said to me in the church, before La Combe, "It is now, my sister, that you must think of fleeing, you are charged with crimes of a deep dye." I was not moved in the least, but replied with my usual tranquility, "If I am guilty of such crimes I cannot be too severely punished; wherefore I will not flee or go out of the way. I have made an open profession of dedicating myself to God entirely. If I have done things offensive to Him, whom I would wish both to love, and to cause to be loved by the whole world, even at the expense of my life, I ought by my punishment to be made an example to the world; but if I am innocent, for me to flee is not the way for my innocence to be believed."

Similar attempts were made to ruin Father La Combe. He was grossly misrepresented to the king, and an order procured for his arrest and imprisonment in the Bastile.

Although on his trial he appeared quite innocent, and they could not find anything whereupon to ground a condemnation, yet they made the king believe he was a dangerous man in the article of religion. He was then shut up in a certain fortress of the Bastile for life; but as his enemies heard that the captain in that fortress esteemed him, and treated him kindly, they had him removed into a much worse place. God, who beholds everything, will reward every man according to his works. I know by an interior communication that he is very well content, and fully resigned to God.

La Mothe now endeavored more than ever to induce me to flee, assuring me that, if I went to Montargis, I should be out of all trouble; but that if I did not, I should pay for it. He insisted on my taking himself for my director, to which I could not agree. He decried me wherever he went, and wrote to his brethren to do the same. They sent me very abusive letters, assuring me that, if I did not put myself under his direction, I was undone. I have the letters by me still. One father desired me in this case to make a virtue of necessity. Nay, some advised me to pretend to put myself under his direction, and to deceive him. I abhorred the thought of deceit. I bore everything with the greatest tranquility, without taking any care to justify or defend myself, leaving it entirely to God to order as he should please about me. Herein he was graciously pleased to increase the peace of my soul, while every one seemed to cry against me, and to look on me as an infamous creature, except those few who knew me well by a near union of spirit. At church I heard people behind me exclaim against me, and even some priests say it was necessary to cast me out of the church. I left myself to God without reserve, being quite ready to endure the most rigorous pains and tortures, if such were His will.

I never made any solicitation either for Father La Combe or myself, though charged with that among other things. Willing to owe everything to God, I have no dependence on any creature. I would not have it said that any but God had made Abraham rich. Gen. 14:23. To lose all for Him is my best gain; and to gain all without Him would be my worst loss. Although at this time so general an outcry was raised against me, God did not fail to make use of me to gain many souls to Himself. The more persecution raged against me the more children were given me, on whom the Lord conferred great favors through His handmaid.

One must not judge of the servants of God by what their enemies say of them, nor by their being oppressed under calumnies without any resource. Jesus Christ expired under pangs. God uses the like conduct toward His dearest servants, to render them conformable to His Son, in whom He is always well pleased. But few place that conformity where it ought to be. It is not in voluntary pains or austerities, but in those which are suffered in a submission ever equal to the will of God, in a renunciation of our whole selves, to the end that God may be our all in all, conducting us according to His views, and not our own, which are generally opposite to His. All perfection consists in this entire conformity with Jesus Christ, not in shining things which men esteem. It will only be seen in eternity who are the true friends of God. Nothing pleases Him but Jesus Christ, and that which bears His mark or character.

They were continually pressing me to flee, though the Archbishop had spoken to myself, and bidden me not to leave Paris. But they wanted to give the appearance of criminality both to me and to Father La Combe by my flight. They knew not how to make me fall into the hands of the official. If they accused me of crimes, it must be before other judges. Any other judge would have seen my innocence; the false witnesses would have run the risk of suffering for it. They continually spread stories of horrible crimes; but the official assured me that he had heard no mention of any. He was afraid lest I should retire out of his jurisdiction.

They then made the king believe "that I was a heretic, that I carried on a literary correspondence with Molinos (I, who never knew there was a Molinos in the world, till the Gazette had told me of it) that I had written a dangerous book; and that on those accounts it would be necessary to issue an order to put me in a convent, that they might examine me. I was a dangerous person, it would be proper for me to be locked up, to be allowed no commerce with any one; since I continually held assemblies," which was very false. To support this calumny my handwriting was counterfeited, and a letter was forged as from me, importing, that I had "great designs, but feared that they would prove abortive, through the imprisonment of Father La Combe, for which reason I had left off holding assemblies at my house, being too closely watched; but that I would hold them at the houses of other persons." This forged letter they showed the king, and upon it an order was given for my imprisonment.

This order would have been put in execution two months sooner than it was, had I not fallen very sick. I had inconceivable pains and a fever. Some thought that I had a gathering in my head. The pain I suffered for five weeks made me delirious. I had also a pain in my breast and a violent cough. Twice I received the holy sacrament, as I was thought to be expiring. One of my friends had acquainted Father La Mothe, (not knowing him to have had any hand in F. La Combe's imprisonment) that she had sent me a certificate from the inquisition in Father La Combe's favor, having heard that his own was lost. This answered a very good purpose; for they had made the king believe that he had run away from the inquisition; but this showed the contrary.

Father La Mothe then came to me, when I was in excessive pain, counterfeiting all the affection and tenderness in his power, and telling me "that the affair of Father La Combe was going on very well, that he was just ready to come out of prison with honor, that he was very glad of it. If he had only this certificate, he would soon be delivered. Give me it then," said he, "and he will be immediately released." At first I made a difficulty of doing it. "What! said he, will you be the cause of ruining poor Father La Combe, having it in your power to save him, and cause us that affliction, for want of what you have in your hands." I yielded, ordering it to be brought and given him. But he suppressed it, and gave out that it was lost. It never could be got from him again. The Ambassador from the Court of Turin sent a messenger to me for this certificate, designing the proper use of it to serve Father La Combe. I referred him to Father La Mothe. The messenger went to him and asked him for it. He denied I had given it to him, saying, "Her brain is disordered which makes her imagine it." The man came back to me and told me his answer. The persons in my chamber bore witness that I had given it to him. Yet all signified nothing; it could not be got out of his hands; but on the contrary, he insulted me, and caused others also to do it, though I was so weak that I seemed to be at the very gates of death.

They told me they only waited for my recovery to cast me into prison. He made his brethren believe that I had treated him ill. They wrote to me that it was for my crimes that I suffered; and that I should put myself under the control of Father La Mothe, otherwise I should repent it; that I was mad and ought to be bound; and was a monster of pride, since I would not suffer myself to be conducted by Father La Mothe. Such was my daily feast in the extremity of my pain; deserted of my friends, and oppressed by my enemies; the former being ashamed of me, through the calumnies which were forged and industriously spread; the latter let loose to persecute me; under all which I kept silence, leaving myself to the Lord.

There was not any kind of infamy, error, sorcery, or sacrilege, of which they did not accuse me. As soon as I was able to be carried to the church in a chair, I was told I must speak to the prebend. (It was a snare concerted between Father La Mothe and the Canon at whose house I lodged). I spoke to him with much simplicity, and he approved of what I said. Yet, two days after they gave out that I had uttered many things, and accused many persons; and from hence they procured the banishment of sundry persons with whom they were displeased, persons whom I had never seen or of whom I never heard. They were men of honor. One of them was banished, because he said my little book is a good one. It is remarkable that they say nothing to those who prefixed their approbations, and that, far from condemning the book, it has been reprinted since I have been in prison, and advertisements of it have been posted up at the Archbishop's palace, and all over Paris. In regard to others, when they find faults in their books, they condemn the books and leave the person at liberty; but as for me, my book is approved, sold and spread, while I am kept a prisoner for it.

The same day that those gentlemen were banished, I received a lettre de cachet, or sealed order to repair to the Convent of the Visitation of St. Mary's, in a suburb of Saint Antoine. I received it with a tranquility which surprised the bearer exceedingly. He could not forbear expressing it, having seen the extreme sorrow of those who were only banished. He was so touched with it as to shed tears. And although his order was to carry me off directly, he was not afraid to trust me, but left me all the day, desiring me to repair to Saint Mary's in the evening. On that day many of my friends came to see me, and found me very cheerful, which surprised such of them as knew my case. I could not stand, I was so weak, having the fever every night, it being only a fortnight since I was thought to be expiring. I imagined they would leave me my daughter and maid to serve me.

Chapter Twenty

On January 29, 1688, I went to Saint Mary's. There they let me know I must neither have my daughter nor a maid to serve me, but must be locked up alone in a chamber. Indeed it touched me to my heart when my daughter was taken from me. They would neither allow her to be in that house, nor anybody to bring me any news of her. I was then obliged to sacrifice my daughter, as if she were mine no longer. The people of the house were prepossessed with so frightful an account of me, that they looked at me with horror. For my jailer they singled out a nun, who, they thought, would treat me with the greatest rigor, and they were not mistaken therein.

They asked me who was now my confessor. I named him; but he was seized with such a fright that he denied it; though I could have produced many persons who had seen me at his confessional. So then they said they had caught me in a lie; I was not to be trusted. My acquaintance then said they knew me not, and others were at liberty to invent stories, and say all manner of evil of me. The woman, appointed for my keeper, was gained over by my enemies, to torment me as a heretic, an enthusiast, one crackbrained and a hypocrite. God alone knows what she made me suffer. As she sought to surprise me in my words, I watched them, to be more exact in them; but I fared the worse for it. I made more slips and gave her more advantages over me thereby, beside the trouble in my own mind for it. I then left myself as I was, and resolved, though this woman would bring me to the scaffold, by the false reports she was continually carrying to the prioress, that I would simply resign myself to my lot; so I re-entered into my former condition.

Monsieur Charon the Official, and a Doctor of Sorbonne, came four times to examine me. Our Lord did me the favor which He promised to His apostles, to make me answer much better than if I had studied. Luke 21:14,15. They said to me, if I had explained myself, as I now did, in the book entitled, Short and Easy Method of Prayer, I would not now have been here. My last examination was about a counterfeit letter, which they read and let me see. I told them the hand was no way like mine. They said it was only a copy; they had the original at home. I desired a sight of it, but could not obtain it. I told them I never wrote it, nor did I know the person to whom it was addressed; but they took scarcely any notice of what I said.

After this letter was read, the official turned to me and said, "You see, madam, that after such a letter there was foundation enough for imprisoning you." "Yes, sir," said I, "if I had written it." I showed them its falsehoods and inconsistencies, but all in vain. I was left two months, and treated worse and worse, before either of them came again to see me. Till then I had always some hope that, seeing my innocence, they would do me justice; but now I saw that they did not want to find me innocent, but to make me appear guilty.

The official alone came the next time, and told me, "I must speak no more of the false letter; that it was nothing." "How nothing," said I, "to counterfeit a person's writing, and to make one appear an enemy to the State!" He replied, "We will seek out the author of it." "The author," said I, "is no other than the Scrivener Gautier." He then demanded where the papers were which I wrote on the Scriptures. I told him, "I would give them up when I should be out of prison; but was not willing to tell with whom I had lodged them."

About three or four days before Easter he came again, with the doctor, and a verbal process was drawn up against me for rebelling, in not giving up papers. Copies of my writings were then put into their hands; for I had not the originals. I know not where those who got them from me have put them; but I am firm in the faith that they will all be preserved, in spite of the storm. The prioress asked the official how my affair went. He said, very well, and that I should soon be discharged; this became the common talk; but I had a presentiment of the contrary.

I had an inexpressible satisfaction and joy in suffering, and being a prisoner. The confinement of my body made me better relish the freedom of my mind. Saint Joseph's day was to me a memorable day; for then my state had more of Heaven than of earth beyond what any expression can reach. This was followed, as it were, with a suspension of every favor then enjoyed, a dispensation of new sufferings. I was obliged to sacrifice myself anew, and to drink the very dregs of the bitter draught.

I never had any resentment against my persecutors, though I well knew them, their spirit and their actions. Jesus Christ and the saints saw their persecutors, and at the same time saw that they could have no power except it were given them from above. John 19:11.

Loving the strokes which God gives, one cannot hate the hand which He makes use of to strike with.

A few days after, the official came, and told me he gave me the liberty of the cloister, that is, to go and come in the house. They were now very industrious in urging my daughter to consent to a marriage, which had it taken place, would have been her ruin. To succeed herein, they had placed her with a relation of the gentleman whom they wanted her to marry. All my confidence was in God, that He would not permit it to be accomplished, as the man had no tincture of Christianity, being abandoned both in his principles and morals.

To induce me to give up my daughter they promised me an immediate release from prison and from every charge under which I labored. But if I refused, they threatened me with imprisonment for life and with death on the scaffold. In spite of all their promises and threatening, I persistently refused.

Soon after, the official and doctor came to tell the prioress I must be closely locked up. She represented to them that the chamber I was in, was small, having an opening to the light or air, only on one side, through which the sun shone all the day long, and being the month of July, it must soon cause my death. They paid no regard. She asked why I must be thus closely locked up. They said I had committed horrible things in her house, even within the last month, and had scandalized the nuns. She protested the contrary, and assured them the whole community had received great edification from me, and could not but admire my patience and moderation. But it was all in vain. The poor woman could not refrain from tears, at a statement so remote from the truth.

They then sent for me, and told me I had done base things in the last month. I asked what things? They would not tell me. I said then that I would suffer as long and as much as it should please God; that this affair was begun on forgeries against me, and so continued. That God was witness of everything. The doctor told me, that to take God for a witness in such a thing was a crime. I replied nothing in the world could hinder me from having recourse to God. I was then shut up more closely than at first, until I was absolutely at the point of death, being thrown into a violent fever, and almost stifled with the closeness of the place, and not permitted to have any assistance.

In the time of the ancient law, there were several of the Lord's martyrs who suffered for asserting and trusting in the one true God. In the primitive church of Christ the martyrs shed their blood, for maintaining the truth of Jesus Christ crucified. Now there are martyrs of the Holy Ghost, who suffer for their dependence on Him, for maintaining His reign in souls, and for being victims of the Divine will.

It is this Spirit which is to be poured out on all flesh, as the prophet Joel states. The martyrs of Jesus Christ have been glorious martyrs, He having drunk up the confusion of that martyrdom; but the martyrs of the Holy Spirit are martyrs of reproach and ignominy. The Devil no more exercises his power against their faith or belief, but directly attacks the dominion of the Holy Spirit, opposing His celestial motion in souls, and discharging his hatred on the bodies of those whose minds he cannot hurt. Oh, Holy Spirit, a Spirit of love, let me ever be subjected to Your will, and, as a leaf is moved before the wind, so let me be moved by Your Divine breath. As the impetuous wind breaks all that resists it, so break you all that oppose Your Empire.

Although I have been obliged to describe the procedure of those who persecute me, I have not done it out of resentment, since I love them at my heart, and pray for them, leaving to God the care of defending me, and delivering me out of their hands, without making any movement of my own for it. I have apprehended and believed that God would have me write everything sincerely, that His name may be glorified; that the things done in secret against His servants should one day be published on the housetops; for the more they strive to conceal them from the eyes of men, the more will God in His own time make them all manifest.

August 22, 1688, it was thought I was about coming out of prison, and everything seemed to tend toward it. But the Lord gave me a sense that, far from being willing to deliver me they were only laying new snares to ruin me more effectually, and to make Father La Mothe known to the king, and esteemed by him. On the day mentioned, which was my birthday, being forty years of age, I awaked under an impression of Jesus Christ in an agony, seeing the counsel of the Jews against Him. I knew that none but God could deliver me out of prison, and I was satisfied that He would do it one day by His own right hand, though ignorant of the manner, and leaving it wholly to Himself.

In the order of Divine Providence my case was laid before Madame de Maintenon, who became deeply interested in the account given her of my sufferings, and at length procured my release. A few days afterward I had my first interview with the Abbe Fenelon.

Coming out of Saint Mary's I retired into the community of Mad. Miramion, where I kept my bed of a fever three months, and had an imposthume in my eye. Yet at this time I was accused of going continually out, holding suspected assemblies, together with other groundless falsehoods. In this house my daughter was married to Mons. L. Nicholas Fouquet, Count de Vaux. I removed to my daughter's house, and on account of her extreme youth, lived with her two years and an half. Even there my enemies were ever forging one thing after another against me. I then wanted to retire quite secretly, to the house of the Benedictines at Montargis, (my native place) but it was discovered, and both friends and enemies jointly prevented it.

The family in which my daughter was married being of the number of Abbe Fenelon's friends, I had the opportunity of often seeing him at our house. We had some conversations on the subject of a spiritual life, in which he made several objections to my experiences therein. I answered them with my usual simplicity, which, as I found, gained upon him. As the affair of Molinos at that time made a great noise, the plainest things were distrusted, and the terms used by mystic writers exploded. But I so clearly expounded everything to him, and so fully solved all his objections, that no one more fully imbibed my sentiments than he; which has since laid the foundation of that persecution he has suffered. His answers to the Bishop of Meaux evidently show this to all who have read them.

I now took a little private house, to follow the inclination I had for retirement; where I sometimes had the pleasure of seeing my family and a few particular friends. Certain young ladies of Saint Cyr. having informed Mad. Maintenon, that they found in my conversation something which attracted them to God, she encouraged me to continue my instructions to them. By the fine change in some of them with whom before she had not been well pleased, she found she had no reason to repent of it.

She then treated me with much respect; and for three years after, while this lasted, I received from her every mark of esteem and confidence. But that very thing afterward drew on me the most severe persecution. The free entrance I had into the house, and the confidence which some young ladies of the Court, distinguished for their rank and piety, placed in me, gave no small uneasiness to the people who had persecuted me. The directors took umbrage at it, and under pretext of the troubles I had some years before, they engaged the Bishop of Chartres, Superior of Saint Cyr, to present to Mad. Maintenon that, by my particular conduct, I troubled the order of the house; that the young women in it were so attached to me, and to what I said to them, that they no longer hearkened to their superiors. I then went no more to Saint Cyr. I answered the young ladies who wrote to me, only by letters unsealed, which passed through the hands of Mad. Maintenon.

Soon after I fell sick. The physicians, after trying in vain the usual method of cure, ordered me to repair to the waters of Bourbon. My servant had been induced to give me some poison. After taking it, I suffered such exquisite pains that, without speedy succor, I should have died in a few hours. The man immediately ran away, and I have never seen him since. When I was at Bourbon, the waters which I threw up burned like spirits of wine. I had no thought of being poisoned, till the physicians of Bourbon assured me of it. The waters had but little effect. I suffered from it for above seven years.

God kept me in such a disposition of sacrifice, that I was quite resigned to suffer everything, and to receive from His hand all that might befall me, since for me to offer in any way to vindicate myself, would be only beating the air. When the Lord is willing to make any one suffer, He permits even the most virtuous people to be readily blinded toward them; and I may confess that the persecution of the wicked is but little, when compared with that of the servants of the church, deceived and animated with a zeal which they think right. Many of these were now, by the artifices made use of, greatly imposed on in regard to me. I was represented to them in an odious light, as a strange creature. Since, therefore, I must, O my Lord, be conformable to

You, to please You; I set more value on my humiliation, and on seeing myself condemned of everybody, than if I saw myself on the summit of honor in the world. How often have I said, even in the bitterness of my heart, that I should be more afraid of one reproach of my conscience, than of the outcry and condemnation of all men!

Chapter Twenty-one

At this time I had my first acquaintance with the Bishop of Meaux. I was introduced by an intimate friend, the Duke of Chevreuse. I gave him the foregoing history of my life, and he confessed, that he had found therein such an unction as he had rarely done in other books, and that he had spent three days in reading it, with an impression of the presence of God on his mind all that time.

I proposed to the bishop to examine all my writings, which he took four or five months to do, and then advanced all his objections; to which I gave answers. From his unacquaintance with the interior paths, I could not clear up all the difficulties which he found in them.

He admitted that looking into the ecclesiastical histories for ages past, we may see that God has sometimes made use of laymen, and of women to instruct, edify, and help souls in their progress to perfection. I think one of the reasons of God's acting thus, is that glory may not be ascribed to any, but to Himself alone. For this purpose, He has chosen the weak things of this world, to confound such as are mighty. 1 Cor. 1:27.

Jealous of the attributes which men pay to other men, which are due only to Himself, He has made a paradox of such persons, that He alone may have the glory of His own works. I pray God, with my whole heart, sooner to crush me utterly, with the most dreadful destruction, than to suffer me to take the least honor to myself, of anything which He has been pleased to do by me for the good of others. I am only a poor nothing. God is all-powerful. He delights to operate, and exercise His power by mere nothings.

The first time that I wrote a history of myself, it was very short. In it I had particularized my faults and sins, and said little of the favors of God. I was ordered to burn it, to write another, and in it to omit nothing anyway remarkable that had befallen me. I did it. It is a crime to publish secrets of the King; but it is a good thing to declare the favors of the Lord our God, and to magnify His mercies.

As the outcry against me became more violent, and Madame Maintenon was moved to declare against me, I sent to her through the Duke of Beauvilliers, requesting the appointment of proper persons to examine my life and doctrines, offering to retire into any prison until fully exculpated. My proposal was rejected. In the meantime, one of my most intimate friends and supporters, Mons. Fouquet, was called away by death. I felt his loss very deeply, but rejoiced in his felicity. He was a true servant of God.

Determined to retire out of the way of giving offense to any, I wrote to some of my friends, and bade them a last farewell; not knowing whether I were to be carried off by the indisposition which I then had, which had been a constant fever for forty days past, or to recover from it.

Referring to the Countess of G. and the Duchess of M., I wrote, "When these ladies and others were in the vanities of the world, when they patched and painted, and some of them were in the way to ruin their families by gaming and profusion of expense in dress, nobody arose to say anything against it; they were quietly suffered to do it. But when they have broken off from all this, then they cry out against me, as if I had ruined them. Had I drawn them from piety into luxury, they would not make such an outcry. The Duchess of M. at her giving herself up to God, thought herself obliged to quit the court, which was to her like a dangerous rock, in order to bestow her time on the education of her children and the care of her family, which, till then, she had neglected. I beseech you, therefore, to gather all the memorials you can against me; if I am found guilty of the things they accuse me of, I ought to be punished more than any other, since God has brought me to know Him and love Him, and I am well assured that there is no communion between Christ and Belial."

I sent them my two little printed books, with my commentaries on the Holy Scriptures. I also, by their order, wrote a work to facilitate their examination, and to spare them as much time and trouble as I could, which was to collect a great number of passages out of approved writers, which showed the conformity of my writings with those used by the holy penmen. I caused them to be transcribed by the quire, as I had written them, in order to send them to the three commissioners. I also, as occasion presented, cleared up the dubious and obscure places. I had written them at a time when the affairs of Molinos had not broken out, I used the less precaution in expressing my thoughts, not imagining that they would ever be turned into an evil sense. This work was entitled, 'The Justifications.' It was composed in fifty days, and appeared to be very sufficient to clear up the matter. But the Bishop of Meaux would never suffer it to be read.

After all the examinations, and making nothing out against me, who would not have thought but they would have left me to rest in peace? Quite otherwise, the more my innocence appeared, the more did they, who had undertaken to render me criminal, put every spring in motion to effect it. I offered the Bishop of Meaux to go to spend some time in any community within his diocese, that he might be better acquainted with me. He proposed to me that of Saint Mary de Meaux, which I accepted; but in going in the depth of winter I had like to have perished in the snow, being stopped four hours, the coach having entered into it, and being almost buried in it, in a deep hollow. I was taken out at the door with one maid. We sat upon the snow, resigned to the mercy of God, and expected nothing but death. I never had more tranquility of mind, though chilled and soaked with the snow, which melted on us. Occasions like these are such as show whether we are perfectly resigned to God or not. This poor girl and I were easy in our minds, in a state of entire resignation, though sure of dying if we passed the night there, and seeing no likelihood of anyone coming to our succor. At length some wagoners came up, who with difficulty drew us through the snow.

The bishop, when he heard of it, was astonished, and had no little self-complacency to think that I had thus risked my life to obey him so punctually. Yet afterward he denounced it as artifice and hypocrisy.

There were times indeed when I found nature overcharged; but the love of God and His grace rendered sweet to me the very worst of bitters. His invisible hand supported me; else I had sunk under so many probations. Sometimes I said to myself, "All your waves and your billows are gone over me," (Psalm 42:7). "You have bent your bow and set me as a mark for the arrow; you have caused all the arrows of your quiver to enter into my veins" (Lamentations 3:12,13). It seemed to me as if everyone thought he was in the right to treat me ill, and rendered service to God in doing it. I then comprehended that it was the very manner in which Jesus Christ suffered. He was numbered with the transgressors, (Mark 15:28). He was condemned by the sovereign pontiff, chief priests, doctors of the law, and judges deputed by the Romans, who valued themselves on doing justice. Happy they who by suffering for the will of God under all the like circumstances, have so near a relation to the sufferings of Jesus Christ!

For six weeks after my arrival at Meaux, I was in a continual fever, nor had I recovered from my indisposition, when I was waited on by the bishop, who would fain have compelled me to give it under my hand, that I did not believe the Word incarnate, (or Christ manifest in the flesh). I answered him, that "through the grace of God, I know how to suffer, even to death, but not how to sign such a falsehood." Several of the nuns who overheard this conversation, and perceiving the sentiments of the bishop, they joined with the Prioress, in giving a testimonial, not only of my good conduct, but of their belief in the soundness of my faith.

The bishop some days after, brought me a confession of faith, and a request to submit my books to the church, that I may sign it, promising to give me a certificate, which he had prepared. On my delivering my submission signed, he, notwithstanding his promise, refused to give the certificate. Some time after, he endeavored to make me sign his pastoral letter, and acknowledge that I had fallen into those errors, which he there lays to my charge, and made many demands of me of the like absurd and unreasonable nature, threatening me with those persecutions I afterward endured, in case of noncompliance. However, I continued resolute in refusing to put my name to falsehoods. At length, after I had remained about six months at Meaux, he gave me the certificate. Finding Mad. Maintenon disapproved of the certificate he had granted, he wanted to give me another in place of it. My refusal to deliver up the first certificate enraged him, and as I understood they intended to push matters with the utmost violence, "I thought that although I were resigned to whatever might fall out, yet I ought to take prudent measures to avoid the threatening storm." Many places of retreat were offered me; but I was not free in my mind to accept of any, nor to embarrass anybody, nor involve in trouble my friends and my family, to whom they might attribute my escape. I took the resolution of continuing in Paris, of living there in some private place with my maids, who were trusty and sure, and to hide myself from the view of the world. I continued thus for five or six months. I passed the day alone in reading, in praying to God, and in working. But the December 27, 1695, I was arrested, though exceedingly indisposed at that time, and conducted to Vincennes. I was three days in the custody of Mons. des Grez, who had arrested me; because the king would not consent to my being put into prison; saying several times over, that a convent was sufficient. They deceived him by still stronger calumnies. They painted me in his eyes, in colors so black, that they made him scruple his goodness and equity. He then consented to my being taken to Vincennes.

I shall not speak of that long persecution, which has made so much noise, for a series of ten years' imprisonments, in all sorts of prisons, and of a banishment almost as long, and not yet ended, through crosses, calumnies, and all imaginable sorts of sufferings. There are facts too odious on the part of divers persons, which charity induces me to cover.

I have borne long and sore languishings, and oppressive and painful maladies without relief. I have been also inwardly under great desolations for several months, in such sort that I could only say these words, "My God, my God, why have you forsaken me!" All creatures seemed to be against me. I then put myself on the side of God, against myself.

Perhaps some will be surprised at my refusing to give the details of the greatest and strongest crosses of my life, after I have related those which were less. I thought it proper to tell something of the crosses of my youth, to show the crucifying conduct which God held over me. I thought myself obliged to relate certain facts, to manifest their falsehood, the conduct of those by whom they had passed, and the authors of those persecutions of which I have been only the accidental object, as I was only persecuted, in order to involve therein persons of great merit; whom, being out of their reach by themselves, they, therefore, could not personally attack, but by confounding their affairs with mine. I thought I owed this to religion, piety, my friends, my family, and myself.

While I was prisoner at Vincennes, and Monsieur De La Reine examined me, I passed my time in great peace, content to pass the rest of my life there, if such were the will of God. I sang songs of joy, which the maid who served me learned by heart, as fast as I made them. We together sang your praises, O my God! The stones of my prison looked in my eyes like rubies; I esteemed them more than all the gaudy brilliancies of a vain world. My heart was full of that joy which You give to them who love You, in the midst of their greatest crosses. When things were carried to the greatest extremities, being then in the Bastile, I said, "O, my God, if you are pleased to render me a new spectacle to men and angels, Your holy will be done!"

DECEMBER, 1709.

Here she left off her narrative, though she lived a retired life above seven years after this date. What she had written being only done in obedience to the commands of her director. She died June 9, 1717, at Blois, in her seventieth year.

METHOD OF PRAYER
 catch

Preface

    This little treatise, conceived in great simplicity, was not originally intended for publication. It was written for a few individuals, who were desirous to love God with their whole heart, some of whom, because of the profit they received in reading the manuscript, wished to obtain copies of it; and on this account alone, it was committed to the press. It still remains in its original simplicity, without any censure on the various divine leadings of others. We submit the whole to the judgment of those who are skilled and experienced in divine matters; requesting them, however, not to decide without first entering into the main design of the Author, which is to induce the world to love God and to serve Him with comfort and success, in a simple and easy manner, adapted to those who are unqualified for learned and deep researches, and are, indeed, incapable of anything but a hearty desire to be truly devoted to God. An unprejudiced reader may find, hidden under the most common expressions, a secret unction, which will excite him to seek after that Sovereign Good, whom all should wish to enjoy. In speaking of the attainment of perfection, the word facility is used, because God is indeed found with facility when we seek Him within ourselves. But, in contradiction to this, some perhaps may urge that passage in the gospel of John, "You will seek me, and will not find me" (John 7:34). This apparent difficulty, however, is removed by another passage, where He, who cannot contradict Himself, has said to all, "Seek and you will find" (Matthew 7:7). It is true, indeed, that he who would seek God, and is yet unwilling to forsake his sins, shall not find Him, because he seeks not aright; and therefore it is added, "You will die in your sins." On the other hand, he who diligently seeks God in his heart, and that he may draw near unto Him sincerely forsakes sin, shall infallibly find Him. A life of devotion appears so formidable, and the Spirit of Prayer of such difficult attainment, that most persons are discouraged from taking a single step towards it. The difficulties inseparable from all great undertakings are, indeed, either nobly surmounted, or left to subsist in all their terrors, just as success is the object of despair or hope. I have therefore endeavored to show the facility of the method proposed in this treatise, the great advantages to be derived from it, and the certainty of their attainment by those that faithfully persevere. Oh, were we once truly sensible of the goodness of God toward His poor creatures, and of His infinite desire to communicate Himself unto them, we would not allow imaginary difficulties to affright us, nor despair of obtaining that good which He is so earnest to bestow. "He, that spared not his own son, but delivered him up for us all; how shall he not, with him, also freely give us all things" (Romans 8:32). But we want courage and perseverance; we have both to a high degree in our temporal concerns, but want them in "the one thing needful" (Luke 10:42). If any think that God is not easily to be found in this way of Simple Love and Pure Adherence, let them not, on my testimony, alter their opinion, but rather make trial of it, and their own experience will convince them that the reality far exceeds all my representations of it. Beloved reader, peruse this little treatise with a humble, sincere and candid spirit, and not with an inclination to criticize, and you will not fail to reap some degree of profit from it. It was written with a hearty desire that you might wholly devote yourself to God; receive it, then, with a like desire for your own perfection. For nothing more is intended by it than to invite the simple and childlike to approach their Father, who delights in the humble confidence of His children, and is grieved at the smallest instance of their diffidence or distrust. With a sincere desire, therefore, to forsake sin, seek nothing from the unpretending method here proposed but the love of God, and you shall undoubtedly obtain it. "Without setting up our opinions above those of others, we mean only, with truth and candor, to declare, from our own experience and the experience of others, the happy effects produced by simply following our Lord. As this treatise was intended only to instruct in Prayer, there are many things which we respect and esteem, totally omitted, as not immediately relative to our main subject. It is, however, certain, that nothing will be found herein to offend, provided it be read in the spirit with which it was written; and it is still more certain, that those who in right earnest make trial of the way, will find we have written the Truth. It is You alone, Oh Holy Jesus, who loves simplicity and innocence, "and whose delight is to dwell with the children of men" (Proverbs 7:3), with those who are, indeed, willing to become "little children," it is You alone, who can render this little work of any value by imprinting it on the hearts of all who read it, and leading them to seek You within themselves, where You repose as in the manger, waiting to receive proofs of their love, and to give them testimony of Yours. Yet alas, they may still lose these unspeakable advantages by their negligence and insensibility. But it belongs to You, the Uncreated Love, Your silent and eternal word. It belongs to You to awaken, attract, and convert; to make Yourself be heard, tasted, and beloved. I know You can do it, and I trust You will do it by this humble work which belongs entirely to You, proceeds wholly from You, and tends only to You. And, oh most Gracious and adorable Savior, to You be all the glory!

Chapter One

What a dreadful delusion has prevailed over the greater part of mankind, in supposing that they are not called to a state of prayer' whereas all are capable of prayer, and are called to it, as all are called to and are capable of salvation. Prayer is the application of the heart to God, and the internal exercise of love. Paul has enjoined us to "pray without ceasing" (1 Thessalonians 5:17), and our Lord says unto you all, "watch and pray" (Mark 10:33, 37), all therefore may, and all ought to practice prayer. I grant that meditation is attainable but by few, for few are capable of it, and therefore, my beloved brethren who are athirst for salvation, meditative prayer is not the prayer which God requires of you, nor which we would recommend. Let all pray that we should be one by prayer, as we should live by love "counsel you to buy of me gold tried in the fire, that you may be rich," this is much more easily obtained than we can conceive, "Come, all you that are athirst, to these living waters," nor lose your precious moments in "hewing out cisterns, broken cisterns that will hold no water" (John 7:37, Jeremiah 2:13).

Come, you famished souls, who find naught whereon to feed, come, and you shall be fully satisfied! Come, you poor afflicted ones, who groan beneath your load of wretchedness and pain, and you shall find ease and comfort. Come, you sick, to your Physician, and be not fearful of approaching Him because you are filled with diseases; expose them to His view and they shall be healed!

Children, draw near to your Father, and He will embrace you in the arms of love! Come, you poor, stray, wandering sheep, return to your Shepherd! Come, sinners, to your Savior! Come, you dull, ignorant, and illiterate, you who think yourselves the most incapable of prayer. You are more peculiarly called and adapted thereto. Let all without exception come, for Jesus Christ has called all. Yet let not those come who are without a heart; they are not asked; for there must be a heart, that there may be love. But who is without a heart? O come, then, give this heart to God; and here learn how to make the donation. All who are desirous of prayer may easily pray, enabled by those ordinary graces and gifts of the Holy Spirit which are common to all men. Prayer is the guide to perfection and the sovereign good; it delivers us from every vice, and obtains us every virtue; for the one great means to become perfect is to walk in the presence of God. He Himself has said, "walk in my presence and be you perfect" (Genesis 17:1). It is by prayer alone, that we are brought into this presence, and maintained in it without interruption. You must then learn a species of prayer, which may be exercised at all times; which does not obstruct outward employments; and which may be equally practiced by princes, kings, prelates, priests and magistrates, soldiers and children, tradesmen, laborers, women and sick persons. It cannot, therefore, be the prayer of the head, but of the heart; not a prayer of the understanding alone, which is so limited in its operations that it can have but one object at one time; but the prayer of the heart is not interrupted by the exercises of reason. Indeed, nothing can interrupt this prayer, but irregular and disordered affections. And when once we have tasted of God, and the sweetness of His love, we shall find it impossible to relish aught but Himself. Nothing is so easily obtained as the possession and enjoyment of God, for "in Him we live, move, and have our being;" and He is more desirous to give Himself into us, than we can be to receive Him. All consists in the manner of seeking Him, and to seek aright, is easier and more natural to us than breathing. Though you think yourselves ever so stupid, dull, and incapable of sublime attainments, yet, by prayer, you may live in God Himself with less difficulty or interruption than you live in the vital air. Will it not then be highly sinful to neglect prayer? But this I trust you will not, when you have learnt the method, which is exceedingly easy.

Chapter Two

There are two ways of introducing a soul into prayer, which should for some time be pursued; the one is Meditation, the other is Reading accompanied with Meditation. Meditative Reading is the choosing some important practical or speculative truth, always preferring the practical, and proceeding as follows. Whatever truth you have chosen, read only a small portion of it, endeavoring to taste and digest it, to extract the essence and substance thereof, and proceed no farther while any savor or relish remains in the passage. When this subsides, take up your book again and proceed as before, seldom reading more than half a page at a time, for it is not the quantity that is read, but the manner of reading, that yields us profit. Those who read fast reap no more advantage than a bee would by only skimming over the surface of the flower, instead of waiting to penetrate into it and extract its sweets. Much reading is rather for scholastic subjects than divine truths. Indeed, to receive real profit from spiritual books, we must read as I have described; and I am certain, if that method were pursued, we should become gradually habituated to and more fully disposed for prayer. Meditation, which is the other method, is to be practiced at an appropriate season, and not in the time of reading. I believe the best manner of meditating is as follows. When, by an act of lively faith, you are placed in the presence of God, recollect some truth wherein there is substance and food; pause gently and sweetly thereon, not to employ the reason, but merely to calm and fix the mind. For you must observe, that your principal exercise should ever be the presence of God; your subject, therefore, should rather serve to stay the mind, than exercise the understanding. From this procedure, it will necessarily follow, that the lively faith in God immediately present in our inmost soul will produce an eager and vehement pressing inwardly into ourselves, and a restraining all our senses from wandering abroad. This serves to extricate us speedily from numberless distractions, to remove us far from external objects, and to bring us nigh unto our God, who is only to be found in our inmost centre, which is the Holy of Holies wherein He dwells. He has even promised "to come and make his abode with him that does his will" (John 14:23). Saint Augustine accuses himself of wasting his time, by not having from the first sought God in this manner of prayer. When we are thus fully introverted, and warmly penetrated throughout with a living sense of the Divine Presence; when the senses are all recollected, and withdrawn from the circumference to the centre, and the soul is sweetly and silently employed on the truths we have read, not in reasoning, but in feeding thereon, and in animating the will by affection, rather than fatiguing the understanding by study; when the affections are in this state, however difficult it may appear at first, it is, as I shall hereafter show, easily attainable. We must allow them sweetly to repose, and peacefully to drink in that of which they have tasted. For as a person may enjoy the flavor of the finest, yet receive no nourishment from it, if he does not cease the action and swallow the food, he will receive no nourishment. So, when our affections are enkindled, if we endeavor to stir them up yet more, we extinguish their flame, and the soul is deprived of its nourishment. We should, therefore, in stillness and repose, with respect, confidence and love, swallow the blessed food of which we have tasted. This method is, indeed, highly necessary, and will advance the soul farther in a short time, than any other in course of years. I have mentioned that our direct and principal exercise should consist in the contemplation of the Divine Presence. We should be also exceedingly watchful and diligent in recalling our dissipated senses, as the most easy method of overcoming distractions; for a direct contest and opposition only serves to irritate and augment them; whereas, by sinking down under a sense and perception of a present God, and by simply turning inwards, we wage insensibly a very advantageous, though indirect war with them. It is proper here to caution beginners against wandering from truth to truth, and from subject to subject. The right way to penetrate every divine truth, to enjoy its full relish, and to imprint it on the heart, is dwelling on it while its savor continues. Though recollection is difficult in the beginning, from the habit the soul has acquired of being always from home; yet, when by the violence it hath done itself, it becomes a little accustomed to it, it will soon be rendered perfectly easy, and become delightful. Such is the experimental taste and sense of His Presence, and such the efficacy of those graces, which that God bestows, Whose one will towards His creatures is to communicate Himself unto them!

Chapter Three

Those who have not learnt to read, are not, on that account, excluded from prayer; for the great book which teaches all things, and which is legible as well internally as externally, is Jesus Christ Himself. The method they should practice is this. They should first learn this fundamental truth, that "the kingdom of God is within them" (Luke 17:21), and that it is there, only it must be sought. It is as incumbent on the clergy to instruct their parishioners in prayer as in their catechism. It is true, they tell them the end of their creation; but should they not also give them sufficient instructions how they may attain it. They should be taught to begin by an act of profound adoration and abasement before God; and closing the corporeal eyes, endeavor to open those of the soul. They should then collect themselves inwardly, and, by a lively faith in God, as dwelling within them, pierce into the Divine Presence; not suffering the senses to wander abroad, but withholding them as much as may be in due subjection. They should then repeat the Lord's prayer in their native tongue, pondering a little upon the meaning of the words, and the infinite willingness of that God Who dwells within them, to become, indeed, their Father. In this state let them pour out their wants before Him; and when they have pronounced the endearing word, Father, remain a few moments in a respectful silence, waiting to have the will of this their heavenly Father made manifest unto them.

Again, beholding themselves in the state of a feeble child, sorely bruised by repeated falls, and defiled in the mire, destitute of strength to keep up, or of power to cleanse himself, they should lay their deplorable situation open to their Father's view in humble confusion; now sighing out a few words of love and plaintive sorrow, and again sinking into profound silence before Him. Then, continuing the Lord's prayer, let them beseech this King of Glory to reign in them, yielding to His love the just claim He has over them, and resigning up themselves wholly to His divine government. If they feel an inclination to peace and silence, let them discontinue the words of the prayer so long as this sensation holds; and when it subsides, go on with the second petition, "Your will be done on earth, as it is in heaven" upon which these humble supplicants must beseech God to accomplish, in them, and by them, all His will; and must place their hearts and freedom into His hands, to be disposed of as He pleases. And finding that the best employment of the will is to love, they should desire to love God with all their strength, and implore Him for His pure love; but all this sweetly and peacefully. Continue like this with the rest of the prayer, in which the clergy may instruct them. But they should not overburden themselves with frequent repetitions of set forms or studied prayers (Matthew 6:7); for the Lord's prayer, once repeated as I have just described, will produce abundant fruit.

At other times they should place themselves as sheep before their Shepherd, looking up to Him for their true substantial food. "Oh Divine Shepherd, You feed Your flock with Yourself, and are, indeed, their daily nourishment!" They may also represent unto Him the necessities of their families, but all upon this principle, and in this one great view of faith, that God is within them. The ideas we form of the Divine Being fall infinitely short of what He is, but a lively faith in His presence is sufficient, for we must not form any image of the Deity, though we may of the Second Person in the ever blessed Trinity, beholding Him in the various states of His Incarnation, from His birth to His crucifixion, or in some other state or mystery, provided the soul always seeks for those views in its inmost ground or centre. Again, we may look to Him as our Physician, and present to His healing influence all our maladies; but always without violence or perturbation, and from time to time with pauses of silence, that being intermingled with the action, the silence may be gradually extended, and our own exertion lessened; till at length, by continually yielding to God's operations, they gain the complete ascendancy; as shall be hereafter explained. When the Divine Presence is granted us, and we gradually relish silence and repose, this experimental feeling and taste of the Presence of God introduces the soul into the second degree of prayer, which, by proceeding in the manner I have described, is attainable as well by the illiterate as the learned. Some favored souls, indeed, are indulged with it even from the beginning.

Chapter Four

Some call the second degree of prayer, "The Prayer of Contemplation," "The Prayer of Faith and Stillness," and others call it, "The Prayer of Simplicity." I shall here use this latter as being more just than any of the former, which imply a much more exalted state of prayer than that I am now treating of. When the soul has been for some time exercised in the way I have mentioned, it finds that it is gradually enabled to approach God with facility; recollection is attended with much less difficulty; and that prayer becomes easy, sweet and delightful; it knows that this is the true way of finding God; and feels His name is as ointment poured forth. But the method must now be altered, and that which, I prescribe, followed with courage and fidelity, without being disturbed at the difficulties we may encounter therein. First, as soon as the soul by faith places itself in the Presence of God, and becomes recollected before Him, let it remain thus for a little time in a profound and respectful silence. But if at the beginning in forming the act of faith, it feels some little pleasing sense of the Divine Presence; let it remain there without being troubled for a subject, and proceed no farther, but carefully cherish this sensation while it continues. As soon as it abates, the will may be excited by some tender affection; and if by the first moving thereof, it finds itself reinstated in sweet peace, let it there remain. The smothered fire must be gently fanned; but as soon as it is kindled, we must cease that effort, lest we extinguish it by our own activity. I would warmly recommend it to all, never to finish prayer, without remaining some little time after in a respectful silence. It is also of the greatest importance for the soul to go to prayer with courage, and such a pure and disinterested love, as seeks nothing from God, but the ability to please Him, and to do His will. For a servant who only proportions his diligence to his hope of reward, renders himself unworthy of all reward. Go then to prayer, not that you may enjoy spiritual delights, but that you may be either full or empty, just as it pleases God this will preserve you in an evenness of spirit, in desertion as well as in consolation, and prevent your being surprised at aridity or the apparent repulses of God.

Chapter Five

Though God has no other desire than to impart Himself to the loving soul that seeks Him, yet He frequently conceals Himself that the soul may be roused from sloth, and impelled to seek Him with fidelity and love. But with what abundant goodness does He recompense the faithfulness of His beloved. And how sweetly are these apparent withdrawings of Himself succeeded by the consoling caresses of love?

At these seasons we are apt to believe, either that it proves our fidelity, and evinces a greater ardor of affection, to seek Him by an exertion of our own strength and activity; or, that this exertion will induce Him the more speedily to revisit us. No, no, my dear souls, believe me, this is not the right procedure in this degree of prayer; with patient love, with self-abasement and humiliation, with the reiterated breathings of an ardent but peaceful affection, and with silence full of the most profound respect, you must wait the return of the Beloved. Thus only you will demonstrate that it is Himself alone, and His good pleasure, that you seek; and not the selfish delights of your own sensations. Hence it is said, "Be not impatient in the time of dryness and obscurity; suffer the suspension and delays of the consolations of God; cleave unto him, and wait upon him, patiently, that your life may increase and be renewed." (Ecclesiastes 2:2-3)

Be you, therefore, patient in prayer, though, during life, you can do nothing but wait the return of the Beloved, in deep humiliation, calm contentment, and patient resignation to His will. And yet how this most excellent prayer may be intermingled with the sighings of plaintive love! This conduct, indeed, is most pleasing to the heart of Jesus; and, above all others, will, as it were, compel Him to return.

Chapter Six

We should now begin to abandon and give up our whole existence unto God, from the strong and positive conviction, that the occurrence of every moment is agreeable to His immediate will and permission, and just such as our state requires. This conviction will make us resigned in all things; and accept of all that happens, not as from the creature, but as from God Himself. But I conjure you, my dearly beloved, who sincerely wish to give up yourselves to God, that after you have made the donation, you will not snatch yourselves back again. Remember, a gift once presented, is no longer at the disposal of the donor. Abandonment is a matter of the greatest importance in our process; it is the key to the inner court; so that whosoever knows truly how to abandon himself, soon becomes perfect. We must, therefore, continue steadfast and immovable therein, nor listen to the voice of natural reason. Great faith produces great abandonment. We must confide in God, "hoping against hope." (Romans 4:18) Abandonment is the casting off all selfish care, that we may be altogether at the Divine Disposal. All Christians are exhorted to this resignation; for it is said to all, "Be not anxious for tomorrow; for your Heavenly Father knows all that is necessary for you." (Matthew 20:25) "In all your ways acknowledge him, and he shall direct your paths." (Proverbs 3:6) "Commit your ways unto the Lord, and your thoughts shall be established." (Proverbs 16:3) "Commit your ways unto the Lord, and he himself will bring it to pass." (Psalm 36:5) Our abandonment then should be as fully applied to external as internal things, giving up all our concerns into the hands of God, forgetting ourselves, and thinking only of Him; by which the heart will remain always disengaged, free, and at peace. It is practiced by continually losing our own will in the will of God; by renouncing every particular inclination as soon as it arises, however good it may appear, that we may stand in indifference with respect to ourselves, and only will that which God from eternity has willed; by being resigned in all things, whether for soul or body, whether for time or eternity; by leaving what is past in oblivion, what is to come to providence, and devoting the present moment to God. This brings God's eternal order, and is as infallible a declaration to us of His will as it is inevitable and common to all; by attributing nothing that befalls us to the creature, but regarding all things in God, and looking upon all, excepting only our sins, as infallibly proceeding from Him. Surrender yourselves, then, to be led and disposed of just as God pleases, with respect both to your outward and inward state.

Chapter Seven

Be patient under all the sufferings which God is pleased to send you. If your love to Him be pure, you will not seek Him less on Calvary, than on Tabor; and, surely, He should be as much loved on that as on this, since it was on Calvary He made the greater display of His Love for you. Be not like those, who give themselves to Him at one season, and withdraw from Him at another. They give themselves only to be caressed; and wrest themselves back again, when they come to be crucified, or at least turn for consolation to the creature.

No, beloved souls, you will not find consolation in aught, but in the love of the Cross, and in total abandonment. "Whosoever favors not the Cross, favors not the things that be of God." (Matthew 16:23) It is impossible to love God without loving the Cross; and a heart that favors the Cross, finds the bitterest things to be sweet. "A famished soul finds bitter things sweet" (Job 6:1) because it finds itself hungering for God in proportion as it hungers for the Cross. God gives the Cross, and the Cross gives us God. We may be assured, that there is an internal advancement, where there is an advancement in the way of the Cross. Abandonment and the Cross go hand in hand together. As soon as suffering presents itself, and you feel a repugnance against it, resign yourself immediately unto God with respect to it, and give yourself up to Him in sacrifice; you shall find, that, when the Cross arrives, it will not be so very burdensome, because you had disposed yourself to a willing reception of it. This, however, does not prevent your feeling its weight as some have imagined; for when we do not feel the Cross, we do not suffer it. A sensibility of sufferings constitutes a principal part of the sufferings themselves. Jesus Christ Himself was willing to suffer its utmost rigors. We often bear the Cross in weakness, at other times in strength; all should be equal to us in the will of God.

Chapter Eight

It may be objected, that, by this method, we shall have no mysteries imprinted on our minds, but it is quite the reverse; because it is the peculiar means of imparting them to the soul. Jesus Christ, to whom we are abandoned, and whom "we follow as the way, whom we hear as the truth, and who animates us as the life" (John 14:6) He does this by imprinting Himself on the soul, impresses the characters of His different states; and to bear all the states of Jesus Christ is far more sublime, than merely to reason concerning them. Paul bore in his body the states of Jesus Christ. "I bear in my body," says he, "the marks of the Lord Jesus" (Galatians 6:17), but he does not say that he reasoned thereon. In our acts of resignation, Jesus Christ frequently communicates some peculiar views or revelations of His states. These we should thankfully receive, and dispose ourselves for what appears to be His will Indeed, having no other choice, but that of ardently reaching after Him, of dwelling ever with Him, and of sinking into nothingness before Him, we should accept indiscriminately all His dispensations, whether obscurity or illumination, fruitfulness or barrenness, weakness or strength, sweetness or bitterness, temptations, distractions, pain, weariness, or doubtings; and none of all these should, for one moment, retard our course.

God engages some, for whole years, in the contemplation and enjoyment of a particular mystery; the simple view or contemplation of which gathers the soul inward, provided it be faithful. But as soon as God is pleased to withdraw this view from the soul, it should freely yield to the deprivation. Some are very uneasy at feeling their inability to meditate on certain mysteries; but this disquietude has no just foundation, since an affectionate attachment to God includes every species of devotion. For whosoever in repose is united to God alone, is, indeed, most excellently and effectually applied to every divine mystery. The love of God comprehends, in itself, the love of all that appertains to Him.

Chapter Nine

It is thus we acquire virtue, with facility and certainty; for, as God is the fountain and principle of all virtue, we possess all in the possession of Himself; and in proportion as we approach towards this possession, in like proportion do we rise into the most eminent virtues. For all virtue is but as a mask, an outside appearance changeable as our garments, if it does not spring up, and issue from within; and then, indeed, it is genuine, essential, and permanent. "The beauty of the King's daughter proceeds from within" said David. (Psalm 14:14) These souls, above all others, practice virtue in the most eminent degree, though they advert not to virtue in particular; to whom they are united, carries them to the most extensive practice of it; He is exceedingly jealous over them, and prohibits them the taste of any pleasure but in Himself. What a hungering for sufferings have those souls, who thus glow with Divine Love. How prone to precipitate into excessive austerities, were they permitted to pursue their own inclinations! They think of nothing except how they may please their Beloved. As their self-love abates, they neglect and forget themselves; and as their love to God increases, so do self-detestation and disregard to the creature. Oh was this easy method acquired, a method so suited to all, to the dull and ignorant as well as to the acute and learned, how easily would the whole Church of God be reformed! Love only is required. "Love," says Saint Augustine, "and then do what you please." For when we truly love, we cannot have so much as a will to anything that might offend the Object of our affections.

Chapter Ten

I will even affirm, that, in any other way, it is next to an impossibility ever to acquire a perfect mortification of the senses and passions. The reason is obvious; the soul gives vigor and energy to the senses, and the senses raise and stimulate the passions. A dead body has neither sensations nor passions, because its connection with the soul is dissolved. All endeavors merely to rectify the exterior, impel the soul yet farther outward into that about which it is so warmly and zealously engaged. It is in these matters that its powers are diffused and scattered abroad, for its application being immediately directed to austerities, and other externals, it thus invigorates the very senses it is aiming to subdue. For the senses have no other spring from whence to derive their vigor, than the application of the soul to themselves; the degree of their life and activity is proportioned to the degree of attention which the soul bestows upon them; and this life of the senses stirs up and provokes the passions, instead of suppressing or subduing them. Austerities may, indeed, enfeeble the body, but, for the reasons just mentioned, can never take off the keenness of the senses, or lessen their activity. The only method to effect this is inward recollection; by which the soul is turned wholly and altogether inward, to possess a present God. If the soul directs all its vigor and energy towards this centre of its being, the simple act separates and withdraws it from the senses; the exercising all its powers internally leaves them faint and impotent; and the nearer it draws to God the farther is it separated from the senses, and the less are the passions influenced by them. Hence it is, that those, in whom the attractions of grace are very powerful, find the outward man weak, feeble, and even liable to faintings. I do not mean to discourage mortification; for it should ever accompany prayer, according to the strength and state of the person, or as obedience will allow. But, I say that mortification should not be our principal exercise; nor should we prescribe ourselves such and such austerities, but follow simply and merely the internal attractions of grace; and being possessed and occupied with the Divine Presence (without thinking particularly on mortification) God will enable us to perform every species of it; and most assuredly He will give no relaxation to those who abide faithful in their abandonment to Him, until He has mortified in them everything that remains to be mortified. We have only then to continue steadfast in the utmost attention to God, and all things will be rightly performed. All are not capable of outward austerities, but all are capable of this. In the mortification of the eye and ear, which continually supply the busy imagination with new objects, there is little danger of falling into excess. But God will teach us this also, and we have only to follow where His Spirit guides. The soul has a double advantage by proceeding thus, for, in withdrawing from outward objects, it draws the nearer to God; and in approaching Him, besides the secret sustaining and preserving power and virtue received, it is the farther removed from sin, the nearer the approach is made; so that conversion becomes habitual.

Chapter Eleven

"Be you truly converted unto that God from whom you have so deeply revolted" (Isaiah 31:6). To be truly converted is to avert wholly from the creature, and, turn wholly unto God. For the attainment of salvation it is absolutely necessary that we should forsake outward sin and turn unto righteousness, but this alone is not perfect conversion, which consists in a total change of the whole man from an outward to an inward life. When the soul is once turned to God a wonderful facility is found in continuing steadfast in conversation; and the longer it remains thus converted, the nearer it approaches, and the more firmly it adheres to God; and the nearer it draws to Him, of necessity it is the farther removed from the creature, which is so contrary to Him, so that it is so effectually established and rooted in its conversion that it becomes habitual, and, as it were, natural. Now we must not suppose that this is effected by a violent exertion of its own powers; for it is not capable of, nor should it attempt any other cooperation with Divine Grace, than that of endeavoring to withdraw itself from external objects and to turn inwards. After which it has nothing farther to do than to continue steadfast in adherence to God. God has an attractive virtue which draws the soul more and more powerfully to Himself, the nearer it approaches towards Him, and, in attracting, He purifies and refines it; just as with a gross vapor exhaled by the sun, which, as it gradually ascends, is rendered pure. The vapor, indeed, contributes to its exhalation only by its passiveness; but the soul cooperates with the attractions of God, by a free and affectionate correspondence. This kind of introversion is both easy and efficacious, advancing the soul naturally and without constraint, because God Himself is its centre. Every centre has a powerfully attractive virtue. The more pure and exalted it is, the stronger and more irresistible are its attractions. But besides the potent magnetism of the centre itself, there is, in every creature, a correspondent tendency to reunion with its peculiar centre which is vigorous and active in proportion to the spirituality and perfection of the subject. As soon as anything is turned towards its centre its own gravitation instigates and accelerates it thereto, unless it be withheld by some invincible obstacle. A stone held in the hand is no sooner disengaged than by its own weight it falls to the earth as to its centre; so also water and fire, when unobstructed, tend and flow incessantly to their principle or centre. Now, when the soul, by its efforts to abandon outward objects, and gather itself inwards, is brought into the influence of this central tendency, without any other exertion, it falls gradually by the weight of Divine Love into its proper centre; and the more passive and tranquil it remains, and the freer from self motion and self exertion, the more rapidly it advances, because the energy of the central active virtue is unobstructed and has full liberty for action. All our care and attention should, therefore, be to acquire inward recollection. Do not be discouraged by the pains and difficulties we encounter in this exercise, which will soon be recompensed, on the part of our God, by such abundant supplies of grace as will render the exercise perfectly easy, provided we be faithful in meekly withdrawing our hearts from outward distractions and occupations, and returning to our centre with affections lull of tenderness and serenity. When at any time the passions are turbulent, a gentle retreat inwards unto a Present God, easily deadens and pacifies them; and any other way of contending with them rather irritates than appeases them.

Chapter Twelve

The soul that is faithful in the exercise of love and adherence to God above described, is astonished to feel Him gradually taking possession of their whole being. It now enjoys a continual sense of that Presence, which is become as it were natural to it; and this, as well as prayer, is the result of habit. The soul feels an unusual serenity gradually being diffused throughout all its faculties; and silence now wholly constitutes its prayer; while God communicates an intuitive love, which is the beginning of ineffable blessedness. Oh that I were permitted to pursue this subject and describe some degrees of the endless progression of subsequent states! But I now write only for beginners; and shall, therefore, proceed no farther, but wait our Lord's time for publishing what may be applicable to every conceivable degree of stature in Christ Jesus. We must, however, urge it as a matter of the highest import, to cease from self action and self exertion, that God Himself may act alone. He said, by the mouth of His Prophet David, "Be still, and know that I am God." But the creature is so infatuated with a lore and attachment to its own workings, that it imagines nothing at all is done, if it does not perceive and distinguish all its operations. It is ignorant that its inability minutely to observe the manner of its motion is occasioned by the swiftness of its progress; and that the operations of God, in extending and diffusing their influence, absorb those of the creature. The stars may be seen distinctly before the sun rises; but as his light advances, their rays are gradually absorbed by His and they become invisible, not from the want of light in themselves, but from the superior effulgence of the chief luminary. The case is similar here; for there is a strong and universal light which absorbs all the little distinct lights of the soul; they grow faint and disappear under its powerful influence, and self activity is now no longer distinguishable, yet those greatly err who accuse this prayer of idleness, a charge that can arise only from inexperience. If they would but make some efforts towards the attainment of this prayer, they would soon experience the contrary of what they suppose and find their accusation groundless. This appearance of inaction is, indeed, not the consequence of sterility and want, but of fruitfulness and abundance which will be clearly perceived by the experienced soul, who will know and feel that the silence is full and unctuous, and the result of causes totally the reverse of apathy and barrenness. There are two kinds of people that keep silence; the one because they have nothing to say, the other because they have too much; it is so with the soul in this state; the silence is occasioned by the superabundance of matter, too great for utterance. To be drowned, and to die of thirst, are deaths widely different; yet water may, in some sense, be said to cause both; abundance destroys in one case, and want in the other. So in this state the abundance and overflow of grace still the activity of self; and, therefore, it is of the utmost importance to remain as silent as possible. The infant hanging at the mother's breast is a lively illustration of our subject. It begins to draw the milk by moving its little lips; but when the milk flows abundantly, it is content to swallow, and suspends its suction. It would only hurt itself if it did otherwise. It would spill the milk and be obliged to quit the breast.

We must act in like manner in the beginning of Prayer, by exerting the lips of the affections; but as soon as the milk of Divine Grace flows freely, we have nothing to do but, in repose and stillness, sweetly to imbibe it; and when it ceases to flow, we must again stir up the affections as the infant moves its lips. Whoever acts otherwise cannot turn this grace to advantage, which is bestowed to allure and draw the soul into the repose of Love, and not into the multiplicity of Self. But what becomes of this child, who gently and without motion drinks in the milk? Who would believe that it can thus receive nourishment? Yet the more peacefully it feeds, the better it thrives. What, I say, becomes of this infant? It drops gently asleep on its mother's bosom. So the soul that is tranquil and peaceful in prayer, sinks frequently into a mystic slumber, wherein all its powers are at rest; till at length it is wholly fitted for that state, of which it enjoys these transient anticipations. In this process the soul is led naturally, without effort, art, or study. The Interior is not a stronghold to be taken by storm and violence, but a kingdom of peace, which is to be gained only by love. If any will thus pursue the little path I have pointed out, it will lead them to intuitive prayer. God demands nothing extraordinary nor difficult; on the contrary, He is best pleased by a simple and childlike conduct. That which is most sublime and elevated in religion is the easiest attained. The most necessary sacraments are the least difficult. It is thus also in natural things. If you would go to sea, embark on a river, and you will be conveyed to it insensibly and without exertion. Would you go to God, follow this sweet and simple path, and you will arrive at the desired object, with an ease and expedition that will amaze you. Oh that you would but once make the trial, how soon would you find that all I have advanced falls short of the reality, and that your own experience will carry you infinitely beyond it. Is it fear that prevents you from instantly casting yourself into those arms of love, which were widely extended on the cross only to receive you? From where can your fears arise? What risk do you run, in depending solely on your God, and abandoning yourself wholly unto Him. Ah, He will not deceive you, unless by bestowing an abundance beyond your highest hopes. But those who expect all from themselves will inevitably be deceived, and must suffer this rebuke of God by His prophet Isaiah, "you have wearied yourselves in the multiplicity of your ways, and have not said let us rest in peace" (Isaiah).

Chapter Thirteen

The soul advanced thus far has no need of any other preparation than its quietude, for now the Presence of God, which is the great effect, or rather continuation of Prayer, begins to be infused, and almost without intermission. The soul enjoys transcendent blessedness, and feels that "it no longer lives, but that Christ lives in it"; and that the only way to find Him is introversion. No sooner do the bodily eyes close than the soul is wrapped up in Prayer. It is amazed at so great a blessing, and enjoys an internal converse, which external matters cannot interrupt. The same may be said of this species of prayer that is said of wisdom, "all good things come together with her" (Wisdom 7:11). For the virtues flow from this soul into exertion with so much sweetness and facility that they appear natural and spontaneous; and the living spring within breaks forth so freely and abundantly into all goodness that it becomes even insensible to evil. Let it then remain faithful in this state; and beware of choosing or seeking any other disposition whatsoever than this simple rest as a preparative either to confession or communion, to action or prayer, for its sole business is to expand itself for the full reception of the Divine infusions. I would not be understood to speak of the preparations necessary for the sacraments, but of the most perfect dispositions in which they can be received.

Chapter Fourteen

"The Lord is in His Holy Temple, let all the earth keep silence before him" (Habakkuk 2:20). Inward silence is absolutely indispensable, because the Word is essential and eternal, and necessarily requires dispositions in the soul in some degree correspondent to His nature, as a capacity for the reception of Himself. Hearing is a sense formed to receive sounds, and is rather passive than active, admitting, but not communicating sensation; and if we would hear, we must lend the ear for that purpose. So Christ, the eternal Word, without whose Divine inspeaking the soul is dead, dark, and barren, when He would speak within us, requires the most silent attention to His all quickening and efficacious voice. Hence it is so frequently enjoined us in Sacred Writ, to hear and be attentive to the voice of God. Of the numerous exhortations to this effect I shall quote a few. "Hearken unto me, my people, and give ear unto me, Oh my nation!" (Isaiah), and again, "Hear me, all you whom I carry in my bosom, and bear within my bowels" (Isaiah), and farther by the Psalmist, "Hearken, Oh daughter and consider, and incline your ear; forget also your own people, and your father's house; so shall the King greatly desire your beauty" (Psalm xlv. 10, 11). We should forget ourselves, and all self-interest, and listen and be attentive to the voice of our God. These two simple actions, or rather passive dispositions, attract His love to that beauty which He Himself communicates. Outward silence is very requisite for the cultivation and improvement of inward; and indeed it is impossible we should become truly internal without the love and practice of outward silence and retirement. God says, by the mouth of His prophet, "I will lead her into solitude, and there will I speak to her heart" (Hosea 2:14); and unquestionably the being internally occupied and engaged with God is wholly incompatible with being busied and employed in the numerous trifles that surround us. When through imbecility or unfaithfulness we become dissipated, or as it were un-centered, it is of immediate importance to turn again gently and sweetly inward; and thus we may learn to preserve the spirit and unction of prayer throughout the day. If prayer and recollection were wholly confined to any appointed half-hour or hour, we should reap but little fruit.

Chapter Fifteen

Self-examination should always precede Confession, and in the nature and manner of it should be conformable to the state of the soul. The business of those that are advanced to the degree of which we now treat, is to lay their whole souls open before God, who will not fail to enlighten them, and enable them to see the peculiar nature of their faults. This examination, however, should be peaceful and tranquil, and we should depend on God for the discovery and knowledge of our sins, rather than, on the diligence of our own scrutiny. When we examine with constraint, and in the strength of our own endeavors, we are easily deceived and betrayed by self-love into error; "we believe the evil good, and the good evil" (Isaiah 5: 20); but when we lie in full exposure before the Sun of Righteousness, His Divine beams render the smallest atoms visible. It follows from hence that we must forsake self, and abandon our souls to God as well in examination as Confession. When souls have attained to this species of prayer no fault escapes reprehension; on every commission they are instantly rebuked by an inward burning and tender confusion. Such is the scrutiny of Him who suffers no evil to be concealed; and under His purifying influence the one way is to turn affectionately to our Judge, and bear with meekness the pain and correction He inflicts. He becomes the incessant

Examiner of the soul; it can now, indeed, no longer examine itself, and if it be faithful in its resignation, experience will convince the soul that it is a thousand times more effectually examined by His Divine Light than by the most active and vigorous self inspection. Those who tread these paths should be informed of a matter respecting their confession in which they are apt to err. When they begin to give an account of their sins, instead of the regret and contrition they had been accustomed to feel, they find that love and tranquility sweetly pervade and take possession of their souls. Now those who are not properly instructed are desirous of withdrawing from this sensation, to form an act of contrition, because they have heard, and with truth, that it is requisite - but they are not aware that they lose thereby the genuine contrition, which is this intuitive love, infinitely surpassing any effect produced by self-exertion, and comprehending the other acts in itself as in one principal act, in much higher perfection than if they were distinctly perceived, and varied in their sensation. Be not then troubled about other things when God acts so excellently in you and for you. To hate sin in this manner is to hate it as God does. The purest love is that which is of His immediate operation in the soul: why should it then be so eager for action. Let it remain in the state He assigns it, agreeable to the instructions of Solomon: "Put your confidence in God; remain in quiet, where he has placed you". The soul will also be amazed at finding a difficulty in calling faults to remembrance: this, however, should cause no uneasiness; first, because this forgetfulness of our faults is some proof of our purification from them; and in this degree of advancement it is best. Secondly, because when confession is our duty God will not fail to make known to us our greatest faults, for then He Himself examines, and the soul will feel the end of examination more perfectly accomplished than it could possibly have been by the utmost exertion of its own endeavors. These instructions, however, would be altogether unsuitable to the preceding degrees while the soul continues in its active state, wherein it is right and necessary it should in all things use the utmost industry in proportion to the degree of its advancement. It is those that have arrived at this more advanced state whom I would exhort to follow these instructions, and not to vary their one simple occupation even on approaching the communion; they should remain in silence, and suffer God to act freely and without limitation. Who can better receive the Body and Blood of Christ than he in whom the Holy Spirit is indwelling?

Chapter Sixteen

If, while reading, you feel yourself recollected, lay aside the book and remain in stillness; at all times read but little, and cease to read when you are thus internally attracted. The soul that is called to a state of inward silence should not encumber itself with long vocal prayers; whenever it does pray vocally, and finds a difficulty therein, and an attraction to silence, it should not use constraint by persevering, but yield to the internal drawings, unless the repeating such prayers be a matter of obedience. In any other case, it is much better not to be burdened with and tied down to the repetition of set forms, but wholly given up to the leadings of the Holy Spirit; and herein, indeed, is every species of devotion inclusively fulfilled in a most eminent degree.

Chapter Seventeen

The soul should not be surprised at feeling itself unable to offer up to God such petitions as it had formerly made with freedom and facility; for now the Spirit makes intercession for it according to the will of God, that "Spirit which helps our infirmities: for we know not what we should pray for as we ought; but the Spirit itself makes intercession for us, with groaning, which cannot be uttered" (Romans 8:26). We must cooperate with, and second the designs of God, which tend to divest us of all our own operations, that in the place thereof His own may be substituted. Let this then be done in you, and suffer not yourself to be attached to anything, however good it may appear; for it is no longer good if it in any measure turns you aside from that which God wills of you: the Divine Will is preferable to all things else. Shake off then all attachments to the interests of self, and live on faith and resignation; here it is that genuine faith begins truly to operate. Should we either wander among externals, or sink into dissipation, or commit a fault, we must instantly turn inwards; for having departed thereby from our God, we should as soon as possible return again unto Him, and suffer in His presence whatever sensations He is pleased to impress. On the commission of a fault it is of great importance to guard against vexation and disquietude, which springs from a secret root of pride and a love of our own excellence; we are hurt by feeling what we are; and if we discourage ourselves or despond, we are the more enfeebled; and from our reflections on the fault a chagrin arises, which is often worse than the fault itself. The truly humble soul is not surprised at defects or failings; and the more miserable and wretched it beholds itself, the more it abandons itself unto God, and press for a nearer and more intimate alliance with Him, that it may avail itself of His eternal strength. We should be induced to act thus, as God Himself has said, "I will make you understand what you should do; I will teach you the way by which you should go; and I will have my eye continually upon you for a guide" (Psalm 32:8).

Chapter Eighteen

A direct contest and struggle with distractions and temptations rather serves to augment them, and withdraws the soul from that adherence to God, which should ever be its principal occupation. The surest and safest method for conquest is simply to turn away from the evil and draw yet nearer and closer to our God. A little child, on perceiving a monster, does not wait to fight with it, and will scarcely turn its eyes towards it, but quickly shrinks into the bosom or its mother, in total confidence of safety; so likewise should the soul turn from the dangers of temptation to God. God is in the midst of her, says the Psalmist, "She shall not be moved; God shall help her, and that right early" (Psalm 16:5). If we do otherwise, and in our weakness attempt to attack our enemies, we shall frequently feel ourselves wounded, if not totally defeated; but, by casting ourselves into the simple Presence of God, we shall find instant supplies of strength for our support. This was the succor sought for by David, "The Lord always before me: because he is at my right hand, I shall not be moved. Therefore my heart is glad, and my glory rejoices: my flesh also shall rest in hope" (Psalm 16:8-9). And it is said in Exodus, "The Lord shall fight for you, and you shall hold your peace."

Chapter Nineteen

Supplication and sacrifice are comprehended in prayer, which, according to Saint John, is "an incense, the smoke whereof ascends unto God;" therefore it is said in the Apocalypse that "unto the Angel was given much incense, that he should offer it with the prayers of all Saints". Prayer is the effusion of the heart in the Presence of God: "I have poured out my soul before God" says the mother of Samuel. (1 Samuel 1:15) The prayer of the wise men at the feet of Christ in the stable of Bethlehem, was signified by the incense they offered: for prayer being the energy and fire of love, melting, dissolving, and sublimating the soul, and causing it to ascend unto God; therefore, in proportion as the soul is melted and dissolved, in like proportion do odors issue from it; and these odors proceed from the intense fire of love within. This is illustrated in the Canticles where the spouse says, "While the King sits on his couch, my spikenard sends forth the smell thereof". The couch is the ground or centre of the soul; and when God is there, and we know how to dwell with Him, and abide in His Presence, the sacred power and influence thereof gradually dissolves the adoration of the soul, and, as it melts, odors issue forth: hence it is, that the Beloved says of His spouse, in seeing her soul melt when He spoke, "Who is this that comes out of the wilderness, like pillars of smoke perfumed with myrrh and frankincense?" (Cant. 5:6; 3:6). Thus does the soul ascend unto God, by giving up self to the destroying and annihilating power of Divine Love: this, indeed, is a most essential and necessary sacrifice in the Christian religion, and that alone by which we pay true homage to the sovereignty of God; as it is written, "The power of the Lord is great, and he is honored only by the humble" (Ecclesiastes 3:20). By the destruction of the existence of self within us, we truly acknowledge the supreme existence of our God; for unless we cease to exist in self, the Spirit of the Eternal Word cannot exist in us: now it is by the giving up of our own life, that we give place for His coming; and "in dying to ourselves, He lives and abides in us." We should, indeed, surrender our whole being unto Christ Jesus: and cease to live any longer in ourselves, that He may become our life; "that being dead, our life may be hid with Christ in God" (Colossians 3:3). "Pass you into me," says God, "all you who earnestly seek after me" (Ecclesiastes 24:16). But how is it we pass into God. We leave and forsake ourselves, that we may be lost in Him; and this can be effected only by annihilation; which being the true prayer of adoration, renders unto God alone, all "Blessing, honor, glory and power, for ever and ever" (Revelation 5:13). This is the prayer of truth: "It is worshipping God in spirit and in truth" (John 4:23). "In spirit," because we enter into the purity of that Spirit which prays within us, and are drawn forth and freed from our own carnal and corrupt manner of praying; "In truth because we are thereby placed in the great Truth of the All of God, and the nothing of the creature. There are but these two truths, the All, and the nothing; everything else is falsehood. We can pay due honor to the All of God, only in our own annihilation; which is no sooner accomplished, than He, who never suffers a void in nature, instantly fills us with Himself. Did we but know the virtue and the blessings which the soul derives from this prayer, we should willingly be employed therein without ceasing. "It is the pearl of great price: it is the hidden treasure" (Matthew 13:44- 45), which, whoever finds, sells freely all that he has to purchase it: "It is the well of living water, which springs up unto everlasting life": It is the adoration of God "in spirit and in truth" (John 4:14-23), and it is the full performance of the purest evangelical precepts. Jesus Christ assures us, that the "Kingdom of God is within us" (Luke), and this is true in two senses: First, when God becomes so fully the Master and Lord in us, that nothing resists His dominion; then is our interior His kingdom: And again, when we possess God, who is the Supreme Good, we possess His kingdom also, wherein there is fullness of joy, and where we attain the end of our creation: thus it is said, " to serve God, is to reign." The end of our creation, indeed, is to enjoy our God, even in this life; but alas, how few there are who think of this seriously.

Chapter Twenty

Some persons, when they hear of the prayer of silence, falsely imagine, that the soul remains stupid, dead, and inactive. But, unquestionably, it acts therein, more nobly and more extensively than it had ever done before; for God Himself is the mover, and the soul now acts by the agency of His Spirit. When Saint Paul speaks of our being led by the Spirit of God, it is not meant that we should cease from action; but that we should act through the internal agency of His Grace. This is finely represented by the Prophet Ezekiel's vision of the "wheels, which had a Living Spirit; and wherever the Spirit was to go, they went; they ascended, and descended, as they were moved; for the Spirit of Life was in them, and they returned not when they went" (Ezekiel). Thus the soul should be equally subservient to the will of that Vivifying Spirit where it is informed, and scrupulously faithful to follow only as that moves. These motions now never tend to return, in reflection on the creatures or itself; but go forward, in an incessant approach towards the chief end. This action of the soul is attended with the utmost tranquility, when it acts of itself, the act is forced and constrained; and, therefore, it can the more easily perceive and distinguish it: but when it acts under the influence of the Spirit of Grace, its action is so free, so easy, and so natural, that it almost seems as if it did not act at all: "He has set me at large, he has delivered me, because He delighted in me" (Psalm 15:19). When the soul is in its central tendency, or, in other words, is returned through recollection into itself; from that moment the central attraction becomes a most potent action, infinitely surpassing in its energy every other species. Nothing, indeed, can equal the swiftness of this tendency to the centre: and though an action, yet it is so noble, so peaceful, so full of tranquility, so natural and spontaneous, that it appears to the soul as if it did not act at all. When a wheel rolls slowly we can easily distinguish its parts; but when its motion is rapid we can distinguish nothing. So the soul, which rests in God, has an activity exceedingly noble and elevated, yet altogether peaceful: and the more peaceful it is, the swifter is its course; because it is proportionately given up to that Spirit, by which it is moved and directed. This attracting spirit is no other than God Himself,

Who, in drawing us, causes us to run unto Him. How well did the spouse understand this when she said, "Draw me, and we will run after You. Draw me unto You, O my Divine centre, by the secret springs of my existence, and all my powers and senses shall follow the potent magnetism!" This simple attraction is both an ointment to heal, and a perfume to allure: "we follow," says she, "the fragrance of your perfumes;" and though so powerfully magnetic it is followed by the soul freely, and without constraint; for it is equally delightful as forcible; and while it attracts by its potency, it charms with its sweetness. "Draw me," says the spouse, "and we will run after You." She speaks of and to herself: "Draw me," behold the unity of the centre which attracts! "We will run," behold the correspondence and course of all the senses and powers, in following that attraction! Instead then of promoting idleness, we promote the highest activity, by inculcating a total dependence on the Spirit of God as our moving principle; for "it is in him we live, and move, and have our being." (Acts 17:28) This meek dependence on the Spirit of God is indispensably necessary to reinstate the soul in its primeval unity and simplicity, that it may thereby attain the end of its creation. We must, therefore, forsake our multifarious activity, to re-enter the simplicity and unity of God, in Whose image we were originally formed. "The Spirit is one and manifold" (Wisdom 7:22), and His unity does not preclude His multiplicity. We enter into His unity when we are united unto His Spirit, and have one and the same Spirit with Him; and we are multiplied in respect to the outward execution of His will, without any departure from our state of union: so that when we are wholly moved by the Divine Spirit, which is infinitely active, our activity must, indeed, differ widely in its energy and degree from that which is merely our own. We must yield ourselves to the guidance of Wisdom, which is more moving than any motion. (Wisdom 7:24); and by abiding in dependence on its action, our activity will be truly efficient. "All things were made by the Word, and without him was not anything made, that was made" (John 1:3). God originally formed us in His own likeness; and He now informs us with the Spirit of His Word, that "Breath of Life" (Genesis 2:7), which was inbreathed at our creation, in the participation whereof the image of God consisted; and this life is a life of unity, simple, pure, intimate, and always fruitful. The Devil having broken and deformed the Divine Image in the soul, the agency of the same Word, whose Spirit was inbreathed at our creation, is absolutely necessary for its renovation; and it can only be renewed by our being passive under Him who is to renew it: but who can restore the Image of God within us in its primeval form, save He who is the Essential Image of the Father. Our activity should, therefore, consist in enduring to acquire and maintain such a state as may be most susceptible of Divine impressions, most flexile to ail the operations of the Eternal Word. While a tablet is unsteady, the painter is unable to delineate a true copy: so every act of our own selfish and proper spirit is productive of false and erroneous lineaments; it interrupts the work, and defeats the design of this adorable Painter; we must then remain in peace and move only when He moves us. "Jesus Christ has the Life, in himself," (John 5:26) and He should be the life of every living thing. As all action is estimable only in proportion to the dignity of the efficient principle, this action is in-contestably more noble than any other. Actions produced by a Divine principle, are Divine; but creaturely actions, however good they appear, are only human, or at best virtuous, even when accompanied by Grace. Jesus Christ says, He has the life in Himself. All other beings have only a borrowed life; but the Word has the life in Himself, and being communicative of His nature He desires to communicate it to man. We should, therefore, make room for the influx of this Life, which can only be done by the election of the Adamlcal life, the suppression of the activity of self. This is agreeable to the assertion of Saint Paul: "If any man be in Christ he is a new creature: old things have passed away, behold all things have become new." (2 Corinthians 5:17), but this state can be accomplished only by dying to ourselves and to all our own activity, that the activity of God may be substituted in its place. Instead, therefore, of prohibiting activity, we enjoin it; but in absolute dependence on the Spirit of God, that His activity may take place of our own. This can only be effected by the concurrence of the creature; and this concurrence can only be yielded by moderating and restraining our own activity, that the activity of God may gradually gain the ascendancy, and finally absorb all that is ours as distinguishable from it. Jesus Christ has exemplified this in the Gospel: Martha did what was right; but because she did it in her own spirit Christ rebuked her. The spirit of man is restless and turbulent; for which reason it does little, though it would appear to do much. "Martha," says Christ, "you are careful and troubled about many things, but one thing is needful; and Mary has chosen that good part which shall not be taken away from her" (Luke 10:41-42). And what was it that Mary had chosen! Repose, tranquility, and peace. She apparently ceased to act, that the Spirit of Christ might act in her; she ceased to live, that Christ might be her life. This shows us how necessary it is to renounce ourselves and all our own activity, to follow Jesus Christ. We cannot follow Him without being animated with His Spirit. Now that His Spirit may gain admission in us it is necessary that our own proper spirit should be first expelled: "He that is joined unto the Lord," says Saint Paul, "is one spirit with him" (1Corinthians 6:17); and David said, "It was good for him to draw near unto the Lord, and to put his trust in him" (Psalm). This drawing near unto God; is the beginning of Union. Divine Union has its commencement, its progression, and its consummation. It is first an inclination and tendency towards God: when the soul is introverted in the manner before described, it gets within the influence of the central attraction, and acquires an eager desire after Union: on a nearer approach unto God, it adheres to Him; and growing stronger and stronger in its adhesion, it finally becomes one; that is, "One Spirit with Him:" and it is thus that the spirit which had wandered and strayed from God, returns again to its proper source. Into this process, which is the Divine motion, and the Spirit of Jesus Christ, we must necessarily enter. Saint Paul says, "If any man has not the Spirit of Christ, he is none of his" Romans 8:9): therefore, to be Christ's, we must be filled with His Spirit, and to be filled with His Spirit we must be emptied of our own. The Apostle, in the same passage, proves the necessity of this Divine influence or motion: "As many" says he, "as are led by the Spirit of God, they are the sons of God" (Romans 8:14). The Spirit of Divine Filiation is then the Spirit of Divine action or motion: he, therefore, adds, "You have not received the spirit of bondage again to fear; but you have received the Spirit of Adoption whereby we, cry, Abba, Father. This Spirit is no other than the Spirit of Christ, through which we participate in His Filiation; And this Spirit bears witness with our Spirit, that you are the children of God" (Romans 8:16). When the soul lends itself to the influence and motions of this blessed Spirit, it feels the testimony of its Divine Filiation; and it feels also, with superadded joy, that it has received not the Spirit of bondage, but of Liberty, even the liberty of the children of God. It then finds that it acts freely and sweetly, though with vigor and infallibility. The Spirit of Divine action is so necessary in all things, that Saint Paul, in the same passage, found that necessity on our ignorance with respect to what we pray for: "The Spirit," says he, "also helps our infirmities: for we know not what we should pray for as we ought, but the Spirit itself makes intercession for us, with groaning which cannot be uttered." This is positive; if we know not what we stand in need of, nor pray, as we ought to do, for those things which are necessary; and if the Spirit which is in us, and to which we resign ourselves, asks and intercedes for us; should we not give unlimited freedom to its action, to its ineffable groaning in our behalf? This Spirit is the Spirit of the Word, which is always heard, as He says Himself: "Now that you hear me always" (John xi. 42); and if we freely admit this Spirit to pray and intercede in us, we also shall be always heard. The reason of this is given us by the same Apostle, that skilful Mystic, and Master of the Internal life, where he adds, "He that searches the heart, knows what is the mind of the Spirit; because he makes intercession for the saints, according to the will of God" (Rom. viii. 27). That is to say, the Spirit demands only that which is conformable to the will of God; and the will of God is, that we should be saved: that we should become perfect: He, therefore, intercedes for that which is necessary for so great an end. Why should we then burden ourselves with superfluous cares, and fatigue and weary ourselves in the multiplicity of our ways, without ever saying, "Let us rest in peace." God Himself invites us to cast our cares, our anxieties, upon Him; and He complains in Isaiah, with ineffable goodness, that the soul had expended its powers and its treasures on a thousand external objects, and mistook its path to happiness, which was attainable by means much more facile: "Wherefore," says God, "do you spend money for that which is not bread? And do you labor for that which does not satisfy? Hearken diligently unto me, and eat that which is good, and let your soul delight itself in fatness" (Isaiah 55:2). Did we but know the blessedness of thus hearkening unto God, and how greatly the soul is strengthened and invigorated thereby, "All flesh would surely be silent before the Lord" (Zechariah 2:13); all would cease and be still, as soon as He appears. But to engage us farther in a boundless resignation, God assures us, by the same Prophet, that we should fear nothing in this abandonment, because He takes care of us, surpassing the highest tenderness of which we can form an idea: "Can a woman" says He, "forget her sucking child, that she should not have compassion on the son of her womb? Yes, she may forget; yet will I not forget you" (Isaiah). O blessed assurance, pregnant with consolation! Who, after this, shall be fearful of resigning themselves wholly to the dispensations and guidance of their God?

Chapter Twenty-one

Acts are distinguished into External and Internal. External acts are those which bear relation to some sensible object, and are either morally good or evil, merely according to the nature of the principle from which they proceed. I intend here to speak only of Internal acts, those energies of the soul, by which it turns internally to some objects, and averts from others. If during my application to God I should form a will to change the nature of my act, I thereby withdraw myself from God, and turn to created objects, and that in a greater or less degree according to the strength of the act: and if, "when I am turned towards the creature, I would return to God, I must necessarily form, an act for that purpose; and the more perfect this act is, the more complete is the conversion. Till conversion is perfected many reiterated acts are necessary; for it is generally progressive, though with some it is almost instantaneous. My act, however, should consist in a continual turning unto God, an exertion of every faculty and power of the soul purely for Him, agreeably to the instructions of the Son of Sirach: "Re-unite all the motions of your heart in the holiness of God" and to the example of David, "I will keep my whole strength for you" (Psalm 58:10), which is done by earnestly re-entering into one's self. As Isaiah says, "Return to your heart" (Isaiah); for we have strayed from our heart by sin, and it is our heart only that God requires, "My son gave me your heart, and let my eye observe your ways" (Proverbs 23:26). To give the heart to God is to have the whole eternal energy of the soul ever centering in Him, that we may be rendered conformable to His will. We must, therefore, continue invariably turned to God from our very first application to Him. But the soul being weak and unstable, and accustomed to turn, to external objects, is consequently prone to dissipation. This evil, however, will be counteracted if the soul, on perceiving the aberration, by a pure act of return to God, instantly replaces itself again in Him; and this act subsists as long as the conversion by the powerful influence of a sure and unfeigned return to God lasts: and as many reiterated acts form a habit, the soul contracts this habit of conversion, and that act which was before interrupted and distinct becomes continual. The soul should not then be perplexed about forming an act which already subsists, and which, indeed, it cannot attempt to form without difficulty and constraint; it even finds that it is withdrawn from its proper state under pretence of seeking that which is in reality acquired, seeing the habit is already formed and is confirmed in habitual conversion and habitual love. It is seeking one act by the help of many, instead of continuing attached to God by one simple act alone. We may remark that at times we form with facility many distinct yet simple acts, which shows that we have wandered, and that we re-enter our heart after having strayed from it; yet when we have re-entered we should remain there in peace. We err, therefore, in supposing that we do not form acts; we form them continually, but they should be in their nature conformable to the degree of our spiritual advancement. The greatest difficulty with most spiritual people arises from their not clearly comprehending this matter. Now some acts are transient and distinct, others are continual; and again, some are direct, and others reflex. All cannot form the first, neither are all in a state suited to form the last. The first are adapted to those who have strayed, and who require a distinguishable exertion, proportioned to the degree of their deviation, which, if inconsiderable, an act of the most simple kind is sufficient. By the continued act I mean that whereby the soul is altogether turned toward God in a direct tendency, which always subsists, and which it does not renew unless it has been interrupted. The soul being thus turned is in charity, and abides therein, "and he that dwells in love dwells in God" (1 John 4:16). The soul then, as it were, exists and reposes in this habitual act, but free from sloth or torpor; for still there is an un-intermitted act subsisting, which is a sweet sinking into the Deity, whose attraction becomes more and more powerful; and in following this potent attraction, the soul presses farther, and sinks continually deeper, into the ocean of Divine Love, maintaining an activity infinitely more powerful, vigorous, and effectual than that which served to accomplish its first return. Now the soul that is thus profoundly and vigorously active, being wholly given up to God, does not perceive its activity, because it is direct and not reflex; and this is the cause why some, who do not express themselves properly, say that they do not act at all; but it is a mistake, for they were never more truly or nobly active: they should rather say that they did not distinguish their acts than that they did not act. I allow they do not act of themselves, but they are drawn, and they follow the attraction. Love is the weight which sinks them into God, as into an infinite sea, wherein they descend with inconceivable rapidity from one profound depth to another. It is then an impropriety to say that we do not form acts, but the manner of their formation is not alike in all. The cause of the mistake is this, all who know they should act are desirous of acting distinguishably and perceptibly. But this cannot be: distinct and sensible acts are for beginners, and acts of a higher nature for those in a more advanced state. To stop in the former, which are weak and of little profit, is to debar one's self of the latter; and again, to attempt the latter without having passed through the former is a no less considerable error. All things should then be done in their season. Every state has its commencement, its progress, and its consummation; and it is an unhappy error to stop in the beginning. There is even no art but what has its progress: and at first we must labor with diligence and toil, but at last we shall reap the harvest of our industry. When the vessel is in port the mariners are obliged to exert all their strength, that they may clear her thence and put to sea; but at length they turn her with facility as they please. In like manner, while the soul remains in sin and creaturely entanglements, very frequent and strenuous endeavors are requisite to effect its freedom; the cords which withhold it must be loosed; and then by strong and vigorous efforts it gathers itself inwards, pushing off gradually from the old port; and in leaving that at a distance it proceeds to the interior, the haven to which it wishes to steer. When the vessel is thus turned, in proportion as she advances on the sea, she leaves the land behind; and the farther she departs from the old harbor, the less difficulty and labor is requisite in moving her forward: at length she begins to get sweetly under sail and now proceeds so swiftly in her course that the oars which have become useless are laid aside. How is the pilot now employed? He is content with spreading the sails and holding the rudder. To spread the sails is to lay one's self before God in the prayer of simple exposition, that we may be acted upon by His Spirit: to hold the rudder is to restrain our hearts from wandering from the true course, recalling it gently, and guiding it steadily to the dictates of the Blessed Spirit, which gradually gain possession and dominion of the heart, just as the wind by degrees fills the sails and impels the vessel. While the winds are fair the pilot and mariners rest from their labors, and the vessel glides rapidly along without their toil; and when they thus repose and leave the vessel to the wind, they make more way in one hour than they had done in a length of time by all their former efforts: were they even now to attempt using the oar they would not only fatigue themselves, but retard the vessel by their ill-timed labors. This is the manner of acting we should pursue interiorly it will, indeed, advance us in a short time, by the Divine impulsion, infinitely farther than a whole life spent in reiterated acts of self-exertion; and whosoever will take this path will find it easier than any other. If the wind is contrary and blows a storm, we must cast anchor to withhold the vessel: our anchor is a firm confidence and hope in our God, waiting patiently the calming of the tempest and the return of a favorable gale as David waited patiently for the Lord, and He inclined unto him and heard his cry. (Psalm) We must, therefore, be resigned to the Spirit of God, giving up ourselves wholly to His Divine Guidance.

Chapter Twenty-two

If all who labored for the conversion of others were to introduce them immediately into prayer and the interior life, and make it their main design to gain and win over the heart, numberless as well as permanent conversions would certainly ensue. On the contrary, few and transient fruits must attend that labor which is confined to outward matters; such as burdening the disciple with a thousand precepts for external exercises, instead of leaving the soul to Christ by the occupation of the heart to Him. If ministers were solicitous thus to instruct their parishioners; shepherds, while they watched their flocks, might have the Spirit of the primitive Christians, and the husbandman at the plough maintain a blessed intercourse with his God; the manufacturer, while he exhausts his outward man with labor, would be renewed in internal strength; and every species of vice would shortly disappear and every parishioner become a true follower of the Good Shepherd. O when once the heart is gained, how easily is all moral evil corrected! It is, therefore, that God, above all things, requires the heart. It is the conquest of the heart alone that can extirpate those dreadful vices which are so predominant, such as drunkenness, blasphemy, lewdness, envy, and theft. Jesus Christ would become the universal and peaceful Sovereign, and the face of the Church would be wholly renewed. The decay of internal piety is unquestionably the source of the various errors that have arisen in the Church; all which would speedily be sapped and overthrown should inward religion be re-established. Errors are only so far prejudicial to the soul as they tend to weaken faith and deter from prayer; and if, instead of engaging our wandering brethren in vain disputes, we could but teach them simply to believe and diligently to pray, we should lead them sweetly unto God. O how inexpressibly great is the loss sustained by mankind from the neglect of the interior life! And how tremendous must the great day of retribution be to those who are entrusted with the care of souls, for not having discovered and dispensed to their flock this hidden treasure. Some excuse themselves by saying that this is a dangerous way; pleading the incapacity of simple persons to comprehend spiritual matters. But the Oracles of Truth affirm the contrary: "The Lord loves those who walk simply" (Proverbs 12:22). And where can be the danger of walking in the only true way, which is Jesus Christ, of giving up ourselves to Him, fixing our eye continually upon Him, placing all our confidence in His grace, and tending with all the strength of our soul to His pure Love? The simple ones, so far from being incapable of this perfection, are, by their docility, innocence, and humility, peculiarly adapted and qualified for its attainment; and as they are not accustomed to reasoning, they are less employed in speculations, less tenacious of their own opinions. Even from their want of learning, they submit more freely to the teachings of the Divine Spirit; whereas others, who are blinded by self-sufficiency and enslaved by prejudice, give great resistance to the operations of Grace. We are told in Scripture "that unto the simple God gives the understanding of his law" (Psalm130); and we are also assured that God loves to commune freely with them: "The Lord cares for the simple; was reduced to extremity, and he saved me" (Psalm). To warn Spiritual Fathers against preventing the little ones from coming to Christ, He Himself said to His Apostles, "Suffer little children to come unto me, for of such is the kingdom of Heaven" (Matthew). It was the endeavor of the Apostles to prevent children from going to our Lord, which occasioned this gracious charge. Man frequently applies a remedy to the outward body, whilst the disease lies at the heart. The cause of our being so unsuccessful in reforming mankind, especially those of the uneducated, is our beginning with external matters; all our labors in this field do but produce such fruit as endures not: but if the key of the interior be first given, the exterior would be naturally and easily reformed. To teach man to seek God in his heart, to think of Him, to return to Him whenever he finds that he has wandered from Him, and to do and to suffer all things with a single eye to please Him, is the natural and ready process; it is leading the soul to the very source of Grace, wherein is to be found all that is necessary for sanctification. I, therefore, conjure you all, O you who have the care of souls, to put them at once into this way, which is Jesus Christ; nay, it is He Himself who conjures you, by the Precious Blood He has shed for those entrusted to you, "to speak to the heart of Jerusalem" (Isaiah). O you dispensers of His grace, you preachers of His word, you ministers of His sacraments, establish His Kingdom and that it may indeed be established, make Him ruler over the hearts of His subjects! It is the heart alone that can oppose His sovereignty, it is by the subjection of the heart that His sovereignty is most highly exalted: "Give glory to the holiness of God, and he shall become your sanctification" (Isaiah 8:13). Compose catechisms particularly to teach prayer, not by reasoning nor by method, for the simple are incapable thereof; but to teach the prayer of the heart, not of the understanding; the prayer of God's Spirit, not of man's invention. Alas, by wanting them to pray in elaborate forms, and to be curiously critical therein, you create their chief obstacles. The children have been led astray from the best of Fathers, by your endeavoring to teach them too refined, too polished a language. Go then, you poor children, to your Heavenly Father; speak to Him in your natural language; and though it be ever so rude and barbarous in the opinion of men, it is not so to Him. A Father is much better pleased with an address which love and respect in the child throws into disorder, because He knows it proceeds from the heart, than by a formal and barren harangue, though ever so elaborate in the composition. The simple and undisguised emotions of filial love are infinitely more expressive than all language and all reasoning. By forming instructions how to love by rule and method the Essential Love, men have in a great measure estranged themselves from Him. O how unnecessary is it to teach an art of loving! The language of love, though natural to the lover, is nonsense and barbarism to him who loves not. The best way to learn the love of God is to love Him. The ignorant and simple, because they proceed with more cordiality and simplicity, often become most perfect therein. The Spirit of God needs none of our arrangements and methods; when it pleases Him, He turns shepherds into prophets: and, so far from excluding any from the Temple of Prayer, He throws wide the gates, that all may enter; while Wisdom cries aloud in the highways, "Whoso is simple let him turn in hither" (Proverbs 9:4); and to the fools she says "Come eat of my bread, and drink of the wine which I have mingled" (Proverbs 9:5). And does not Jesus Christ Himself thank His Father for having hid the secrets of his kingdom from the wise and prudent and revealed them unto babes?1 (Matthew 11:25).

Chapter Twenty-three

It is impossible to attain Divine Union solely by the activity of meditation, or by the meltings of the affections, or even by the highest degree of luminous and distinctly - comprehended prayer. There are many reasons for this, the chief of which are as follow:

First, according to scripture "No man shall see God and live" (Exodus 33:20). Now all the exercises of discursive prayer, and even of active contemplation, while esteemed as the summit and end of the passive, and not merely as a preparative to it, are still living exercises by which we cannot see God; that is to say, be united with Him; for all that is of man's own power or exertion must first die, be it ever so noble, ever so exalted. Saint John relates "That there was a great silence in heaven" (Revelation 8:1). Now heaven represents the foundation and centre of the soul, wherein, ere the Majesty of God appears, all must be hushed to silence. All the efforts, nay, the very existence of self-sufficiency must be destroyed, because nothing is opposite to God but self-sufficiency; and all the malignity of man is in this failing, as in the power of its evil nature, insomuch that the purity of a soul increases in proportion as it loses this quality; till at length that which had been a fault, while the soul lived in self-sufficiency and so acted, becomes no longer such, from the purity and innocence it has acquired by departing from that which caused the dissimilitude between it and God. Secondly, to unite two things so opposite, as the impurity of the creature and the purity of God, the simplicity of God and the multiplicity of man, much more is requisite than the impotent efforts of the creature: no less than a singular and efficacious operation of the Almighty can ever accomplish this, for things must be reduced to some familiarity before they can blend and become one. Can the impurity of dross be united with the purity of gold? What then does God do? He sends His own Wisdom before Him, as the last fire shall be sent upon earth to destroy by its activity all that is impure therein and as nothing can resist the power of that fire, in like manner this Wisdom dissolves and destroys all the impurities of the creature and disposes it for Divine Union. This impurity, so opposite to Union, consists in self-sufficiency and activity. This is the source and fountain of all that defilement and corruption which can never be allied to Essential Purity; the rays of the sun may glance, indeed, upon filth and mire, but can never be united with them. Activity obstructs Union; for God being an Infinite Stillness, the soul, in order to be united to Him, must participate in this stillness, else the contrariety between stillness and activity would prevent assimilation. Therefore, the soul can never arrive at Divine Union but by the repose or stillness of the will, nor can it ever become One with God but by being re-established in the purity of its first creation, that is, in this central repose. God purifies the soul by His Wisdom, as refiners do metals in the furnace. Gold cannot be purified but by fire, which gradually separates from and consumes all that is earthy and heterogeneous: it must be melted and dissolved, and all impure mixtures taken away by casting it again and again into the furnace; thus it is refined from all internal corruption, and even exalted to a state incapable of farther purification. The goldsmith now no longer discovers any adulterate mixture; its purity is perfect, its simplicity complete. The fire no longer touches it; and were it to remain an age in the furnace its purity would not be increased nor its substance diminished. Then is it fit for the most exquisite workmanship: and if thereafter this gold seems obscured or defiled, it is no more than an accidental defilement contracted by its contiguity to some impure body; but this is only superficial, and widely different from its former impurity, which was hidden in the very centre and ground of its nature and, as it were, identified with it. Those, however, who are ignorant of this process and its blessed effects would be apt to despise and reject the vessel of pure gold sullied by some external pollution, and prefer an impure and gross metal that appeared superficially bright and polished. Further, the goldsmith never mingles together the pure and the impure gold, lest the dross of the one should corrupt the other; before they can be united they must first be equally refined; lie therefore plunges the impure metal into the furnace till all its dross is purged away and it becomes fully prepared for incorporation and union with the pure gold.

This is what Saint Paul means when he declares that "the fire shall try every man's work of what sort it is" (1 Corinthians 3:13). He adds, "If any man's work be burnt, he shall suffer loss; yet he himself shall be saved, yet so as by fire" (15 verse). He here intimates that there is a species of works so degraded by impure mixtures that though the mercy of God accepts them, yet they must pass through the fire to be purged from the contamination of self; and it is in this sense that God is said to "examine and judge our righteousness" (Psalm 14:3), because that, "by the deeds of the law, there shall no flesh be justified, but by the righteousness of God, which is by faith in Jesus Christ" (Romans 3:20). Thus we see that the Divine Justice and Wisdom, as an unremitting fire, must devour and destroy all that is earthly, sensual, and carnal, and all self-activity, before the soul can be fitted for and capable of Union with God. Now this purification can never be accomplished by the industry of fallen man; on the contrary, he submits to it always with reluctance: he is so enamored of self, and so averse to its destruction, that did not God act upon him powerfully and with authority, he would for ever resist. It may, perhaps, be objected here that as God never robs man of his free will he can always resist the Divine Operations, and that I therefore err in saying God acts thus absolutely and without the consent of man. Let me, however, explain myself. By man's giving a passive consent, God, without usurpation, may assume full power and entire guidance; for having, in the beginning of his conversion, made an unreserved surrender of himself to all that God wills of him or by him, he thereby gave an active consent to whatsoever God thereafter might operate or require. But when God begins to burn, destroy, and purify, then the soul, not perceiving the salutary design of these operations, shrinks from them: and as the gold seems rather to blacken than brighten when first put into the furnace, so it conceives that its purity is lost and that its temptations are sins; insomuch that if an active and explicit consent were then requisite the soul could scarcely give it, nay, often would withhold it. The utmost the soul can do is to remain firm in a passive disposition, enduring as well as it is able all these Divine Operations, which it neither can nor will obstruct. In this manner, therefore, the soul is purified from all proper, distinct, perceptible, and multiplied operations which constitute the great dissimilitude between it and God: it is rendered, by degrees, conformed, and then uniform; and the passive capacity of the creature is elevated, ennobled, and enlarged, though in a secret and hidden manner, and therefore called mystical: but in all these operations the soul must concur passively. It is true, indeed, that at the beginning of its purification activity is requisite; which as the Divine Operations become stronger and stronger it must gradually cease, yielding itself up to the impulses of the Divine Spirit, till wholly absorbed in Him. But this is often a difficult and tedious process. We do not then say, as some have falsely supposed, that there is no need of action in the process of Divine Purification; on the contrary, we affirm it is the gate; at which, however, we would not have those stop who are to obtain ultimate perfection, which is impractical, except the first helps are laid aside: for, however necessary they may have been at the entrance of the road, they become afterwards mere clogs, and greatly detrimental to those who adhere to them, preventing them from ever arriving at the end of their course. This made Saint Paul say, "Forgetting those things which are behind and reaching forth to those which are before, I press toward the mark for the prize of the high calling in Christ Jesus." (Philippians 3:13). Would you not say that he had lost his senses, who, having undertaken an important journey, should fix his abode at the first inn because he had been told that many travelers who had come that way had lodged in the house and made it their place of residence. All that we would wish then is, that souls should press toward the mark, should pursue their journey, and take the shortest and easiest road; not stopping at the first stage, but following the counsel and example of Saint Paul, suffer themselves to be guided and governed by the Spirit of Grace which would infallibly conduct them to the end of their creation, the enjoyment of God. But while we confess that the enjoyment of God is the end for which alone we were created; that without holiness none can attain it: and that to attain it, we must necessarily pass through a severe and purifying process; how strange is it that we should dread and avoid this process, as if that could be the cause of evil or imperfection in the present life, which is to be productive of glory and blessedness in the life to come! None can be ignorant that God is the Supreme Good; that essential blessedness consists in Union with Him; that the Saints are more or less glorified, according as this Union is more or less advanced; and that the soul cannot attain this Union by the mere activity of its own powers: for God communicates Himself to the soul in proportion as its passive capacity is great, noble, and extensive; it cannot be united to God but in simplicity and passivity; and as this Union is beatitude itself, the way to it in simplicity and passivity, instead of being evil, must be good, must be most free from delusion and danger, the safest, the surest, and the best. Would Jesus Christ have made this the most perfect and necessary way had there been evil danger therein? No, all can travel this road to blessedness; and all are called thereto, as to the enjoyment of God, which alone is beatitude, both in this world and the next. I say the enjoyment of God Himself and not His gifts which, as they do not constitute essential beatitude, cannot fully content an immortal spirit: the soul is so noble, so great, that the most exalted gifts of God cannot fill its immense capacity with happiness unless the Giver also bestows Himself. Now the whole desire of the Divine Being is to give Himself to every creature, according to the capacity with which it is endued; and yet, alas, how reluctantly man suffers himself to be drawn to God, how fearful is he to prepare for Divine Union. Some say that we should not attempt, by our own ability, to place ourselves in this state. I grant it: but what a poor subterfuge is this since I have all along asserted and proved that the utmost exertion of the highest created being could never accomplish this of itself, it is God alone must do it. The creature may, indeed, open the window; but it is the sun himself that must give the light. The same persons say again that some may feign to have attained this blessed state: but, alas, none can any more feign this than the wretch who is on the point of perishing with hunger can for a length of time feign to be full and satisfied; some wish or word, some sigh or sign, will inevitably escape him, and betray his famished state. Since then none can attain this blessed state save those whom God Himself leads and places therein, we do not pretend to introduce any into it, but only to point out the shortest and safest road that leads to it: beseeching you not to be retarded in your progress by any external exercises, not to sit down a resident at the first inn, nor to be satisfied with the sweets which are tasted in the milk for babes. If the Water of Eternal Life is shown to some thirsty souls, how inexpressibly cruel would it be, by confining them to a round of external forms, to prevent approaching it, so that their longing shall never be satisfied but they shall perish with thirst! Let us all agree in the way, as we all agree in the end, which is evident and incontrovertible. The way has its beginning, progress, and end; and the nearer we approach the end, the farther is the beginning behind us: it is only by proceeding from one that we can ever arrive at the other. Would you get from the entrance to the distant end of the road without passing over the intermediate space. And surely, if the end is good, holy, and necessary, and the entrance also good, can that be condemnable, as evil, which is the necessary passage, the direct road leading from the one to the other?

O you blind and foolish men, who pride yourselves on science, wisdom, wit, and power, how well do you verify what God has said, that "His Secrets are hidden from the great and wise, and revealed unto babes."

The Way to God
ॐ

"And the glory which You gave me, I have given them; that they may be one even as we are one, (I in them and You in me,) that they may be made perfect in one." — John 17:22

Part One
On The Way to God

The First Degree: Conversion

1. The first degree is the return of the Soul to God, when, being truly converted, it begins to subsist by means of his grace.

The Second Degree: The Effectual Touch in the Will

2. The Soul then receives an effectual Touch in the Will, which invites it to recollection, and instructs it that God is within, and must be sought there; that He is present in the Heart, and must be there enjoyed.

3. This discovery, in the beginning, is the source of very great joy to the Soul, as it is an intimation or pledge of happiness to come; in its very commencement, the road it is to pursue is opened and is shown to be that of the Inward Life. This knowledge is the more admirable, as it is the spring of all the felicity of the Soul, and the solid foundation of interior progress; for those Souls who tend toward God merely by the intellect, even though they should enjoy a somewhat spiritual contemplation, yet can never enter into Intimate Union, if they

do not quit that path and enter this of the Inward Touch, where the whole working is in the Will.

4. Those who are led in this Way, though conducted by a blind abandonment, yet experience a savory knowledge. They never walk by the light of the intellect, like the former, who receive distinct lights to guide them, and who, having a clear view of the road, never enter those impenetrable passes of the hidden Will which are reserved for the latter. The former proceed upon the evidence furnished by their illuminations, assisted by their reason, and they do well; but the latter are destined to pursue blindly an unknown course, which, nevertheless, appears perfectly natural to them, although they seem obliged to feel their way. They go, however, with more certainty than the others, who are subject to be misled in their intellectual illuminations; but these are guided by a supreme Will which conducts them howsoever it will. And further, all the more immediate operations are performed in the Centre of the Soul, that is, in the Three Powers reduced to the Unity of the Will, where they are all absorbed, insensibly following the path prescribed for them by that Touch to which we have before referred.

5. These latter are they who pursue the Way of Faith and absolute Abandonment. They have neither relish nor liberty for any other path; all else constrains and embarrasses them. They dwell in greater aridness than the others, for as there is nothing distinct to which their minds are attached, their thoughts often wander and have nothing to fix them. And as there are differences in Souls, some having more sensible delights, and others being drier, so it is with those who are led by the Will; the former sort have more relish and less solid acquirement, and should restrain their too eager disposition, and suffer their emotions to pass, even when they seem burning with love; the latter seem harder and more insensible, and their state appears altogether natural; nevertheless, there is a delicate something in the depth of the Will, which serves to nourish them, and which is, as it were, the condensed Essence of what the others experience in the intellect and in ardor of purpose.

6. Still, as this support is exceedingly delicate, it frequently becomes imperceptible, and is hidden by the slightest thing. This

gives rise to great suffering, especially in times of tribulation and temptation; for as the relish and support are delicate and concealed, the Will partakes of the same character in a high degree, so that such Souls have none of those strong wills. Their state is more indifferent and insensible, and their way more equable; but this does not hinder them from having as severe and even more serious trouble than others; for nothing being done in them by impulse, everything takes place, as it were, naturally, and their feeble, insensible, hidden Wills cannot be found, to make head against their foes. Their Fidelity, however, often excels that of the others. Notice the striking difference between Peter and John; one seems to be overflowing with extraordinary zeal, and falls away at the voice of a maid servant; the other makes no external manifestation, and remains faithful unto the end.

7. You will ask me, then, if these Souls are urged on by no violent influence, but walk in blindness, do they do the will of God? They do, more truly, although they have no distinct assurance of it; His Will is engraved in indelible characters on their very inmost recesses, so that they perform with a cold and languid, but firm and inviolable, abandonment, what the others accomplish by the drawings of an exquisite delight.

8. Thus they go on under the influence of this divine touch, from one degree to another, by a faith more or less sensibly savory, and experience constant alternations of aridity and enjoyment of the presence of God, but ever finding that the enjoyment becomes continually deeper and less perceptible, and thus more delicate and interior. They discover, too, that in the midst of their aridity, and without any distinct illumination, they are not the less enlightened; for this state is luminous in itself, though dark to the Soul that dwells in it. And so true is this, that they find themselves more acquainted with the truth; I mean that truth implanted in their interior, and which causes everything to yield to the Will of God. This divine Will becomes more familiar to them, and they are enabled, in their insipid way, to penetrate a thousand Mysteries that never could have been discovered by the light of reason and knowledge. They are insensibly and gradually preparing, without being aware of it, for the states that are to follow.

9. The trials of this state are alternations of dryness and facility. The former purified the attachment or tendency and natural relish that we have for the enjoyment of God. So that the whole of this degree is passed in these alternations of enjoyment, aridity, and facility, without any intermixture of temptations, except very transitory ones, or certain faults; for in every state, from the beginning onward, the faults of nature are much more liable to overtake us in times of aridity than in seasons of interior joy, when the Unction of Grace secures us from a thousand evils. In all the preceding states thus far, the Soul is engaged in combating its evil habits, and in endeavoring to overcome them by all sorts of painful Self-denial.

10. In the beginning, when God turned its look inward, he so influenced it against itself, that it was obliged to cut off all its enjoyments, even the most innocent, and to load itself with every kind of affliction. God gives no respite to some in this regard, until the life of Nature, that is, of the exterior senses as manifested in appetites, likes and dislikes, is wholly destroyed.

11. This destruction of the appetites and repugnance's of the outward senses, belongs to the second degree, which I have called the effectual Touch in the Will, and in which the highest and greatest virtue is practiced, especially when the inward drawing is vigorous and the Unction very savory. For there is no sort of contrivance that God does not discover to the Soul, to enable it to conquer and overcome Self in everything; so that at length, by this constant practice, accompanied by the gracious Unction before referred to, the Spirit gets the upper hand of Nature, and the interior part comes under subjection without resistance. There is, then, no further trouble from this source, any more than if all external feeling had been taken away. This state is mistaken, by those who are but little enlightened, for a state of Death; it is, indeed, the Death of the Senses, but there is yet a long way to that of the Spirit.

The Third Degree: Passivity and Interior Sacrifice

12. When we have for some time enjoyed the repose of a victory that has cost us so much trouble, and suppose ourselves

forever relieved from an enemy whose whole power has been destroyed, we enter into the third degree, next in order to the other, which is a Way of Faith more or less savory, according to the state. We enter into a condition of alternate dryness and facility, as I have stated, and in this dryness, the Soul perceives certain exterior weaknesses, natural defects, which, though slight, take it by surprise; it feels, too, that the strength it had received for the struggle, is dying away. This is caused by the loss of our active, inward force; for although the Soul, in the second degree, imagines itself to be in silence before God, it is not entirely so. It does not speak, indeed, either in Heart or by Mouth, but it is in an active striving after God and constant out breathing of Love, so that, being the subject of the most powerful amorous activity, exerted by the Divine Love towards Himself, it is continually leaping, as it were, towards its object, and its activity is accompanied by a delightful and almost constant Peace. As it is from this activity of Love that we acquire the strength to overcome Nature, it is then that we practice the greatest virtues and most severe mortifications.

13. But just in proportion as this activity decays, and is lost in an amorous passivity, so does our strength of resistance sink and diminish, and, as this degree advances, and the Soul becomes more and more passive, it becomes more and more powerless in combat. As God becomes strong within, so do we become weak. Some regard this impossibility of resistance as a great temptation, but they do not see that all our labor, aided and assisted by Grace, can only accomplish the conquest of our Outward Senses, after which God takes gradual possession of our Interior, and becomes Himself our purifier. And as He required all our watchfulness while He continued us in amorous activity, so He now requires all our Fidelity to let Him work, while He begins to render Himself Lord by the subjection of the Flesh to the Spirit.

14. For it must be observed that all our outward Perfection depends upon, and must follow the inward; so that when we are employed in active devotion, however simple, we are actively engaged against ourselves just as simply.

15. The second degree accomplishes the destruction of the Outward Senses, the third, that of the Inward and this is brought about by means of this savory passivity. But as God is then working within, He seems to neglect the outward, and hence the reappearance of defects, though feebly and only in a time of aridity, which we thought extinct.

16. The nearer we approach the termination of the third degree, the longer and more frequent are our aridities, and the greater our weakness. This is a purification which serves to destroy our internal feelings, as the amorous activity put an end to our external, and in each degree, there are alternations of dryness and enjoyment. The dryness serves as a purifier of the joy that is to follow; it is always painful from its barrenness and weakness. As soon as we cease, from inability, to practice mortifications of our own fashioning, those of Providence take their place — the crosses which God dispenses according to our degree. These are not chosen by the Soul; but the Soul, under the interior guidance of God, receives such as He appoints.

The Fourth Degree: Naked Faith

17. The fourth degree is Naked Faith; here we have nothing but inward and outward desolation; for the one always follows the other.

18. Every degree has its beginning, progress, and consummation.

19. All that has hitherto been granted and acquired with so much labor, is here gradually taken away.

20. This degree is the longest, and only ends with total death, if the Soul be willing to be so desolated as to die wholly to Self. For there is an infinite number of Souls that never pass the first degrees, and of those who reach the present state there are very few in whom its perfect work is accomplished.

21. This desolation takes place in some with violence, and although they suffer more distress than others, yet they have less reason to complain, for the very severity of their affliction is a sort of consolation. There are others who experience only a

feebleness and a kind of disgust for everything, which has the appearance of being a failure in duty and unwillingness to obey.

22. We are first deprived of our voluntary works, and become unable to do what we did in the preceding degrees; and as this increases, we begin to feel a general inability in respect to everything, which, instead of diminishing, enlarges day by day. This weakness and inability gradually taking possession of us, we enter upon a condition in which we say: "For that which I do, I allow not; for what I would, that do I not; but what I hate, that do I." (Romans 7:15)

23. After being thus deprived of all things, both inward and outward, which are not essential, the work begins upon those which are; and in proportion as the virtuous life becoming a Christian, which we regarded with so much complacency, disappears, we are likewise spoiled of a certain interior delight and substantial support. As this support becomes weaker and more subtle, the more perceptible becomes its loss. It is to be remarked, however, that there is no loss except to our own consciousness, as it still exists in the Soul, but imperceptibly and without apparent action. If it were not hidden, the death and loss of Self could not be accomplished. But it retires within, and shuts itself up so closely that the Soul is not aware of its presence.

24. Do you ask why this course is pursued? The whole object of the Way thus far has been to cause the Soul to pass from multiplicity to the distinct sensible without multiplicity; from the distinct sensible to the distinct insensible; then to the sensible indistinct, which is a general delight much less attractive than the other. It is vigorous in the beginning and introduces the Soul into the perceived, which is a purer and less exquisite pleasure than the first; from the perceived, into Faith sustained and working by Love; passing in this Way from the sensible to the spiritual, and from the spiritual to Naked Faith, which, causing us to be dead to all spiritual experiences, makes us die to ourselves and pass into God, that we may live henceforth from the Life of God only.

25. In the economy of Grace, then, we begin with sensible things, continue with those which are spiritual, and end

by leading the Soul gradually into its centre, and uniting it with God.

26. The more deeply this imperceptible support retires, the more does it knit the Soul together, so that it cannot continue to multiply itself among a thousand things which it can no longer either affect or even perceive; and, entirely stripped, it is gradually obliged to desert even itself.

27. It is stripped without mercy, then, equally and at the same time, of everything both within and without, and what is worst of all, is delivered over to temptations; and the more fully it is thus given up to temptation, the more completely is it deprived of strength to resist them from without; thus it is weakened still farther at the very time when it is subjected to more violent attacks, and finally its internal support is removed, which, while it served as a refuge and asylum, would be an evidence of the Goodness of God, and of its Faithfulness to itself.

28. So you may see a man pursued by a powerful adversary; he fights, and defends himself as well as he is able, always contriving, however, to get nearer and nearer to a Stronghold of Safety; but the longer he fights the weaker he becomes, while the strength of his opponent is constantly increasing. What shall he do? He will gain the portal of the stronghold as adroitly as he can, for there he will find abundant aid. But, on reaching it, he sees that it is closed, and finds that, far from rendering him any assistance, the keepers have barricaded every loophole of refuge; he must fall into the hands of his powerful enemy, whom he recognizes, when, defenseless and in despair, he has given himself up, as his best and truest friend.

29. Be sure, then, that this degree comprehends all these things; the privation of every good, the accumulation of all sorts of weaknesses, powerlessness of defense, no interior asylum; God himself often appears angry; and, to crown all, temptations.

30. Willingly, I think I hear you say, provided I might be sure that my Will was not in harmony with the malignity of Nature and the weaknesses of the senses. Ah, you would be too happy; but that cannot be. In proportion as you become enfeebled and destitute of every operation and activity of Love,

however insignificant, the Will, which was founded in that vigor of Love, becoming weaker day by day, gradually disappears; and vanishing thus, it is certain that it takes no part in anything that is passing in the man, but is separate. But as it does not manifest itself anywhere, by any sign, it affords no assured support to the Soul, but the contrary; for, no longer finding the Will in an attitude of resistance, the Soul believes that it is consenting to everything, and that it has joined in with the animal will, which is the only one perceptible.

31. You will, perhaps, remind one that I have before stated that, in the first contest of amorous activity, Nature and the Senses had become, as it were, extinguished and subdued. It is true; but the Spirit of Self, by the very victories that Grace had thus acquired for it, has become high-minded, more tenacious of what it esteems good, and still more indomitable. God, who is determined to subdue it, makes use for that purpose, of an apparent resurrection of that same nature which the Soul supposed dead. But observe that He does not use Nature until He has extracted its malignity, destroyed it and separated the superior Will from that which rendered it violent and criminal. He extracts the venom of the viper, and then uses it as an antidote to the Spirit. Whoever shall become acquainted with the admirable Economy of Grace and the Wisdom of God in bringing man to a total sacrifice of Self, will be filled with delight, and, insensible as he may be, will expire with Love. The little traces of it which have been revealed to my Heart, have often overwhelmed me with ecstasy and transport.

32. Fidelity in this degree requires us to suffer Spoliation to the whole extent of the designs of God, without being anxious about ourselves, sacrificing to God all our interests both for time and for eternity. Nothing must be made a pretext for reserving or retaining the slightest atom, for the least reservation is the cause of an irreparable loss, as it prevents our death, from being total. We must let God work his absolute pleasure, and suffer the winds and tempests to beat upon us from every quarter, submerged, as we may often be, beneath the tumultuous billows.

33. A wonderful thing is here perceived; far from being estranged by our suffering and wretched state, it is then that God

appears; and if any weakness has been apparent, He gives us some token of his immediate presence, as if to assure the Soul for a moment, that He was with it in its tribulation. I say for a moment, for it is of no service subsequently, as a support, but is rather intended to point out the Way and invite the Soul to the further loss of Self.

34. These states are not continuous in their violence; there are remissions, which, while they afford space for taking breath, serve, at the same time, to render the subsequent trial more painful. For Nature will make use of anything to sustain its life, as a drowning man will support himself in the water by clinging to the blade of a razor, without adverting to the pain it causes him, if there be nothing else within his reach.

The Fifth Degree: Mystical Death

35. Attacked thus on all sides by so many enemies, without life and without support, we have no recourse but to expire in the arms of Love. When death is complete, the most terrible states cause no further trouble. We do not recognize death from the fact of having passed through all these states, but by an absolute want of power to feel pain, to think of or care for Self, and, by our indifference to remaining there forever, without manifesting the slightest sign of vitality. Life is evidenced by a Will for or repugnance to something; but here, in this death of the Soul, all things are alike. It remains dead and insensible to everything that concerns itself, and, let God reduce it to what extremity He will, feels no repugnance. It has no choice between being Angel or Demon, because it has no longer any eyes for Self. It is then that God has placed all its enemies beneath his footstool, and, reigning supreme, takes and possesses it the more fully, as it has the more completely deserted itself. But this takes place by degrees.

36. There remains for a long time, even after death, a trace of the living heat, which is only gradually dissipated. All states effect somewhat towards cleansing the Soul, but here the process is completed.

37. We do not die spiritually, once for all, as we do naturally; it is accomplished gradually; we vibrate between life and death, being sometimes in one and sometimes in the other, until death has finally conquered life. And so it is in the resurrection; an alternate state of life and death, until life has finally overcome death.

38. Not that the new life does not come suddenly. He who was dead, finds himself living, and can never afterward doubt that he was dead and is alive again; but it is not then established; it is rather a disposition toward living, then a settled state of life.

39. The first life of Grace began in the sensible, and sank continually inward toward the Centre, until, having reduced the Soul to Unity, it caused it to expire in the arms of Love; for all experience this death, but each by means peculiar to himself. But the life that is now communicated arises from within; it is, as it were, a living germ which has always existed there, though unobserved, and which demonstrates that the life of Grace has never been wholly absent, however it may have been suffered to remain hidden. There it remained even in the midst of death; nor was it less death because life was concealed in it; as the silkworm lies long dead in the chrysalis, but contains a germ of life that awakes it to a resurrection. This new life, then, buds in the Centre, and grows from there; thence it gradually extends over all the faculties and senses, impregnating them with its own life and fecundity.

40. The Soul, endued with this vitality, experiences an infinite contentment; not in itself, but in God; and this especially when the life is well advanced.

41. But, before entering upon the effects of this admirable life, let me say, that there are some who do not pass through these painful deaths; they only experience a mortal languor and fainting, which annihilate them, and cause them to die to all.

42. Many spiritual persons have given the name of death, to the earlier purifications, which are, indeed, a death in relation to the life communicated, but not a total death. They result in an

extinguishment of some one of the lives of Nature, or of Grace; but that is widely different from a general extinction of all life.

43. Death has various names, according to our different manner of expression or conception. It is called a departure, that is, a separation from Self in order that we may pass into God; a loss, total and entire, of the Will of the creature, which causes the Soul to be wanting to itself, that it may exist only in God. Now, as this Will is in everything that subsists in the creature, however good and holy it may be, all these things must necessarily be destroyed, so far as they so subsist, and so far as the good will of man is in them, that the Will of God alone may remain. Everything born of the will of the flesh and the will of man, must be destroyed. Then nothing but the Will of God is left, which becomes the principle of the new life, and, gradually animating the old extinguished will, takes its place and changes it into Faith.

44. From the time that the Soul expires mystically, it is separated generally from everything that would be an obstacle to its perfect Union with God; but it is not, for all that, received into God. This causes it the most extreme suffering. You will object here, that, if it be wholly dead, it can no longer suffer. Let me explain.

45. The Soul is dead as soon as it is separated from Self; but this death or mystic decease is not complete until it has passed into God. Until then, it suffers very greatly, but its suffering is general and indistinct, and proceeds solely from the fact that it is not yet established in its proper place.

46. The suffering which precedes death, is caused by our repugnance to the means that are to produce it. This repugnance returns whenever these means recur, or grow sharper; but in proportion as we die we become more and more insensible, and seem to harden under the blows, until at last death comes in truth through an entire cessation of all life. God has unrelentingly pursued our life into all its covert hiding places; for so malignant is it, that when hard pressed, it fortifies itself in its refuges, and makes use of the holiest and most reasonable pretexts for existence; but, being persecuted and followed into its last retreat,

in a few souls (alas! how few!) it is obliged to abandon them altogether.

47. No pain then remains arising from the means which have caused our death, and which are exactly the opposite to those which used to maintain our life; the more reasonable and holy the latter are in appearance, the more unreasonable and defiled is the look of the other.

48. But after death — which is the cause of the Soul's departure from Self, that is, of its losing every Self-appropriation whatever; for we never know how strongly we cling to objects until they are taken away, and he who thinks that he is attached to nothing, is frequently grandly mistaken, being bound to a thousand things, unknown to himself — after death, I repeat, the Soul is entirely rid of Self, but not at first received into God. There still exists a something, I know not exactly what, a form, a human remnant; but that also vanishes. It is a tarnish which is destroyed by a general, indistinct suffering, having no relation to the means of death, since they are passed away and completed; but it is an uneasiness arising from the fact of being turned out of Self, without being received into its great Original. The Soul loses all possession of Self, without which it could never be united to God; but it is only gradually that it becomes fully possessed of Him by means of the new life, which is wholly divine.

Union with God: But Not Yet Recognized

49. As soon as the Soul has died in the embraces of the Lord, it is united to Him in truth and without any intermediate; for in losing everything, even its best possessions, it has lost the means and intermediates which dwelt in them; and even these greatest treasures themselves were but intermediates. It is, then, from that moment, united to God immediately, but it does not recognize it, nor does it enjoy the fruits of its Union, until He animates it and becomes its vivifying principle. A bride fainting in the arms of her husband, is closely united to him, but she does not enjoy the blessedness of the union, and may even be unconscious of it; but when he has contemplated her for some time, fainting from excess of love, and recalls her to life by his

tender caresses, then she perceives that she is in possession of him whom her Soul loves, and that she is possessed by him.

Part Two

On Union With God

The Resurrection

50. The Soul thus possessed of God, finds that He is so perfectly Lord over it, that it can no longer do anything but what He pleases and as He pleases; and this state goes on increasing. Its powerlessness is no longer painful but pleasant, because it is full of the Life and Power of the Divine Will.

51. The dead Soul is in Union, but it does not enjoy the fruits of it until the moment of its Resurrection, when God, causing it to pass into Him, gives it such pledges and assurances of the consummation of its Divine Marriage, that it can no longer doubt: for this immediate Union is so spiritual, so refined, so divine, so intimate, that it is equally impossible for the Soul to conceive or to doubt it. For we may observe that the whole way whereof we speak, is infinitely removed from any imagination; these Souls are not in the least imaginative, having nothing in the intellect, and are perfectly protected from deceptions and illusions, as everything takes place within.

52. During their passage through the Way of Faith, they had nothing distinct, for distinctness is entirely opposed to Faith, and they could not enjoy anything of that sort, having only a certain generality as a foundation upon which everything was communicated to them. But it is far otherwise when the life becomes advanced in God; for though they have nothing distinct for themselves, they have for others, and their illumination for the use of others, though not always received by those for whom it was intended, is the more certain as it is more immediate, and as it were natural.

53. When God raises a Soul, that is to say, receives it into Himself, and the living germ, which is no other than the Life and

Spirit of the Word, begins to appear, it constitutes the Revelation in it of Jesus Christ, (Galatians 1:16) who lives in us by the loss of the life of Adam subsisting in Self.

54. The Soul is thus received into God, and is there gradually changed and transformed into Him, as food is transformed into the one who has partaken of it. All this takes place without any loss of its own individual existence, as has been elsewhere explained.

55. When transformation begins, it is called annihilation, since in changing our form, we become annihilated as to our own, in order to take on His. This operation goes on constantly during life, changing the Soul more and more into God, and conferring upon it a continually increasing participation in the divine qualities, making it unchangeable, immovable, etc. But He also renders it fruitful in, and not out of, Himself.

56. This fruitfulness extends to certain persons whom God gives and attaches to the Soul, communicating to it his Love, full of Charity. For the love of these divine Souls for the persons thus bestowed upon them, while it is far removed from the natural feelings, is infinitely stronger than the love of parents for their children, and though it appears eager and precipitate, it is not so, because he, who exhibits it, merely follows the movement impressed upon him.

57. To make this intelligible, we must know that God did not deprive the senses and faculties of their life, to leave them dead; for though there might be life in the Centre of the Soul, they would remain dead if that life were not also communicated to them. It increases by degrees, animates all the powers and senses which, until then, had remained barren and unfruitful, enlarges them in proportion to its communication, and renders them active, but with an activity derived and regulated from God, according to His own designs. Persons in a dying or dead condition, must not condemn the activity of such Souls, for they could never have been put in divine motion if they had not passed through the most wonderful death. During the whole period of Faith, the Soul remains motionless; but after God has infused into it the Divine Activity, its sphere is vastly extended;

but, great as it may be, it cannot execute a Self-originated movement.

The Life In God

58. There is no more to be said here of degrees; that of Glory being all that remains, every means being left behind, and the future consisting in our enjoying an infinite stretch of life, and that more and more abundantly. (John 10:10) As God transforms the Soul into Himself, his life is communicated to it more plentifully. The Love of God for the creature is incomprehensible, and his assiduity inexplicable; some Souls He pursues without intermission, prevents them, seats Himself at their door, and delights Himself in being with them and in loading them with the marks of his Love. He impresses this chaste, pure, and tender love upon the Heart. Saint Paul and Saint John the Evangelist, felt the most of this maternal affection. But to be as I have described it, it must be bestowed upon the Soul in the state of Grace of which I have just spoken; otherwise, such emotions are purely natural.

59. The prayer of the state of Faith is an absolute silence of all the powers of the Soul, and a cessation of every working, however delicate, especially toward its termination. The Soul in that state, perceiving no more prayer, and not being able to set apart fixed seasons for it, since all such exercises are taken away, is led to think that it has absolutely lost all kind of devotion. But when life returns, Prayer returns with it, and accompanied by a marvelous facility; and as God takes possession of the senses and faculties, its devotion becomes sweet, gentle, and very spiritual, but always to God. Its former devotion caused it to sink within itself, that it might enjoy God, but that which it now has, draws it out of Self, that it may be more and more lost and changed in God.

60. This difference is quite remarkable, and can only be accomplished by experience. The Soul is silent in the state of death, but its stillness is barren, and accompanied by a frantic rambling, which leaves no mark of silence save the impossibility of addressing God, either with the lips or the heart. But after the

Resurrection, its silence is fruitful and attended by an exceedingly pure and refined Unction, which is deliciously diffused over the senses, but with such a purity, that it occasions no stay and contracts no taint.

61. It is now impossible for the Soul to take what it has not, or to put off what it has. It receives with passive willingness whatever impressions are made upon it. Its state, however overwhelming, would be free from suffering, if God, who moves it towards certain free things, gave them the necessary correspondence. But as their state will not bear it, it becomes necessary that what God wills they should have, should be communicated by means of suffering for them.

62. It would be wrong for such persons to say that they do not wish these means; that they desire God only. He is anxious that they should die to a certain interior support of Self, which causes them to say that they desire God only, and if they were to reject these means, they would withdraw themselves from the order of God, and arrest their progress. But, being given simply as means, though fruitful in grace and virtue, however secret and concealed, they finally disappear when the Soul finds itself united with the means in God, and He communicates Himself directly. Then God withdraws the means, upon which he no longer impresses any movement in the direction of the person to whom they are attached; because it might then serve as a stay, its utility being at last recognized. The Soul can then no longer have what it had, and remains in its first death in respect to them, though still very closely united.

63. In this state of Resurrection comes that ineffable silence, by which we not only subsist in God, but commune with Him, and which, in a Soul thus dead to its own working, and general and fundamental Self-appropriation, becomes a flux and reflux of Divine Communion, with nothing to sully its purity; for there is nothing to hinder it.

64. The Soul then becomes a partaker of the ineffable communion of the Trinity, where the Father of Spirits imparts his spiritual fecundity, and makes it one Spirit with Himself. Here it is that it communes with other Souls, if they are sufficiently pure

to receive its communications in silence, according to their degree and state; here, that the ineffable secrets are revealed, not by a momentary illumination, but in God Himself, where they are all hid, the Soul not possessing them for itself, nor being ignorant of them.

65. Although I have said that the Soul then has something distinct, yet it is not distinct in reference to itself, but to those with whom it communes; for what it says is said naturally and without attention, but seems extraordinary to the hearers, who, not finding the thing in themselves, notwithstanding it may be there, consider it as something distinct and wonderful, or perhaps fanatical. Souls that are still dwelling among gifts, have distinct and momentary illuminations, but these latter have only a general illumination, without defined beams, which is God Himself; whence they draw whatever they need, which is distinct whenever it is required by those with whom they are conversing, and without any of it remaining with themselves afterwards.

The Transformation

66. There are a thousand things that might be said about the inward and celestial life of the Soul thus full of life in God, which He dearly cherishes for Himself, and which He covers externally with abasement, because He is a jealous God. But it would require a volume, and I have only to fulfill your request. God is the life and Soul of this Soul, which thus uninterruptedly lives in God, as a fish in the sea, in inexpressible happiness, though loaded with the sufferings which God lays upon it for others.

67. It has become so simple, especially when its transformation is far advanced, that it goes its way perpetually without a thought for any creature or for itself. It has but one object, to do the will of God. But as it has to do with many of the creatures who cannot attain to this state, some of them cause it suffering by endeavoring to compel it to have a care for Self, to take precautions, and so on, which it cannot do; and others by their want of correspondence to the Will of God.

68. The crosses of such Souls are the most severe, and God keeps them under the most abject humiliations and a very common and feeble exterior, though they are his delight. Then Jesus Christ communicates Himself in all his states, and the Soul is clothed upon both with his inclinations and sufferings. It understands what man has cost Him, what his faithlessness has made Him suffer, what is the redemption of Jesus Christ, and how He has borne his children.

69. The Transformation is recognized by the want of distinction between God and the Soul, it not being able any longer to separate itself from God; everything is equally God, because it has passed into its Original Source, is reunited to its All, and changed into Him. But it is enough for me to sketch the general outlines of what you desire to know; experience will teach you the rest, and having shown you what I ought to be to you, you may judge of what I am in our Lord.

70. In proportion as its Transformation is perfected, the Soul finds a more extended quality in itself. Everything is expanded and dilated, God making it a partaker of His infinity; so that it often finds itself immense, and the whole earth appears but as a point in comparison with this wonderful breadth and extension. Whatever is in the order and will of God, expands it; everything else contracts it; and this contraction restrains it from passing out. As the Will is the means of effecting the transformation, and the Center is nothing else but all the faculties united in the will, the more the Soul is transformed, the more its will is changed and passed into that of God, and the more God Himself wills for the Soul. The Soul acts and works in this Divine Will, which is thus substituted for its own, so naturally, that it cannot tell whether the will of the Soul is become the Will of God, or the Will of God become the will of the Soul.

71. God frequently exacts strange sacrifices from Souls thus transformed in Him; but it costs them nothing, for they will sacrifice everything to Him without repugnance. The smaller sacrifices cost the most, and the greater ones the least, for they are not required until the Soul is in a state to grant them without difficulty, to which it has a natural tendency. This is what is said of Jesus Christ on his coming into the world; "Then said I, Lo, I

come: in the volume of the book it is written of me; I delight to do thy will, O my God; yea, thy law is within my heart." (Psalm 11:7-8) As soon as Christ comes into any Soul to become its living principle, He says the same thing of it; He becomes the eternal Priest who unceasingly fulfills within the Soul his sacerdotal office. This is sublime indeed, and continues until the victim is carried to glory.

72. God destines these Souls for the assistance of others in the most tangled paths; for, having no longer any anxiety in regard to themselves, nor anything to lose, God can use them to bring others into the way of his pure, naked and assured Will. Those who are still Self-possessed, could not be used for this purpose; for, not having yet entered into a state where they follow the Will of God blindly for themselves, but always mingling it with their own reasoning, and false wisdom, they are not by any means in a condition to withhold nothing in following it blindly for others. When I say withhold nothing, I mean of that which God desires in the present moment; for He frequently does not permit us to point out to a person all that hinders him, and what we see must come to pass in respect to him, except in general terms, because he cannot bear it. And though we may sometimes say hard things, as Christ did to the Capernaites, He nevertheless bestows a secret strength to bear it; at least He does so to the Souls whom He has chosen solely for Himself; and this is the Touchstone.

SPIRITUAL TORRENTS
ଔଃଊ

Part One

Chapter One

As soon as a soul is brought under divine influence, and its return to God is true and sincere, after the first cleansing which confession and contrition have effected, God imparts to it a certain instinct to return to Him in a most complete manner, and to become united to Him. The soul feels then that it was not created for the amusements and trifles of the world, but that it has a centre and an end, to which it must be its aim to return, and out of which it can never find true repose. This instinct is very deeply implanted in the soul, more or less in different cases, according to the designs of God; but all have a loving impatience to purify themselves, and to adopt the necessary ways and means of returning to their source and origin, like rivers, which, after leaving their source, flow on continuously, in order to precipitate themselves into the sea. You will observe that some rivers move gravely and slowly, and others with greater velocity; but there are rivers and torrents which rush with frightful impetuosity, and which nothing can arrest. All the burdens which might be laid upon them, and the obstructions which might be placed to impede their course, would only serve to redouble their violence. It is thus with souls. Some go on quietly towards perfection, and never reach the sea, or only very late, contented to lose themselves in some stronger and more rapid river, which carries them with itself into the sea. Others, which form the second class, flow on more vigorously and promptly than the first. They even carry with them a number of rivulets; but they are slow and idle in comparison with the last class, which rush onward with so much impetuosity, that they are utterly useless. They are not available for navigation, nor can any merchandise be trusted upon them, except at certain parts and at certain times. These are bold and mad rivers, which dash against the rocks, which terrify by their noise, and which stop at nothing. The second class is more agreeable and more useful; their gravity is pleasing, they are all laden with merchandise, and we sail upon them without fear or peril. Let us look, with divine aid, at these three classes of persons, under the three figures that I have proposed; and we will commence with the first, in order to conclude happily with the last.

Chapter Two

The first souls are those who, after their conversion, give themselves up to meditation, or even to works of charity. They perform some exterior austerities; endeavor, little by little, to purify themselves, to rid themselves of certain notable sins, and even of voluntary venial ones. They endeavor, with all their little strength, to advance gradually, but it is feebly and slowly. As their source is not abundant, the dryness sometimes causes delay. There are even periods, in times of aridity, when they dry up altogether. They do not cease to flow from the source, but it is so feebly as to be barely perceptible. These rivers carry little or no merchandise, and, therefore, for the public need, it must be taken to them. It is necessary, at the same time, that art should assist nature, and find the means of enlarging them, either by canals, or by the help of other rivers of the same kind, which are joined together and united to it, which rivers thus joined increase the body of water, and, helping each other, put themselves in a condition to carry a few small boats, not to the sea, but to some of the chief rivers, of which we shall speak later. Such beings have usually little depth of spiritual life. They work outwardly, and rarely quit their meditations, so that they are not fit for great things. In general they carry no merchandise - that is to say, they can impart nothing to others; and God seldom uses them, unless it be to carry a few little boats - that is, to minister to bodily necessities; and in order to be used, they must be discharged into the canals of sensible graces, or united to some others in religion, by which means several, of medium grace, manage to carry the small boat, but not into the sea itself, which is God - into that they never enter in this life, but only in the next. It is not that souls are not sanctified in this way. There are many people, who pass for being very virtuous, who never get beyond it, God giving them lights conformed to their condition, which are sometimes very beautiful, and are the admiration of the religious world. The most highly favored of this class are diligent in the practice of virtue; they devise thousands of holy inventions and practices to lead them to God, and to enable them to abide in His presence; but all is accomplished by their own efforts, aided and supported by grace, and their own works appear to exceed the work of God, His work only concurring with theirs. The spiritual life of this class only thrives in proportion to their work. If this work be removed, the progress of grace within them is arrested. They resemble pumps, which only yield water in proportion as they are agitated. You will observe in them a great tendency to assist themselves by means of their natural sensibilities, a vigorous activity, a desire to be always doing something more and something new to promote their perfection, and, in their seasons of barrenness, an anxiety to rid themselves of it. They are subject to great variation, sometimes they do wonders, at other times they languish and decline. They have no evenness of conduct, because, as the greater part of their religion is in these natural sensibilities, whenever it happens that their sensibilities are dry, either from want of work on their part, or from a lack of correspondence on the part of God, they fall into discouragement, or else they redouble their efforts, in the hope of recovering of themselves what they have lost. They never possess, like others, a profound peace or calmness in the midst of distractions; on the contrary, they are always on the alert to struggle against them or to complain of them. Such minds must not be directed to passive devotion; this would be to ruin them irrecoverably, taking from them their means of access to God. For as with a person who is compelled to travel, and who has neither boat nor carriage, nor any other alternative than that of going on foot, if you remove his feet, you place advancement beyond his reach; so with these souls; if you take away their works, which are their feet, they can never advance. And I believe this to be the cause of the contests which now agitate the religious world. Those who are in the passive way, conscious of the blessedness they experience in it, would compel all to walk with them; those, on the contrary, who are in what I have termed the state of meditation, would confine all to their way, which would involve inestimable loss. What must be done then? We must take the middle course, and see for which of the two ways souls are fitted. This may be known in some by the opposition they have to remaining at rest, and allowing themselves to be led by the Spirit of God; by a confusion of faults and defects into which they fall without being conscious of them; or, if they are possessed of natural prudence, by a certain skill in concealing their faults from others and from themselves; by their adherence to their sentiments, and by a number of other indications which cannot be explained. The way to deliver them from such a state would be, to lead them to live less in the intellect and more in the affections, and if it be manifest that they are gradually substituting the one for the other, it is a sign that a spiritual work is being carried on within them. I am at a loss to understand why so loud a cry is raised against those books and writers that treat of the inner life. I maintain that they can do no harm, unless it be to some who are willing to lose themselves for the sake of their own pleasure, to whom not only these things, but everything else, would be an injury. But they can do no injury to those humble souls who are desirous for perfection, because it is impossible for any to understand them to whom the special light is not accorded; and whatever others may read, they cannot rightly understand those conditions which, being beyond the range of imagination, can be known only by experience. Perfection goes on with a steady advancement corresponding to the progress of the inner life. Not that there are no persons advanced in sanctification who have faults in appearance even greater than those of others, but they are not the same either as to their nature or their quality. The second reason why I say that such books can do no harm is, that they demand so much natural death, so much breaking off, so many things to be conquered and destroyed, that no one would ever have strength for the undertaking without sincerity of purpose; or even if anyone undertook it, it would only produce the effect of meditation, which is to endeavor to destroy itself. As for those who wish to lead others in their groove, and not in God's, and to place limits to their further advancement - as for those, I say, who know but one way, and would have all the world to walk in it, the evils which they bring upon others are irremediable, for they keep them all their lives stopping at certain things which hinder God from blessing them infinitely. It seems to me that we must act in the divine life as in a school. The scholars are not kept always in the same class, but are passed on to others more advanced. Oh human science! You are so little worth, and yet with you men do not fail to take every precaution! Oh science mysterious and divine! You are so great and so necessary; and yet they neglect you, they limit you, they contract you, they do violence to you! Oh, will there never be a school of religion! Alas! By wishing to make it a study, man has marred it. He has sought to give rules and limits to the Spirit of God, who is without limit. Oh poor powerless souls! You are better fitted to answer God's purposes, and, if you are faithful, your devotion will be more pleasing to Him, than that of those great intellects which make prayer a study rather than a devotion. More than this, I say that such souls as these, who appear so powerless and so incapable, are worthy of consideration, provided they only knock at the door, and wait with a humble patience until it be opened to them. Those persons of great intellect and subtle understanding who can not remain a moment in silence before God, who make a continual Babel, who are so well able to give an account of their devotion in all its parts, who go through it always according to their own will, and with the same method, who exercise themselves as they will on any subject which suggests itself to them, who are so well satisfied with themselves and their light, who expatiate upon the preparation and the methods for prayer, will make but little advance in it; and after ten or twenty years of this exercise, will always remain the same. Alas! When it is a question of loving a miserable creature, do they use a method for that? The most ignorant in such a matter are the most skilful. It is the same, and yet very different, with divine love. Therefore, if one who has never known such religion comes to you to learn it, teach him to love God much, and to let himself go with a perfect abandonment into love, and he will soon know it. If it be a nature slow to love, let him do his best, and wait in patience till love itself make itself beloved in its own way, and not in yours.

Chapter Three

The second class is like those large rivers which move with a slow and steady course. They flow with pomp and majesty; their course is direct and easily followed; they are charged with merchandise, and can go on to the sea without mingling with other rivers; but they are late in reaching it, being grave and slow. There are even some who never reach it at all, and these, for the most part, lose themselves in other larger rivers, or else turn aside to some arm of the sea. Many of these rivers serve to carry merchandise, and are heavily laden with it. They may be kept back by sluices, and turned off at certain points. Such are the souls in the passive way of sight. Their strength is very abundant; they are laden with gifts, and graces, and celestial favors; they are the admiration of their generation and numbers of saints who shine as stars in the Church have never passed this limit. This class is composed of two kinds. The first commenced in the ordinary way, and have afterwards been drawn to passive contemplation. The others have been, as it were, taken by surprise; they have been seized by the heart, and they feel themselves loving without having learned to know the object of their love. For there is this difference between divine and human love, that the latter supposes a previous acquaintance with its object, because, as it is outside of it, the senses must be taken to it, and the senses can only be taken to it because it is communicated to them. The eyes see and the heart loves. It is not so with divine love. God, having an absolute power over the heart of man, and being its origin and its end, it is not necessary that He should make known to it what He is. He takes it by assault, without giving it battle. The heart is powerless to resist Him, even though He may not use an absolute and violent authority, unless it be in some cases where He permits it to be so, in order to manifest His power. He takes hearts, then, in this way, making them burn in a moment; but usually He gives them flashes of light which dazzle them, and lift them nearer to Himself. These persons appear much greater than those of whom

I shall speak later, to those who are not possessed of a divine discernment, for they attain outwardly to a high degree of perfection, God eminently elevating their natural capacity, and replenishing it in an extraordinary manner; and yet they are never really brought to a state of annihilation to self, and God does not usually so draw them out of their own being that they become lost in Himself. Such characters as these are, however, the wonder and admiration of men. God bestows on them gifts upon gifts, graces upon graces, visions, revelations, inward voices, ecstasies, ravishments, and more. It seems as though God's only care was to enrich and beautify them, and to communicate to them His secrets. All joys are theirs. This does not imply that they bear no heavy crosses, no fierce temptations. These are the shadows which cause their virtues to shine with greater brilliancy; for these temptations are thrust back vigorously, the crosses are borne bravely; they even desire more of them. They are all flame and fire, enthusiasm and love. God uses them to accomplish great things, and it seems as though they only need to desire a thing in order to receive it from God, He finding His delight in satisfying all their desires and doing all their will. Yet in the same path there are various degrees of progression, and some attain a far higher standard of perfection than others; their danger lies in fixing their thoughts upon what God has done for them, thus stopping at the gifts, instead of being led through them to the Giver. The design of God in the bestowal of His grace, and in the profusion with which He gives it, is to bring them nearer to Himself; but they make use of it for an utterly different end. They rest in it, reflect upon it, look at it, and appropriate it; and hence arise vanity, complaisance, self-esteem, the preference of themselves to others, and often the destruction of religious life. These people are admirable, in themselves considered; and sometimes by a special grace they are made very helpful to others, particularly if they have been brought from great depths of sin. But usually they are less fitted to lead others than those who come after; for being near to God themselves, they have a horror of sin, and often a shrinking from sinners, and never having experienced the miseries they see in others, they are astonished, and unable to render either help or advice. They expect too great perfection, and do not lead on to it little by little, and if they meet with weak ones, they do not aid them in proportion to their own advancement, or in accordance with God's designs, but often even seek to avoid them. They find it difficult to converse with those who have not reached their own level, preferring a solitary life to all the ministry of love. If such persons were heard in conversation by those not divinely enlightened, they would be believed equal to the last class, or even more advanced. They make use of the same terms such as death, loss of self, and annihilation; and it is quite true that they do die in their own way, that they are annihilated and lose themselves, for often their natural sensibilities are lost or suspended in their seasons of devotion; they even lose the habit of making use of them. Thus these souls are passive, but they have light, and love, and strength in themselves; they like to retain something of their own, it may be even their virtues, but in so delicate a form that only the Divine eye can detect it. Such as these are so laden with merchandise that their course is very slow. What must be done with them, then, to lead them out of this way? There is a more safe and certain path for them, even that of faith. They need to be led from the sensible to the supernatural, from that which is known and perceived to the very deep, yet very safe, darkness of faith. It is useless to endeavor to ascertain whether these things be of God or not, since they must be surpassed; for if they are of God, they will be carried on by Him, if only we abandon ourselves to Him; and if they are not of God, we shall not be deceived by them, if we do not stay at them. This class of people find far greater difficulty in entering the way of faith than the first, for as what they already possess is so great, and so evidently from God, they will not believe that there is anything higher in the Church of God. Therefore they cling to it. O God, how many spiritual possessions there are which appear great virtues to those who are not divinely enlightened, and which appear great and dangerous defects to those who are so. For those in this way regard as virtues what others look upon as subtle faults; and even the light to see them in their true colors is not given to them. These people have rules and regulations for their obedience, which are marked by prudence; they are strong and vigorous, though they appear dead. They are indeed dead as to their own wants, but not as to their foundation. Such souls as these often possess an inner silence, a certain sinking into God, which they distinguish and express well; but they have not that secret longing to be nothing, like the last class. It is true they desire to be nothing by a certain perceptible annihilation, a deep humility, an abasement under the immense weight of God's greatness. All this is an annihilation in which they dwell without being annihilated. They have the feeling of annihilation without the reality, for the soul is still sustained by its feelings, and this state is more satisfactory to it than any other, for it gives more assurance. This class usually is only brought into God by death, unless it is some privileged ones, whom God designs to be the lights of His Church, or whom He designs to sanctify more eminently; and such He robs by degrees of all their riches. But as there are few sufficiently courageous to be willing, after so much blessedness, to lose it all, few pass this point, God's intention perhaps being that they should not pass it, and that, as in the Father's house there are many mansions, they should only occupy this one. Let us leave the causes with God.

Chapter Four

What shall we say of the souls in this third way, unless it be that they resemble torrents which rise in high mountains? They have their source in God Himself, and they have not a moment's rest until they are lost in Him. Nothing stops them, and no burdens are laid upon them. They rush on with a rapidity which alarms even the most confident. These torrents flow without order, here and there, wherever they can find a passage, having neither regular beds nor an orderly course. They sometimes become muddy by passing through ground which is not firm, and which they bear away with them by their rapidity. Sometimes they appear to be irrecoverably lost, then they reappear for a time, but it is only to precipitate themselves in another abyss, still deeper than the former one. It is the sport of these torrents to show themselves, to lose themselves, and to break themselves upon the rocks. Their course is so rapid as to be indiscernible; but finally, after many precipices and abysses, after having been dashed against rocks, and many times lost and found again, they reach the sea, where they are lost to be found no more. And there, however poor, mean, useless, destitute of merchandise the poor torrent may have been, it is wonderfully enriched, for it is not rich with its own riches, like other rivers, which only bear a certain amount of merchandise or certain rarities, but it is rich with the riches of the sea itself. It bears on its bosom the largest vessels; it is the sea which bears them, and yet it is the river, because the river being lost in the sea, has become one with it. It is to be remarked, that the river or torrent thus precipitated into the sea does not lose its nature, although it is so changed and lost as not to be recognized. It will always remain what it was, yet its identity is lost, not as to reality, but as to quality; for it so takes the properties of salt water that it has nothing peculiar to itself, and the more it loses itself and remains in the sea, the more it exchanges its own nature for that of the sea. For what, then, is not this poor torrent fitted? Its capacity is unlimited, since it is the same as that of the sea; it is capable of enriching the whole earth. O happy loss! Who can set you forth? Who can describe the gain which has been made by this useless and good for nothing river, despised and looked upon as a mad thing, on which the smallest boat could not be trusted, because, not being able to restrain itself, it would have dragged the boat with it. What do you say of the fate of this torrent, O great rivers which flow with such majesty, which are the delight and admiration of the world and glory in the quantity of merchandise spread out upon you? The fate of this poor torrent, which you regard with contempt, or at best with compassion, what has it become? What use can it serve now, or rather, what use can it not serve? What does it lack? You are now its servants, since the riches which you possess are only the overflow of its abundance, or a fresh supply which you are carrying to it. But before speaking of the happiness of a soul thus lost in God, we must begin with its origin and go on by degrees. The soul, as we have said, having proceeded from God, has a continual propensity to return to Him, because, as He is its origin, He is also its final end. Its course would be interminable if it were not arrested or interrupted by sin and unbelief. Therefore the heart of man is perpetually in motion, and can find no rest till it returns to its origin and its centre, which is God. It's like fire, which, being removed from its sphere, is in continual agitation, and does not rest till it has returned to it, and then, by a miracle of nature, this element, so active itself as to consume everything by its activity, is at perfect rest. O poor soul who are seeking happiness in this life! You will never find it out of God. Seek to return to Him, there all your longings and troubles, your agitations and anxieties, will be reduced to perfect rest. It is to be remarked, that in proportion as fire approaches its centre, it always approaches rest, although its swiftness increases. It is the same with the soul, as soon as sin ceases to hold it back, it seeks indefatigably to find God; and if it were not for sin, nothing could impede its course, which would be so speedy, that it would soon attain its end. But it is also true that, in proportion as it approaches God, its speed is augmented, and at the same time becomes more peaceful; for the rest, or rather the peace, since it is not at rest, but is pursuing a peaceful course, increases so that its peace redoubles its speed, and its speed increases its peace. The hindrances, then, arise from sins and imperfections, which arrest for a time the course of the soul, more or less, according to the magnitude of the fault. Then the soul is conscious of its activity, as though when fire was going on towards its centre, it encountered obstacles, such as pieces of wood or straw, it would resume its former activity in order to consume these obstacles or barriers, and the greater the obstacle the more its activity would increase. If it were a piece of wood, a longer and stronger activity would be needed to consume it, but if it were only a straw, it would be burned up in a moment, and would but very slightly impede its course. You will notice that the obstacles which the fire would encounter would only impart to it a fresh stimulus to surmount all which prevented its union with its centre; again, it is to be remarked, that the more obstacles the fire might encounter, and the more considerable they might be, the more they would retard its course; and if it were continually meeting with fresh ones, it would be kept back, and prevented from returning whence it came. We know by experience, that if we continually add fuel to fire, we shall keep it down, and prevent its rising. It is the same with the souls of men. Their instincts and natural propensities lead them towards God. They would advance incessantly, were it not for the hindrances they meet. These hindrances are sins and imperfections, which prove the greater obstacles in the way of their return to God, according as they are serious and lasting; so that if they continue in sin, they will never reach their end. Those, therefore, who have not sinned so grossly as others, should advance much more rapidly. This usually is the case, and yet it seems as though God took pleasure in making "grace abound where sin has most abounded" (Romans 5:20). I believe that one of the reasons of this, to be found in those who have not grossly sinned, is their estimation of their own righteousness, and this is an obstacle more difficult to surmount then even the grossest sins, because we cannot have so great an attachment to sins which are so hideous in themselves, as we have to our own righteousness; and God, who will not do violence to liberty, leaves such hearts to enjoy their holiness at their own pleasure, while He finds His delight in purifying the most miserable. And in order to accomplish His purpose, He sends a stronger and fiercer fire, which consumes those gross sins more easily than a slower fire consumes smaller obstacles. It even seems as though God loved to set up His throne in these criminal hearts, in order to manifest His power, and to show how He can restore the disfigured soul to its original condition, and even make it more beautiful than it was before it fell. Those then who have greatly sinned, and for whom I now write, are conscious of a great fire consuming all their sins and hindrances; they often find their course impeded by besetting sins, but this fire consumes them again and again, till they are completely subdued. And as the fire thus goes on consuming, the obstacles are more and more easily surmounted, so that at last they are no more than straws, which, far from impeding its course, only make it burn the more fiercely. Let us then take the soul in its original condition, and follow it through its various stages, if God, who inspires these thoughts, which only occur to me as I write, wills that we should do so. As God's design for the soul is that it should be lost in Himself, in a manner unknown to ordinary Christians, He begins His work by imparting to it a sense of its distance from Him. As soon as it has perceived and felt this distance, the natural inclination which it has to return to its source, and which has been, as it were, deadened by sin, is revived. Then the soul experiences true sorrow for sin, and is painfully conscious of the evil which is caused by this separation from God. This sentiment thus implanted in the soul leads it to seek the means of ridding itself of this trouble, and of entering into a certain rest which it sees from afar, but which only redoubles its anxiety, and increases its desire to pursue it until it finds it. Some of those who are thus exercised, having never been taught that they must seek to have God within them, and not expect to find Him in outward righteousness, give themselves up to meditation, and seek without what can only be found within. This meditation, in which they seldom succeed, because God, who has better things in store for them, does not permit them to find any rest in such an experience, only serves to increase their longing; for their wound is at the heart, and they apply the plaster externally, which does but foster the disease, instead of healing it. They struggle a long time with this exercise, and their struggling does but increase their powerlessness; and unless God, who Himself assumes the charge of them, sends some messenger to show them a different way, they will lose their time, and will lose it just so long as they remain unaided. But God, who is abundant in goodness, does not fail to send them help, though it may be but passing and temporary. As soon, then, as they are taught that they cannot advance because their wound is an internal one, and they are seeking to heal it by external applications; when they are led to seek in the depths of their own hearts what they have sought in vain out of themselves - then they find, with an astonishment which overwhelms them, that they have within them a treasure which they have been seeking far off. Then they rejoice in their new liberty and they marvel that prayer is no longer a burden, and that the more they retire within themselves, the more they taste of a certain mysterious something which ravishes them and carries them away, and they would wish ever to love thus, and thus to be buried within themselves. Yet what they experience, delightful as it may appear, does not stop them, if they are to be led into pure faith, but leads them to follow after something more, which they have not yet known. They are now all ardor. They seem already to be in Paradise; for what they possess within themselves is infinitely sweeter than all the joys of earth, these they can leave without pain; they would leave the whole world to enjoy for one hour their present experience. They find that prayer has become their continual attitude and their love increases day by day, so that their one desire is always to love and never to be interrupted. And as they are not now strong enough to be undisturbed by conversation, they shun and fear it; they love to be alone, and to enjoy the caresses of their Beloved. They have within themselves a Counselor, who lets them find no pleasure in earthly things, and who does not suffer them to commit a single fault, without making them feel by His coldness how much sin is displeasing to Him. This coldness of God, in times of transgression, is to them the most terrible chastisement. It seems as though God's only care were to correct and reprove them, and His one purpose to perfect them. It is a surprise to themselves and to others that they change more in a month by this way, and even in a day, than in several years by the other. Oh God, it belongs only to You to correct and to purify the hearts of Your children! God has yet another means of chastising the soul, when it is further advanced in the divine life, by making Himself more fully known to it after it falls; then the poor soul is covered with confusion; it would rather bear the most severe chastisement than this goodness of God after it has sinned. These persons are now so full of their own feelings that they want to impart them to others; they long to teach the whole world to love God; their sentiments towards Him are so deep, so pure, and so disinterested, that those who hear them speak, if they are not divinely enlightened, believe them to have attained the height of perfection. They are fruitful in good works; there is no reasoning here, nothing but a deep and burning love. The soul feels itself seized and held fast by a divine force which ravishes and consumes it. It is like intoxicated persons, who are so possessed with wine that they do not know what they are doing, and are no longer masters of themselves. If such as these try to read, the book falls from their hands, and a single line suffices them; they can hardly get through a page in a whole day, however assiduously they may devote themselves to it, for a single word from God awakens that secret instinct which animates and fires them, so that love closes both their mouth and their eyes. They cannot utter verbal prayers, being unable to pronounce them. A heart which is unaccustomed to this does not know what it means; for it has never experienced anything like it before, and it does not understand why it cannot pray, and yet it cannot resist the power which overcomes it. It cannot be troubled, nor be fearful of doing wrong, for He who holds it bound does not permit it either to doubt that it is He who thus holds it, or to strive against it, for if it makes an effort to pray, it feels that He who possesses it closes its lips, and compels it, by a sweet and loving violence, to be silent. Not that the creature cannot resist and speak by an effort, but besides doing violence to himself he loses this divine peace, and feels that he is becoming dry. He must allow himself to be moved upon by God at His will, and not in his own way. The soul in this state imagines itself to be in an inward silence, because its working is so gentle, so easy, and so quiet that it does not perceive it. It believes itself to have reached the summit of perfection, and it sees nothing before it but enjoyment of the wealth it possesses. These Christians, so ardent and so desirous after God, begin to rest in their condition, and gradually and insensibly to lose the loving activity in seeking after God which formerly characterized them, being satisfied with their joy which they substituted for God Himself; and this rest would be to them an irreparable loss, if God, in His infinite goodness, did not draw them out of this state to lead them into one more advanced. But before speaking of it, let us look at the imperfections of this stage.

Chapter Five

The soul in the degree of which I have just spoken can and does make great advances, going from love to love, and from cross to cross; but it falls so frequently, and is so selfish, that it may be said to move only at a snail's pace, although it appears to itself and to others to progress infinitely. The torrent is now in a flat country, and has not yet found the slope of the mountain down which it may precipitate itself, and take a course which is never to be stopped. The faults of those in this degree are a certain self-esteem, more hidden and deeply rooted than it was before they had received these graces and favors from God; a certain secret contempt for others whom they see so far behind themselves, and a certain hardness for sin and sinners; a zeal of St John before the descent of the Holy Ghost, when he wanted to call down fire from heaven upon the Samaritans to consume them; a certain confidence in their own safety and virtue; a secret pride, which causes them to grieve specially over the faults which they commit in public. They appropriate the gifts of God, and treat them as though they were their own. They forget weakness and poverty in the strength which they possess; so that they lose all self-distrust. Though all this and much more is to be found in persons in this degree, they are themselves unconscious of it; but these faults will make themselves known in time. The grace which they feel so strongly in themselves being an assurance to them that they have nothing to fear, they allow themselves to speak without being divinely commissioned. They are anxious to communicate what they feel to every one else. It is true that they are of use to others, for their burning words take hold of the hearts of those who hear them; but apart from the fact that they cannot do the good they would do, if God would have them impart to others what they have received, they are giving out of their necessity and not of their abundance; so that they exhaust themselves; as you have seen several pools of water under a fountain. The fountain alone gives out of its abundance, and the pools only send into each other of the fullness which is communicated to them; but if the fountain be closed or turned aside, and the pools cease to overflow, then as they are cut off from the source, they dry up. This is precisely what happens to those in this degree. They want to be constantly sending out their waters, and it is not till late that they perceive that the water which they had was only for themselves, and that they are not in a state to communicate it, because they are not connected with the source. They are like bottles of scent which are left open. They find so much sweetness in the odor which they emit that they do not perceive the loss they themselves sustain. Yet they appear to practice virtue without any effort, since they are occupied only with a general love, without reason or motive. If you ask them what they do during the day, they will tell you that they love; but if you ask why they love, they will tell you that they do not know; they only know that they love, and that they burn with desire to suffer for the object of their love. You may ask if it is not the sight of the sufferings of their Beloved which inspires them with the longing to suffer with Him, but they will reply that the thought of His sufferings did not even enter their mind. Neither is it the desire to imitate the virtues which they see in

Him, for they do not think of them, nor the sight of His beauty which enraptures them, for they do not look at it. Only they feel in the depths of their heart a deep wound, yet so delightful that they rest in their pain, and find their pleasure in their grief. They believe now that they have arrived at the consummation of all, for though they are full of the faults I have mentioned, and many others yet more dangerous, which are better perceived in the following degree than in this, they rest in their fancied perfection, and stopping at the means, which they mistake for the end, they would remain stationary, if God did not bring the torrent, which is now like a peaceful lake on a mountaintop, to the brow of the hill in order to precipitate it, and to start it on a course which will be more or less rapid according to the depth of its fall. It appears to me that even the most advanced in this degree have a habit of concealing their faults, both from themselves and others, always finding excuses and extenuations; not designedly, but from a certain love of their own excellence, and a habitual dissimulation under which they hide themselves. The faults which cause them the deepest solicitude are those which are most apparent to others. They have a hidden love of self, stronger than ever, and esteem for their own position, a secret desire to attract attention, an affected modesty, a facility in judging others, and a preference for private devotion rather than domestic duties, which renders them the cause of many of the sins of those around them. This is of great importance. The soul, feeling itself grown so strongly and sweetly, desires to be always alone and in prayer, which gives rise to two evils. The first, that in its seasons of greatest liberty it spends too much time in solitude; the second, that when its vigor of love is exhausted, as it often is in this way, it has not the same strength in times of dryness; it finds it difficult to remain so long in prayer; it readily shortens the time; its thoughts wander to exterior objects; then it is discouraged and cast down, thinking that all is lost, and does everything in its power to restore itself to the presence and favor of God. But if such persons were strong enough to live an even life, and not to seek to do more in seasons of abundance than in times of barrenness, they would satisfy everyone. As it is, they are troublesome to those around them, to whom they cannot condescend, making it a favor to lay themselves out for the satisfaction of others. They preserve an austere silence when it is unnecessary, and at other times talk incessantly of the things of God. A wife has scruples about pleasing her husband, entertaining him, walking with him, or seeking to amuse him, but has none about speaking uselessly for two hours with religious devotees. This is a horrible abuse. We ought to be diligent in the discharge of all duties, whatever their nature may be and even if they do cause us inconvenience, we shall yet find great profit in doing this, not perhaps in the way we imagine, but in hastening the crucifixion of self. It even seems as though our Lord shows that such sacrifice is pleasing to Him by the grace which He sheds upon it. I knew a lady who, when playing at cards with her husband in order to please him, experienced such deep and intimate communion with God as she never felt in prayer, and it was the same with everything she did at her husband's desire; but if she neglected these things for others which she thought better, she was conscious that she was not walking in the will of God. This did not prevent her often committing faults, because the attractions of meditation and the happiness of devotion, which are preferred to these apparent losses of time, insensibly draw the soul away, and lead it to change its course, and this by most people is looked upon as sanctity. However, those who are to be taught the way of faith are not suffered long to remain in these errors, because, as God designs to lead them on to better things, He makes them conscious of their deficiency. It often happens, too, that persons by means of this death to self, and acting contrary to their natural inclinations, feel themselves more strongly drawn to their inward rest; for it is natural to man to desire most strongly what it is most difficult for him to obtain, and to desire most intensely those things which he most earnestly resolves to avoid. This difficulty of being able to enjoy only a partial rest increases the rest, and causes them even in activity to feel themselves acted upon so powerfully that they seem to have two souls within them, the inner one being infinitely stronger than the outer. If they leave their duties in order to give the time to devotion, they will find it an empty well, and all its joy will be lost. By devotion I do not mean compulsory prayer, which is gone through as a duty that must not be avoided; neither do I understand by activity the labors of their own choice, but those which come within the range of positive duty. If they have spare time at their disposal, by all means let them spend it in prayer; nor must they lay upon themselves unnecessary burdens, and call them obligations. When the taste for meditation is very great, the soul does not usually fall into these last named errors, but rather into the former one, that of courting retirement. I knew a person who spent more time in prayer when it was painful to her than when she felt it a delight, struggling with the disinclination; but this is injurious to the health, because of the violence which it does to the senses and the understanding, which being unable to concentrate themselves upon any one object, and being deprived of the sweet communion which formerly held them in subjection to God, endure such torment, that the subject of it would rather suffer the greatest trial than the violence which is necessary to enable it to fix its thoughts on God. The person to whom I alluded sometimes passed two or three hours successively in this painful devotion, and she has assured me that the strangest austerities would have been delightful to her in comparison with the time thus spent. But as a violence so strong as this in subjects so weak is calculated to ruin both body and mind, I think it is better not in any way to regulate the time spent in prayer by our varying emotions. This painful dryness of which I have spoken belongs only to the first degree of faith, and is often the effect of exhaustion; and yet those who have passed through it imagine themselves dead, and write and speak of it as the most sorrowful part of the spiritual life. It is true they have not known the contrary experience, and often they have not the courage to pass through this, for in this sorrow the soul is deserted by God, who withdraws from it His sensible helps, but it is nevertheless caused by the senses, because, being accustomed to see and to feel, and never having experienced a similar privation, they are in despair, which however is not of long duration, for the forces of the soul are not then in a state to bear for long such a pressure; it will either go back to seek for spiritual food, or else it will give all up. This is why the Lord does not fail to return. Sometimes He does not even suffer the prayer to cease before He reappears; and if He does not return during the hour of prayer, He comes in a more in day. It seems as though He repented of the suffering He has caused to the soul of His beloved, or that He would pay back with usury what she has suffered for His love. If this consolation last for many days, it becomes painful. She calls Him sweet and cruel. She asks Him if He has only wounded her that she may die. But this kind Lover laughs at her pain, and applies to the wound a balm so sweet, that she could ask to be continually receiving fresh wounds, that she might always find a new delight in a healing which not only restores her former health, but imparts one yet more abundant. Hitherto it has only been a play of love, to which the soul would easily become accustomed if her Beloved did not change His conduct. O poor hearts who complain of the flights of love! You do not know that this is only a farce, an attempt, a specimen of what is to follow. The hours of absence mark the days, the weeks, the months, and the years. You must learn to be generous at your own expense, to suffer your Beloved to come and go at His pleasure. I seem to see these young brides. They are at the height of grief when their Beloved leaves them. They mourn His absence as if it were death, and endeavor, as far as they can, to prevent His departure. This love appears deep and strong, but it is not so by any means. It is the pleasure they derive from the sight of their Beloved which they mourn after. It is their own satisfaction they seek, for if it were the pleasure of their Beloved, they would rejoice in the pleasure which He found apart from them, as much as in that which He found with them. So it is self interested love, though it does not appear such to them; on the contrary, they believe that they only love Him for what He is. It is true, poor souls, you do love Him for what He is, but you love Him because of the pleasure you find in what He is. You reply that you are willing to suffer for your Beloved. True, provided He will be the witness and the companion of your suffering. You say you desire no recompense. I agree; but you do desire that He should know of your suffering, and approve of it. You want Him to take pleasure in it. Is there anything more plausible than the desire that He for whom we suffer should know it, and approve of it, and take delight in it? Oh, how much you are out in your reckoning! Your jealous Lover will not permit you to enjoy the pleasure which you take in seeing His satisfaction with your sorrow. You must suffer without His appearing to see it, or to approve of it, or to know it. That would be too great a gratification. What pain would we not suffer on such conditions! What, to know that our Beloved sees our woes, and takes an infinite pleasure in them! This is too great a pleasure for a generous heart. Yet I am sure the greatest generosity of those in this degree never goes beyond this. But to suffer without our Beloved being aware of it, when He seems to despise what we do to please Him, and to turn away from it; to have only scorn for what formerly seemed to charm Him; to see Him repay with a terrible coldness and distance what we do for His sake alone, and with terrible flights all our pursuit of Him; to lose without complaint all that He had formerly given as pledges of His love, and which we think we have repaid by our love, our fidelity, and our suffering; not only uncomplainingly to suffer ourselves. To be thus despoiled, but to see others enriched with our spoils, and nevertheless not to cease to do what would please our absent Lover; not to cease following after Him; and if by unfaithfulness or surprise we stop for a moment, to redouble our speed, without fearing or contemplating the precipices, although we fall a thousand times, till we are so weary that we lose our strength, and die from continual fatigue; when, perhaps, if our Beloved turns and looks upon us, His glance restores life by the exquisite pleasure it gives; until at last He becomes so cruel that He lets us die for want of help. All this, I say, belongs not to this state, but to that which follows. I must remark here, that the degree of which I have been speaking is of very long duration, at least unless God intends the soul to make great advances; and many, as I have said, never pass it.

Chapter Six

The torrent having come to the brow of the hill, enters at the same time into the second degree of the passive way. This soul, which was so peacefully resting on the mountaintop, had no thought of leaving it. However, for want of a declivity, these waters of Heaven by their stay upon earth were becoming tainted; for there is this difference between stagnant waters which have no outlet, and those which are in motion and have an outlet, that the first, with the exception of the sea, and those large lakes which resemble it, grow putrid, and their want of motion causes their destruction. But when, after leaving their source, they have an easy outlet, the more rapidly they flow, the more they are preserved. You will remember I remarked before of this soul, that as soon as God imparted to it the gift of passive faith, He gave it at the same time an instinct to seek after Him as its centre; but in its unfaithfulness it stifles by its repose this instinct to seek God, and would remain stationary, if God did not revive this instinct by bringing it to the edge of the mountain, whence it is compelled to precipitate itself. At first it is sensible that it has lost that calmness which it expected to retain for ever. Its waters, formerly so tranquil, begin to be noisy, a tumult is seen in its waves; they run and dash over. But where do they run? Alas, as they imagine, it is to their own destruction. If it were in their power to desire anything, they would wish to restrain themselves, and return to their former calm. But this is impossible. The declivity is found; they must be precipitated from slope to slope. It is no longer a question of abyss or of loss. The water, that is the soul, always reappears, and is never lost in this degree. It is embroiled and precipitated; one wave follows another, and the other takes it up and crashes it by its precipitation. Yet this water finds on the slope of the mountain certain flat places where it takes a little relaxation. It delights in the clearness of its waters; and it sees that its falls, its course, this breaking of its waves upon the rocks, have served to render it more pure. It finds itself delivered from its noise and storms, and thinks it has now found its resting place. And it believes this the more readily because it cannot doubt that the state through which it has just passed has greatly purified it, for it sees that its waters are clearer, and it no longer perceives the disagreeable odor which certain stagnant parts had given to it on the top of the mountain; it has even acquired a certain insight into its own condition; it has seen by the troubled state of its passions, the waves, that they were not lost, but only asleep. As when it was descending the mountain, on its way to this level, it thought it was losing its way, and had no hope of recovering its lost peace, so now that it no longer hears the dash of its waves, that it finds itself flowing calmly and pleasantly along the sand, it forgets its former trouble, and never imagines there will be a return of it. It sees that it has acquired fresh purity, and does not fear that it will again become soiled; for here it is not stagnant, but flows as gently and brightly as possible. Ah, poor torrent! You think you have found your resting place, and are firmly established in it! You begin to delight in your waters. The swans glide upon them, and rejoice in their beauty. But what is your surprise while, as you are flowing along so happily, you suddenly encounter a steeper slope, longer and more dangerous than the first! Then the torrent recommences its tumult. Formerly it was only a moderate noise; now it is insupportable. It descends with a crash and a roar greater than ever. It can hardly be said to have a bed, for it falls from rock to rock, and dashes down without order or reason; it alarms every one by its noise; all fear to approach it. Ah, poor torrent! What will you do? You drag away in your fury all that comes in your way; you feel nothing but the declivity down which you are hurried, and you think you are lost. Nay, do not fear; you are not lost, but the time of your happiness is not yet come. There must be many more disturbances and losses before then. You have but just commenced your course. At last this dashing torrent feels that it has gained the foot of the mountain and another level spot. It resumes its former calm, and even a deeper one; and after having passed it may be years in these changes, it enters the third degree, before speaking of which I will touch upon the condition of those who enter it, and the first steps in it. The soul having passed some time in the tranquility of which we have spoken, which it imagines it has secured for ever, and having, as it supposes, acquired all the virtues in their full extent, believing all its passions to be dead; when it is expecting to enjoy with the greatest safety a happiness it has no fear of losing, is astonished to find that, instead of mounting higher, or at least remaining in its present position, it comes to the slope of the mountain. It begins, to its amazement, to be sensible of an inclination for the things it had given up. It sees its deep calm suddenly disturbed and distractions come in crowds, one upon another and the soul finds only stones in its path, dryness and aridity. A feeling of distaste comes into prayer. Its passions, which it thought were dead, but which were only asleep, all revive. It is completely astonished at this change. It would like either to return to the top of the mountain, or at least to remain where it is; but this cannot be. The declivity is found, and the soul must fall, not into sin, but into a privation of the previous degree and of feeling. It does its best to rise after it falls; it does all in its power to restrain itself, and to cling to some devotional exercises and it makes an effort to recover its former peace; it seeks solitude in the hope of recovering it. But its labor is in vain. It resigns itself to suffer its dejection, and hates the sin which has occasioned it. It longs to put things right, but can find no means of doing it and the torrent must go on its way; it drags with it all that is opposed to it. Then, seeing that it no longer finds support in God, it seeks it in the creature, but it finds none; and its unfaithfulness only increases its apprehension. At last, the poor bride, not knowing what to do, weeping everywhere the loss of her Beloved, is filled with astonishment when He again reveals Himself to her. At first she is charmed at the sight, as she feared she had lost Him for ever. She is all the more happy, because she finds that He has brought with Him new wealth, a new purity, a great distrust of self. She has no longer the desire to stop, as she formerly had; she goes on continuously, but peacefully and gently, and yet she has fears lest her peace should be disturbed. She trembles lest she should again lose the treasure which is all the dearer to her because she had been so sensible of its loss. She is afraid she may displease Him, and that He will leave her again. She tries to be more faithful to Him, and not to make an end of the means. However, this repose carries away the soul, ravishes it, and renders it idle. It cannot help being sensible of its peace, and it desires to be always alone. It has again acquired a spiritual greediness. To rob it of solitude is to rob it of life. It is still more selfish than before, what it possesses being more delightful. It seems to be in a new rest. It is going along calmly, when all at once it comes to another descent, steeper and longer than the former one. It is suddenly seized with a fresh surprise; it endeavors to hold itself back, but in vain; it must fall; it must dash on from rock to rock. It is astonished to find that it has lost its love for prayer and devotion. It does violence to itself by continuing in it. It finds only death at every step. That which formerly revived it is now the cause of its death. Its peace has gone, and has left a trouble and agitation stronger than ever, caused as much by the passions, as by crosses, which increase outwardly, and which it has no strength to bear. It arms itself with patience; it weeps, groans, and is troubled. The Bride complains that her Beloved has forsaken her; but her complaints are unheeded. Life has become death to her. All that is good she finds difficult, but has an inclination towards evil which draws her away. But she can find no rest in the creature, having tasted of the Creator. She dashes on more vehemently; and the steeper the rocks, and the greater the obstacles which oppose her course, the more she redoubles her speed. She is like the dove from the ark, which, finding no rest for the sole of its foot, was obliged to return. But alas, what could the poor dove have done if, when it desired to re-enter the ark, Noah had not put out his hand to take it in? It could only have fluttered round about the ark, seeking rest but finding none. So this poor dove flutters round the ark till the Divine Noah, having compassion on her distress, opens the door and receives her to Himself. Oh, wonderful and loving invention of the goodness of God! He only eludes the search of the soul to make it flee more quickly to Him. He hides Himself that He may be sought after. He apparently lets her fall, that He may have the joy of sustaining her and raising her up. Oh, strong and vigorous ones, who have never experienced these artifices of love, these apparent jealousies, these flights, lovely to the soul which has passed them, but terrible to those who experience them! You, I say, who do not know these flights of love, because you are satisfied with the abiding presence of your Beloved; or, if He hide Himself, it is for so short a time that you cannot judge of the joy of His presence by the pain of a long absence; you have never experienced your weakness, and your need of His help; but those who are thus forsaken learn to lean no longer on themselves, but only on the Beloved. His rigors have rendered His gentleness the more needful for them. These persons often commit faults through sheer weakness, and because they are deprived of all sensible support; and these faults so fill them with shame, that, if they could, they would hide themselves from their Beloved. Alas, in the terrible confusion into which they are thrown, He gives them a glimpse of Himself. He touches them with His scepter, like another Ahasuerus (Esther 5:2), that they may not die; but His tender caresses only serve to increase their confusion at the thought of having displeased Him. At other times He makes them sensible, by His severity, how much their unfaithfulness displeases Him. Oh, if they could sink into dust, they would. They would do anything to repair the injury done to

God; and if, by any slight neglects, which appear crimes to them, they have offended their neighbor, what return are they not willing to make? But it is pitiful to see the state of that one who has driven away her Beloved. She does not cease to run after Him, but the faster she goes, the further He seems to leave her behind; and if He stops, it is only for a moment, that she may recover breath. She feels now that she must die; for she no longer finds life in anything; all has become death to her; prayer, reading, conversation - all is dead. She loses the joy of service, or rather, she dies to it, performing it with so much pain and weariness, that it is as death to her. At last, after having fought well, but uselessly, after a long succession of conflicts and rest, of lives and deaths, she begins to see how she has abused the grace of God, and that this state of death is better for her than life. As she sees her Beloved returning, and finds that she possesses Him more purely, and that the state which preceded her rejoicing was a purification for her, she abandons herself willingly to death, and to the coming and going of her Beloved, giving Him full liberty to go and come as He will. She receives instruction as she is able to bear it. Little by little she loses her joy in herself, and is thus prepared for a new condition. But before speaking of it, let me say, that in proportion as the soul advances, its joys become short, simple, and pure, and its privations long and agonizing, until it has lost its own joy, to find it no more. And this is the third degree, that of death, burial, and decay. This second degree ends in death, and goes no further.

Chapter Seven

Section One

You have seen dying persons who, after they have been believed to be dead, have all at once assumed a new strength, and retained it until their death; as a lamp whose oil is spent flickers in the surrounding darkness, but only to die out the more quickly. Thus the soul casts out flames, which only last for a moment. It has bravely resisted death; but its oil is spent. The Sun of Righteousness has so withered it up, that it is forced to die. But does this Sun design anything else with its fierce rays, except the consumption of the soul? And the poor soul thus burned thinks that it is frozen! The truth is that the torment it suffers prevents its recognizing the nature of its pain. So long as the Sun was obscured by clouds, and gave out rays to a certain extent moderated, it felt the heat, and thought it was burning, while in reality it was but slightly warmed. But when the Sun flashed full upon it, then the soul felt itself burning, without believing that it was so much as warmed. Oh loving deceit! Oh sweet and cruel Love! Have you lovers only to deceive them thus? You wound these hearts, and then hide your darts, and make them pursue after that which has wounded them. You attract them, and show yourself to them, and when they long to possess you, you flee from them. When you see the soul reduced to the last extremity, and out of breath from its constant pursuit, you show yourself for a moment that it may recover life, only to be killed a thousand times with ever increasing severity. Oh rigorous Lover! Innocent murderer! Why dost Thou not kill with a single blow? Why give wine to an expiring heart, and restore life in order to destroy it afresh? This is Thy sport. You wound to the death; and when You see the victim on the point of expiring, You heal one wound in order to inflict another! Alas, usually we die but once; and the very cruelest murderers in times of persecution, though they prolonged life, it is true, yet were content to destroy it but once. But You, less compassionate than they, take away our life time after time, and restore it again. Oh life, which cannot be lost without so many deaths! Oh death, which can only be attained by the loss of so many lives! Perhaps this soul, after You have devoured it in Your bosom, will enjoy its Beloved. That would be too great happiness. For it must undergo another torture. It must be buried and reduced to ashes. But perhaps it will then arrive at the end of its sufferings, for bodies which decay suffer no longer. Oh, it is not thus with the soul. It suffers continually; and burial, decay, and nothingness are even more sensibly felt by it than death itself. This degree of death is extremely long, and as I have said that very few pass the other degrees, so I say that far less pass this one. Many people have been astonished to see very holy persons, who have lived like angels, die in terrible anguish, and even despairing of their salvation. It is because they have died in this mystical death; and as God wished to promote their advancement, because they were near their end, He redoubled their Sorrow. The work of stripping the soul must be left wholly to God. He will do the work perfectly, and the soul will second the spoliation and the death, without putting hindrances in the way. But to do the work for ourselves is to lose everything, and to make a vile state of a divine one. There are persons who, hearing of this spoliation, have effected it for themselves, and remain always stationary; for as the stripping is their own work, God does not clothe them with Himself. The design of God in stripping the soul is to clothe it again. He only impoverishes that He may enrich, and He substitutes Himself for all that He takes away, which cannot be the case with those whose spoliation is their own work. They indeed lose the gifts of God, but they do not possess God Himself in exchange. In this degree the soul has not learned to let itself be stripped, emptied, impoverished, killed; and all its efforts to sustain itself will but be its irreparable loss, for it is seeking to preserve a life which must be lost. As a person wishing to cause a lamp to die out without extinguishing it, would only have to cease to supply it with oil, and it would die out of itself; but if this person, while persistently expressing a wish that the lamp should go out, continued replenishing it with oil from time to time, the lamp would never go out. It is the same with the soul in this degree, which holds on, however feebly, to life. If it consoles itself, does not suffer itself to be killed, in a word, if it performs any actions of life whatever, it will thereby retard its death. Oh poor soul, fight no longer against death, and you will live by your death. I seem to see a drowning man before me; he makes every effort to rise to the surface of the water; he holds on to anything that offers itself to his grasp; he preserves his life so long as his strength holds out; he is only drowned when that strength fails. It is thus with Christians. They endeavor as long as possible to prevent their death; it is only the failure of all power which makes them die. God, who wishes to hasten this death, and who has compassion upon them, cuts off the hands with which they cling to a support, and thus obliges them to sink into the deep. Crosses become multiplied, and the more they increase, the greater is the helplessness to bear them, so that they seem as though they never could be borne. The most painful part of this condition is, that the trouble always begins by some fault in the sufferer, who believes he has brought it upon himself. At last the soul is reduced to utter self despair. It consents that God should deprive it of the joy of His gifts, and admits that He is just in doing it. It does not even hope to possess these gifts again. When those who are in this condition see others who are manifestly living in communion with God, their anguish is redoubled, and they sink in the sense of their own nothingness. They long to be able to imitate them, but finding all their efforts useless, they are compelled to die. They say in the language of Scripture, "The thing which I greatly feared is come upon me". (Job 3:25) What, they say, to lose God, and to lose Him for ever, without the hope of ever finding Him again. To be deprived of love for time and for eternity. To be unable to love Him whom I know to be so worthy of my affection! Oh, is it not sufficient, Divine Lover, to cast off your spouse, to turn away from her, without compelling her to lose love, and lose it, as it seems, for ever? She believes she has lost it, and yet she never loved more strongly or more purely. She has indeed lost the vigor, the sensible strength of love; but she has not lost love itself; on the contrary, she possesses it in a greater degree than ever. She cannot believe this, and yet it is easily known; for the heart cannot exist without love. If it does not love God, its affection is concentrated upon some other object - but here the bride of Christ is far from taking pleasure in anything. She regards the revolt of her passions and her involuntary faults as terrible crimes, which draw upon her the hatred of her Beloved. She seeks to cleanse and to purify herself, but she is no sooner washed than she seems to fall into a slough yet more filthy and polluted than that from which she has just escaped. She does not see that it is because she runs that she contracts defilement, and falls so frequently, yet she is so ashamed to run in this condition, that she does not know where to hide herself. Her garments are soiled; she loses all she has in the race. Her Bridegroom aids in her spoliation for two reasons, the first, because she has soiled her beautiful garments by her vain complaisance's, and has appropriated the gifts of God in reflections of self-esteem. The second, because in running, her course will be impeded by this burden of appropriation; even the fear of losing such riches would lessen her speed. Oh poor soul! What have you become? Formerly you waste the delight of the

Bridegroom, when He took such pleasure in adorning and beautifying you; now you are so naked, so ragged, so poor, that you dare neither to look upon yourself nor to appear before Him. Those who gaze upon you, who, after having so much admired you, see you now so disfigured, believe that either you have grown mad, or that you have committed some great crime, which has caused your Beloved to abandon you. They do not see that this jealous Husband, who desires that His bride should be His alone, seeing that she is amusing herself with her ornaments, that she delights in them, that she is in love with herself, and that she sometimes ceases looking at Him in order to look at herself, and that her love to Him is growing cold because her self-love is so strong. He is stripping her, and taking away all her beauties and riches from before her eyes. In the abundance of her wealth, she takes delight in contemplating herself. She sees good qualities in herself, which engage her affection, and alienate it from her Bridegroom. In her foolishness she does not see that she is only fair with the beauties of her Beloved; and that if He removed these, she would be so hideous that she would be frightened at herself. More than this, she neglects to follow Him wherever He goes; she fears lest she may spoil her complexion, or lose her jewels. Oh jealous Love, how well is it that You come to chastise this proud one, and to take from her what You have given, that she may learn to know herself, and that, being naked and destitute, nothing may impede her course. In this way our Lord strips the soul little by little, robbing her of her ornaments, all her gifts, positions, and favors. That is, as to her perception or conscious possession of them, which are like jewels that weigh her down; then He takes away her natural capacity for good, which are her garments; after which He destroys her personal beauty, which sets forth divine virtue, which she finds it impossible to practice. This spoliation commences with the graces, gifts, and favors of conscious love. The bride sees that her husband takes from her, little by little, the riches He had bestowed upon her. At first she is greatly troubled by this loss; but what troubles her the most, is not so much the loss of her riches, as the anger of her Beloved; for she thinks it is in anger that He thus takes back His gifts. She sees the abuse she had made of them, and the delight she had been taking in them, which so fills her with shame that she is ready to die of confusion. She lets Him do as He will, and dares not say, "Why do You take from me what You have given?" For she sees that she deserves it, and looks on in silence. Though she keeps silence, it is not so profound now as afterwards; it is broken by mingled sobs and sighs. But she is astonished to find, when she looks at her Bridegroom, that He appears to be angry with her for weeping over His justice towards her, in no longer allowing her the opportunity of abusing His gifts, and for thinking so lightly of the abuse she has made of them. She tries then to let Him know that she does not care about the loss of His gifts, if only He will cease His anger towards her. She shows Him her tears and her grief at having displeased Him. It is true that she is so sensible of the anger of her Beloved that she no longer thinks of her riches. After allowing her to weep for a long time, her Lover appears to be appeased. He consoles her, and with His own hand He dries her tears. What a joy it is to her to see the new goodness of her Beloved, after what she has done! Yet He does not restore her former riches, and she does not long for them, being only too happy to be looked upon, consoled, and caressed by Him. At first she receives His caresses with so much confusion, that she dare not lift her eyes, but forgetting her past woes in her present happiness, she loses herself in the new caresses of her Beloved, and thinking no more of her past miseries, she glories and rests in these caresses, and thereby compels the Bridegroom to be angry again, and to despoil her anew. It must be observed that God despoils the loss little by little; and the weaker the souls may be, the longer the spoliation continues; while the stronger they are, the sooner it is completed, because God despoils them oftener and of more things at once. But however rough this spoliation may be, it only touches superfluities on the outside, that is to say, gifts, graces, and favors. This leading of God is so wonderful, and is the result of such deep love to the soul, that it would never be believed, except by those who have experienced it; for the heart is so full of itself, and so permeated with self-esteem, that if God did not treat it thus, it would be lost. It will perhaps be asked, "if the gifts of God are productive of such evil consequences, why are they given?" God gives them, in the fullness of His goodness, in order to draw the soul from sin, from attachment to the creature, and to bring it back to Himself. But these same gifts with which He gratifies it He uses that He may wean it from earth and from self to love Him. We use these gifts to excite our self-love and self-admiration, to amuse ourselves with them; and self-love is so deeply rooted in man, that it is augmented by these gifts; for he finds in himself new charms, which he had not discovered before; he delights in them, and appropriates to himself what belongs only to God. It is true, God could deliver him from it, but He does not do it, for reasons known only to Himself. The soul, thus despoiled by God, loses a little of its self love, and begins to see that it was not so rich as it fancied, but that all its virtue was in Christ; it sees that it has abused His grace, and consents that He should take back His gifts. The bride says, "I shall be rich with the riches of my Bridegroom, and though He may keep them, yet, from my union in heart and will with Him, they will still be mine." She is even glad to lose these gifts of God; she finds herself unencumbered, better fitted for walking. Gradually she becomes accustomed to this spoliation; she knows it has been good for her; she is no longer grieved because of it; and, as she is so beautiful, she satisfies herself that she will not cease to please her Bridegroom by her natural beauty and her simple garments, as much as she could with all her ornaments.

Section Two

When the poor bride is expecting always to live in peace, in spite of this loss, and sees clearly the good which has resulted to her from it, and the harm she had done to herself by the bad use which she had made of the gifts which now have been taken from her, she is completely astonished to find that the Bridegroom, who had only given her temporary peace because of her weakness, comes with yet greater violence to tear off her clothing from her. Alas, poor bride! What will you do now? This is far worse than before, for these garments are necessary to her, and it is contrary to all propriety to suffer herself to be stripped of them. Oh, it is now that she makes all the resistance in her power. She brings forward all the reasons why her Bridegroom should not thus leave her naked. She tells Him that it will bring reproach upon Himself. "Alas!" she cries, "I have lost all the virtues which You have bestowed upon me, Your gifts, the sweetness of Your love! But still I was able to make an outward profession of virtue; I engaged in works of charity; I prayed assiduously, even though I was deprived of Your sensible benefits, but I cannot consent to lose all this. I was still clothed according to my position, and looked upon by the world as Your bride, but if I lose my garments, it will bring shame upon You." "It matters not, poor soul; you must consent to this loss also. You do not yet know yourself; you believe that your raiment is your own, and that you can use it as you will. But though I acquired it at such a cost, you have given it back to me as if it were payment on your part for the labors I have endured for You. Let it go; you must lose it." The soul having done its best to keep it, let it go, little by little, and finds itself gradually despoiled. It finds no inclination for anything; on the contrary, all is distasteful to it. Formerly it had aversions and difficulties, without absolute powerlessness; but here all power is taken from it. Its strength of body and mind fails entirely; the inclination for better things alone remains, and this is the last robe, which must finally be lost. This is done very gradually, and the process is extremely painful, because the bride sees all the while that it has been caused by her own folly. She dares not speak, lest she may irritate the Bridegroom, whose anger is worse to her than death. She begins to know herself better, to see that she is nothing in herself, and that all belongs to her Bridegroom. She begins to distrust herself, and, little by little, she loses her self-esteem. But she does not yet hate herself, for she is still beautiful, though naked. From time to time she casts a pitiful look towards the Bridegroom, but she says not a word. She is grieved at His anger. It seems to her that the spoliation would be of little moment if she had not offended Him, and if she had not rendered herself unworthy to wear her nuptial robes. Although she was confused when at the first her riches were taken from her, her confusion at the sight of her nakedness is infinitely more painful. She cannot bear to appear before her Bridegroom, so deep is her shame. But she must remain, and run hither and thither in this state. What, is it not even permitted to her to hide herself? No; she must appear thus in public. The world begins to think less highly of her. It says, "Is this that bride who was once the admiration of angels and of men? See how she has fallen." These words increase her confusion, because she is well aware that her Bridegroom has dealt justly with her. She does what she can to induce Him to clothe her a little, but He will do nothing, after having thus stripped her of all, for her garments would satisfy her by covering her, and would prevent her seeing herself as she is. It is a great surprise to a soul that thinks itself far advanced towards perfection to see itself thus despoiled all at once. It imagines the old sins, from which it was once purged, must have returned. But it is mistaken. The secret is, that she was so bidden by her garments as to be unable to see what she was. It is a terrible thing for a soul to be thus stripped of the gifts and graces of God, and it is impossible that any should know or imagine what it is without the actual experience of it.

Section Three

All this would be but little if the bride still retained her beauty; but the Bridegroom robs her of that also. Hitherto she has been despoiled of gifts, graces, and favors (facility for good). She has lost all good works, such as outward charity, care for the poor, readiness to help others, but she has not lost the divine virtues. Here, however, these too must be lost, so far as their practice is concerned, or rather the habit of exercising them, as acquired by herself, in order to appear fair. In reality, they are all the while being more strongly implanted. She loses virtue as virtue, but it is only that she may find it again in Christ. This degraded bride becomes, as she imagines, filled with pride. She, who was so patient, who suffered so easily, finds that she can suffer nothing. Her senses revolt her by continual distractions. She can no longer restrain herself by her own efforts, as formerly; and what is worse, she contracts defilement at every step. She complains to her Beloved that the watchmen that go about the city have found her and wounded her. I ought, however, to say that persons in this condition do not sin willingly. God usually reveals to them such a deep seated corruption within themselves, that they cry with Job, "Oh, that You would hide me in the grave, that You would keep me in secret, until Your wrath be past!" (Job 14:13). It must not be supposed that either here or at any other stage of progress God suffers the soul really to fall into sin; and so truly is this the case, that though they appear in their own eyes the most miserable sinners, yet they can discover no definite sin of which they are guilty, and only accuse themselves of being full of misery, and of having only sentiments contrary to their desires. It is to the glory of God that, when He makes the soul most deeply conscious of its inward corruption, He does not permit it to fall into sin. What makes its sorrow so terrible is that it is overwhelmed with a sense of the purity of God, and that purity makes the smallest imperfection appear as a heinous sin, because of the infinite distance between the purity of God and the impurity of the creature. The soul sees that it was originally created pure by God, and that it has contracted not only the original sin of Adam, but thousands of actual sins, so that its confusion is greater than can be expressed. The reason why Christians in this condition are despised by others, is not to be found in any particular faults which are observed in them, but because, as they no longer manifest the same ardor and fidelity which formerly distinguished them, the greatness of their fall is judged from this, which is a great mistake. Let this serve to explain or modify any statements or representations in the sequel, which may appear to be expressed too strongly, and which those who do not understand the experience might be liable to misinterpret. Observe, also, that when I speak of corruption, of decay, etc., I mean the destruction of the old man by the central conviction, and by an intimate experience of the depth of impurity and selfishness which there is in the heart of man, which, bringing him to see himself as he is apart from God, causes him to cry with David, "I am a worm and no man" (Psalm 22:6), and with Job, "If I wash myself with snow water, and make my hands never so clean, yet shall You plunge me in the ditch, and mine own clothes shall abhor me" (Job 9:30-31). It is not, then, that this poor bride commits the faults of which she imagines herself guilty, for in heart she was never purer than now; but her senses and natural powers, particularly the senses, being unsupported, wander away. Besides which, as the speed of her course towards God redoubles, and she forgets herself more, it is not to be wondered at that in running she soils herself in the muddy places through which she passes; and as all her attention is directed towards her Beloved, although she does not perceive it by reason of her own condition, she thinks no more of herself, and does not notice where she steps. So that, while believing herself most guilty, she does not willingly commit a single sin; though all her sins appear voluntary to herself, they are rather faults of surprise, which often she does not see until after they are committed. She cries to her Bridegroom, but He does not heed her, at least not perceptibly, though He sustains her with an invisible hand. Sometimes she tries to do better, but then she becomes worse; for the design of her Bridegroom in letting her fall without wounding herself, (Psalm 37:24) is that she should lean no longer on herself; that she should recognize her helplessness; that she should sink into complete self despair; and that she should say, "My soul chooses death rather than life" (Job 7:15). It is here that the soul begins truly to hate itself, and to know itself as it would never have done if it had not passed through this experience. All our natural knowledge of self, whatever may be its degree, is not sufficient to cause us really to hate ourselves. "He that loves his life shall lose it; and he that hates his life in this world, shall keep it unto life eternal." It is only such an experience as this which can reveal to the soul its infinite depth of misery. No other way can give true purity; if it give any at all, it is only superficial, and not in the depth of the heart, where the impurity is seated. Here God searches the inmost recesses of the soul for that hidden impurity which is the effect of the self-esteem and self-love which He designs to destroy. Take a sponge which is full of impurities, wash it as much as you will, you will clean the outside, but you will not render it clean throughout unless you press it; in order to squeeze out all the filth. This is what God does. He squeezes the soul in a painful manner, but He brings out from it that which was the most deeply hidden. I say, then, that this is the only way in which we can be purified radically; and without it we should always be filthy, though outwardly we might appear very clean. It is necessary that God should make the soul thoroughly sensible of its condition. We could never believe, without the experience, of what nature left to itself is capable of. Yes, indeed, our own being, abandoned to itself, is worse than all devils. Therefore we must not believe that the soul in this state of misery is abandoned by God. It was never better sustained; but nature is, as it were, left a little alone, and makes all these ravages without the soul in itself taking any part in them. This poor desolate bride, running hither and thither in search of her Beloved, not only soils herself grievously, as I have said, by falling into faults of surprise and self-esteem, but she wounds herself with the thorns that come in her way. She becomes so wearied at length that she is forced to die in her race for want of help; that is, to expect nothing from herself or her own activity. That which is productive of the highest good to the soul in this condition is that God manifests no pity towards it; and when He desires to promote its advancement, He lets it run even to death; if He stops it for a moment, by doing which He ravishes and revives it, it is because of its weakness, and in order that its weariness may not compel it to rest. When He sees that it is becoming disheartened and inclined to give up the race altogether, He looks upon it for a moment, and the poor bride finds herself wounded anew by this look. She would willingly say to Him, "Alas, why have You thus compelled me to run? Oh, that I could find You; and see You face to face!" But alas, when she seems to lay hold of Him, He flees from her again. "I sought You," she cries, "but I found You not" As this look from her Bridegroom has increased her love, she redoubles her speed in order to find Him, nevertheless she was delayed just so long as the look lasted, that is, in sensible joy. This is why the Bridegroom does not often cast such looks upon her, and only when He sees that her courage is failing. The soul then dies at the end of its race, because all its active strength is exhausted; for though it had been passive, it had not lost its active strength, though it had been unconscious of it. The bride said, "Draw me, we will run after You". She ran indeed, but how? By the loss of all; as the sun travels incessantly, yet without quitting his repose. In this condition she so hates herself, that she can hardly suffer herself. She thinks her Bridegroom has good reason to treat her as He does, and that it is His indignation against her which makes Him leave her. She does not see that it is in order to make her run that He flees, that it is in order that He may purify her that He suffers her to become so soiled. When we put iron in the fire, to purify it and to purge it from its dross, it appears at first to be tarnished and blackened, but afterwards it is easy to see that it has been purified. Christ only makes His bride experience her own weakness, that she may lose all strength and all support in herself, and that, in her self-despair, He may carry her in His arms, and she may be willing to be thus borne; for whatever her course may be, she walks as a child; but when she is in God, and is borne by Him, her progress is infinite, since it is that of God Himself. In addition to all this degradation, the bride sees others adorned with her spoils. When she sees a holy soul, she dare not approach it. She sees it adorned with all the ornaments which her Bridegroom has taken from her; but though she admires it, and sinks into the depths of nothingness, she cannot desire to have these ornaments again, so conscious is she of her unworthiness to wear them. She thinks it would be a profanation to put them upon a person so covered with mud and defilement. She even rejoices to see that, if she fills her Beloved with horror, there are others in whom He can take delight, and whom she regards as infinitely happy in having gained the love of her God. As for the ornaments, though she sees others decorated with them, she does not suppose that these are the sources of their happiness. If she sees any blessedness in the possession of them, it is because they are the tokens of the love of her Beloved. When she is thus sensible of her littleness in the presence of such as these, whom she regards as queens, she does not know the good which will result to her from this nakedness, death, and decay. Her Bridegroom only unclothes her that He may be Himself her clothing. "Put on the Lord Jesus Christ," says Saint Paul (Romans 13: 1-4). He only kills her that He may be her life. "If we be dead with Christ, we believe that we shall also live with Him." He only annihilates her that she may be transformed in Himself. This loss of virtue is only brought about by degrees, as well as the other losses, and this apparent inclination for evil is involuntary; for that evil which makes us so vile in our own eyes is really no evil at all. The things which bring defilement to these persons are certain faults which only lie in the feelings. As soon as they see the beauty of a virtue, they seem to be incessantly falling into the contrary vice. For example, if they love truth, they speak hastily or with exaggeration, and fancy they lie at every moment, although in fact they do but speak against their sentiments. It is thus with all the other virtues, the more important these virtues are, and the more strongly they cling to them, because they appear the more essential, the greater is the force with which they are torn from them.

Section Four

This poor soul, after having lost its all, must at last lose its own life by an utter self-despair, or rather it must die worn out by terrible fatigue. Prayer in this degree is extremely painful, because the soul being no longer able to make use of its own powers, of which it seems to be entirely deprived, and God having taken from it a certain sweet and profound calm which supported it, is left like those poor children whom we see running here and there in search of bread, yet finding no one to supply their need, so that the power of prayer seems to be as entirely lost as if we had never possessed it; but with this difference, that we feel the pain occasioned by the loss, because we have proved its value by its possession, while others are not sensible of the loss, because they have never known its enjoyment. The soul, then, can find no support in the creature; and if it feels itself carried away by the things of earth, it is only by impetuosity. It can find nothing to satisfy it. Not that it does not seek to abandon itself to the things in which it formerly delighted. But alas, it finds in them nothing but bitterness, so that it is glad to leave them again, taking nothing back but sadness at its own unfaithfulness. The imagination goes altogether astray, and is scarcely ever at rest. The three powers of the soul, the understanding, the memory, and the will, by degrees lose their life, so that at length they become altogether dead, which is very painful to the soul, especially as regards the will, which had been tasting I know not what of sweetness and tranquility, which comforted the other powers in their deadness and powerlessness. This unexplainable something which sustains the soul at its foundation, as it were, is the hardest of all to lose, and that which the soul endeavors the most strenuously to retain; for as it is too delicate, so it appears the more divine and necessary. It would consent willingly to be deprived of the two other powers, and even of the will, so far as it is a distinct and perceived thing, if only this something might be left; for it could bear all its labors if it may have within itself the witness that it is born of God. However, this must be lost, like the rest - that is, as to the sentiment. Then the soul enters into the sensible realization of all the misery with which it is filled. And it is this which really produces the spiritual death; for whatever misery the soul might endure, if this, I know not what, were not lost, it would not die; and if, on the other hand, this were lost without the soul being conscious of its misery, it would be supported, and would not die. It can easily understand that it must give up all dependence upon its own feelings or upon any natural support, but to lose an almost imperceptible comfort, and to fall from weakness, to fall into the mire, to this it cannot consent. This is where reason fails, this is where terrible fears fill the heart, which seems to have only sufficient life to be sensible of its death. It is, then, the loss of this imperceptible support, and the experience of this misery, which causes death. We should be very careful, in such times as these, not to let our senses be led away willingly to creatures, seeking willingly consolation and diversion. I say willingly, for we are incapable of mortifications and attentions reflected upon ourselves, and the more we have mortified ourselves, the stronger will be the bearing in the contrary direction, without being aware of it; like a madman, who goes wandering about, if you attempt to keep him too rigorously within bounds, apart from its being useless, it would retard his death. What must we do then? We must be careful to give no support to the senses, to suffer them, and to let them find recreation in innocent ways; for as they are not capable of an inward operation, by endeavoring to restrain them we should injure health, and even mental strength. What I say applies only to this degree; for if we were to make this use of the senses in the time of the strength and activity of grace, we should do wrong; and our Lord Himself in His goodness makes us see the conduct that we should pursue; for at first, He puts such a pressure on the senses, they have no liberty. They only have to desire something in order to be deprived of it. God orders it thus that the senses may be drawn from their imperfect operation, to be confined within the heart; and in severing them outwardly, He binds them inwardly so gently, that it costs them little to be deprived of everything; they even find more pleasure in this deprivation than in the possession of all things. But when they are sufficiently purified, God, who wishes to draw the soul out of itself with a contrary movement, permits the senses to expand outwardly, which appears to the soul as a great impurity. However, it has now happened seasonably, and to endeavor to order things otherwise, would be to purify ourselves in a different way from that which God desires, and therefore to defile ourselves anew. This does not prevent our making mistakes in this outward development of the senses; but the confusion which it occasions us, and our fidelity in making use of it, is the furnace in which we are most quickly purified, by dying the soonest to our selves. It is here also that we lose the esteem of men. They look on us with contempt, and say, "Are not these the persons whom we formerly admired? How are they become thus disfigured?" "Alas!" we reply, "look not upon me. It is the sun which has thus discolored me." It is at this point that we suddenly enter the third degree, that of burial and decay.

Chapter Eight

The torrent, as we have said, has passed through every imaginable vicissitude. It has been dashed against rocks; indeed, its course has been but a succession of falls from rock to rock; but it has always reappeared, and we have never seen it really lost. Now it begins to lose itself in gulf after gulf. Formerly it still had a course, though it was so precipitate, so confused, and so irregular; but here it is engulfed with a yet greater precipitation in unsearchable depths. For a long time it disappears altogether from view, then we perceive it slightly, but more by hearing than by sight, and it only appears to be again precipitated in a deeper gulf. It falls from abyss to abyss, from precipice to precipice, until at last it falls into the depths of the sea, where, losing all form, it is lost to be found no more, having become one with the sea itself. The soul, after many deaths, expires at last in the arms of Love; but it does not even perceive those arms. It has no sooner expired, than it loses all vital action, all desire, inclination, tendency, choice, repugnance, and aversion. As it draws near to death, it grows weaker; but its life, though languishing and agonizing, is still life, and "while there is life there is hope," even though death be inevitable. The torrent must be buried out of sight. Oh God, what is this? What were only precipices become abysses. The soul falls into a depth of misery from which there is no escape. At first this abyss is small, but the further the soul advances, the stronger does it appear, so that it goes from bad to worse; for it is to be remarked, that when we first enter a degree, there clings to us much that we have brought in with us, and at the end we already begin to feel symptoms of that which is to come. It is also noticeable that each degree contains within it an infinitude of others. A man, after his death and before his burial, is still among the living. He still has the face of a man, though he is an object of terror; thus the soul, in the commencement of this degree, still bears some resemblance to what it was before; there remains in it a certain secret impression of God, as there remains in a dead body a certain animal heat which gradually leaves it. The soul still practices devotion and prayer, but this is soon taken away from it. It must lose not only all prayer, every gift of God, but God Himself to all appearance - that is, so far as He was possessed selfishly by the ego. And not lose Him for one, two, or three years, but for ever. All facility for good, all active virtue, are taken from it; it is left naked and despoiled of everything. The world, which formerly esteemed it so much, begins to fear it. Yet it is no visible sin which produces the contempt of men, but a powerlessness to practice its former good works with the same facility. Formerly whole days were spent in the visitation of the sick, often even against natural inclination; such works as these can be practiced no longer. The soul will soon be in an entire oblivion. Little by little, it loses everything in such a degree, that it is altogether impoverished. The world tramples it under foot, and thinks no more of it. Oh poor soul, you must see yourself treated thus, and see it with terror, without being able to prevent it. It must suffer itself to be buried, covered with earth, and trodden under foot by all men. It is here that heavy crosses are borne, and all the heavier that they are believed to be merited. The soul begins to have a horror of itself. God casts it so far off, that He seems determined to abandon it for ever. Poor soul, you must be patient, and remain in your sepulcher. It is content to remain there, though in terrible suffering, because it sees no way of escape from it; and it sees, too, that it is its only fit place, all others being even sadder to it. It flees from men, knowing that they regard it with aversion. They look upon this forlorn Bride as an outcast, who has lost the grace of God, and who is only fit to be buried in the earth. The heart endures its bitterness; but, alas, how sweet this state is even now, and how easy it would be to remain in the sepulcher, if it were not necessary to decay. The old man becomes gradually corrupted. Formerly there were weaknesses and failings, now the soul sees a depth of corruption of which it had hitherto been ignorant, for it could not imagine what were its self-esteem and selfishness. Oh God, what horror this soul suffers in seeing itself thus decaying! All troubles, the contempt and aversion of man, affect it no longer. It is even insensible to the deprivation of the Sun of Righteousness; it knows that His light does not penetrate the tomb. But to feel its own corruption, that it cannot endure. What would it not rather suffer? But it must experience, to the very depths of its being, what it is. And yet, if I could decay without being seen by God, I should be content. What troubles me is the horror which I must cause Him by the sight of my corruption. Poor desolate one! What can you do? It should suffice you, one would think, to bear this corruption, without loving it. But now you are not even sure that you do not desire it! The soul is in darkness, without being able to judge whether its terrible thoughts proceed from itself or from the evil one. It is no longer troubled at being cast off by God; it is so conscious of its demerit that it consents to the deprivation of the sensible presence of God. But it cannot endure the thought that the taint of its corruption reaches even to God. It does not wish to sin. Let me decay, is its cry, and find my home in the depths of hell, if only I may be kept free from sin. It no longer thinks of love, for it believes itself to be incapable of affection. It is, in its own opinion, worse than when it was in a state of nature, since it is in the state of corruption usual to the body deprived of life. At length by degrees the soul becomes accustomed to its corruption. It feels it less, and finds it natural, except at certain times, when it is tried by various temptations, whose terrible impressions cause it much anguish. Ah, poor torrent! Were you not better off on the mountain-top than here? You had then some slight corruption, it is true; but now, though you flow rapidly, and nothing can stop you, you pass through such filthy places, so tainted with sulfur and saltpeter, that you bear away their odors with you. At last the soul is reduced to a state of nothingness, and has become like a person who does not exist, and never will exist; it does nothing, either good or ill. Formerly it thought of itself, now it thinks no longer. All that is of grace is done as if it were of nature, and there is no longer either pain or pleasure. All that there is, is that its ashes remain as ashes, without the hope of ever being anything but ashes. It is utterly dead, and nothing affects it either from without or within - that is, it is no longer troubled by any sensible impressions. At last, reduced to nonentity, there is found in the ashes a germ of immortality, which lives beneath these ashes, and in due time will manifest its life. But the soul is in ignorance of it, and never expects to be revived or raised from the dead. The faithfulness of the soul in this condition consists in letting itself be buried, crushed, trampled on, without making any more movement than a corpse, without seeking in any way to prevent its putrefaction. There are those who wish to apply balm to themselves. No, no; leave yourselves as you are. You must know your corruption, and see the infinite depth of depravity that is in you. To apply balm is but to endeavor by good works to hide your corruption. Oh, do it not! You will wrong yourselves. God can suffer you; why cannot you suffer yourselves? The soul, reduced to nothingness, must remain in it, without wishing to change its state; and it is then that the torrent loses itself in the sea, never to find itself in itself again, but to become one with the sea. It is then that this corpse feels without feeling, that it is gradually re-animated, and assumes a new lift; but this is done so gradually that it seems like a dream. And this brings us to the last degree, which is the commencement of the divine and truly inner life, including numberless smaller degrees, and in which the advancement is infinite - just as this torrent can perpetually advance in the sea, and imbibe more of its nature, the longer it remains in it.

Chapter Nine

When the torrent begins to lose itself in the sea, it can easily be distinguished. Its movement is perceptible, until at length it gradually loses all form of its own, to take that of the sea. So the soul, leaving this degree, and beginning to lose itself, yet retains something of its own; but in a short time it loses all that it had peculiar to itself. The corpse which has been reduced to ashes is still dust and ashes; but if another person were to swallow those ashes, they would no longer have an identity, but would form part of the person who had taken them. The soul hitherto, though dead and buried, has retained its own being; it is only in this degree that it is really taken out of itself. All that has taken place up to this point has been in the individual capacity of the creature; but here the creature is taken out of his own capacity to receive an infinite capacity in God Himself. And as the torrent, when it enters the sea, loses its own being in such a way that it retains nothing of it, and takes that of the sea, or rather is taken out of itself to be lost in the sea; so this soul loses the human in order that it may lose itself in the divine, which becomes its being and its subsistence, not essentially, but mystically. Then this torrent possesses all the treasures of the sea, and is as glorious as it was formerly poor and miserable. It is in the tomb that the soul begins to resume life, and the light enters insensibly. Then it can be truly said that "The people which sat in darkness saw great light; and to them which sat in the region and shadow of death light is sprung up" (Matthew 4:16). There is a beautiful figure of this resurrection in Ezekiel (Ezekiel 37), where the dry bones gradually assume life. Then there is that other passage, "The hour is coming, and now is, when the dead shall hear the voice of the Son of God; and they that hear shall live" (John 5:25). O you who are coming out of the sepulcher, you feel within yourselves a germ of life springing up little by little, you are quite astonished to find a secret strength taking possession of you, your ashes are reanimated, you feel yourselves to be in a new country. The poor soul which only expected to remain at rest in its grave, receives an agreeable surprise. It does not know what to think. It supposes that the sun must have shed upon it a few scattered rays through some opening or chink, whose brightness will only last for a moment. It is still more astonished when it feels this secret vigor permeating its entire being, and finds that it gradually receives a new life, to lose it no more for ever, unless it be by the most flagrant unfaithfulness. But this new life is not like the former one. It is a life in God. It is a perfect life. The soul lives no longer and works no longer of itself, but God lives, acts, and operates in it (Galatians 2:20); and this goes on increasing, so that it becomes perfect with God's perfection, rich with God's riches, and loving with God's love. The soul sees now that whatever it owned formerly had been in its own possession, now it no longer possesses, but is possessed. It only takes a new life in order to lose it in God; or rather it only lives with the life of God; and as He is the principle of life, the soul can want nothing. What a gain it has made by all its losses! It has lost the created for the Creator, the nothing for the All in all. All things are given to it, not in itself, but in God; not to be possessed by itself, but to be possessed by God. Its riches are immense, for they are God Himself. It feels its capacity increasing day by day to immensity, every virtue is restored to it, but in God. It must be remarked, that as it was only despoiled by degrees, so it is only enriched and vivified by degrees. The more it loses itself in God, the greater its capacity becomes; just as the more the torrent loses itself in the sea, the more it is enlarged, having no other limits than those of the sea, it participates in all its properties. The soul becomes strong and firm, it has lost all means, but it has found the end. This divine life becomes quite natural to it. As it no longer feels itself, sees itself, or knows itself, so it no longer sees or understands or distinguishes anything of God as distinct or outside of itself. It is no longer conscious of love, or light, or knowledge; it only knows that God is, and that it no longer lives except in God. All devotion is action, and all action is devotion - all is the same; the soul is indifferent to all, for all is equally God. Formerly it was necessary to exercise virtue in order to perform virtuous works; here all distinction of action is taken away, the actions having no virtue in themselves, but all being God, the meanest action equally with the greatest, provided it is in the order of God and at His time. For all that might be of the natural choice, and not in this order, would have another effect, leading the soul out of God by unfaithfulness. Not that it would be brought out of its degree or its loss, but out of the divine plan, which makes all things one and all things God. So the soul is indifferent as to whether it be in one state or another, in one place or another. All is the same to it, and it lets itself be carried along naturally. It ceases to think, to wish, or to choose for itself, but remains content, without care or anxiety, no longer distinguishing its inner life to speak of it. Indeed it may be said not to possess one. It is no longer in itself, it is all in God. It is not necessary for it to shut itself up within itself, it does not hope to find anything there, and does not seek for it. If a person were altogether penetrated with the sea, having sea within and without, above and below, on every side, he would not prefer one place to another, all being the same to him. So the soul does not trouble itself to seek anything or to do anything; that is, of itself, by itself, or for itself. It remains as it is. But what does it do? Nothing, always nothing. It does what it is made to do, it suffers what it is made to suffer. Its peace is unchangeable, but always natural. It has, as it were, passed into a state of nature and yet how different from those altogether without God! The difference is, that it is compelled to action by God without being conscious of it, whereas formerly it was nature that acted. It seems to itself to do neither right nor wrong, but it lives satisfied, peaceful, doing what it is made to do in a steady and resolute manner. God alone is its guide, for at the time of its loss, it lost its own will. And if you were to ask, what are its desires, it could not tell. It can choose for itself no longer. All desire is taken away, because, having found its centre, the heart loses all natural inclination, tendency, and activity, in the same way as it loses all repugnance and contrariety. The torrent has no longer either a declivity or a movement, it is in repose, and at its end. But with what satisfaction is this soul satisfied? With the satisfaction of God, immense, general, without knowing or understanding what it is that satisfies it, for here all sentiments, tastes, views, particular opinions, however delicate they may be, are taken from it. That certain vague, indefinable something, which formerly occupied without occupying it, is gone, and nothing remains to it. But this insensibility is very different to that of death, burial, and decay. That was a deprivation of life, a distaste, a separation, the powerlessness of the dying united with the insensibility of the dead; but this is a deviation above all these things, which does not remove them, but renders them useless. A dead man is deprived of all the functions of life by the powerlessness of death; but if he were to be raised gloriously, he would be full of life, without having the power to preserve it by means of the senses, and being placed above all means by virtue of his germ of immortality, he would no longer feel that which animated him, although he would know himself to be alive. In this degree God cannot be tasted, seen, or felt, being no longer distinct from ourselves, but one with us. The soul has neither inclination nor taste for anything. In the period of death and burial it experienced this, but in a very different manner. Then it arose from distaste and powerlessness, but now it is the effect of plenitude and abundance; just as if a person could live on air, he would be full without feeling his plenitude, or knowing in what way he had been satisfied; he would not be empty and unable to eat or to taste, but free from all necessity of eating by reason of his satisfaction, without knowing how the air, entering by all his pores, had penetrated equally at all parts. The soul here is in God, as in the air which is natural to it, and it is no more sensible of its fullness than we are of the air we breathe. Yet it is full, and nothing is wanting to it; therefore all its desires are taken from it. Its peace is great, but not as it was before. Formerly it was an inanimate peace, a certain sepulture, from which there sometimes escaped exhalations which troubled it. When it was reduced to ashes, it was at peace; but it was a barren peace, like that of a corpse, which would be at peace in the midst of the wildest storms of the sea. It would not feel them, and would not be troubled by them, its state of death rendering is insensible. But here the soul is raised, as it were, to a mountaintop, from which it sees the waves rolling and tossing, without fearing their attacks; or rather it is at the bottom of the sea, where there is always tranquility, even while the surface is agitated. The senses may suffer their sorrows, but at the centre there is always the same calm tranquility, because He who possesses it is immutable. This, of course, supposes the faithfulness of the soul; for in whatever state it may be, it is possible for it to recede and fall back into itself. But here the soul progresses infinitely in God; and it is possible for it to advance incessantly; just as, if the sea had no bottom, anyone falling into it would sink to infinitude, and going down to greater and greater depths of the ocean, would discover more and more of its beauties and treasures. It is even thus with the soul whose home is in God. But what must it do in order to be faithful to God? Nothing, and less than nothing. It must simply suffer itself to be possessed, acted upon, and moved without resistance, remaining in the state which is natural to it, waiting for what every moment may bring to it, and receiving it from Him, without either adding to or taking from it; letting itself be led at all times and to any place, regardless of sight or reason, and without thinking of either; letting itself go naturally into all things, without considering what would be best or most plausible; remaining in the state of evenness and stability in which God has placed it, without being troubled to do anything, but leaving to God the care of providing its opportunities, and of doing all for it; not making definite acts of abandonment, but simply resting in the state of abandonment in which it already is, and which is natural to it. The soul is unable to act in any way of itself without a consciousness of unfaithfulness. It possesses all things by having nothing. It finds a facility for every duty, for speaking and for acting, no longer in its own way, but in God's. Its faithfulness does not consist in ceasing from all activity, like one who is dead, but in doing nothing except by the principle which animates it. A soul in this state has no inclination of its own in anything, but lets itself go as it is led, and beyond that does nothing. It cannot speak of its state, for it does not see it; though there is so much that is extraordinary, it is no longer as it was in the former degrees, where the creature had some part in it, that which was in a great measure its own; but here the most wonderful things are perfectly natural, and are done without thought. It is the same principle that gives life to the soul which acts in it and through it. It has a sovereign power over the hearts of those around it, but not of itself. As nothing belongs to it, it can make no reserves; and if it can say nothing of a state so divine, it is not because it fears vanity, for that no longer exists; it is rather because what it has, while possessing nothing, passes all expression by its extreme simplicity and purity. Not that there are not many things which are but the accessories of this condition, and not the centre, of which it can easily speak. These accessories are like the crumbs which fall from that eternal feast of which the soul begins to partake in time; they are but the sparks which prove the existence of a furnace of fire and flame; but it is impossible to speak of the principle and the end, because only so much can be imparted as God is pleased to give at the moment to be either written or spoken. It may be asked, is the soul unconscious of its faults, or does it commit none? It does commit them, and is more conscious of them than ever, especially in the commencement of its new life. The faults committed are often more subtle and delicate than formerly. The soul knows them better, because its eyes are open; but it is not troubled by them, and can do nothing to rid itself of them. It is true that, when it has been guilty of unfaithfulness or sin, it is sensible of a certain cloud; but it passes over, without the soul itself doing anything to dispel it, or to cleanse itself; apart from which, any efforts it might make would be useless, and would only serve to increase its impurity; so that it would be deeply sensible that the second stain was worse than the first. It is not a question of returning to God, because a return presupposes a departure; and if we are in God, we have but to abide in Him; just as, when there arises a little cloud in the middle region of air, if the wind blows, it moves the clouds, but does not dissipate them; if, on the contrary, the sun shines forth, they will soon be dispelled. The more subtle and delicate the clouds are, the more quickly they will be dissipated. Oh, if we had sufficient fidelity never to look at ourselves, what progress might we not make! Our sights of ourselves resemble certain plants in the sea, which, just so long as their support lasts, prevent bodies from falling. If the branches are very delicate, the weight of the body forces them down, and we are only delayed for a moment; but if we look at ourselves willingly and long, we shall be delayed just so long a time as the look may occupy, and our loss will be great indeed. The defects of this state are certain light emotions or sights of self, which are born and die in a moment. Certain winds of self, which pass over the calm sea, and cause ripples; but these faults are taken from us little by little, and continually become more delicate. The soul, on leaving the tomb, finds itself, without knowing how, clothed with the inclinations of Christ; not by distinct and natural views of Him, but by its natural condition, finding these inclinations just when they are needed, without thinking of them; as a person who possesses a hidden treasure might find it unexpectedly in the time of his need. The soul is surprised when, without having reflected on the mind and disposition of Christ, it finds them naturally implanted within it. These dispositions of Christ are lowliness, meekness, submission, and the other virtues which He possessed. The soul finds that all these are acting within it, but so easily, that they seem to have become natural to it. Its treasury is in God alone, where it can draw upon it ceaselessly in every time of need, without in any degree diminishing it. It is then that it really "puts on" Jesus Christ (Romans 13:14); and it is henceforth He who acts, speaks, moves in the soul, the Lord Jesus Christ being its moving principle. Now those around it do not inconvenience it; the heart is enlarged to contain them. It desires neither activity nor retreat, but only to be each moment what God makes it to be. As in this condition the soul is capable of infinite advancement, I leave those who are living in it to write of it, the light not being given me for the higher degrees, and my soul not being sufficiently advanced in God to see or to know them. All that I shall add is, that it is easy to see by the length of the road necessary to be taken in order to arrive at God that the end is not so soon attained as we are apt to imagine, and that even the most spiritual and enlightened mistake the consummation of the passive way of light and love for the end of this one, when in reality it is but the commencement. I must also remark, that what I have said touching the mind of Christ commences as soon as we enter the way of naked faith. Although the soul in the former degrees has no distinct sights of Christ, it has nevertheless a desire to be conformed to His image. It covets the cross, lowliness, poverty; then this desire is lost, and there remains a secret inclination for the same things, which continually deepens and simplifies, becoming every day more intimate and more hidden. But here the mind of Christ is the mind of the soul, natural and habitual to it, as something no longer distinct from itself, but as its own being and its own life Christ exercising it without going out of the soul, and the soul exercising it with Him, in Him, without going out of Him; not like something distinct, which it knows, sees, attempts, practices, but as that which is natural to it. All the actions of life, such as breathing, are done naturally, without thought, rule, or measure; and they are done unconsciously by the person who does them. It is thus with the mind of Christ in this degree, which continually develops, as the soul is more transformed in Him, and becomes more thoroughly one with Him. But are there no crosses in this condition? As the soul is strong with the strength of God Himself, God lays upon it more crosses and heavier ones than before; but they are borne divinely. Formerly the cross charmed it; it was loved and cherished; now it is not thought of, but is suffered to go and come; and the cross itself becomes God, like all other things. This does not involve the cessation of suffering, but of the sorrow, the anxiety, the bitterness of suffering. It is true that the crosses are no longer crosses, but God. In the former stages, the cross is virtue, and is exalted more and more as the condition is more advanced. Here the soul feels it to be God, like the rest; all that constitutes the life of this soul, all that it has, moment by moment, being God to it. The outward appearance of these persons is quite ordinary, and nothing unusual is observed in them except by those who are capable of understanding them. All is seen in God, and in its true light; therefore this state is not subject to deception. There are no visions, revelations, ecstasies, ravishments, or translations. All these things do not belong to this state, which is above them all. This way is simple, pure, and naked, seeing nothing out of God; and thus seeing all as God sees it, and with His eyes.

Part Two

Chapter One

This is where true liberty begins; not, as some imagine, a liberty which necessitates idleness; that would be imprisonment rather than liberty, fancying ourselves free because, having an aversion to our own works, we no longer practice them. The liberty of which I speak is of a different nature; it does all things easily which God would have done, and the more easily in proportion to the duration and the painfulness of the incapacity to do them which we have previously experienced. I confess I do not understand the resurrection state of certain Christians, who profess to have attained it, and who yet remain all their lives powerless and destitute - for here the soul takes up a true life. The actions of a raised man are the actions of life, and if the soul remain lifeless, I say that it may be dead or buried, but not risen. A risen soul should be able to perform without difficulty all the actions which it has performed in the past, only they would be done in God. Did not Lazarus, after his resurrection, exercise all the functions of life as formerly, and Jesus Christ after His resurrection was willing to eat and to converse with men. And so of those who believe themselves to be risen with Christ, and who are nevertheless stunted in their spiritual growth and incapable of devotion, I say, that they do not possess a resurrection life, for there everything is restored to the soul a hundred fold. There is a beautiful illustration of this in the case of Job, whose history I consider a mirror of the spiritual life. First God robbed him of his wealth, which we may consider as setting forth gifts and graces. Then of his children, this signifies the destruction of natural sensibilities, and of our own works, which are as our children and our most cherished possessions. Then God deprived him of his health, which symbolizes the loss of virtue. Then He touched his person, rendering him an object of horror and contempt. It even appears that this holy man was guilty of sin, and failed in resignation; he was accused by his friends of being justly punished for his crimes; there was no healthy part left in him. But after he had been brought down to the dunghill, and reduced as it were to a corpse, did not God restore everything to him, his wealth, his children, his health, and his life? It is the same with spiritual resurrection, everything is restored, with a wonderful power to use it without being defiled by it, clinging to it without appropriating it as before. All is done in God, and things are used as though they were not used. It is here that true liberty and true life are found. "If we have been planted in the likeness of Christ's death, we shall be also in the likeness of His resurrection" (Romans 6:5) Can there be freedom where there are powerlessness and restrictions? No, "If the Son shall make you free, you shall be free indeed," but with His liberty. This is where true liberty begins. Nothing that God desires is difficult to us, or costs us anything; and if a person is called to preach, to instruct, etc, he does it with a marvelous facility, without the necessity of preparing a discourse, being well able to practice what Jesus commanded His disciples, "Take no thought how or what you shall speak, for I will give you a mouth and wisdom, which all your adversaries shall not be able to gainsay nor resist" (Matthew 10:19; Luke 21:15). This is not given till after an experience of powerlessness; and the deeper that experience has been, the greater is the liberty. But it is useless to endeavor to force ourselves into this condition; for as God would not be the source, we should not realize the desired results. It may well be said of this risen life, that all good things are given with it. In this state, the soul cannot practice the virtues as virtues; it is not even conscious of them; but all the virtues have become so habitual to it, that it practices them naturally, almost instinctively. When it hears others speak of deep humiliation, it is surprised to find that it experiences nothing of the kind; and if it sought to humble itself, it would be astonished, as though it were guilty of unfaithfulness, and would even find it impossible, because the state of annihilation through which it has passed has placed it below all humiliation; for in order to be humbled, we must be something, and nothingness cannot be brought lower; its present state has placed it above all humility and all virtue by its transformation into God, so that its powerlessness arises both from its annihilation and its elevation. Those persons have nothing outwardly to distinguish them from others, unless it be that they do no harm to anyone; for, so far as the exterior is concerned, they are very ordinary, and therefore do not attract observation, but live in a state of quiet rest, free from all care and anxiety. They experience a deep joy, arising from the absence of all fear, or desire, or longing, so that nothing can disturb their repose or diminish their joy. David possessed this experience when he said, "The Lord is my light and my salvation, whom shall I fear? The Lord is the strength of my life; of whom shall I be afraid" (Psalm 27:1). A heart ravished with joy no longer looks at itself, nor thinks of itself; and its joy, though great, is not an object of contemplation. The soul is in a state of ravishment and ecstasy which cause no uneasiness, because God has enlarged its capacity almost to infinitude. Those ecstasies which cause the loss of consciousness are the effect of human imperfection, and are nevertheless the admiration of men. God is, as it were, drawing the soul out of itself that it may be lost in Him; but as it has neither sufficient purity nor strength to bear the process, it becomes necessary, either that God should cease thus to draw it, which involves the cessation of the ecstasy, or that nature should succumb and die, which not infrequently happens. But in this resurrection life, the ecstasy lasts, not for a few hours only, but for ever, without either violence or variation, God having purified and strengthened the subject of it to the extent necessary to enable it to bear this glorious ravishment. It seems to me that when God goes out of Himself, He creates an ecstasy, but I dare not say this for fear of teaching an error. What I say then is, that the soul drawn out of itself experiences an inward ecstasy; but a happy one, because it is only drawn out of itself in order that it may be drowned and lost in God, quitting its own imperfections and its own limited thoughts to participate in those of God. Oh happy nothingness, where does its blessedness end? Oh poverty stricken, weary ones, how well you are recompensed! Oh unutterable happiness! Oh soul, what a gain you have made in exchange for all your losses! Could you have believed, when you waste lying in the dust, that what caused you so much horror could have procured you so great a happiness as that which you now possess? If it had been told you, you could not have credited it. Learn now by your own experience how good it is to trust in God, and that those who put their confidence in Him shall never be confounded. Oh abandonment, what gladness can you impart to the soul, and what progress it might have made if it had found you at first; from how much weariness it might have been delivered if it had known how to let God work. But, alas, men are not willing to abandon themselves, and to trust only in God. Even those who appear to do it, and who think themselves well established in it, are only abandoned in imagination, and not in reality. They are willing to abandon themselves in one thing and not in another; they wish to compromise with God, and to place a limit to what they will permit Him to do. They want to give themselves up, but on such and such conditions. No; this is not abandonment. An entire and total abandonment excepts nothing, keeps back nothing, neither death, nor life, nor perfection, nor salvation, nor heaven, nor hell. Oh poor souls, give yourselves up utterly in this abandonment; you will get only happiness and blessing from it. Walk boldly on this stormy sea, relying on the word of Jesus, who has promised to take upon Himself the care of all those who will lose their own life, and abandon themselves to Him. But if you sink like Peter, ascribe it to the weakness of your faith. If we had the faith calmly, and without hesitation, to face all dangers, what good should we not receive! What do you fear, trembling heart? You fear to lose yourself? Alas, for all that you are worth, what would that matter? Yes, you will lose yourself if you have strength to abandon yourself to God, but you will be lost in Him. Oh happy loss, I do not know how sufficiently to repeat it. Why can I not persuade every one to make this abandonment? And why do men preach anything less? Alas, men are so blind that they regard all this as folly, as something fit for women and weak minds; but for great minds it is too mean; they must guide themselves by their own meager share of wisdom. This path is unknown to them, because they are wise and prudent in themselves; but it is revealed to babes, who can suffer self to be annihilated, and who are willing to be moved by God at His pleasure, leaving Him to do with them as He will, without resistance, without considering what others will say. Oh, how difficult it is to this proper prudence to become nothing both in its own eyes and in the sight of others! Men say that their one object in life is to glorify God, while it is really their own glorification. But to be willing to be nothing in the sight of God, to live in an entire abandonment, in utter self despair, to give themselves to Him when they are the most discouraged, to leave themselves in His hands, and not to look at self when they are on the very edge of the abyss; it is this that is so rare, and it is this which constitutes perfect abandonment. There sometimes occur in this life wonderful manifestations to the natural senses, but this is not usual; it is like Christ on the Mount of Transfiguration.

Chapter Two

The soul having attained a divine state, is, as I have already said, an immovable rock, proof against all blows or shocks, unless it be when the Lord desires it to do something contrary to custom; then, if it does not yield to His first promptings, it has to suffer the pain of a constraint to which it can offer no resistance, and is compelled by a violence, which cannot be explained, to obey His will. It is impossible to tell the strange proofs to which God subjects the hearts which are perfectly abandoned, and which offer no resistance to Him in anything; neither, if I could speak of them, should I be understood. All that I can say is, that He does not leave them the shadow of anything that could be named, either in God or out of

God. And He so raises them above all by the loss of all, that nothing less than God Himself, either in earth or heaven, can stop them. Nothing can harm them, because there is no longer anything hurtful for them, by reason of their union with God, which, in associating with sinners, contracts no defilement, because of its essential purity. This is more real than I can express. The soul participates in the purity of God; or rather, all natural purity having been annihilated, the purity of God alone exists in its nothingness; but so truly, that the heart is in perfect ignorance of evil, and powerless to commit it, which does not however prevent the possibility of its falling; but this seldom happens here, because the profound nothingness of the soul does not leave anything that can be appropriated to itself; and it is appropriation alone which can cause sin, for that which no longer exists cannot sin. The peace of those in this condition is so invariable and so profound, that nothing either in earth or hell can disturb it for a moment. The lenses are still susceptible to suffering; but when they are overpowered by it, and cry out with the anguish, if they are questioned, or if they examine themselves, they will find nothing in themselves that suffers. In the midst of the greatest pain, they say that they suffer nothing, being unable to admit that they are suffering, because of the divine state of blessedness which reigns in the centre or supreme part. And then there is such an entire and complete separation of the two parts, the inferior and the superior, that they live together like strangers; and the most extraordinary trouble does not interrupt the perfect peace, tranquility, joy, and rest of the superior part; as the joy of the divine life does not prevent the suffering of the inferior. If you wish to attribute any goodness to those who are thus transformed in God, they will object to it, not being able to find anything in themselves that can be named, affirmed, or heard. They are in a complete negation. It is this which causes the difference of terms and expressions employed by writers on this subject, who find a difficulty in making themselves understood, except by those whose experience accords with their own. Another effect of this negation is, that the soul having lost all that was its own, God having substituted Himself, it can attribute nothing either to itself or to God; because it knows God only, of whom it can say nothing. Here all is God to the soul because it is no longer a question of seeing all in God; for to see things in God is to distinguish them in Him. For instance, if I enter a room, I see all that is there in addition to the room itself, though it be placed within it; but if all could be transformed into the room itself, or else were taken out of it, I should see nothing but the room alone. All creatures, celestial, terrestrial, or pure intelligences, disappear and fade away, and there remains only God Himself, as He was before the creation. The soul sees only God everywhere; and all is God; not by thought, sight, or light, but by an identity of condition and a consummation of unity, which rendering it God by participation, without its being able to see itself, prevents it seeing anything anywhere; it can see no created being out of the uncreated, the only uncreated One being all and in all men would condemn such a state, saying it makes us something less than the meanest insect; and so it does, not by obstinacy and firmness of purpose, but by powerlessness to interfere with ourselves. You may ask one in this condition, "Who leads you to do such and such a thing? Is it God who has told you to do it, or has made known to you His will concerning it?" He will reply, "I know nothing, and I do not think of knowing anything. All is God and His will; and I no longer know what is meant by the will of God, because that will has become natural to me." But why should you do this rather than that? "I do not know. I let myself be guided by Him who draws me." Why so? "He draws me because I, being no longer anything, am carried along with God, and am drawn by Him alone. He goes hither and thither. He acts; and I am but an instrument, which I neither see nor regard. I have no longer a separate interest, because by the loss of myself I have lost all self interest. Neither am I capable of giving any reason for my conduct, for I no longer have a conduct, yet I act infallibly so long as I have no other principle than that of the Infallible One." And this blind abandonment is the permanent condition of the soul of which I speak; because having become one with God, it can see nothing but God; for having lost all separateness, self possession, and distinction, it can no longer be abandoning itself, because, in order to abandon ourselves, we must do something, and have the power of disposing of ourselves. The soul is in this condition "hidden with Christ in God" (Colossians 3:3); mingled with Him, as the river of which we have spoken is mingled with the sea, so that it can be separated no more. It has the ebb and flow of the sea, no longer by choice, will, and liberty, but by nature. The immense sea having absorbed its shallow limited waters, it participates in all the movements of the sea. It is the sea which bears it, and yet it is not borne, since it has lost its own being; and having no other motion than that of the sea, it acts as the sea acts. Not because it naturally possesses the same qualities, but because, having lost all its natural qualities, it has no others but those of the sea, without having the power of ever being anything but sea. It is not, as I have said, that it does not so retain its own nature, that, if God so willed it, in a moment it could be separated from the sea; but He does not do this. Neither does it lose the nature of the creature; and God could, if He pleased, cast it off from His divine bosom, but He does not do it, and the creature acts as it were divinely. But it will be said that by this theory I deprive man of his liberty. Not so; he is no longer free except by an excess of liberty, because he has lost freely all created liberty. He participates in the uncreated freedom, which is not contracted, bounded, limited by anything; and the soul's liberty is so great, so broad, that the whole earth appears to it as a speck, to which it is not confined. It is free to do all and to do nothing. There is no state or condition to which it cannot accommodate itself; it can do all things, and yet takes no part in them. Oh glorious state, who can describe you, and what have you to fear or to apprehend? Oh Paul, you could say, "who shall separate us from the love of Christ?" "I am persuaded," says the great apostle, "that neither death, nor life, nor angels, nor principalities, nor powers, nor things present, nor things to come, nor height, nor depth, nor any other creature, shall be able to separate us from the love of God, which is in Christ Jesus our Lord" (Rom. viii. 35, 38, 39). Now these words, "I am persuaded," exclude all doubt. But what was the foundation of Paul's assurance? It was in the infallibility of God alone. The epistles of this great apostle, this mystical teacher, are often read, but seldom understood; yet all the mystic way, its commencement, its progress, its end, are described by St Paul, and even the divine life; but few are able to understand it, and those to whom the light is given see it all there clearer than the day. Ah, if those who find it so difficult to leave themselves to God could only experience this, they would confess that though the way might be arduous, a single day of this life was a sufficient recompense for years of trouble. But by what means does God bring the soul here? By ways altogether opposed to natural wisdom and imagination. He builds up by casting down; He gives life by killing. Oh, if I could tell what He does, and the strange means which He uses to bring us here. But silence, men are not able to hear it. Those who have experienced it know what it is. Here there is no need of place or time. All is alike, all places are good, and wherever the order of God may take us, it is well, because all means are useless and infinitely surpassed. When we have reached the end, there is nothing left to wish for. Here all is God. God is everywhere and in everything, and therefore to the soul all is the same. Its religion is God Himself, always the same, never interrupted; and if sometimes God pours some stream of His glory upon its natural powers and sensibilities, it has no effect upon the centre, which is always the same. The soul is indifferent either to solitude or a crowd, it no longer looks forward to deliverance from the body in order that it may be united to God. It is now not only united, but transformed, changed into the object of its love, which causes it no longer to think of loving; for it loves God with His own love, and naturally, though not inadmissibly.

Chapter Three

A similitude occurs to my mind which appears very appropriate to this subject - it is that of grain. First it is separated from the husk, which sets forth conversion and separation from sin. When the grain is separate and pure, it must be ground, by affliction, crosses, sickness, etc; when it is thus bruised and reduced to flour, there must still be taken from it, not that which is impure, for this is gone, but all that is coarse, that is, the bran. And when there is nothing left but the fine flour, then it is made into bread for food. It appears as though the flour were soiled, blackened, and blighted; that its delicacy and whiteness were taken from it, in order that it may be made into a paste which is far less beautiful than the flour. Lastly, this paste is exposed to the heat of the fire. Now this is precisely what happens to the soul of which I have been speaking. But after the bread is baked, it is fit for the mouth of the king, who not only unites it to himself by contact with it, but eats it, digests it, consumes it, and annihilates it, that it may enter into his composition, and become part of himself. You will observe that though the bread has been eaten by the king, which is the greatest honor it can receive, and is its end, yet it cannot be changed into his substance unless it be annihilated by digestion, losing all its natural form and quality. Oh, how well this sets forth all the conditions of the soul; that of union being very different to that of transformation, in which the soul, in order to become one with God, transformed and changed into Him, must not only be eaten, but digested, that, after having lost all that was its own, it may become one with God Himself. "That they all may be one, as You, Father, are in me, and I in You; that they also may be one in us, I in them, and You in me, that they may be made perfect in one." (John 17:21, 23) "He that is joined unto the Lord is one spirit" (I Corinthians 6:17) This state is very little known, therefore it is not spoken of. Oh state of life, how narrow is the way which leads unto you! Oh love the most pure of all, because You are God Himself. Oh love immense and independent, which nothing can limit or straiten! Yet these people appear quite common, as I have said, because they have nothing outwardly to distinguish them, unless it be an infinite freedom, which is often scandalized by those who are limited and confined within themselves, to whom, as they see nothing better than they have themselves, all that is different to what they possess appears evil. But the holiness of these simple and innocent ones whom they despise is a holiness incomparably more eminent than all which they consider holy, because their own works, though performed with such strictness, have no more strength than the principle in which they originate, which is always the effort, though raised and ennobled, of a weak creature; but those who are consummated in the divine union act in God by a principle of infinite strength; and thus their smallest actions are more agreeable to God than the multitude of heroic deeds achieved by others, which appear so great in the sight of men. Therefore those in this degree do not seek for great things to do, resting contented with being what God makes them at each moment. These do more, without doing anything, for the conversion of a kingdom, than five hundred preachers who have not attained this condition. God sometimes, however, permits these people to be known, though not fully. Many people apply to them for instruction, to whom they communicate a vivifying principle, by means of which many more are won to Christ; but this is done, without care or anxiety, by pure Providence. If people only knew the glory which is rendered to God by such as these, who are scorned by the world, they would be astonished; for it is they who render to God a glory worthy of Himself; because God, acting as God within them, brings into them a glory worthy of Him. Oh, how many Christians, quite seraphic in appearance, are far from this! But in this condition, as in all others, there are souls more or less divine. God hides them in His bosom, and under the veil of a most common life, so that they may be known to Him alone, though they are His delight. Here the secrets of God, in Himself and in the hearts of those in whom He dwells, are revealed; not by word, sight, or light, but by the science of God, which abides in Him; and when such people have to write or speak, they are themselves astonished to find that all flows from a divine centre, without their having been aware that they possessed such treasures. They find themselves in a profound science, without memory or recollection; like an inestimable treasure, which is unobserved until there is a necessity for its manifestation; and it is in the manifestation to others that they find the revelation to themselves. When they write, they are astonished to find themselves writing of things with which they neither knew nor believed themselves to be acquainted. Although, as they write, they cannot doubt their apprehension of them. It is not so with other Christians. Their light precedes their experience, as a person sees from afar the things which he does not possess, and describes what he has seen, known, and heard. But these are persons who hold a treasure within themselves, which they do not see until after the manifestation, although it is in their possession. Yet, after all, this does not well express the idea which I wish to convey. God is in this soul; or rather the soul no longer exists; it no longer acts, but God acts, and it is the instrument. God includes all treasures in Himself, and manifests them through this soul to others; and thus, as it draws them from its centre, it becomes aware of their presence, though it had never reflected upon them before. I am sure that any who have attained this degree will enter into my meaning, and will easily distinguish the difference between the states I have described. Those whom I mentioned first, see things and enjoy them as we enjoy the sun; but the others have become one with the sun itself, which does not enjoy nor reflect upon its own light. This condition is permanent, and its only vicissitude, so far as its centre is concerned, is a greater advancement in God, and as God is infinite, He can continually make the soul more divine by enlarging its capacity, as the water of which we have spoken expands in proportion as it is lost in the sea, with which it mingles incessantly without ever leaving it. It is the same with these souls. All who are in this degree have God, but some more and some less fully. They are all full, but all do not possess an equal plenitude. A little vase when full is as truly filled as a larger one, yet it does not contain an equal quantity. So all these souls are filled with the fullness of God, but it is according to their receptive capacity, which capacity God continually enlarges. Therefore the longer Christians live in this divine condition, the more they expand, and their capacity becomes continually more immense, without anything being left for them to do or desire; for they always possess God in His fullness, and He never leaves an empty corner in their hearts. As they grow and enlarge, He fills them with Himself, as we see with the air. A small room is full of air, but a large one contains more. If you continually increase the size of a room, in the same proportion the air will enter, infallibly though imperceptibly, and thus, without changing its state or disposition, and without any new sensation, the soul increases in capacity and in plenitude. But this growing capacity can only be received in a state of nothingness, because in any; other condition there is an opposition to growth. It may be well here to explain what may appear a contradiction, when I say, that the soul must be brought to nothing in order to pass into God, and that it must lose all that is its own; and yet I speak of capacity which it retains. There are two capacities. One is natural to the creature, and this is narrow and limited - when it is purified, it is fitted to receive the gifts of God, but not God Himself; because what we receive within us must of necessity be less than ourselves, as that which is enclosed in a vase must be of less extent, though it may be of greater value, than the vase which contains it. But the capacity of which I speak here is a capacity to extend and to lose itself more and more in God, after the soul has lost its appropriation, which confined it to itself; and this capacity being no longer restricted nor limited, because its annihilation has deprived it of all form, disposes the soul to flow into God, so that it loses itself, and flows into Him who is beyond comprehension. The more it is lost in Him, the more it develops and becomes immense, participating in His perfections, and being more and more transformed in Him, as water in communication with its source continually mingles with it. God, being our original source, has created us with a nature fit to be united, transformed, and made one with Himself.

Chapter Four

The soul has now nothing to do but to remain as it is, and to follow without resistance all the movements of its Guide. All its movements are of God, and He guides it infallibly. It is not thus in the inferior conditions, unless it be when the soul begins to taste of the centre; but then it is not so infallible, and they would be deceived who applied this rule to any but the most advanced state. It is the duty of this soul to follow blindly with reflection all the movings of God. Here all reflection is banished, and the soul would find a difficulty in indulging in it, even if it desired to do so. But as by an effort it might accomplish it, this habit should be scrupulously avoided; because reflection alone has the power of leading man to enter into himself, and of drawing him out of God. Now, I say, that if man does not go out of God he will never sin, and if he sin, it is because he has gone out of Him, which can only be the effect of appropriation; and the soul can only take itself back from its abandonment by reflex action, which would be to it a hell similar to that into which the great angel fell when, looking with complacency upon himself, and preferring himself to God, he became a devil. And this state would be more terrible as that which had been previously attained was more advanced. It will be objected that suffering is impossible in this condition, not only as to the centre, but also as to the senses, because in order to suffering there must be reflex action, and it is reflection which constitutes the principal and the most painful part of suffering. All this is true in a certain sense; and as it is a fact that souls far less advanced than these suffer sometimes by reflection, sometimes by impression, I maintain that it is also true that those in this degree cannot suffer otherwise than by impression. This does not imply that sorrow may not be unlimited, and far more intense than that which is reflected, as the burning of one brought into actual contact with fire would be much more severe than that of one who is burned by the reflection of fire. It will be said, but God can teach them by means of reflection how to suffer. God will not make use of reflection for this end. He can show them in a moment what they have to suffer by a direct view, and not by a reflected one, as those in heaven see in God that which is in Him, and that which passes out from Him to His creatures, without looking at these things or reflecting upon them, but remaining absorbed and lost in God. It is this which deceives so many spiritually minded people, who imagine that nothing can be either known or suffered but by reflection. On the contrary, this kind of knowledge and suffering is very slight compared to that which is imparted in other ways. All such suffering as can be distinguished and known, though expressed in such exaggerated terms, does not equal that of those who do not know their suffering, and cannot admit that they do suffer, because of the great separation between the two parts. It is true that they suffer extreme pain; it is true that they suffer nothing, and that they are in a state of perfect contentment. I believe that, if such a soul were taken to hell, it would suffer all the cruel tortures of its fate in a complete contentment, because of the beatitude of its transformed centre; and this is the cause of the indifference which they feel towards all conditions. As I have said, this does not prevent their experiencing the extremity of suffering, as the extremity of suffering does not hinder their perfect happiness. Those who have experienced it will be well able to understand me. It is not here as in the passive state of love. There the soul is filled with a love of suffering and of the good pleasure of God. Here it is a loss of the will in God by a state of deification, where all is God without its being recognized as such. The soul is established by its condition in its sovereign, unchangeable good. It is in a perfect beatitude, where nothing can cross its perfect happiness, which is rendered its permanent condition; for many possess it temporarily, or know it temporarily, before it becomes their permanent condition. God gives first the knowledge of the condition, then a desire for it; then He gives it confusedly and indistinctly; and lastly, He makes it a normal condition, and establishes the soul in it for ever. It will be said that when once the soul is established in this condition, nothing more can be done for it. It is just the reverse, there is always an infinitude to be done on the part of God, not on that of the creature. God does not make the life divine all at once, but by degrees. Then, as have said, He enlarges the capacity of the soul, and can continually deify it more and more, God being an unfathomable depth. Oh Lord, "how great is Your goodness, which You have laid up for them that fear You!" (Psalm 31:19). It was the sight of this state of blessedness which elicited such frequent exclamations from David after he had been purified from sin. These persons can no longer be astonished either at any grace that may be given them or at any sin that can be committed, knowing thoroughly both the goodness of God, which causes the one, and the depravity of man, which is the source of the other. Though the whole world might perish, they would not be troubled by it. Is it because they are no longer jealous for the honor of God that they are not troubled by the sin they see around them? No, it is not that, it is that they are jealous for the glory of God as God. God necessarily cares more for His glory than any other can; and all that He does in Himself, and out of Himself in others, He does for Himself. Yet He cannot be troubled by the sins of the world or by the loss of men, although, in order to save them, He became incarnate, and took a mortal body, and gave His life. These Christians also would give a thousand lives to save men; because God, who has transformed them, makes them participate in His qualities, and they see all in the light of God, and although God truly desires the salvation of men, and offers to them all that is necessary for their salvation, though by their own fault it is not efficacious for them, yet He does not fail to promote His glory by their loss; because it is impossible that God should permit anything by which He cannot be glorified, either by justice or by mercy. This is not the intention of those who offend Him, and who render Him active dishonor. On the part of God there is no passive dishonor; so it is unavoidable that, even against the will of the sinner, his sin should redound to the glory of God. Although God's nature cannot be offended, he who sins against Him deserves infinite punishment because of his willingness to offend such infinite goodness; and if he does not professedly oppose God, he yet does so by his actions and his will. And this will is so malicious, that if it could rob God of His divinity, it would do so. It is, then, this malicious will, and not the outward action, which constitutes the offence; for if a person whose will was lost, hidden, and transformed in God were compelled by absolute force to commit sinful actions, it is obvious that he would not sin in committing them. But in conclusion, say that these persons cannot be troubled by sin, because, although they hate it infinitely, they no longer suffer from it, seeing it as God sees it; and though, if it were necessary, they would give their lives to prevent the commission of a single sin, if God so willed it, they are without action, without desire, without inclination, without choice, without impatience, in a state of complete death, seeing things only as God sees them, and judging them only with God's judgment.

POETRY

God Neither Known nor Loved by the World

You linnets, let us try, beneath this grove,
Which shall be loudest in our Maker's praise!
In quest of some forlorn retreat I rove,
For all the world is blind, and wanders from his ways.
That God alone should prop the sinking soul,
Fills them with rage against his empire now:
I traverse earth in vain from pole to pole,
To seek one simple heart, set free from all below.
They speak of love, yet little feel its sway,
While in their bosom many an idol lurks;
Their base desires, well satisfied, obey,
Leave the Creator's hand, and lean upon his works.
'Tis therefore I can dwell with man no more;
Your fellowship, you warblers! suits me best:
Pure love has lost its price, though prized of yore,
Profaned by modern tongues, and slighted as a jest.
My God, who formed you for his praise alone,
Beholds his purpose well fulfilled in you;
Come, let us join the choir before his throne,
Partaking in his praise with spirits just and true.
Yes, I will always love; and, as I ought,
Tune to the praise of love my ceaseless voice;
Preferring love too vast for human thought,
In spite of erring men, who cavil at my choice.
Why have I not a thousand thousand hearts,
Lord of my soul! that they might all be yours?
If you approve - the zeal your smile imparts,
How should it ever fail! can such a fire decline?

Love, pure and holy, is a deathless fire;
Its object heavenly, it must ever blaze:
Eternal love a God must needs inspire,
When once he wins the heart, and fits it for his praise.
Self-love dismissed - 'tis then we live indeed -
In her embrace, death, only death is found:
Come, then, one noble effort, and succeed,
Cast off the chain of self with which thy soul is bound.
Oh! I could cry, that all the world might hear,
You self-tormentors, love your God alone;
Let his unequalled excellence be dear,
Dear to your inmost souls, and make him all your own!
They hear me not - alas! how fond to rove
In endless chase of folly's specious lure!
'Tis here alone, beneath this shady grove,
I taste the sweets of truth - here only am secure.

The Swallow

I am fond of the swallow - I learn from her flight,
Had I skill to improve it, a lesson of love:
How seldom on earth do we see her alight!
She dwells in the skies, she is ever above.
It is on the wing that she takes her repose,
Suspended and poised in the regions of air,
'Tis not in our fields that her sustenance grows,
It is winged like herself - 'tis ethereal fare.
She comes in the spring, all the summer she stays,
And, dreading the cold, still follows the sun -
So, true to our love, we should covet his rays,
And the place where he shines not immediately shun.
Our light should be love, and our nourishment prayer;
It is dangerous food that we find upon earth;
The fruit of this world is beset with a snare,
In itself it is hurtful, as vile in its birth.
'Tis rarely, if ever, she settles below,
And only when building a nest for her young;
Were it not for her brood, she would never bestow

A thought upon anything filthy as dung.
Let us leave it ourselves ('tis a mortal abode),
To bask every moment in infinite love;
Let us fly the dark winter, and follow the road
That leads to the dayspring appearing above.

The Triumph of Heavenly Love Desired

Ah! reign, wherever man is found!
My spouse, beloved and divine!
Then I am rich, and I abound,
When every human heart is thine.
A thousand sorrows pierce my soul,
To think that all are not thine own:
Ah! be adored from pole to pole;
Where is thy zeal? arise; be known!
All hearts are cold, in every place,
Yet earthly good with warmth pursue;
Dissolve them with a flash of grace,
Thaw these of ice, and give us new!

Procedure of Divine Love

'Twas my purpose, on a day,
To embark, and sail away.
As I climbed the vessel's side,
Love was sporting in the tide;
"Come," he said, - "ascend - make haste,
Launch into the boundless waste."
Many mariners were there,
Having each his separate care;
They that rowed us held their eyes
Fixed upon the starry skies;
Others steered, or turned the sails,
To receive the shifting gales.
Love, with power divine supplied,
Suddenly my courage tried;
In a moment it was night,
Ship and skies were out of sight;
On the briny wave I lay,

Floating rushes all my stay.
Did I with resentment burn
At this unexpected turn?
Did I wish myself on shore,
Never to forsake it more?
No – "My soul," I cried, "be still;
If I must be lost, I will."
Next he hastened to convey
Both my frail supports away;
Seized my rushes; bade the waves
Yawn into a thousand graves:
Down I went, and sunk as lead,
Ocean closing o'er my head.
Still, however, life was safe;
And I saw him turn and laugh:
"Friend," he cried, "adieu! lie low,
While the wintry storms shall blow;
When the spring has calmed the main,
You shall rise and float again."
Soon I saw him, with dismay,
Spread his plumes, and soar away;
Now I mark his rapid flight;
Now he leaves my aching sight;
He is gone whom I adore,
'Tis in vain to seek him more.
How I trembled then and feared,
When my love had disappeared!
"Wilt thou leave me thus," I cried,
"Whelmed beneath the rolling tide?"
Vain attempt to reach his ear!
Love was gone, and would not hear.
Ah! return, and love me still;
See me subject to your will;
Frown with wrath, or smile with grace,
Only let me see your face!
Evil I have none to fear,
All is good, if you are near.
Yet he leaves me - cruel fate!
Leaves me in my lost estate -

Have I sinned? Oh, say wherein;
Tell me, and forgive my sin!
King, and Lord, whom I adore,
Shall I see your face no more?
Be not angry; I resign,
Henceforth, all my will to thine:
I consent that you depart,
Though your absence breaks my heart;
Go then, and for ever too:
All is right that you will do.
This was just what Love intended;
He was now no more offended;
Soon as I became a child,
Love returned to me and smiled:
Never strife shall more betide
'Twixt the bridegroom and his bride.

A Child of God Longing to See Him Beloved

There's not an echo round me,
But I am glad should learn,
How pure a fire has found me,
The love with which I burn.
For none attends with pleasure
To what I would reveal;
They slight me out of measure,
And laugh at all I feel.
The rocks receive less proudly
The story of my flame;
When I approach, they loudly
Reverberate his name.
I speak to them of sadness,
And comforts at a stand;
They bid me look for gladness,
And better days at hand.
Far from all habitation,
I heard a happy sound;
Big with the consolation,
That I have often found.

I said, "My lot is sorrow,
　My grief has no alloy;"
The rocks replied-"To-morrow,
　To-morrow brings you joy."
These sweet and sacred tidings,
　What bliss it is to hear!
For, spite of all my chidings,
　My weakness and my fear,
No sooner I receive them,
　Than I forget my pain,
And, happy to believe them,
　I love as much again.
I fly to scenes romantic,
　Where never men resort;
For in an age so frantic
　Impiety is sport.
For riot and confusion
　They barter things above;
Condemning, as delusion,
　The joy of perfect love.
In this sequestered corner,
　None hears what I express;
Delivered from the scorner,
　What peace do I possess!
Beneath the boughs reclining,
　Or roving o'er the wild,
I live as undesigning
　And harmless as a child.
No troubles here surprise me,
　I innocently play,
While Providence supplies me,
　And guards me all the day:
My dear and kind defender
　Preserves me safely here,
From men of pomp and splendor,
　Who fill a child with fear.

Aspirations of the Soul After God

My Spouse! in whose presence I live,
 Sole object of all my desires,
Who knows what a flame I conceive,
 And can easily double its fires!
 How pleasant is all that I meet!
 From fear of adversity free,
 I find even sorrow made sweet;
 Because 'tis assigned me by thee.
 Transported I see thee display
 Your riches and glory divine;
 I have only my life to repay,
 Take what I would gladly resign.
 Thy will is the treasure I seek,
 For you are as faithful as strong;
 There let me, obedient and meek,
 Repose myself all the day long.
 My spirit and faculties fail;
 Oh, finish what love has begun!
 Destroy what is sinful and frail,
And dwell in the soul you have won!
Dear theme of my wonder and praise,
 I cry, who is worthy as you?
 I can only be silent and gaze!
 'Tis all that is left to me now.
 Oh, glory in which I am lost,
Too deep for the plummet of thought;
 On an ocean of Deity tossed,
 I am swallowed, I sink into nought.
 Yet, lost and absorbed as I seem,
 I chant to the praise of my King;
And, though overwhelmed by the theme,
 Am happy whenever I sing.

Gratitude and Love to God

All are indebted much to thee,
 But I far more than all,
From many a deadly snare set free,

And raised from many a fall.
Overwhelm me, from above,
Daily, with thy boundless love.
What bonds of gratitude I feel
No language can declare;
Beneath the oppressive weight I reel,
'Tis more than I can bear:
When shall I that blessing prove,
To return thee love for love?
Spirit of charity, dispense
Thy grace to every heart;
Expel all other spirits thence,
Drive self from every part;
Charity divine, draw nigh,
Break the chains in which we lie!
All selfish souls, whatever they feign,
Have still a slavish lot;
They boast of liberty in vain,
Of love, and feel it not.
He whose bosom glows with thee,
He, and he alone, is free.
Oh blessedness, all bliss above,
When thy pure fires prevail!
Love only teaches what is love:
All other lessons fail:
We learn its name, but not its powers,
Experience only makes it ours.

Happy Solitude - Unhappy Men

My heart is easy, and my burden light;
I smile, though sad, when you are in my sight:
The more my woes in secret I deplore,
I taste your goodness, and I love you more.
There, while a solemn stillness reigns around,
Faith, love, and hope within my soul abound;
And, while the world suppose me lost in care,
The joys of angels, unperceived, I share.
Your creatures wrong you, O you sovereign good!

You are not loved, because not understood;
This grieves me most, that vain pursuits beguile
Ungrateful men, regardless of your smile.
Frail beauty and false honor are adored;
While You they scorn, and trifle with your Word;
Pass, unconcerned, a Savior's sorrows by;
And hunt their ruin with a zeal to die.

Living Water

The fountain in its source,
No drought of summer fears;
The farther it pursues its course,
The nobler it appears.
But shallow cisterns yield
A scanty short supply;
The morning sees them amply filled,
At evening they are dry.

Truth and Divine Love Rejected by the World

O love, of pure and heavenly birth!
O simple truth, scarce known on earth!
Whom men resist with stubborn will;
And, more perverse and daring still,
Smother and quench, with reasonings vain,
While error and deception reign.
Whence comes it, that, your power the same
As His on high from whence you came,
You rarely find a listening ear,
Or heart that makes you welcome here? -
Because you bring reproach and pain,
Wherever you visit, in your train.
The world is proud, and cannot bear
The scorn and calumny you share;
The praise of men the mark they mean,
They fly the place where you are seen;
Pure love, with scandal in the rear,
Suits not the vain; it costs too dear.

Then, let the price be what it may,
Though poor, I am prepared to pay;
Come shame, come sorrow; spite of tears,
Weakness, and heart-oppressing fears;
One soul, as least, shall not repine,
To give you room; come, reign in mine!

Divine Justice Amiable

You have no lightnings, O you Just!
　Or I their force should know;
And, if you strike me into dust,
　My soul approves the blow.
The heart, that values less its ease
　Than it adores your ways,
In your avenging anger sees
　A subject of its praise.
Pleased I could lie, concealed and lost,
　In shades of central night;
Not to avoid your wrath, you know,
　But lest I grieve your sight.
Smite me, O you, whom I provoke!
　And I will love you still:
The well deserved and righteous stroke
　Shall please me, though it kill.
Am I not worthy to sustain
　The worst you can devise;
And dare I seek your throne again,
　And meet your sacred eyes?
Far from afflicting, you are kind;
　And, in my saddest hours,
An unction of your grace I find,
　Pervading all my powers.
Alas! you spare me yet again;
　And, when your wrath should move,
Too gentle to endure my pain,
　You sooth me with your love.
I have no punishment to fear;
　But, ah! that smile from you

Imparts a pang far more severe
Than woe itself would be.

The Soul That Loves God Finds Him Everywhere

O you, by long experience tried,
Near whom no grief can long abide;
My love! how full of sweet content
I pass my years of banishment!
All scenes alike engaging prove
To souls impressed with sacred love!
Wherever they dwell, they dwell in you;
In heaven, in earth, or on the sea.
To me remains nor place nor time;
My country is in every clime;
I can be calm and free from care
On any shore, since God is there.
While place we seek, or place we shun,
The soul finds happiness in none;
But, with a God to guide our way,
'Tis equal joy to go or stay.
Could I be cast where you are not,
That were indeed a dreadful lot;
But regions none remote I call,
Secure of finding God in all.
My country, Lord, are you alone;
Nor other can I claim or own;
The point where all my wishes meet;
My law, my love, life's only sweet!
I hold by nothing here below;
Appoint my journey and I go;
Though pierced by scorn, oppressed by pride,
I feel you good - feel naught beside.
No frowns of men can hurtful prove
To souls on fire with heavenly love;
Though men and devils both condemn,
No gloomy days arise from them.
Ah, then! to his embrace repair;
My soul, you are no stranger there;

There love divine shall be your guard,
And peace and safety your reward.

The Testimony of Divine Adoption

How happy are the new-born race,
Partakers of adopting grace!
How pure the bliss they share!
Hid from the world and all its eyes,
Within their heart the blessing lies,
And conscience feels it there.
The moment we believe, 'tis ours;
And if we love with all our powers
The God from whom it came;
And if we serve with hearts sincere,
'Tis still discernible and clear,
An undisputed claim.
But, ah! if foul and willful sin
Stain and dishonor us within,
Farewell the joy we knew;
Again the slaves of nature's sway,
In labyrinths of our own we stray,
Without a guide or clue.
The chaste and pure, who fear to grieve
The gracious Spirit they receive,
His work distinctly trace;
And, strong in undissembling love,
Boldly assert and clearly prove
Their hearts his dwelling-place.
Oh, messenger of dear delight,
Whose voice dispels the deepest night,
Sweet peace-proclaiming Dove!
With you at hand, to soothe our pains,
No wish unsatisfied remains,
No task but that of love.
'Tis love unites what sin divides;
The centre, where all bliss resides;
To which the soul once brought,
Reclining on the first great cause,

From his abounding sweetness draws
Peace passing human thought.
Sorrow forgoes its nature there,
And life assumes a tranquil air,
Divested of its woes;
There sovereign goodness soothes the breast,
Till then incapable of rest,
In sacred sure repose.

Divine Love Endures No Rival

Love is the Lord whom I obey,
Whose will transported I perform;
The centre of my rest, my stay,
Love's all in all to me, myself a worm.
For uncreated charms I burn,
Oppressed by slavish fear no more,
For One in whom I may discern,
Even when he frowns, a sweetness I adore.
He little loves him who complains,
And finds him rigorous and severe;
His heart is sordid, and he feigns,
Though loud in boasting of a soul sincere.
Love causes grief, but 'tis to move
And stimulate the slumbering mind;
And he has never tasted love
Who shuns a plan so graciously designed.
Sweet is the cross, above all sweets,
To souls enamored with your smiles;
The keenest woe life ever meets,
Love strips of all its terrors, and beguiles.
'Tis just that God should not be dear
Where self engrosses all the thought,
And groans and murmurs make it clear,
Whatever else is loved, the Lord is not.
The love of thee flows just as much
As that of ebbing self subsides;
Our hearts, their scantiness is such,
Bear not the conflict of two rival tides.

Both cannot govern in one soul;
Then let self-love be dispossessed;
The love of God deserves the whole,
And will not dwell with so despised a guest.

Self-diffidence

Source of love, and light of day,
Tear me from myself away;
Every view and thought of mine
Cast into the mould of thine;
Teach, O teach this faithless heart
A consistent constant part;
Or, if it must live to grow
More rebellious, break it now!
Is it thus that I requite
Grace and goodness infinite?
Every trace of every boon
Cancelled and erased so soon!
Can I grieve you, whom I love;
You, in whom I live and move?
If my sorrow touch you still,
Save me from so great an ill!
Oh! the oppressive, irksome weight,
Felt in an uncertain state;
Comfort, peace, and rest, adieu,
Should I prove at last untrue!
Still I choose you, follow still
Every notice of your will;
But, unstable, strangely weak,
Still let slip the good I seek.
Self-confiding wretch, I though
I could serve you as I ought,
Win you, and deserve to feel
All the love you can reveal;
Trusting self, a bruised reed,
Is to be deceived indeed:
Save me from this harm and loss,
Lest my gold turn all to dross!

Self is earthly - faith alone
Makes an unseen world our own;
Faith relinquished, how we roam,
Feel our way, and leave our home!
Spurious gems our hopes entice,
While we scorn the pearl of price;
And, preferring servants' pay,
Cast the children's bread away.

The Acquiescence of Pure Love

Love! if your destined sacrifice am I,
Come, slay your victim, and prepare your fires;
Plunged in your depths of mercy, let me die
The death which every soul that lives desires!
I watch my hours, and see them fleet away;
The time is long that I have languished here;
Yet all my thoughts your purposes obey,
With no reluctance, cheerful and sincere.
To me 'tis equal, whether love ordain
My life or death, appoint me pain or ease;
My soul perceives no real ill in pain;
In ease or health no real good she sees.
One good she covets, and that good alone,
To choose your will, from selfish bias free;
And to prefer a cottage to a throne,
And grief to comfort, if it pleases thee.
That we should bear the cross is your command,
Die to the world and live to self no more;
Suffer, unmoved, beneath the rudest hand,
As pleased when shipwrecked as when safe on shore.

Repose in God

Blest! who, far from all mankind
This world's shadows left behind,
Hears from heaven a gentle strain
Whispering love, and loves again.
Blest! who, free from self-esteem,

Dives into the great Supreme.
All desire beside discards,
Joys inferior none regards.
Blest! who in your bosom seeks
Rest that nothing earthly breaks,
Dead to self and worldly things,
Lost in you, the King of kings!
You that know my secret fire,
Softly speak and soon retire;
Favor my divine repose,
Spare the sleep a God bestows.

Glory to God Alone

Oh loved! but not enough-though dearer far
Than self and its most loved enjoyments are;
None duly loves you, but who, nobly free
From sensual objects, finds his all in thee.
Glory of God! you stranger here below,
Whom man nor knows, nor feels a wish to know;
Our faith and reason are both shocked to find
Man in the post of honor - You behind.
Reason exclaims – "Let every creature fall,
Ashamed, abased, before the Lord of all;"
And faith, overwhelmed with such a dazzling blaze,
Feebly describes the beauty she surveys.
Yet man, dim-sighted man, and rash as blind,
Deaf to the dictates of his better mind,
In frantic competition dares the skies,
And claims precedence of the Only wise.
Oh, lost in vanity, till once self-known!
Nothing is great, or good, but God alone;
When you shall stand before his awful face,
Then, at the last, your pride shall know his place.
Glorious, Almighty, First, and without end!
When will you melt the mountains and descend?
When will you shoot abroad your conquering rays,
And teach these atoms, you have made, your praise?
Your glory is the sweetest heaven I feel;

And, if I seek it with too fierce a zeal,
Your love, triumphant over a selfish will,
Taught me the passion, and inspires it still.
My reason, all my faculties, unite,
To make your glory their supreme delight:
Forbid it, fountain of my brightest days,
That I should rob you, and usurp your praise!
My soul! rest happy in your low estate,
Nor hope, nor wish, to be esteemed or great,
To take the impression of a will divine,
Be that your glory, and those riches thine.
Confess him righteous in his just decrees,
Love what he loves, and let his pleasure please;
Die daily; from the touch of sin recede;
Then you have crowned him, and he reigns indeed.

Self-love and Truth Incompatible

From thorny wilds a monster came,
That filled my soul with fear and shame;
The birds, forgetful of their mirth,
Drooped at the sight, and fell to earth;
When thus a sage addressed mine ear,
Himself unconscious of a fear:
"Whence all this terror and surprise,
Distracted looks and streaming eyes?
Far from the world and its affairs,
The joy it boasts, the pain it shares,
Surrender, without guile or art,
To God an undivided heart;
The savage form, so feared before,
Shall scare your trembling soul no more;
For, loathsome as the sight may be,
'Tis but the love of self you see.
Fix all your love on God alone,
Choose but his will, and hate your own:
No fear shall in your path be found,
The dreary waste shall bloom around,
And you, through all your happy days,

Shall bless his name, and sing his praise."
Oh lovely solitude, how sweet
The silence of this calm retreat!
Here truth, the fair whom I pursue,
Gives all her beauty to my view;
The simple, unadorned display
Charms every pain and fear away.
O Truth, whom millions proudly slight;
O Truth, my treasure and delight;
Accept this tribute to your name,
And this poor heart from which it came!

The Love of God the End of Life

Since life in sorrow must be spent,
So be it - I am well content,
And meekly wait my last remove,
Seeking only growth in love.
No bliss I seek, but to fulfill
In life, in death, your lovely will;
No succors in my woes I want,
Save what you are pleased to grant.
Our days are numbered, let us spare
Our anxious hearts a needless care:
'Tis yours to number out our days;
Ours to give them to your praise.
Love is our only business here,
Love, simple, constant, and sincere;
O blessed days, your servants see,
Spent, O Lord! in pleasing thee!

Love Faithful in the Absence of the Beloved

In vain you woo me to your harmless joys,
You pleasant bowers, remote from strife and noise;
Your shades, the witnesses of many a vow,
Breathed forth in happier days, are irksome now;
Denied that smile 'twas once my heaven to see,
Such scenes, such pleasures, are all past with me.

In vain he leaves me, I shall love him still;
And, though I mourn, not murmur at his will;
I have no cause - an object all divine,
Might well grow weary of a soul like mine;
Yet pity me, great God! forlorn, alone,
Heartless and hopeless, life and love all gone.

Love Pure and Fervent

Jealous, and with love overflowing,
   God demands a fervent heart;
Grace and bounty still bestowing,
   Calls us to a grateful part.
Oh, then, with supreme affection
   His paternal will regard!
If it cost us some dejection,
   Every sigh has its reward.
Perfect love has power to soften
   Cares that might our peace destroy,
Nay, does more - transforms them often,
   Changing sorrow into joy.
Sovereign Love appoints the measure,
   And the number of our pains;
And is pleased when we find pleasure
   In the trials he ordains.

The Entire Surrender

Peace has unveiled her smiling face,
And wooes your soul to her embrace,
   Enjoyed with ease, if you refrain
From earthly love, else sought in vain;
   She dwells with all who truth prefer,
But seeks not them who seek not her.
Yield to the Lord, with simple heart,
   All that you have, and all you art;
Renounce all strength but strength divine;
   And peace shall be for ever thine:
Behold the path which I have trod,

My path, till I go home to God.

The Perfect Sacrifice

I place an offering at your shrine,
From taint and blemish clear,
Simple and pure in its design,
Of all that I hold dear.
I yield you back your gifts again,
Your gifts which most I prize;
Desirous only to retain
The notice of your eyes.
But if, by your adored decree,
That blessing be denied;
Resigned and un-reluctant, see
My every wish subside.
Your will in all things I approve,
Exalted or cast down;
Your will in every state I love,
And even in your frown.

God Hides His People

To lay the soul that loves him low,
Becomes the Only-wise:
To hide beneath a veil of woe,
The children of the skies.
Man, though a worm, would yet be great;
Though feeble, would seem strong;
Assumes an independent state,
By sacrilege and wrong.
Strange the reverse, which, once abased,
The haughty creature proves!
He feels his soul a barren waste,
Nor dares affirm he loves.
Scorned by the thoughtless and the vain,
To God he presses near;
Superior to the world's disdain,
And happy in its sneer.

Oh welcome, in his heart he says,
    Humility and shame!
Farewell the wish for human praise,
    The music of a name!
But will not scandal mar the good
    That I might else perform?
And can God work it, if he would,
    By so despised a worm?
Ah, vainly anxious! - leave the Lord
    To rule you, and dispose;
Sweet is the mandate of his word,
    And gracious all he does.
He draws from human littleness
    His grandeur and renown;
And generous hearts with joy confess
    The triumph all his own.
Down, then, with self-exalting thoughts;
    Your faith and hope employ,
To welcome all that he allots,
    And suffer shame with joy.
No longer, then, you wilt encroach
    On his eternal right;
And he shall smile at your approach,
    And make you his delight.

The Secrets of Divine Love Are To Be Kept

Sun! stay your course, this moment stay -
Suspend the over flowing tide of day,
    Divulge not such a love as mine,
    Ah! hide the mystery divine;
Lest man, who deems my glory shame,
Should learn the secret of my flame.
    O night! propitious to my views,
    Your sable awning wide diffuse;
    Conceal alike my joy and pain,
    Nor draw your curtain back again,
Though morning, by the tears she shows,
    Seems to participate my woes.

You stars! whose faint and feeble fires
 Express my languishing desires,
Whose slender beams pervade the skies,
 As silent as my secret sighs,
 Those emanations of a soul,
That darts her fires beyond the Pole;
Your rays, that scarce assist the sight,
That pierce, but not displace the night;
That shine indeed, but nothing show
 Of all those various scenes below,
 Bring no disturbance, rather prove
 Incentives to a sacred love.
You moon! whose never-failing course
 Bespeaks a providential force,
 Go, tell the tidings of my flame
To Him who calls the stars by name;
Whose absence kills, whose presence cheers;
 Who blots, or brightens, all my years.
 While, in the blue abyss of space,
 Your orb performs its rapid race;
 Still whisper in his listening ears
The language of my sighs and tears;
 Tell him, I seek him, far below,
 Lost in a wilderness of woe.
You thought-composing, silent hours,
 Diffusing peace over all my powers;
 Friends of the pensive, who conceal,
 In darkest shades, the flames I feel;
 To you I trust, and safely may,
The love that wastes my strength away.
 In sylvan scenes and caverns rude,
 I taste the sweets of solitude;
 Retired indeed, but not alone,
I share them with a spouse unknown,
Who hides me here from envious eyes,
 From all intrusion and surprise.
Embowering shades and dens profound!
 Where echo rolls the voice around;
 Mountains! whose elevated heads

A moist and misty veil overspreads;
Disclose a solitary bride
To him I love - to none beside.
You rills, that, murmuring all the way,
Among the polished pebbles stray;
Creep silently along the ground,
Lest, drawn by that harmonious sound,
Some wanderer, whom I would not meet,
Should stumble on my loved retreat.
Enameled meads, and hillocks green,
And streams that water all the scene,
You torrents, loud in distant ears,
You fountains, that receive my tears,
Ah! still conceal, with caution due,
A charge I trust with none but you!
If, when my pain and grief increase
I seem to enjoy the sweetest peace,
It is because I find so fair,
The charming object of my care,
That I can sport and pleasure make
Of torment suffered for his sake.
You meads and groves, unconscious things!
You know not whence my pleasure springs;
You know not, and you cannot know,
The source from which my sorrows flow:
The dear sole cause of all I feel, -
He knows, and understands them well.
You deserts, where the wild beasts rove,
Scenes sacred to my hours of love;
You forests, in whose shades I stray,
Benighted under burning day;
Ah! whisper not how blest am I,
Nor while I live, nor when I die.
You lambs, who sport beneath these shades,
And bound along the mossy glades;
Be taught a salutary fear,
And cease to bleat when I am near:
The wolf may hear your harmless cry,
Whom you should dread as much as I.

How calm, amid these scenes, my mind;
How perfect is the peace I find!
Oh hush, be still, my every part,
My tongue, my pulse, my beating heart!
That love, aspiring to its cause,
May suffer not a moment's pause.
You swift-finned nations, that abide
In seas, as fathomless as wide;
And, unsuspicious of a snare,
Pursue at large your pleasures there;
Poor sportive fools! how soon does man
Your heedless ignorance trepan.
Away! dive deep into the brine,
Where never yet sunk plummet line;
Trust me, the vast leviathan
Is merciful, compared with man;
Avoid his arts, forsake the beach,
And never play within his reach.
My soul her bondage ill endures;
I pant for liberty like yours;
I long for that immense profound,
That knows no bottom and no bound:
Lost in infinity, to prove
The incomprehensible of love.
You birds, that lessen as you fly,
And vanish in the distant sky;
To whom yon airy waste belongs,
Resounding with your cheerful songs;
Haste to escape from human sight;
Fear less the vulture and the kite.
How blest and how secure am I,
When, quitting earth, I soar on high;
When lost, like you I disappear,
And float in a sublimer sphere;
Whence falling, within human view,
I am ensnared and caught like you!
Omniscient God, whose notice deigns,
To try the heart and search the reins,
Compassionate the numerous woes,

I dare not, even to you, disclose;
O save me from the cruel hands
Of men who fear not your commands!
Love, all-subduing and divine,
Care for a creature truly thine;
Reign in a heart, disposed to own
No sovereign but yourself alone;
Cherish a bride who cannot rove,
Nor quit you for a meaner love!

The Vicissitudes Experienced in the Christian Life

I suffer fruitless anguish day by day,
Each moment, as it passes, marks my pain;
Scarce knowing whither, doubtfully I stray,
And see no end of all that I sustain.
The more I strive the more I am withstood;
Anxiety increasing every hour
My spirit finds no rest, performs no good,
And naught remains of all my former power.
My peace of heart is fled, I know not where;
My happy hours, like shadows, passed away;
Their sweet remembrance doubles all my care;
Night darker seems, succeeding such a day.
Dear faded joys and impotent regret,
What profit is there in incessant tears?
Oh you, whom, once beheld, we never forget,
Reveal your love, and banish all my fears!
Alas! he flies me-treats me as his foe,
Views not my sorrows, hears not when I plead;
Woe such as mine, despised, neglected woe,
Unless it shortens life, is vain indeed.
Pierced with a thousand wounds, I yet survive;
My pangs are keen, but no complaint transpires
And, while in terrors of your wrath I live,
Hell seems to loose it less tremendous fires.
Has hell a pain I would not gladly bear,
So your severe displeasure might subside?
Hopeless of ease, I seem already there,

My life extinguished, and yet death denied.
Is this the joy so promised - this the love,
The unchanging love, so sworn in better days?
Ah! dangerous glories! shown me, but to prove
How lovely you, and I how rash to gaze.
Why did I see them? had I still remained
Untaught, still ignorant how fair you are,
My humbler wishes I had soon obtained,
Nor known the torments of a doubting heart.
Deprived of all, yet feeling no desires,
Whence then, I cry, the pangs that I sustain
Dubious and uninformed, my soul inquires,
Ought she to cherish or shake off her pain?
Suffering, I suffer not - sincerely love,
Yet feel no touch of that enlivening flame;
As chance inclines me, unconcerned I move,
All times, and all events, to me the same.
I search my heart, and not a wish is there
But burns with zeal that hated self may fall;
Such is the sad disquietude I share,
A sea of doubts, and self the source of all.
I ask not life, nor do I wish to die;
And, if your hand accomplish not my cure,
I would not purchase with a single sigh
A free discharge from all that I endure.
I groan in chains, yet want not a release;
Am sick, and know not the distempered part;
Am just as void of purpose as of peace;
Have neither plan, nor fear, nor hope, nor heart.
My claim to life, though sought with earnest care,
No light within me, or without me, shows;
Once I had faith, but now in self-despair
Find my chief cordial and my best repose.
My soul is a forgotten thing; she sinks,
Sinks and is lost, without a wish to rise;
Feels an indifference she abhors, and thinks
Her name erased for ever from the skies.
Language affords not my distress a name,-
Yet it is real and no sickly dream;

'Tis love inflicts it; though to feel that flame
   Is all I know of happiness supreme.
When love departs, a chaos wide and vast,
   And dark as hell, is opened in the soul;
When love returns, the gloomy scene is past,
   No tempests shake her, and no fears control.
   Then tell me why these ages of delay?
   Oh love, all-excellent, once more appear;
Disperse the shades, and snatch me into day,
From this abyss of night, these floods of fear!
   No-love is angry, will not now endure
   A sigh of mine, or suffer a complaint;
He smites me, wounds me, and withholds the cure;
Exhausts my powers, and leaves me sick and faint.
He wounds, and hides the hand that gave the blow;
   He flies, he re-appears, and wounds again -
   Was ever heart that loved you treated so?
   Yet I adore you, though it seem in vain.
And will you leave me, whom, when lost and blind,
   You did distinguish and vouchsafe to choose,
   Before your laws were written in my mind,
While yet the world had all my thoughts and views?
   Now leave me, when, enamored of your laws,
   I make your glory my supreme delight?
   Now blot me from your register, and cause
   A faithful soul to perish from your sight?
What can have caused the change which I deplore?
   Is it to prove me, if my heart be true?
   Permit me then, while prostrate I adore,
   To draw, and place its picture in your view.
'Tis yours without reserve, most simply thine;
   So given to you, that it is not my own;
   A willing captive of your grace divine;
And loves, and seeks you, for yourself alone.
   Pain cannot move it, danger cannot scare;
   Pleasure and wealth, in its esteem, are dust;
It loves you, even when least inclined to spare
   Its tenderest feelings, and avows you just.
   'Tis all your own; my spirit is so too,

An undivided offering at your shrine;
It seeks your glory with no double view,
Your glory, with no secret bent to mine.
Love, holy love! and are you not severe,
To slight me, thus devoted, and thus fixed?
Mine is an everlasting ardor, clear
From all self-bias, generous and unmixed.
But I am silent, seeing what I see -
And fear, with cause, that I am self-deceived,
Not even my faith is from suspicion free,
And that I love seems not to be believed.
Live you, and reign forever, glorious Lord!
My last, least offering I present you now -
Renounce me, leave me, and be still adored!
Slay me, my God, and I applaud the blow.

Watching unto God in the Night Season

Sleep at last has fled these eyes,
  Nor do I regret his flight,
More alert my spirits rise,
  And my heart is free and light.
Nature silent all around,
  Not a single witness near;
God as soon as sought is found;
  And the flame of love burns clear.
Interruption, all day long,
  Checks the current of my joys;
Creatures press me with a throng,
  And perplex me with their noise.
Undisturbed I muse all night,
  On the first Eternal Fair;
Nothing there obstructs delight,
  Love is renovated there.
Life, with its perpetual stir,
  Proves a foe to love and me;
Fresh entanglements occur -
  Comes the night, and sets me free.
Never more, sweet sleep, suspend

My enjoyments, always new:
Leave me to possess my friend;
Other eyes and hearts subdue.
Hush the world, that I may wake
To the taste of pure delights;
Oh the pleasures I partake -
God, the partner of my nights!
David, for the selfsame cause,
Night preferred to busy day;
Hearts whom heavenly beauty draws,
Wish the glaring sun away.
Sleep, self-lovers, is for you -
Souls that love celestial know
Fairer scenes by night can view
Than the sun could ever show.

Season of

Season of my purest pleasure,
Sealer of observing eyes!
When, in larger, freer measure,
I can commune with the skies;
While, beneath your shade extended,
Weary man forgets his woes,
I, my daily trouble ended,
Find, in watching, my repose.
Silence all around prevailing,
Nature hushed in slumber sweet,
No rude noise mine ears assailing,
Now my God and I can meet:
Universal nature slumbers,
And my soul partakes the calm,
Breathes her ardor out in numbers,
Plaintive song or lofty psalm.
Now my passion, pure and holy,
Shines and burns without restraint;
Which the day's fatigue and folly
Cause to languish, dim and faint:
Charming hours of relaxation!

How I dread the ascending sun!
　　Surely, idle conversation
Is an evil matched by none.
Worldly prate and babble hurt me;
　　Unintelligible prove;
Neither teach me nor divert me;
　　I have ears for none but love.
Me they rude esteem, and foolish,
　　Hearing my absurd replies;
I have neither art's fine polish,
　　Nor the knowledge of the wise.
Simple souls, and unpolluted
　　By conversing with the great,
Have a mind and taste ill suited
　　To their dignity and state;
All their talking, reading, writing,
　　Are but talents misapplied;
Infants' prattle I delight in,
　　Nothing human choose beside.
'Tis the secret fear of sinning
　　Checks my tongue, or I should say,
When I see the night beginning,
　　I am glad of parting day:
Love this gentle admonition
　　Whispers soft within my breast;
"Choice befits not your condition,
　　Acquiescence suits you best."
Henceforth, the repose and pleasure
　　Night affords me I resign;
And your will shall be the measure,
　　Wisdom infinite! of mine:
Wishing is but inclination
　　Quarrelling with your decrees;
Wayward nature finds the occasion-
　　'Tis her folly and disease.
Night, with its sublime enjoyments,
　　Now no longer will I choose;
Nor the day, with its employments,
　　Irksome as they seem, refuse;

Lessons of a God's inspiring
Neither time nor place impedes;
From our wishing and desiring
Our unhappiness proceeds.

Night

Night! how I love your silent shades,
My spirits they compose;
The bliss of heaven my soul pervades,
In spite of all my woes.
While sleep instills her poppy dews
In every slumbering eye,
I watch to meditate and muse,
In blest tranquility.
And when I feel a God immense
Familiarly impart,
With every proof he can dispense,
His favor to my heart;
My native meanness I lament,
Though most divinely filled
With all the ineffable content
That Deity can yield.
His purpose and his course he keeps;
Treads all my reasonings down;
Commands me out of nature's deeps,
And hides me in his own.
When in the dust, its proper place,
Our pride of heart we lay;
'Tis then a deluge of his grace
Bears all our sins away.
You whom I serve, and whose I am,
Whose influence from on high
Refines, and still refines my flame,
And makes my fetters fly;
How wretched is the creature's state
Who thwarts your gracious power;
Crushed under sin's enormous weight,
Increasing every hour!

The night, when passed entire with thee,
How luminous and clear!
Then sleep has no delights for me,
Lest you should disappear.
My Savior! occupy me still
In this secure recess;
Let reason slumber if she will,
My joy shall not be less.
Let reason slumber out the night;
But if you deign to make
My soul the abode of truth and light,
Ah, keep my heart awake!

The Joy of the Cross

Long plunged in sorrow, I resign
My soul to that dear hand of thine,
Without reserve or fear;
That hand shall wipe my streaming eyes;
Or into smiles of glad surprise
Transform the falling tear.
My sole possession is your love;
In earth beneath, or heaven above,
I have no other store;
And, though with fervent suit I pray,
And importune you night and day,
I ask you nothing more.
My rapid hours pursue the course
Prescribed them by love's sweetest force,
And I your sovereign will,
Without a wish to escape my doom;
Though still a sufferer from the womb,
And doomed to suffer still.
By your command, wherever I stray,
Sorrow attends me all my way,
A never-failing friend;
And, if my sufferings may augment
Your praise, behold me well content -
Let sorrow still attend!

It cost me no regret, that she,
Who followed Christ, should follow me,
And though, wherever she goes,
Thorns spring spontaneous at her feet,
I love her, and extract a sweet
From all my bitter woes.
Adieu! you vain delights of earth,
Insipid sports, and childish mirth,
I taste no sweets in you;
Unknown delights are in the cross,
All joy beside to me is dross;
And Jesus thought so too.
The cross! Oh, ravishment and bliss -
How grateful even its anguish is;
Its bitterness how sweet!
There every sense, and all the mind,
In all her faculties refined,
Tastes happiness complete.
Souls once enabled to disdain
Base sublunary joys, maintain
Their dignity secure;
The fever of desire is passed,
And love has all its genuine taste,
Is delicate and pure.
Self-love no grace in sorrow sees,
Consults her own peculiar ease;
'Tis all the bliss she knows;
But nobler aims true Love employ;
In self-denial is her joy,
In suffering her repose.
Sorrow and love go side by side;
Nor height nor depth can ever divide
Their heaven-appointed bands;
Those dear associates still are one,
Nor till the race of life is run
Disjoin their wedded hands.
Jesus, avenger of our fall,
You faithful lover, above all
The cross has ever borne!

Oh, tell me, - life is in your voice -
How much afflictions were your choice,
And sloth and ease your scorn!
Your choice and mine shall be the same,
Inspirer of that holy flame
Which must for ever blaze!
To take the cross and follow you,
Where love and duty lead, shall be
My portion and my praise.

Joy in Martyrdom

Sweet tenants of this grove!
Who sing without design,
A song of artless love,
In unison with mine:
These echoing shades return
Full many a note of ours,
That wise ones cannot learn,
With all their boasted powers.
O you! whose sacred charms
These hearts so seldom love,
Although your beauty warms
And blesses all above;
How slow are human things,
To choose their happiest lot!
All-glorious King of kings,
Say why we love you not?
This heart, that cannot rest,
Shall thine for ever prove;
Though bleeding and distressed,
Yet joyful in your love:
'Tis happy though it breaks
Beneath your chastening hand;
And speechless, yet it speaks,
What you can understand.

Simple Trust

Still, still, without ceasing,
I feel it increasing,
This fervor of holy desire;
And often exclaim,
Let me die in the flame
Of a love that can never expire!
Had I words to explain
What she must sustain
Who dies to the world and its ways;
How joy and affright,
Distress and delight,
Alternately chequer her days:
You, sweetly severe!
I would make you appear,
In all you are pleased to award.
Not more in the sweet
Than the bitter I meet
My tender and merciful Lord.
This faith, in the dark,
Pursuing its mark,
Through many sharp trials of love,
Is the sorrowful waste
That is to be passed
On the way to the Canaan above.

The Necessity of Self-abasement

Source of love, my brighter sun,
You alone my comfort are;
See, my race is almost run;
Have you left this trembling heart?
In my youth your charming eyes
Drew me from the ways of men;
Then I drank unmingled joys;
Frown of thine saw never then.
Spouse of Christ was then my name;
And, devoted all to thee,
Strangely jealous I became,

Jealous of this self in me.
You to love, and none beside,
Was my darling, sole employ;
While alternately I died,
Now of grief, and now of joy.
Through the dark and silent night
On your radiant smiles I dwelt;
And to see the dawning light
Was the keenest pain I felt.
You my gracious teacher wert;
And thine eye, so close applied,
While it watched your pupil's heart,
Seemed to look at none beside.
Conscious of no evil drift,
This, I cried, is love indeed -
'Tis the giver, not the gift,
Whence the joys I feel proceed.
But, soon humbled and laid low,
Stripped of all you have conferred,
Nothing left but sin and woe,
I perceived how I had erred.
Oh, the vain conceit of man,
Dreaming of a good his own,
Arrogating all he can,
Though the Lord is good alone!
He the graces you have wrought
Makes subservient to his pride;
Ignorant that one such thought
Passes all his sin beside.
Such his folly-proved, at last
By the loss of that repose,
Self-complacence cannot taste,
Only love divine bestows.
'Tis by this reproof severe,
And by this reproof alone,
His defects at last appear,
Man is to himself made known.
Learn, all earth! that feeble man,
Sprung from this terrestrial clod,

Nothing is, and nothing can;
Life and power are all in God.

Love Increased by Suffering

"I love the Lord," is still the strain
This heart delights to sing:
But I reply - your thoughts are vain,
Perhaps 'tis no such thing.
Before the power of love divine
Creation fades away;
Till only God is seen to shine
In all that we survey.
In gulfs of awful night we find
The God of our desires;
'Tis there he stamps the yielding mind,
And doubles all its fires.
Flames of encircling love invest,
And pierce it sweetly through;
'Tis filled with sacred joy, yet pressed
With sacred sorrow too.
Ah love! my heart is in the right-
Amidst a thousand woes,
To you, its ever new delight,
And all its peace it owes.
Fresh causes of distress occur
Wherever I look or move;
The comforts I to all prefer
Are solitude and love.
Nor exile I nor prison fear;
Love makes my courage great;
I find a Savior every where,
His grace in every state.
Nor castle walls, nor dungeons deep,
Exclude his quickening beams;
There I can sit, and sing, and weep,
And dwell on heavenly themes.
There sorrow, for his sake, is found
A joy beyond compare;

There no presumptuous thoughts abound,
No pride can enter there.
A Savior doubles all my joys,
And sweetens all my pains,
His strength in my defense employs,
Consoles me and sustains.
I fear no ill, resent no wrong;
Nor feel a passion move,
When malice whets her slanderous tongue;
Such patience is in love.

Scenes Favorable to Meditation

Wilds horrid and dark with over shadowing trees,
Rocks that ivy and briers enfold,
Scenes nature with dread and astonishment sees,
But I with a pleasure untold;
Though awfully silent, and shaggy, and rude,
I am charmed with the peace you afford;
Your shades are a temple where none will intrude,
The abode of my lover and Lord.
I am sick of your splendor, O fountain of day,
And here I am hid from its beams,
Here safely contemplate a brighter display
Of the noblest and holiest of themes.
You forests, that yield me my sweetest repose,
Where stillness and solitude reign,
To you I securely and boldly disclose
The dear anguish of which I complain.
Here, sweetly forgetting and wholly forgot
By the world and its turbulent throng,
The birds and the streams lend me many a note
That aids meditation and song.
Here, wandering in scenes that are sacred to night,
Love wears me and wastes me away,
And often the sun has spent much of his light
Ere yet I perceive it is day.
While a mantle of darkness envelops the sphere,
My sorrows are sadly rehearsed,

To me the dark hours are all equally dear,
And the last is as sweet as the first.
Here I and the beasts of the deserts agree,
Mankind are the wolves that I fear,
They grudge me my natural right to be free,
But nobody questions it here.
Though little is found in this dreary abode
That appetite wishes to find,
My spirit is soothed by the presence of God,
And appetite wholly resigned.
You desolate scenes, to your solitude led,
My life I in praises employ,
And scarce know the source of the tears that I shed,
Proceed they from sorrow or joy.
There's nothing I seem to have skill to discern,
I feel out my way in the dark,
Love reigns in my bosom, I constantly burn,
Yet hardly distinguish the spark.
I live, yet I seem to myself to be dead,
Such a riddle is not to be found,
I am nourished without knowing how I am fed,
I have nothing, and yet I abound.
Oh, love! who in darkness are pleased to abide,
Though dimly, yet surely I see
That these contrarieties only reside
In the soul that is chosen of thee.
Ah! send me not back to the race of mankind,
Perversely by folly beguiled,
For where, in the crowds I have left, shall I find
The spirit and heart of a child?
Here let me, though fixed in a desert, be free;
A little one whom they despise,
Though lost to the world, if in union with thee,
Shall be holy, and happy, and wise.

The Nativity

'Tis folly all - let me no more be told
Of Parian porticos, and roofs of gold;

Delightful views of nature, dressed by art,
Enchant no longer this indifferent heart;
The Lord of all things, in his humble birth,
Makes mean the proud magnificence of earth;
The straw, the manger, and the moldering wall,
Eclipse its luster; and I scorn it all.
Canals, and fountains, and delicious vales,
Green slopes and plains, whose plenty never fails;
Deep-rooted groves, whose heads sublimely rise,
Earth-born, and yet ambitious of the skies;
The abundant foliage of whose gloomy shades,
Vainly the sun in all its power invades;
Where warbled airs of sprightly birds resound,
Whose verdure lives while Winter scowls around;
Rocks, lofty mountains, caverns dark and deep,
And torrents raving down the rugged steep;
Smooth downs, whose fragrant herbs the spirits cheer;
Meads crowned with flowers; streams musical and clear,
Whose silver waters, and whose murmurs, join
Their artless charms, to make the scene divine;
The fruitful vineyard, and the furrowed plain,
That seems a rolling sea of golden grain:
All, all have lost the charms they once possessed;
An infant God reigns sovereign in my breast;
From Bethlehem's bosom I no more will rove;
There dwells the Savior, and there rests my love.
You mightier rivers, that, with sounding force,
Urge down the valleys your impetuous course!
Winds, clouds, and lightning! and, you waves, whose heads,
Curled into monstrous forms, the seaman dreads!
Horrid abyss, where all experience fails,
Spread with the wreck of planks and shattered sails;
On whose broad back grim Death triumphant rides,
While havoc floats on all your swelling tides,
Your shores a scene of ruin strewed around
With vessels bulged, and bodies of the drowned!
You fish, that sport beneath the boundless waves,
And rest, secure from man, in rocky caves;
Swift-darting sharks, and whales of hideous size,

Whom all the aquatic world with terror eyes!
Had I but faith immoveable and true,
I might defy the fiercest storm, like you:
The world, a more disturbed and boisterous sea,
When Jesus shows a smile, affrights not me;
He hides me, and in vain the billows roar,
Break harmless at my feet, and leave the shore.
Your azure vault where, through the gloom of night,
Thick sown, we see such countless worlds of light!
You moon, whose car, encompassing the skies,
Restores lost nature to our wondering eyes;
Again retiring, when the brighter sun
Begins the course he seems in haste to run!
Behold him where he shines! His rapid rays,
Themselves unmeasured, measure all our days;
Nothing impedes the race he would pursue,
Nothing escapes his penetrating view,
A thousand lands confess his quickening heat,
And all he cheers are fruitful, fair, and sweet.
Far from enjoying what these scenes disclose,
I feel the thorn, alas! but miss the rose:
Too well I know this aching heart requires
More solid gold to fill its vast desires;
In vain they represent his matchless might,
Who called them out of deep primeval night;
Their form and beauty but augment my woe,
I seek the Giver of those charms they show:
Nor, Him beside, throughout the world he made,
Lives there in whom I trust for cure or aid.
Infinite God, you great unrivalled One!
Whose glory makes a blot of yonder sun;
Compared with your, how dim his beauty seems,
How quenched the radiance of his golden beams!
You are my bliss, the light by which I move;
In you alone dwells all that I can love.
All darkness flies when thou art pleased to appear,
A sudden spring renews the fading year;
Wherever I turn I see your power and grace
The watchful guardians of our heedless race;

Your various creatures in one strain agree,
All, in all times and places, speak of thee;
Even I, with trembling heart and stammering tongue,
Attempt your praise, and join the general song.
Almighty Former of this wondrous plan,
Faintly reflected in your image, man -
Holy and just - the greatness of whose name
Fills and supports this universal frame,
Diffused throughout the infinitude of space,
Who are thyself thine own vast dwelling-place;
Soul of our soul, whom yet no sense of ours
Discerns, eluding our most active powers;
Encircling shades attend your awful throne,
That veil your face, and keep you still unknown;
Unknown, though dwelling in our inmost part,
Lord of the thoughts, and Sovereign of the heart!
Repeat the charming truth that never tires,
No God is like the God my soul desires;
He at whose voice heaven trembles, even He,
Great as he is, knows how to stoop to me -
Lo! there he lies - that smiling infant said,
"Heaven, earth, and sea, exist!" - and they obeyed.
Even he, whose being swells beyond the skies,
Is born of woman, lives, and mourns, and dies;
Eternal and immortal, seems to cast
That glory from his brows, and breathes his last.
Trivial and vain the works that man has wrought,
How do they shrink and vanish at the thought!
Sweet solitude, and scene of my repose!
This rustic sight assuages all my woes -
That crib contains the Lord, whom I adore;
And earth's a shade that I pursue no more.
He is my firm support, my rock, my tower,
I dwell secure beneath his sheltering power,
And hold this mean retreat for ever dear,
For all I love, my soul's delight is here.
I see the Almighty swathed in infant bands,
Tied helpless down the thunder-bearer's hands!
And, in this shed, that mystery discern,

Which faith and love, and they alone, can learn.
You tempests, spare the slumbers of your Lord!
You zephyrs, all your whispered sweets afford!
Confess the God, that guides the rolling year;
Heaven, do him homage; and you, earth, revere!
You shepherds, monarchs, sages, hither bring
Your hearts an offering, and adore your King!
Pure be those hearts, and rich in faith and love;
Join, in his praise, the harmonious world above;
To Bethlehem haste, rejoice in his repose,
And praise him there for all that he bestows!
Man, busy man, alas! can ill afford
To obey the summons, and attend the Lord;
Perverted reason revels and runs wild,
By glittering shows of pomp and wealth beguiled;
And, blind to genuine excellence and grace,
Finds not her author in so mean a place.
You unbelieving! learn a wiser part,
Distrust your erring sense, and search your heart;
There soon you shall perceive a kindling flame
Glow for that infant God, from whom it came;
Resist not, quench not, that divine desire,
Melt all your adamant in heavenly fire!
Not so will I requite you, gentle love!
Yielding and soft this heart shall ever prove;
And every heart beneath your power should fall,
Glad to submit, could mine contain them all.
But I am poor, oblation I have none,
None for a Savior, but himself alone:
Whatever I render you, from you it came:
And, if I give my body to the flame,
My patience, love, and energy divine
Of heart, and soul, and spirit, all are thine.
Ah, vain attempt to expunge the mighty score!
The more I pay, I owe you still the more.
Upon my meanness, poverty, and guilt,
The trophy of your glory shall be built;
My self-disdain shall be the unshaken base,
And my deformity its fairest grace;

For destitute of good, and rich in ill,
Must be my state and my description still.
And do I grieve at such a humbling lot?
Nay, but I cherish and enjoy the thought-
Vain pageantry and pomp of earth, adieu!
I have no wish, no memory for you;
The more I feel my misery, I adore
The sacred inmate of my soul the more;
Rich in his love, I feel my noblest pride
Spring from the sense of having naught beside.
In you I find wealth, comfort, virtue, might;
My wanderings prove your wisdom infinite;
All that I have I give you; and then see
All contrarieties unite in thee;
For you have joined them, taking up our woe,
And pouring out your bliss on worms below,
By filling with your grace and love divine
A gulf of evil in this heart of mine.
This is, indeed, to bid the valleys rise,
And the hills sink - 'tis matching earth and skies;
I feel my weakness, thank you and deplore
An aching heart, that throbs to thank you more;
The more I love you, I the more reprove
A soul so lifeless, and so slow to love;
Till, on a deluge of your mercy tossed,
I plunge into that sea, and there am lost.

CPSIA information can be obtained
at www.ICGtesting.com
Printed in the USA
BVHW071244231122
652652BV00002B/73